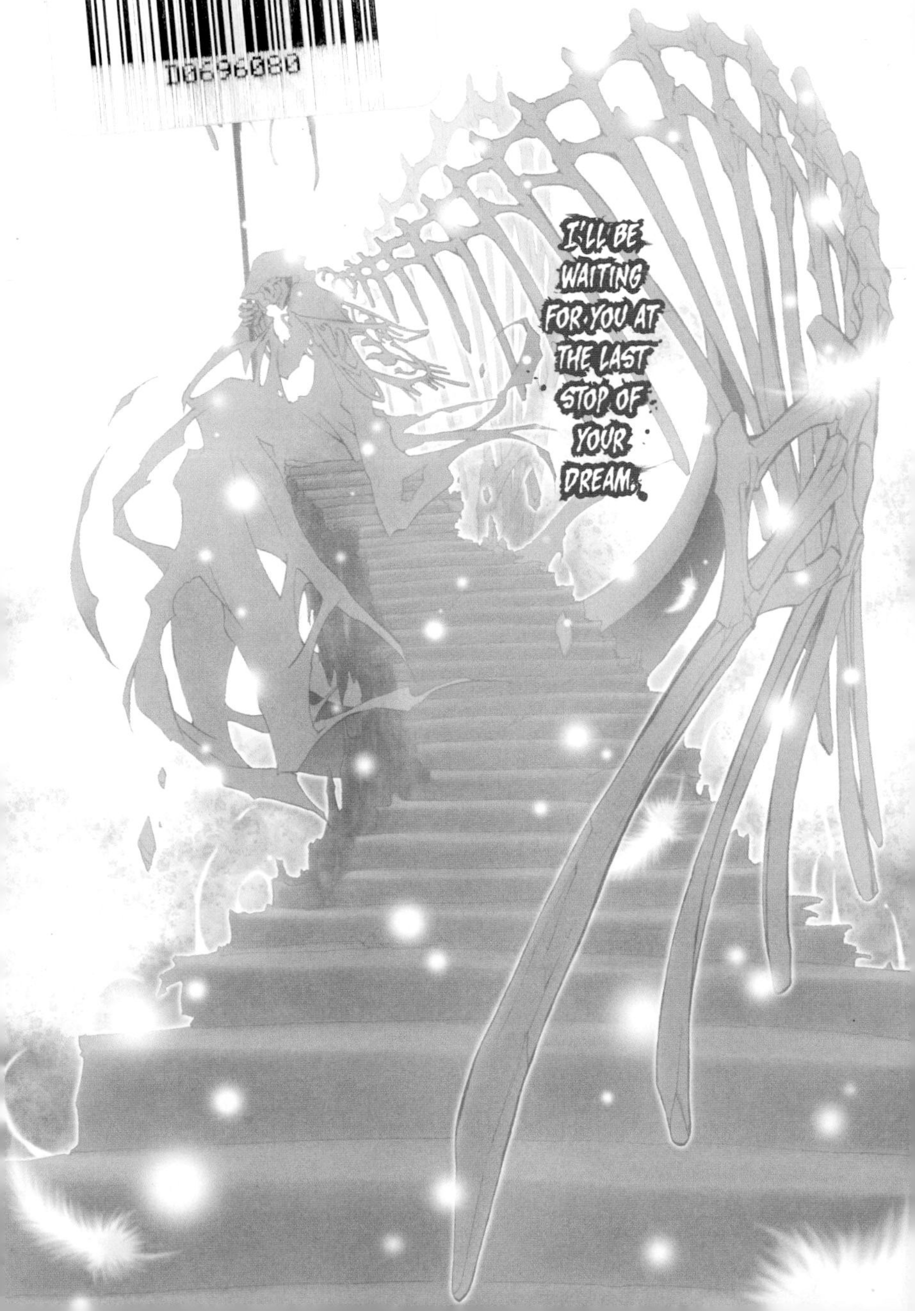
I'LL BE WAITING FOR YOU AT THE LAST STOP OF YOUR DREAM.

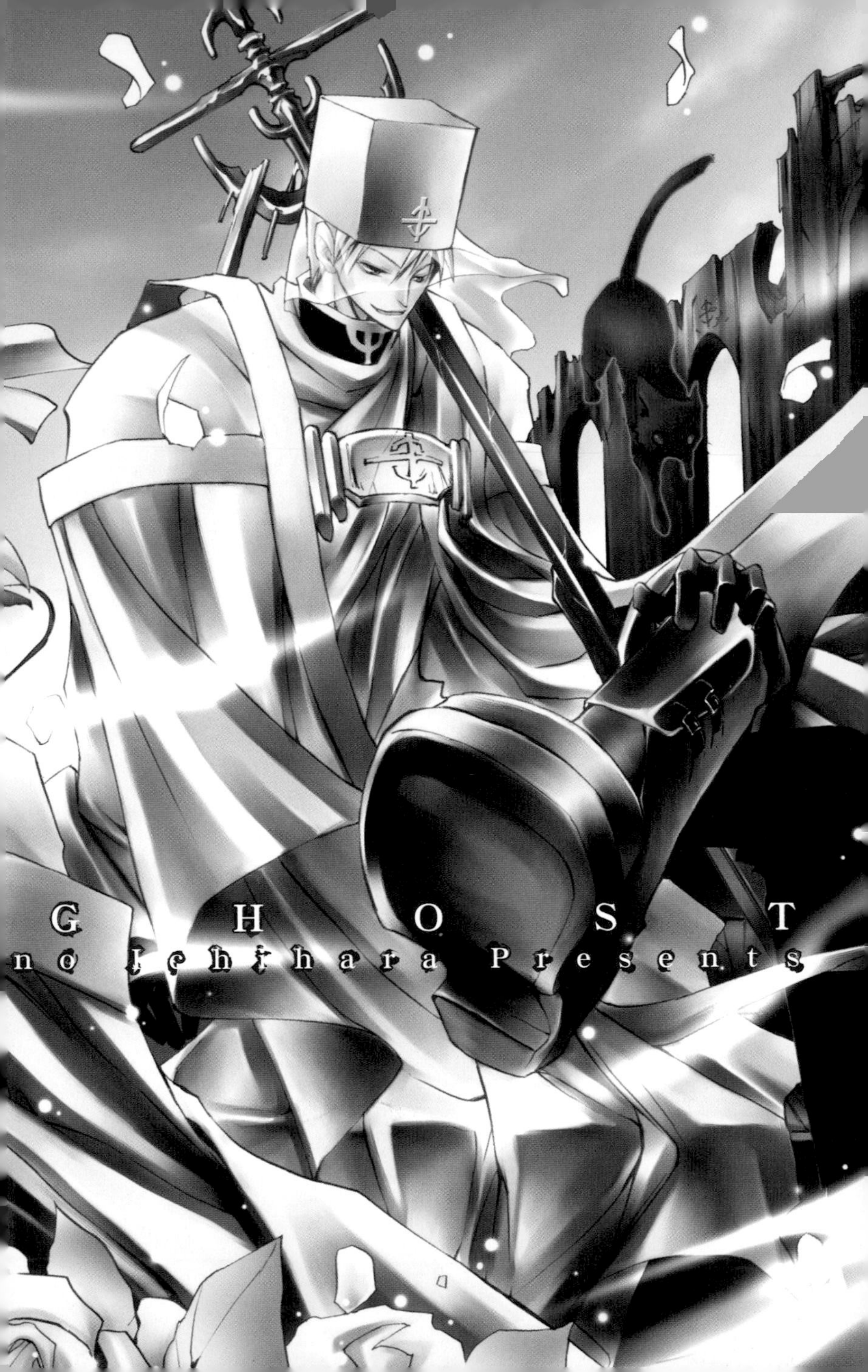
G H O S T
no Ichihara Presents

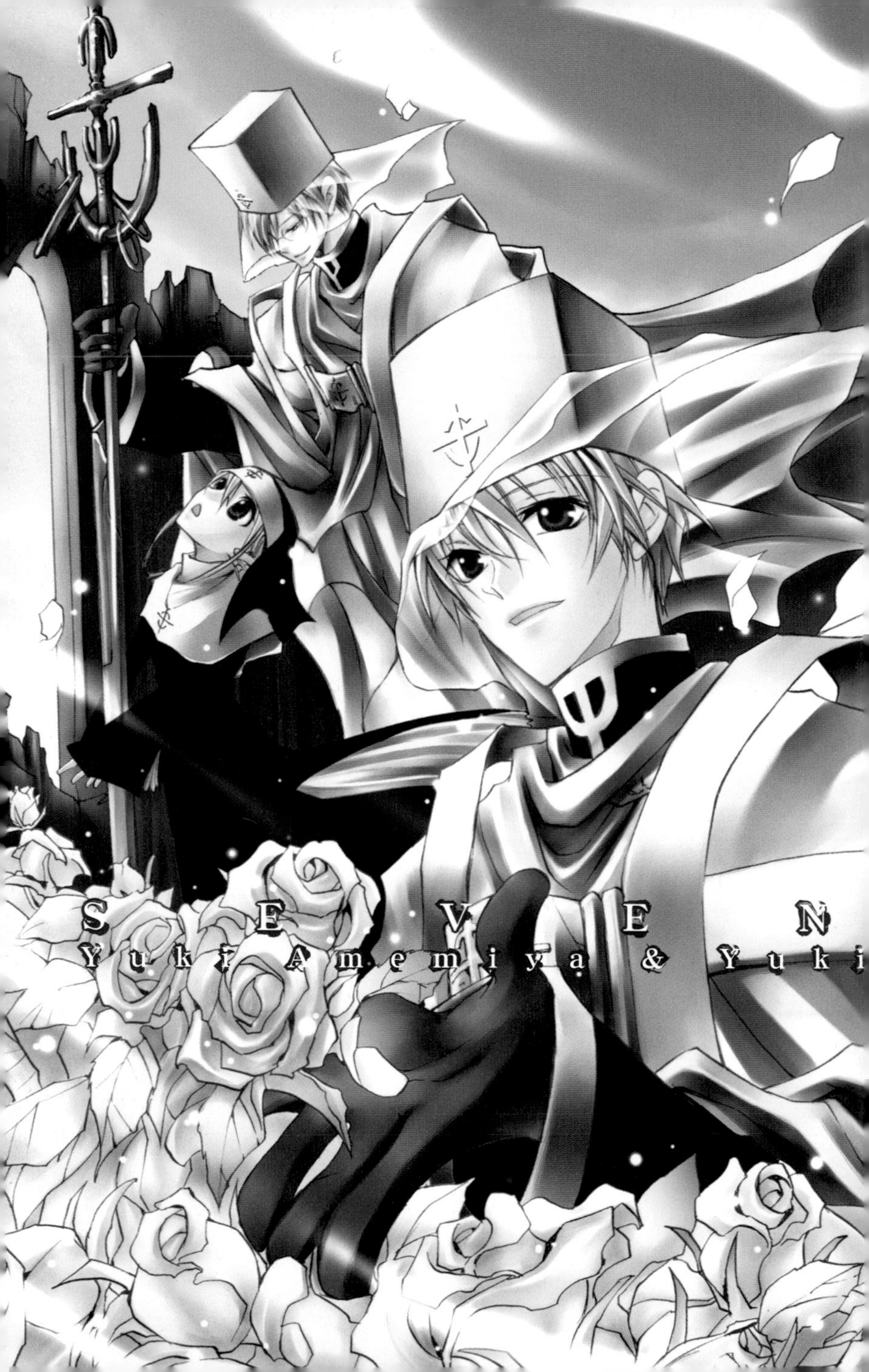
S E V E N
Yuki Amemiya & Yuki

C O N T E N T S

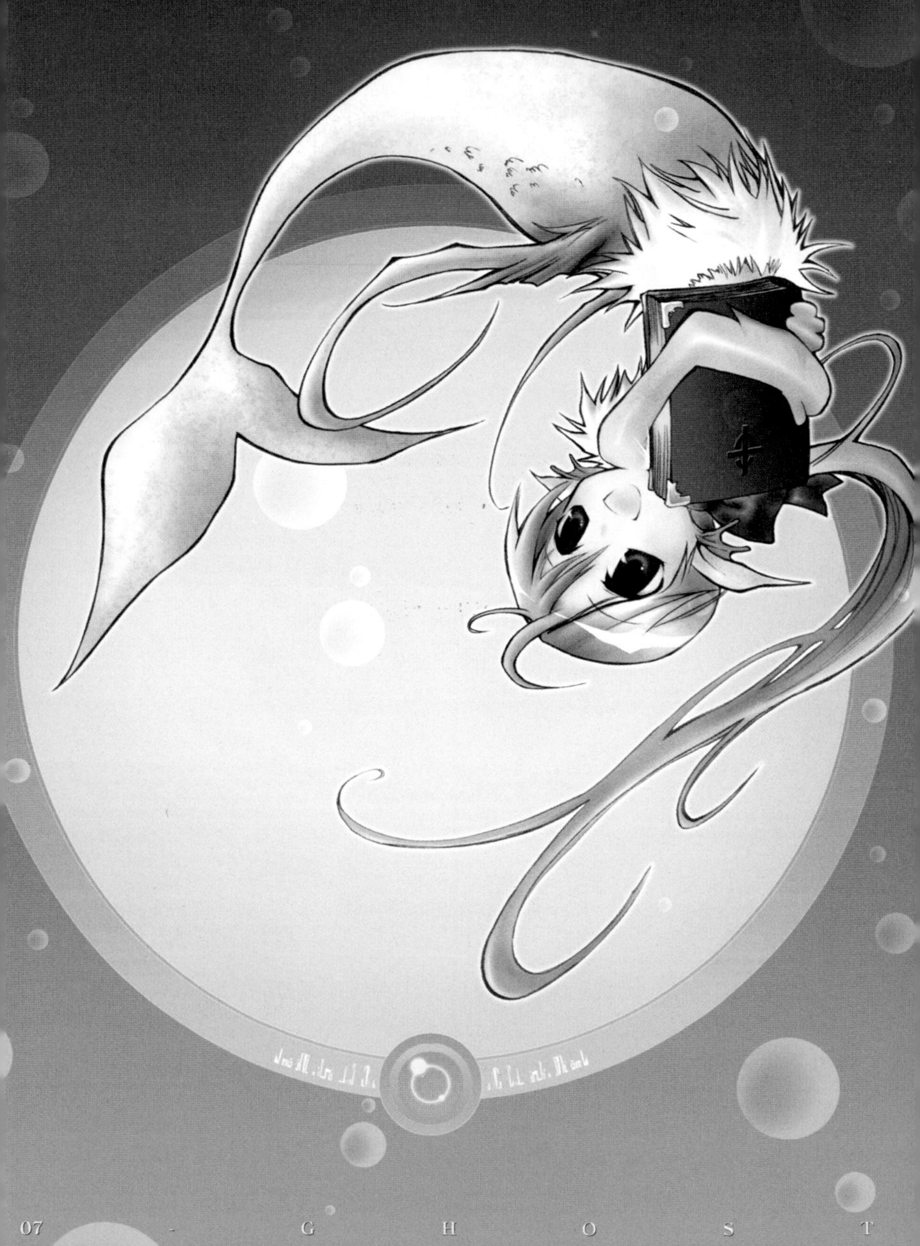

07-GHOST

Yuki Amemiya & Yukino Ichihara

1

go!comi

Translation – Christine Schilling
Adaptation – Mallory Reaves
Retouch and Lettering – Fawn Lau
Production Assistant – Suzy Wells
Production Manager – James Dashiell
Editor – Brynne Chandler

A Go! Comi manga

Published by Go! Media Entertainment, LLC

07-GHOST Vol. 1
© 2005 by Yuki Amemiya/Yukino Ichihara
All rights reserved.
First published in 2005 by Ichijinsha, Inc. Tokyo, Japan.

English Text © 2008 Go! Media Entertainment, LLC. All rights reserved.

Visit us online at www.gocomi.com
e-mail: info@gocomi.com

ISBN 978-1-60510-032-6

First printed in December 2008

1   2   3   4   5   6   7   8   9

Manufactured in the United States of America

Concerning Honorifics

At Go! Comi, we do our best to ensure that our translations read seamlessly in English while respecting the original Japanese language and culture. To this end, the original honorifics (the suffixes found at the end of characters' names) remain intact. In Japan, where politeness and formality are more integrated into every aspect of the language, honorifics give a better understanding of character relationships. They can be used to indicate both respect and affection. Whether a person addresses someone by first name or last name also indicates how close their relationship is.

Here are some of the honorifics you might encounter in reading this book:

-san: This is the most common and neutral of honorifics. The polite way to address someone you're not on close terms with is to use "-san." it's kind of like Mr. or Ms., except you can use "-san" with first names as easily as family names.

-chan: Used for friendly familiarity, mostly applied towards young girls. "-chan" also carries a connotation of cuteness with it, so it is frequently used with nicknames towards both boys and girls (such as "Na-chan" for "Natsu").

-kun: Like "-chan," it's an informal suffix for friends and classmates, only "-kun" is usually associated with boys. It can also be used in a professional environment by someone addressing a subordinate.

-sama: Indicates a great deal of respect or admiration.

Sempai: In school, "sempai" is used to refer to an upperclassman or club leader. It can also be used in the workplace by a new employee to address a mentor or staff member with seniority.

Sensei: Teachers, doctors, writers or any master of a trade are referred to as "sensei." When addressing a manga creator, the polite thing to do is attach "-sensei" to the manga-ka's name (as in Amemiya-sensei).

Onii: This is the more casual term for an older brother. Usually you'll see it with an honorific attached, such as "onii-chan."

Onee: The casual term for older sister, it's used like "onii" with honorifics.

[blank]: Not using an honorific when addressing someone indicates that the speaker has permission to speak intimately with the other person. This relationship is usually reserved for close friends and family.

07-GHOST

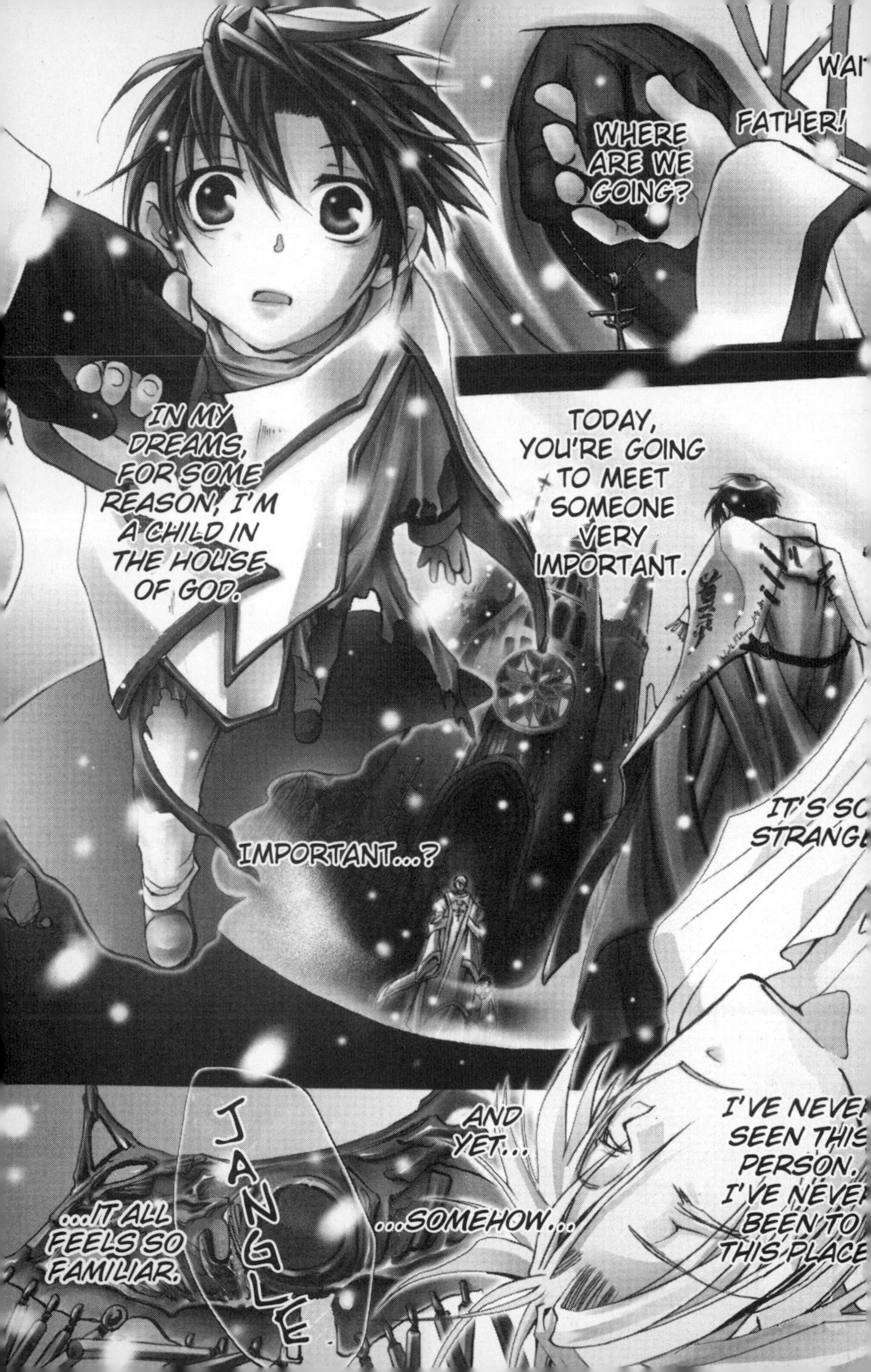
WAI
FATHER!
WHERE ARE WE GOING?
TODAY, YOU'RE GOING TO MEET SOMEONE VERY IMPORTANT.
IN MY DREAMS, FOR SOME REASON, I'M A CHILD IN THE HOUSE OF GOD.
IT'S SO STRANG
IMPORTANT...?
I'VE NEVE SEEN THIS PERSON. I'VE NEVE BEEN TO THIS PLAC
AND YET...
...SOMEHOW...
JANGLE
...IT ALL FEELS SO FAMILIAR.

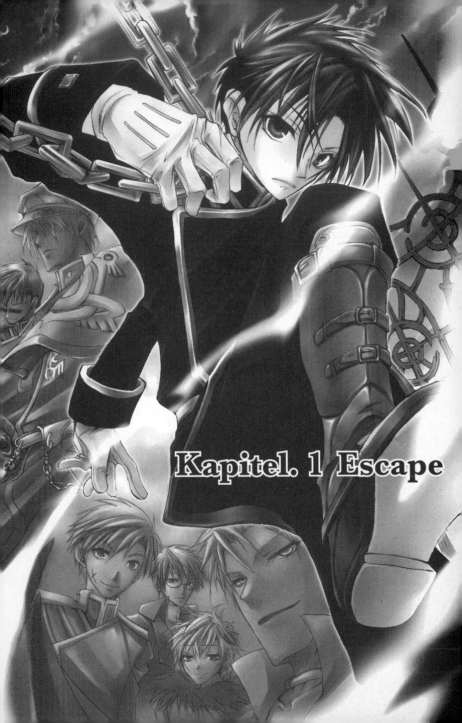

Kapitel. 1 Escape

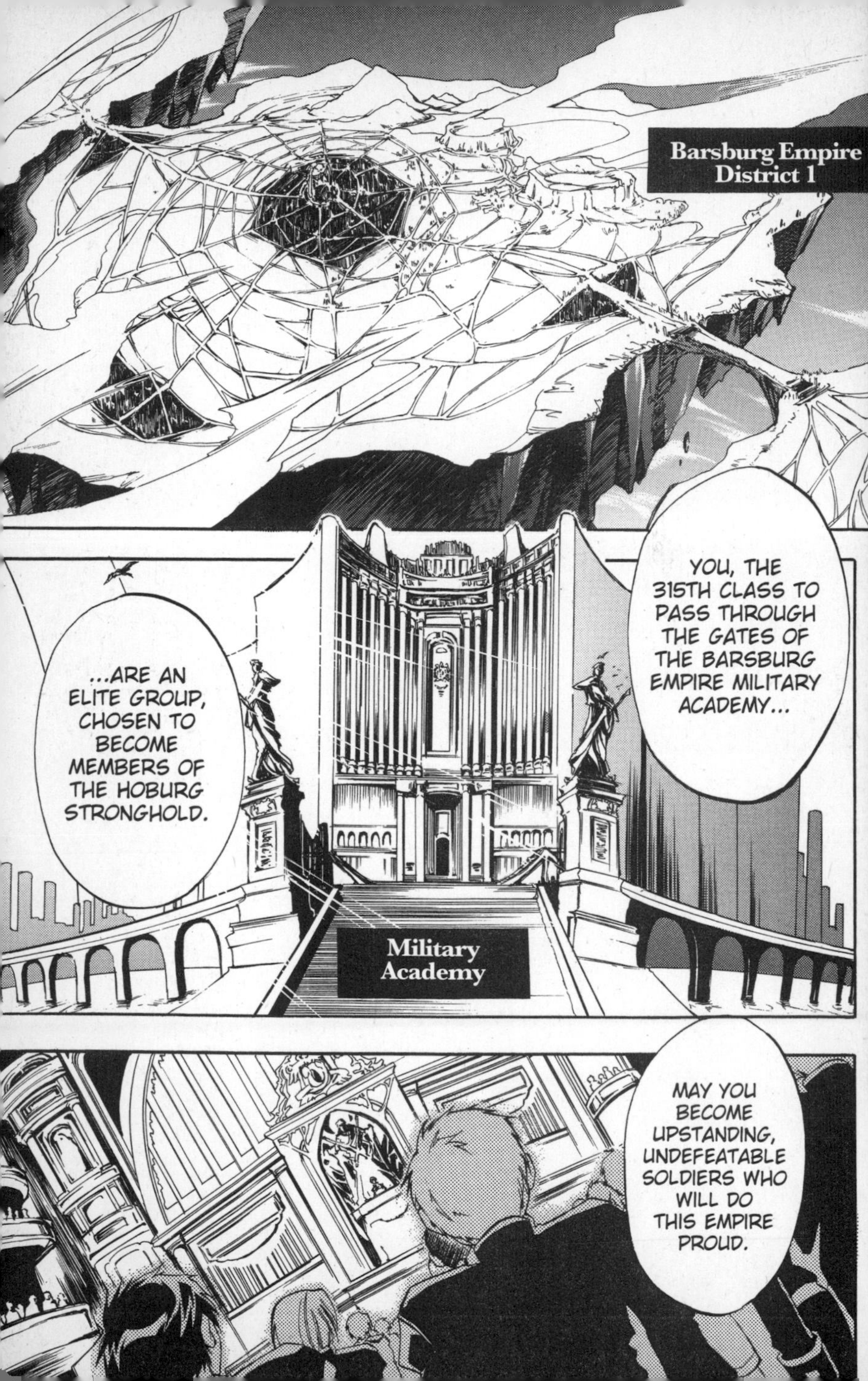
Barsburg Empire District 1
YOU, THE 315TH CLASS TO PASS THROUGH THE GATES OF THE BARSBURG EMPIRE MILITARY ACADEMY...
...ARE AN ELITE GROUP, CHOSEN TO BECOME MEMBERS OF THE HOBURG STRONGHOLD.
Military Academy
MAY YOU BECOME UPSTANDING, UNDEFEATABLE SOLDIERS WHO WILL DO THIS EMPIRE PROUD.

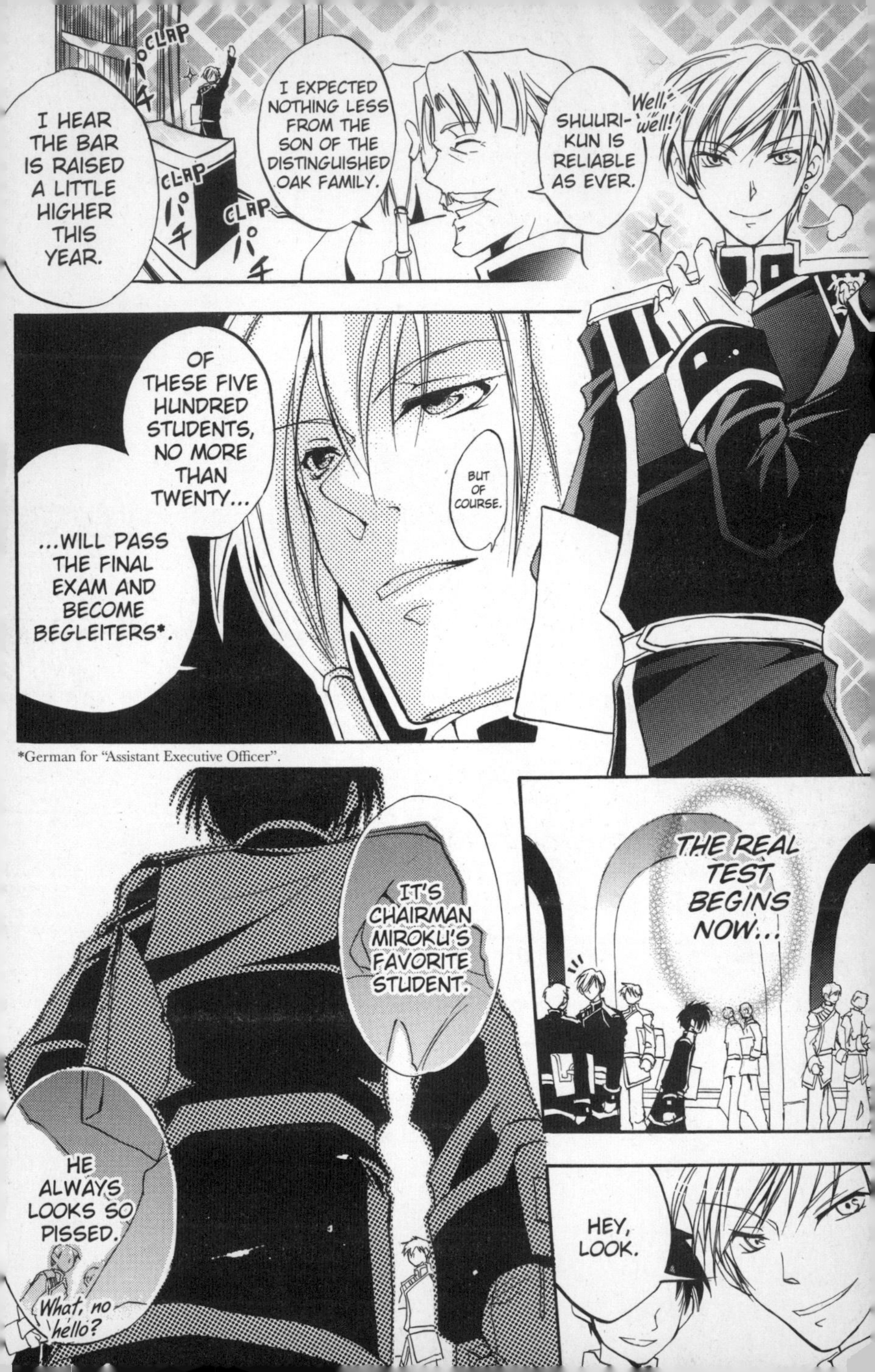
Well, well!
SHUURI-KUN IS RELIABLE AS EVER.
I EXPECTED NOTHING LESS FROM THE SON OF THE DISTINGUISHED OAK FAMILY.
CLAP パチ
CLAP パチ
CLAP パチ
I HEAR THE BAR IS RAISED A LITTLE HIGHER THIS YEAR.
OF THESE FIVE HUNDRED STUDENTS, NO MORE THAN TWENTY...
BUT OF COURSE.
...WILL PASS THE FINAL EXAM AND BECOME BEGLEITERS*.
THE REAL TEST BEGINS NOW...
HEY, LOOK.
IT'S CHAIRMAN MIROKU'S FAVORITE STUDENT.
HE ALWAYS LOOKS SO PISSED.
What, no hello?

*German for "Assistant Executive Officer".

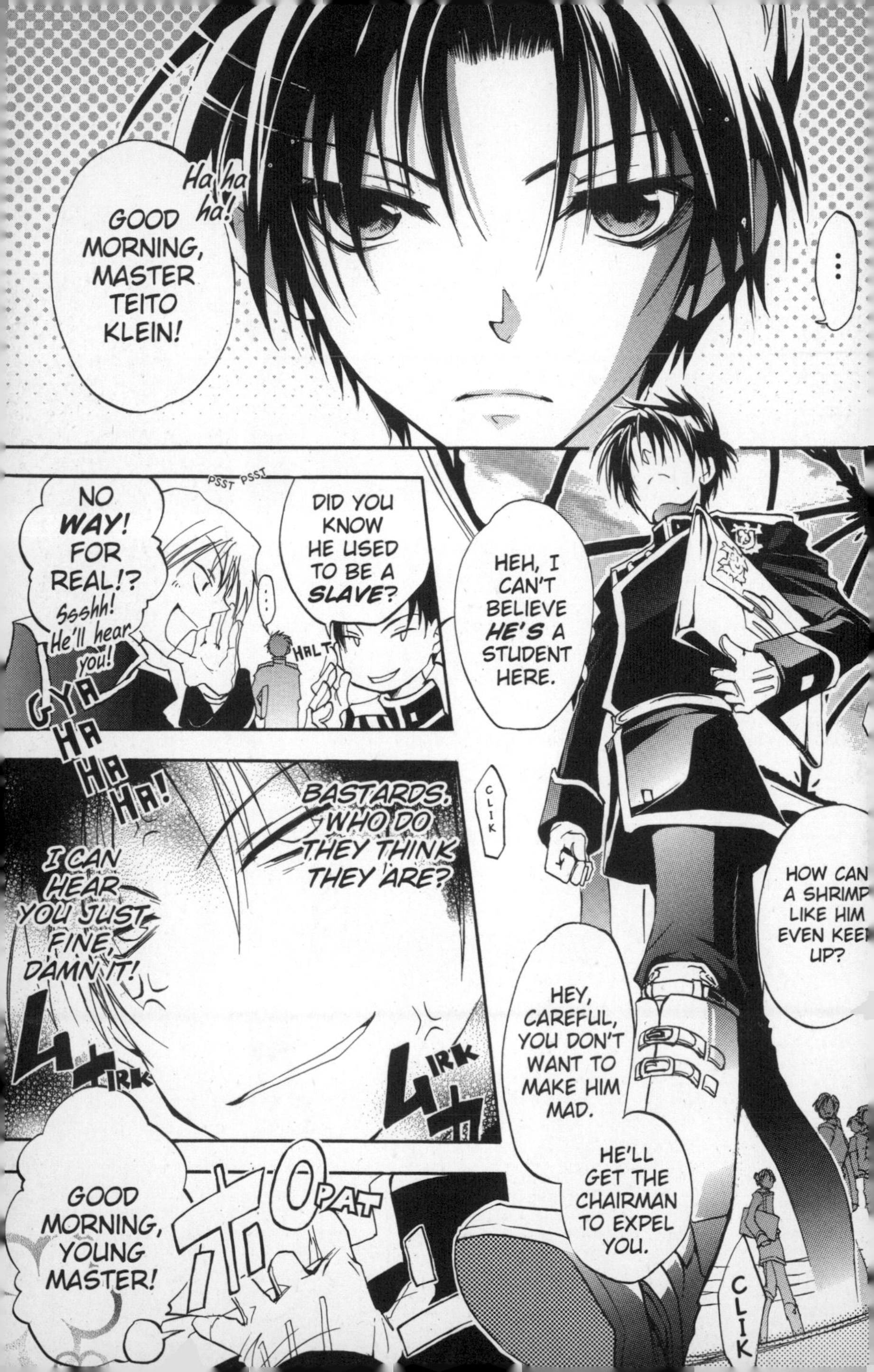
Ha ha ha!
GOOD MORNING, MASTER TEITO KLEIN!
...
HEH, I CAN'T BELIEVE HE'S A STUDENT HERE.
CLIK
HOW CAN A SHRIMP LIKE HIM EVEN KEE UP?
HEY, CAREFUL, YOU DON'T WANT TO MAKE HIM MAD.
HE'LL GET THE CHAIRMAN TO EXPEL YOU.
CLIK
PSST PSST
DID YOU KNOW HE USED TO BE A SLAVE?
NO WAY! FOR REAL!?
Ssshh! He'll hear you!
...
HALT
GYA HA HA HA!
BASTARDS. WHO DO THEY THINK THEY ARE?
I CAN HEAR YOU JUST FINE, DAMN IT!
IRK
IRK
PAT
GOOD MORNING, YOUNG MASTER!

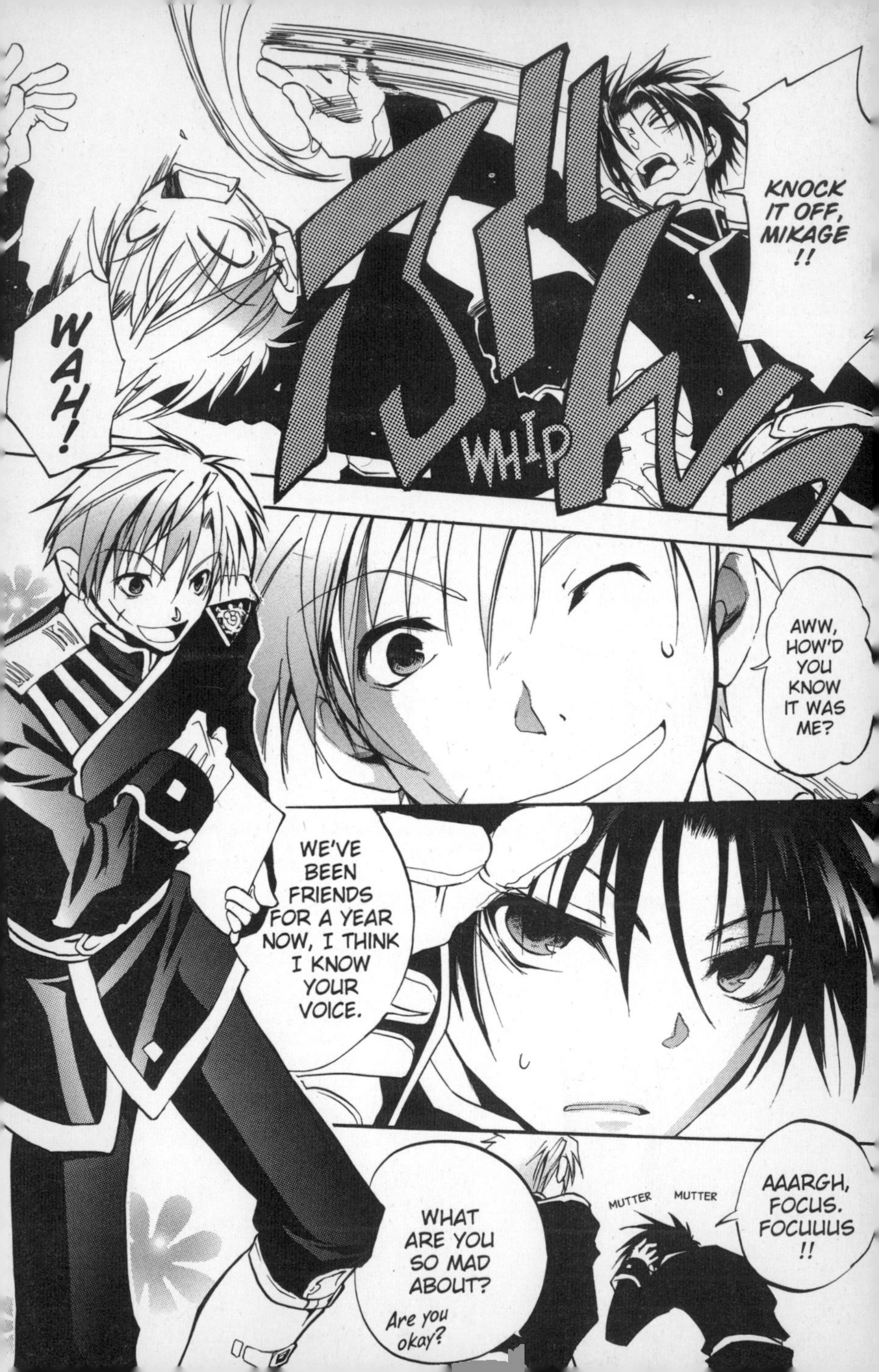
KNOCK IT OFF, MIKAGE!!
WHIP
WAH!
AWW, HOW'D YOU KNOW IT WAS ME?
WE'VE BEEN FRIENDS FOR A YEAR NOW, I THINK I KNOW YOUR VOICE.
AAARGH, FOCUS. FOCUUUS!!
MUTTER MUTTER
WHAT ARE YOU SO MAD ABOUT?
Are you okay?

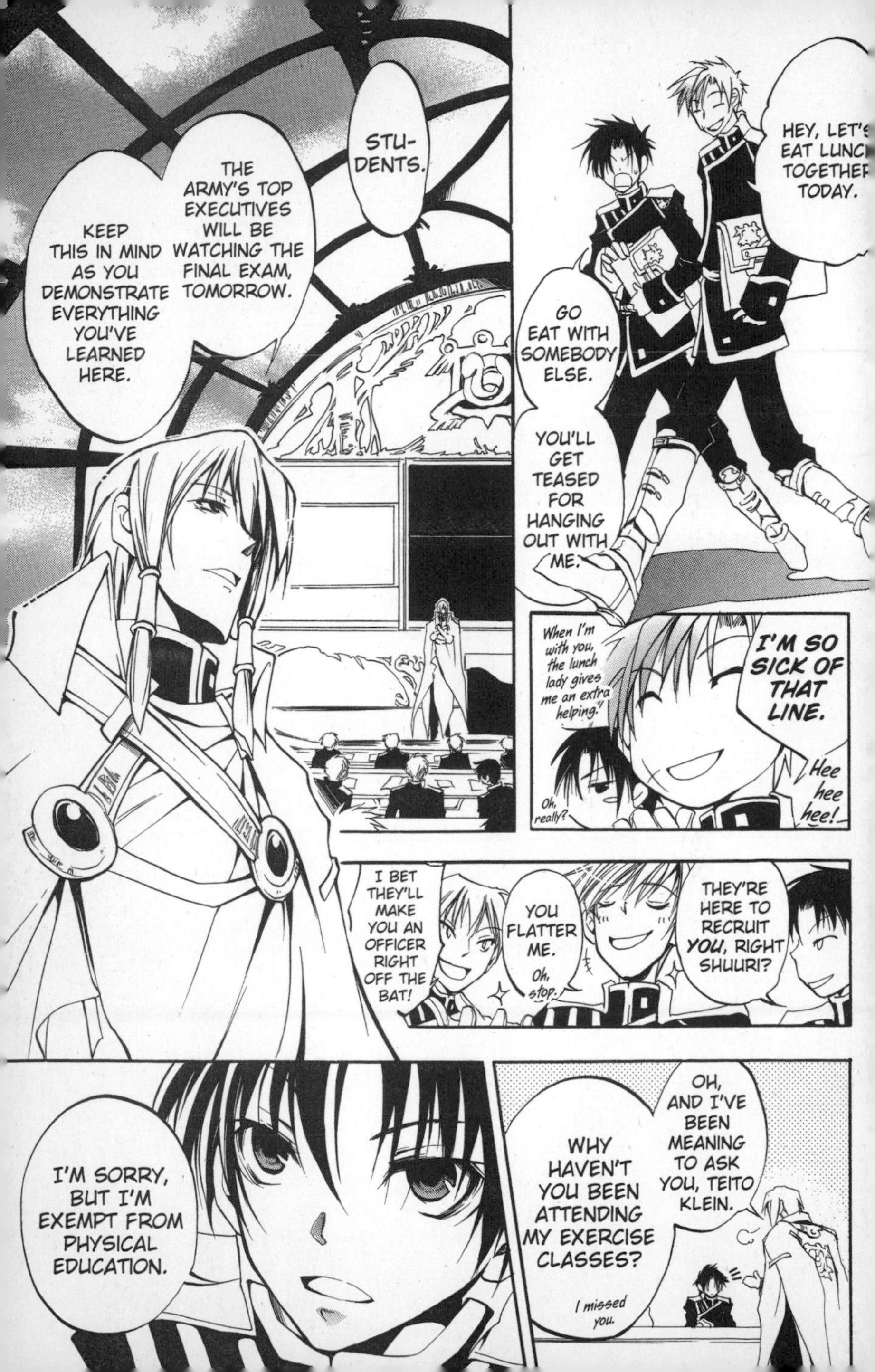
HEY, LET'S EAT LUNC TOGETHER TODAY.
GO EAT WITH SOMEBODY ELSE.
YOU'LL GET TEASED FOR HANGING OUT WITH ME.
I'M SO SICK OF THAT LINE.
When I'm with you, the lunch lady gives me an extra helping.
Hee hee hee!
Oh, really?
THEY'RE HERE TO RECRUIT YOU, RIGHT SHUURI?
YOU FLATTER ME.
Oh, stop.
I BET THEY'LL MAKE YOU AN OFFICER RIGHT OFF THE BAT!
STU- DENTS.
THE ARMY'S TOP EXECUTIVES WILL BE WATCHING THE FINAL EXAM, TOMORROW.
KEEP THIS IN MIND AS YOU DEMONSTRATE EVERYTHING YOU'VE LEARNED HERE.
OH, AND I'VE BEEN MEANING TO ASK YOU, TEITO KLEIN.
WHY HAVEN'T YOU BEEN ATTENDING MY EXERCISE CLASSES?
I missed you.
I'M SORRY, BUT I'M EXEMPT FROM PHYSICAL EDUCATION.

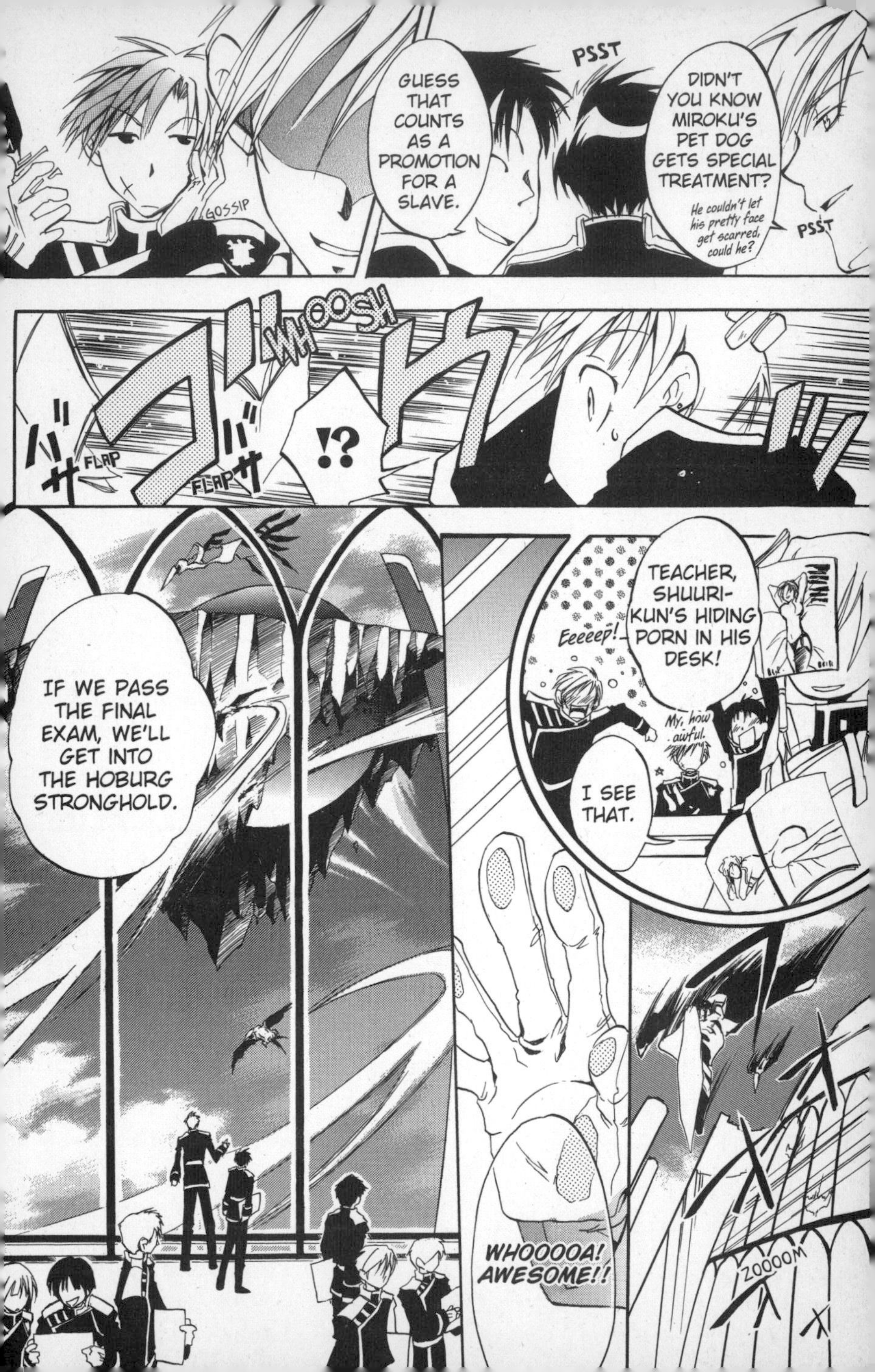
PSST
DIDN'T YOU KNOW MIROKU'S PET DOG GETS SPECIAL TREATMENT?
He couldn't let his pretty face get scarred, could he?
PSST
GUESS THAT COUNTS AS A PROMOTION FOR A SLAVE.
GOSSIP
WHOOSH
!?
FLAP
FLAP
TEACHER, SHUURI-KUN'S HIDING PORN IN HIS DESK!
Eeeeep!
My, how awful.
I SEE THAT.
ZOOOOM
WHOOOOA! AWESOME!!
IF WE PASS THE FINAL EXAM, WE'LL GET INTO THE HOBURG STRONGHOLD.

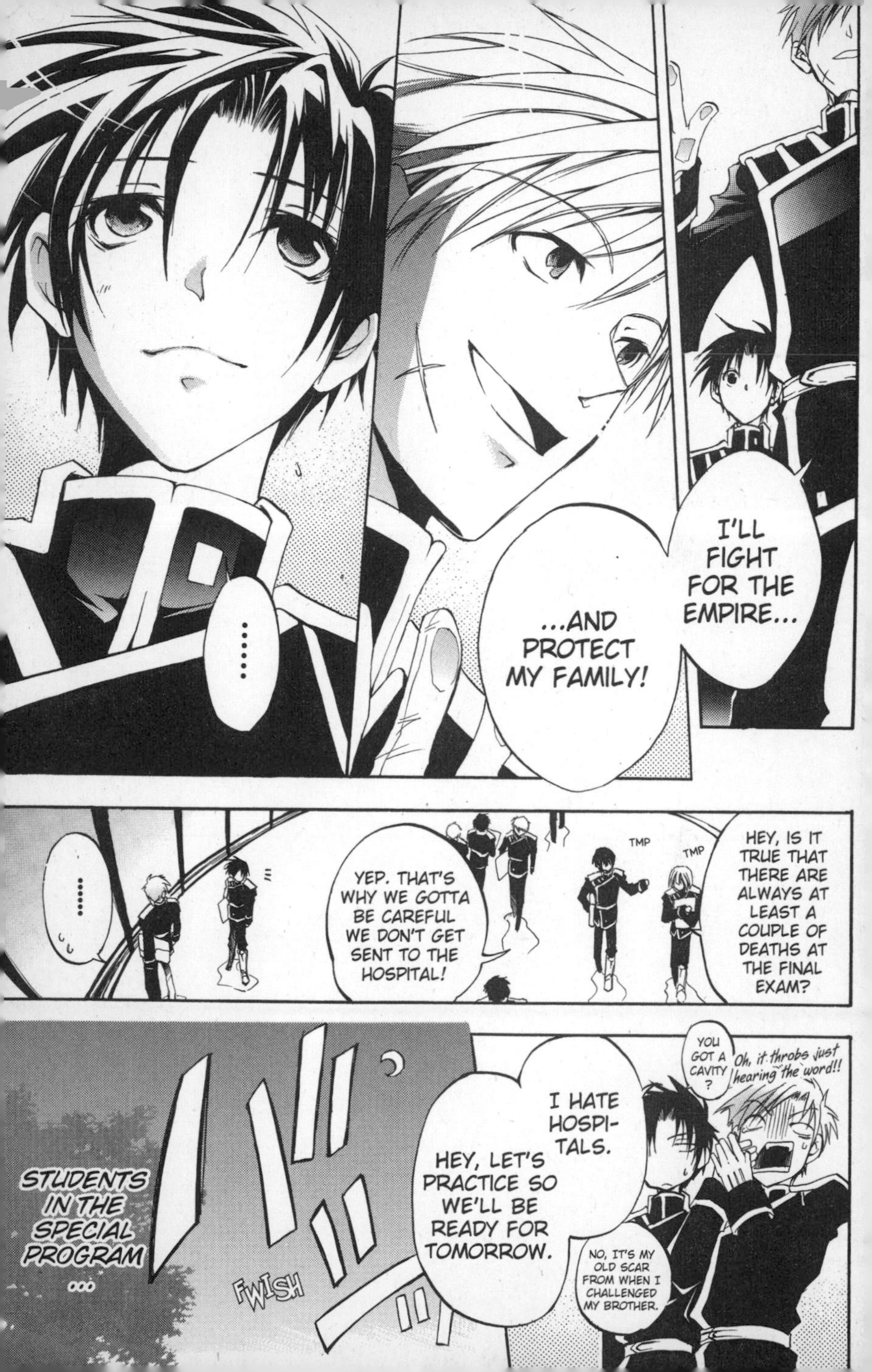
I'LL FIGHT FOR THE EMPIRE...
...AND PROTECT MY FAMILY!
......
HEY, IS IT TRUE THAT THERE ARE ALWAYS AT LEAST A COUPLE OF DEATHS AT THE FINAL EXAM?
TMP
TMP
YEP. THAT'S WHY WE GOTTA BE CAREFUL WE DON'T GET SENT TO THE HOSPITAL!
......
I HATE HOSPI-TALS.
YOU GOT A CAVITY?
Oh, it throbs just hearing the word!!
NO, IT'S MY OLD SCAR FROM WHEN I CHALLENGED MY BROTHER.
HEY, LET'S PRACTICE SO WE'LL BE READY FOR TOMORROW.
FWISH
STUDENTS IN THE SPECIAL PROGRAM...

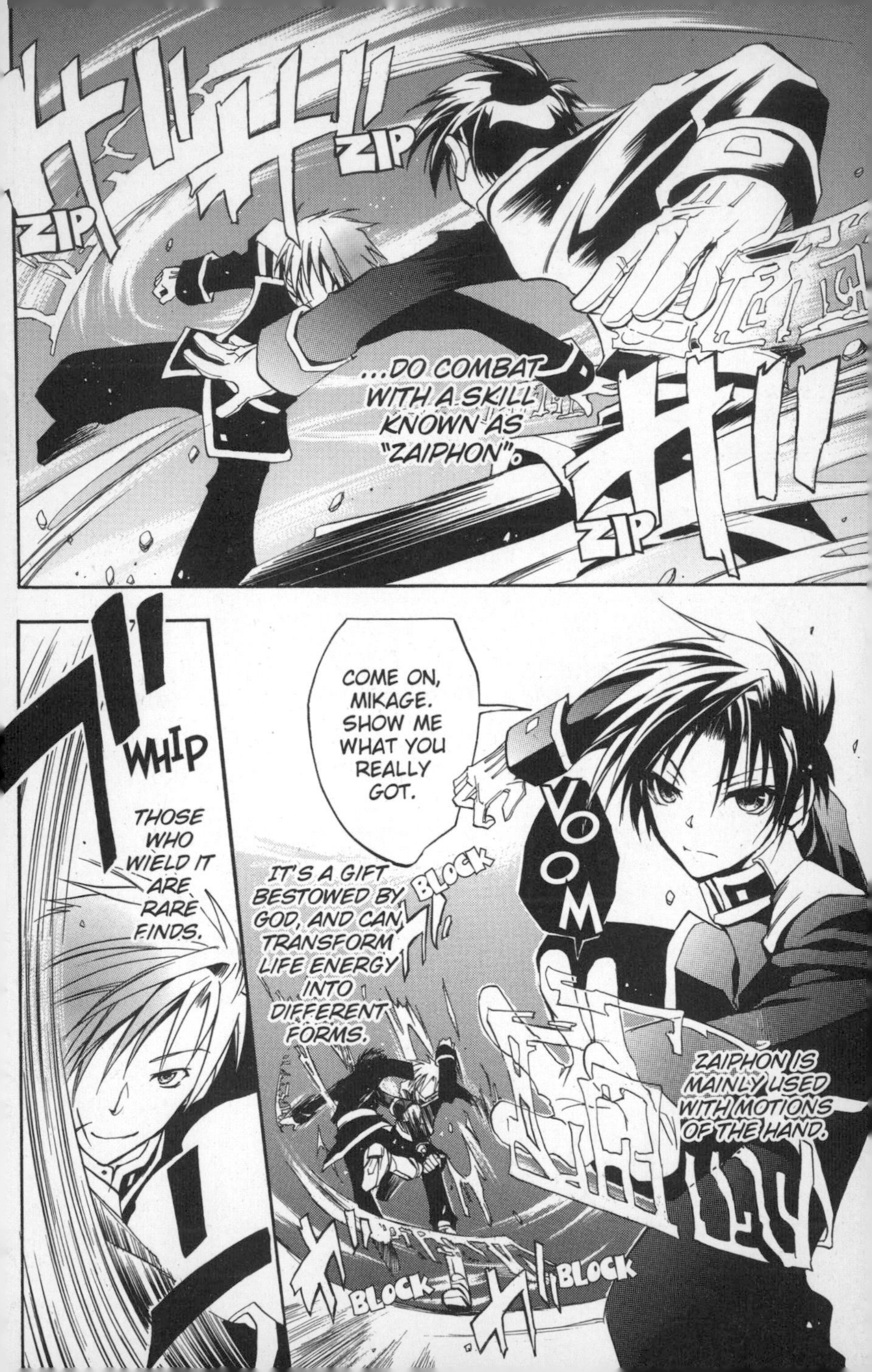
ZIP
ZIP
...DO COMBAT WITH A SKILL KNOWN AS "ZAIPHON".
ZIP
COME ON, MIKAGE. SHOW ME WHAT YOU REALLY GOT.
VOOM
ZAIPHON IS MAINLY USED WITH MOTIONS OF THE HAND.
BLOCK
IT'S A GIFT BESTOWED BY GOD, AND CAN TRANSFORM LIFE ENERGY INTO DIFFERENT FORMS.
BLOCK
BLOCK
THOSE WHO WIELD IT ARE RARE FINDS.
WHIP

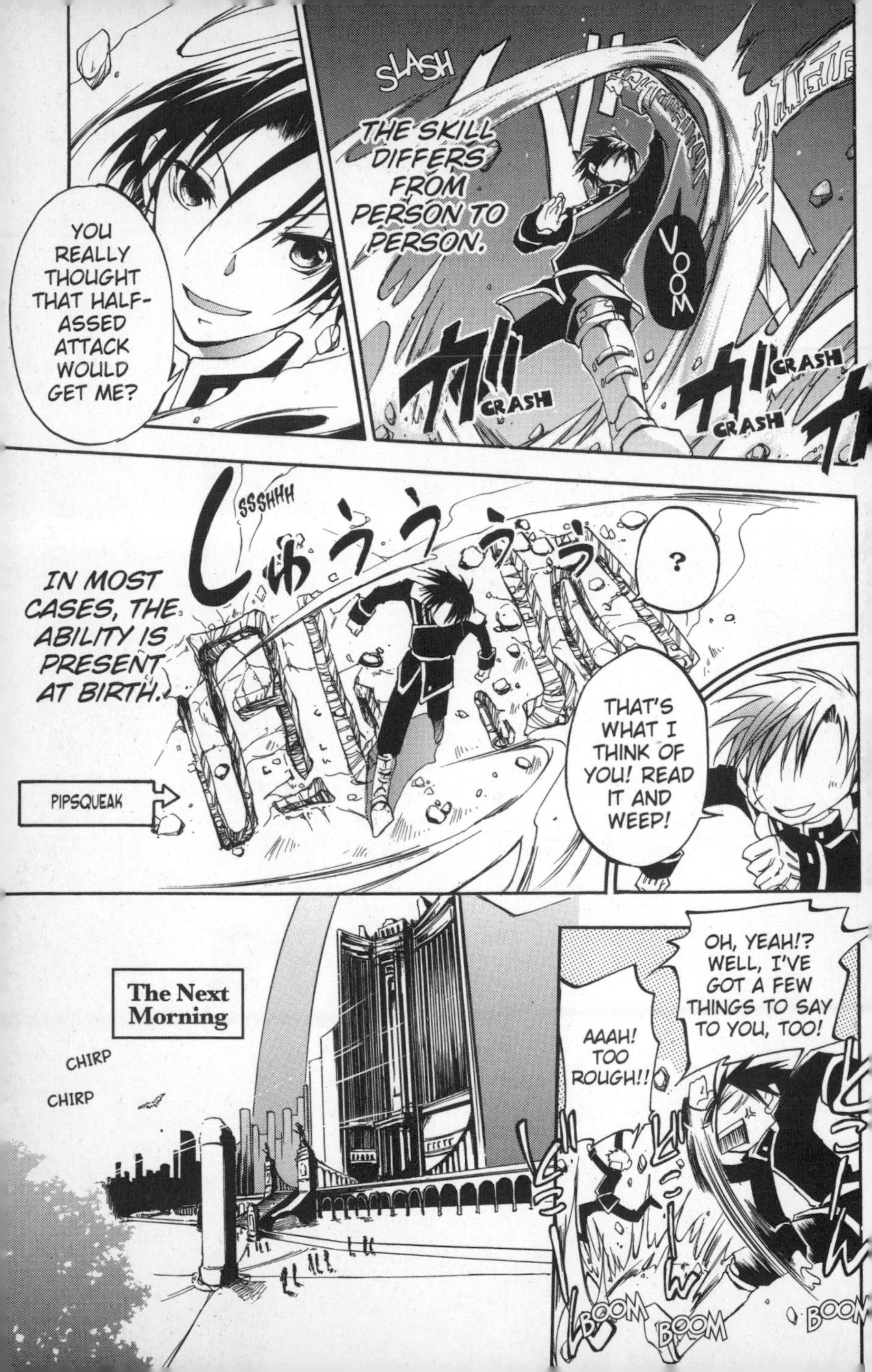
SLASH
THE SKILL DIFFERS FROM PERSON TO PERSON.
VOOM
CRASH
CRASH
CRASH
YOU REALLY THOUGHT THAT HALF-ASSED ATTACK WOULD GET ME?
?
SSSHHH
THAT'S WHAT I THINK OF YOU! READ IT AND WEEP!
IN MOST CASES, THE ABILITY IS PRESENT AT BIRTH.
PIPSQUEAK
OH, YEAH!? WELL, I'VE GOT A FEW THINGS TO SAY TO YOU, TOO!
AAAH! TOO ROUGH!!
BOOM
BOOM
BOOM
The Next Morning
CHIRP
CHIRP

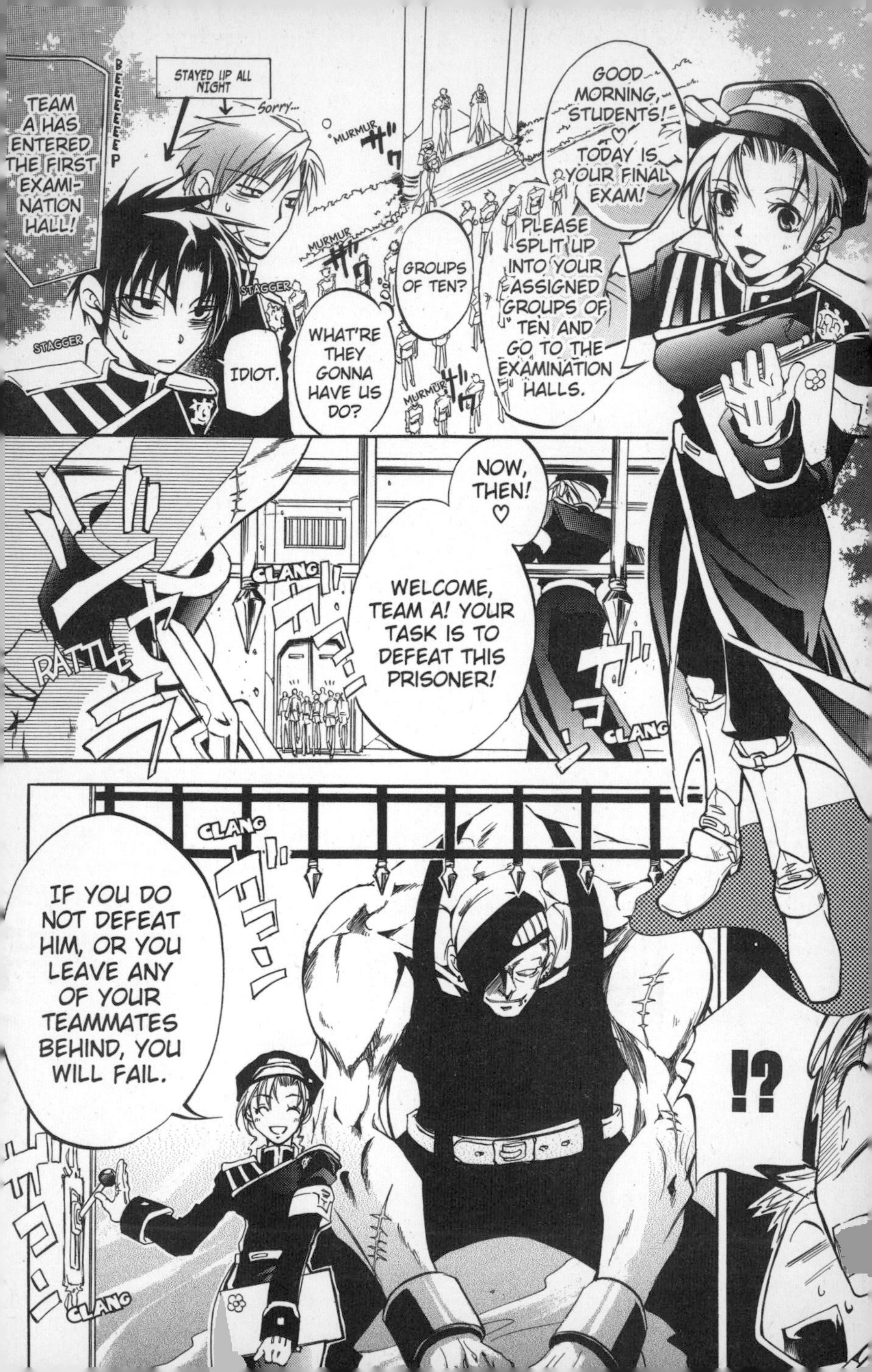
GOOD MORNING, STUDENTS! ♡
TODAY IS YOUR FINAL EXAM!
PLEASE SPLIT UP INTO YOUR ASSIGNED GROUPS OF TEN AND GO TO THE EXAMINATION HALLS.
MURMUR
MURMUR
GROUPS OF TEN?
WHAT'RE THEY GONNA HAVE US DO?
MURMUR
STAYED UP ALL NIGHT
Sorry...
STAGGER
STAGGER
IDIOT.
BEEEEEEEP
TEAM A HAS ENTERED THE FIRST EXAMINATION HALL!
NOW, THEN! ♡
WELCOME, TEAM A! YOUR TASK IS TO DEFEAT THIS PRISONER!
CLANG
CLANG
RATTLE
!?
CLANG
IF YOU DO NOT DEFEAT HIM, OR YOU LEAVE ANY OF YOUR TEAMMATES BEHIND, YOU WILL FAIL.
CLANG

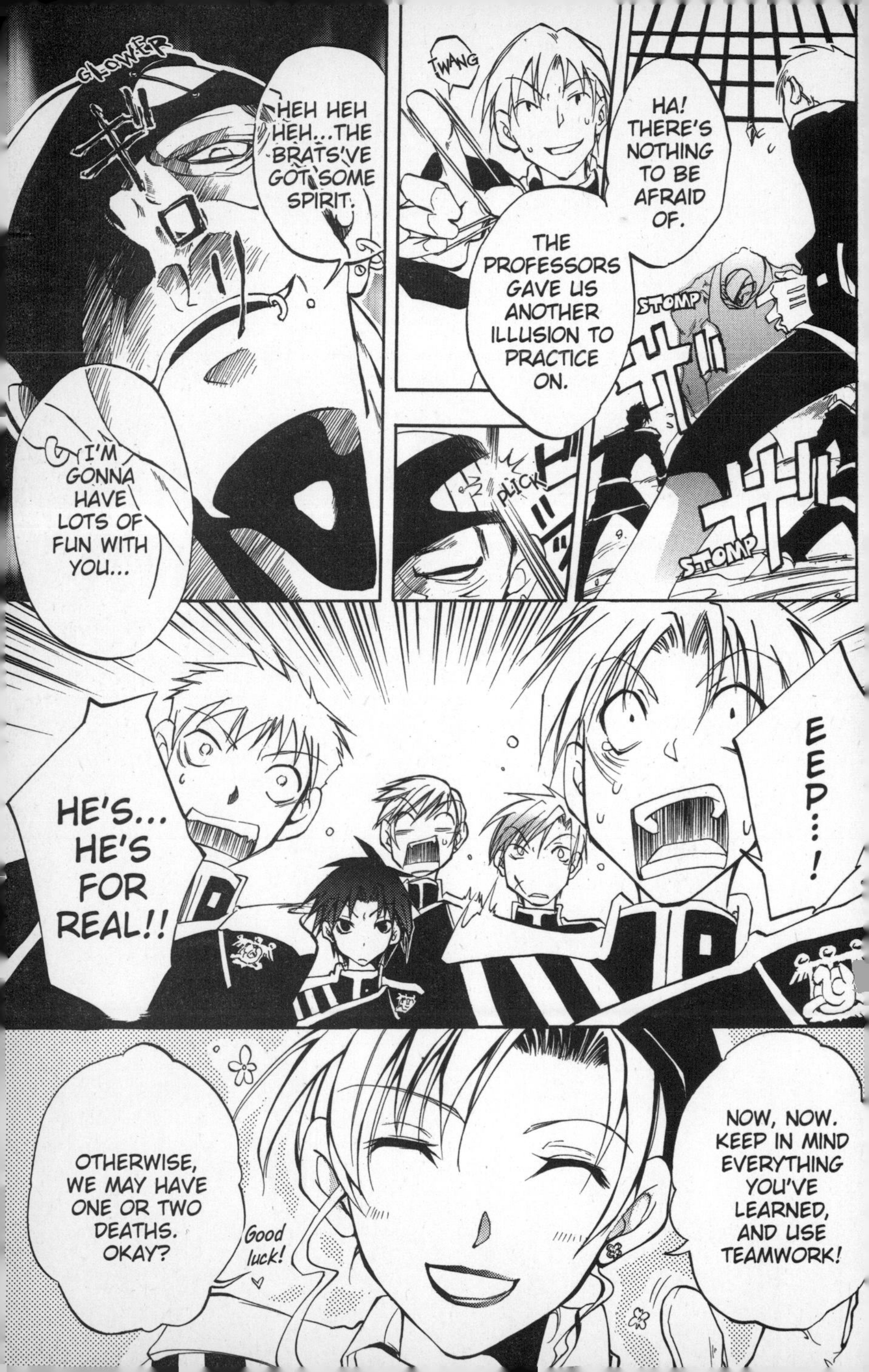
TWANG
HA! THERE'S NOTHING TO BE AFRAID OF.
THE PROFESSORS GAVE US ANOTHER ILLUSION TO PRACTICE ON.
STOMP
STOMP
PLICK
GLOWER
HEH HEH HEH...THE BRATS'VE GOT SOME SPIRIT.
I'M GONNA HAVE LOTS OF FUN WITH YOU...
EEP...!
HE'S... HE'S FOR REAL!!
NOW, NOW. KEEP IN MIND EVERYTHING YOU'VE LEARNED, AND USE TEAMWORK!
Good luck!
OTHERWISE, WE MAY HAVE ONE OR TWO DEATHS. OKAY?

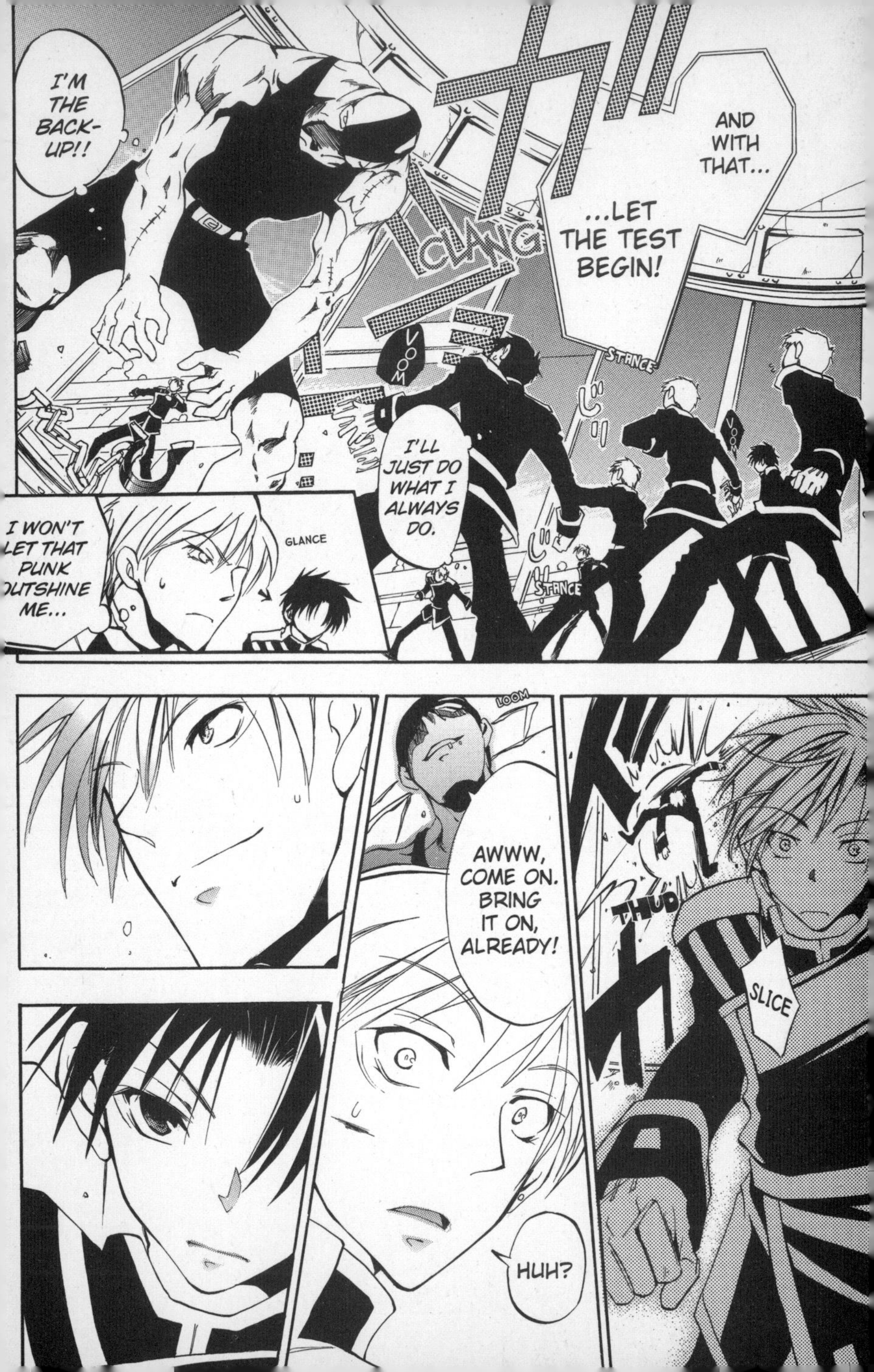
AND WITH THAT...
...LET THE TEST BEGIN!
CLANG
I'M THE BACK-UP!!
STANCE
VOOM
VOOM
I'LL JUST DO WHAT I ALWAYS DO.
STANCE
I WON'T LET THAT PUNK OUTSHINE ME...
GLANCE
THUD
SLICE
LOOM
AWWW, COME ON. BRING IT ON, ALREADY!
HUH?

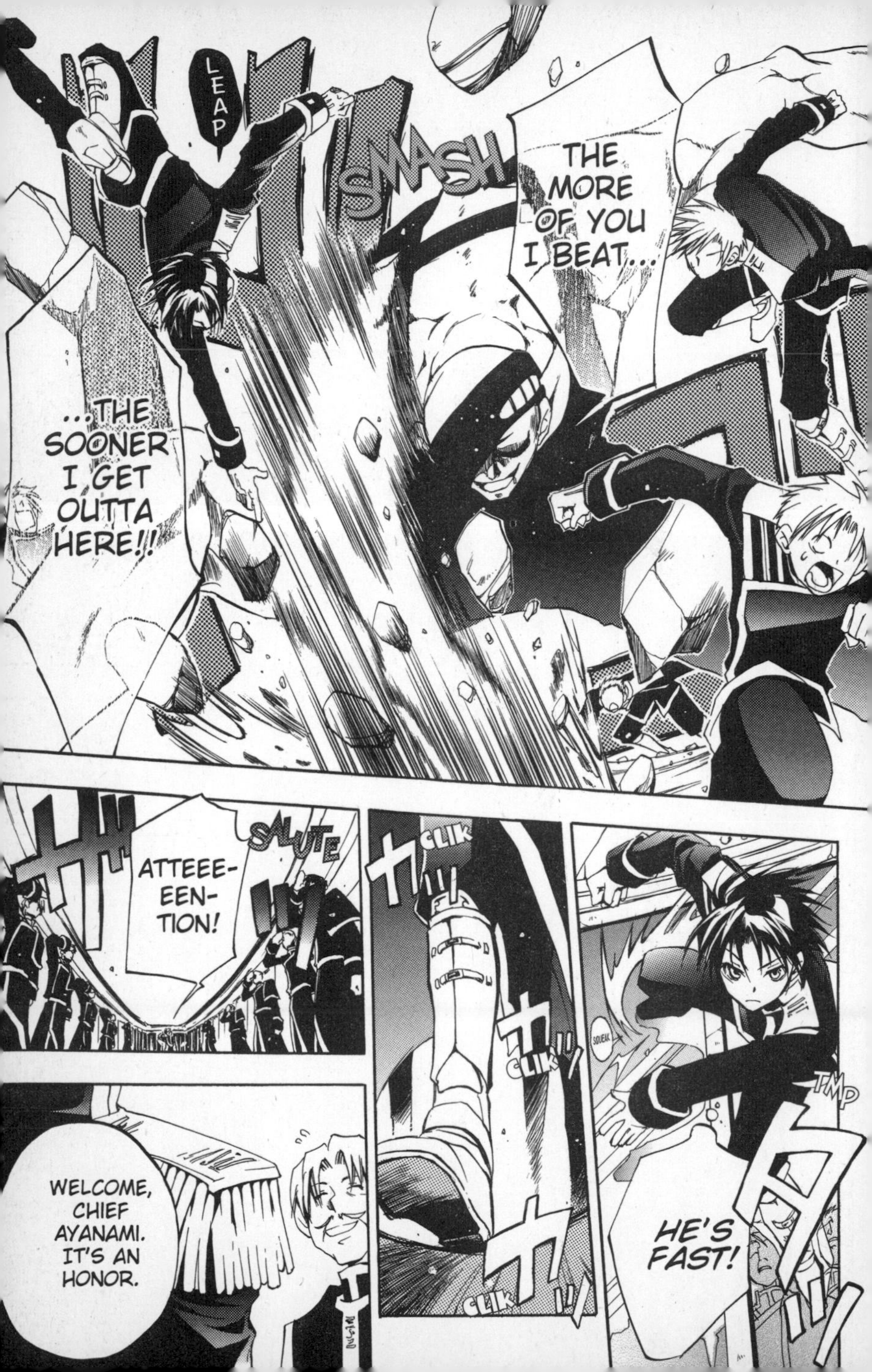
THE MORE OF YOU I BEAT...
SMASH
LEAP
...THE SOONER I GET OUTTA HERE!!
TMP
HE'S FAST!
CLIK
CLIK
CLIK
SALUTE
ATTEEEE-EEN-TION!
WELCOME, CHIEF AYANAMI. IT'S AN HONOR.

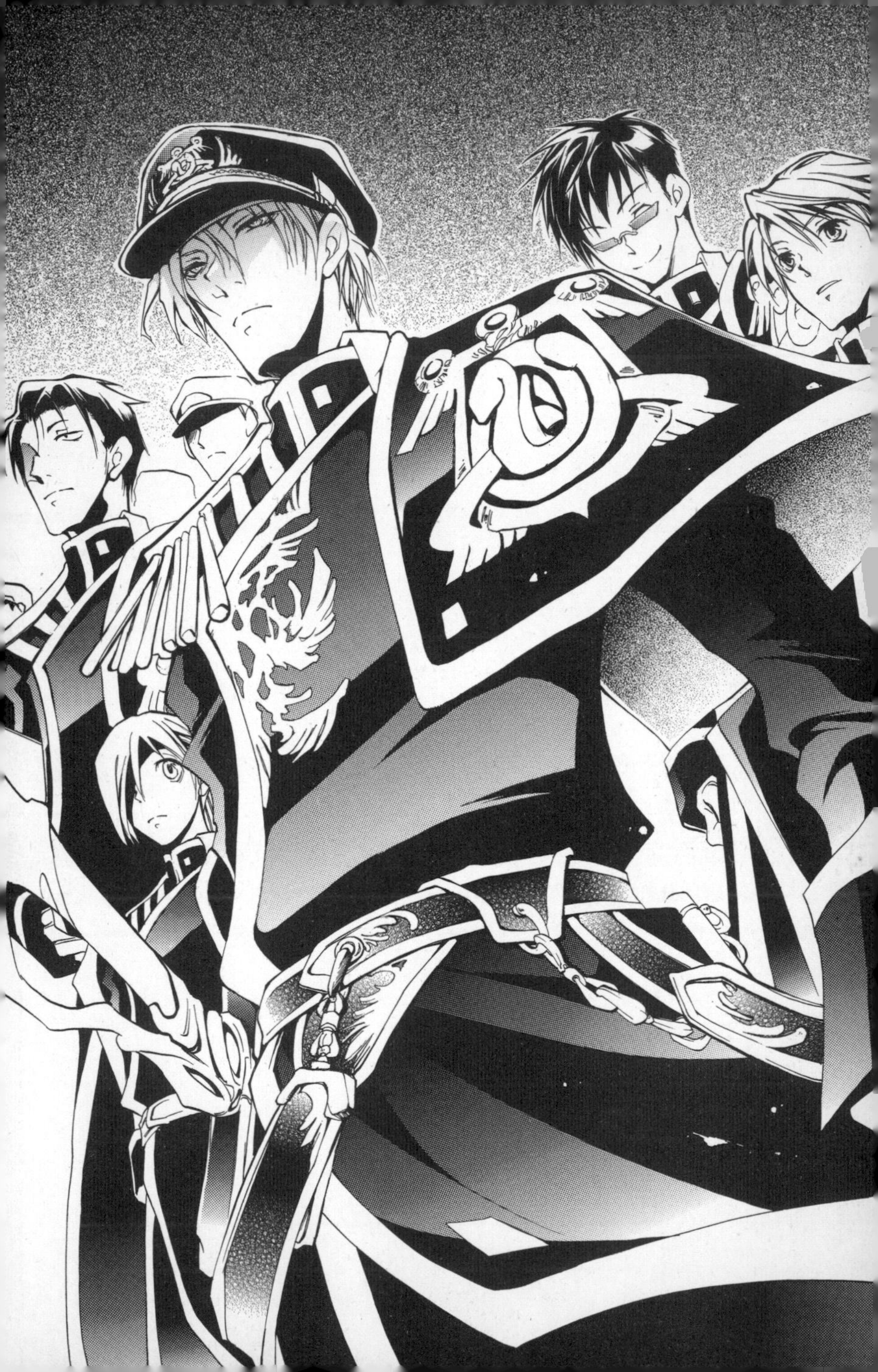

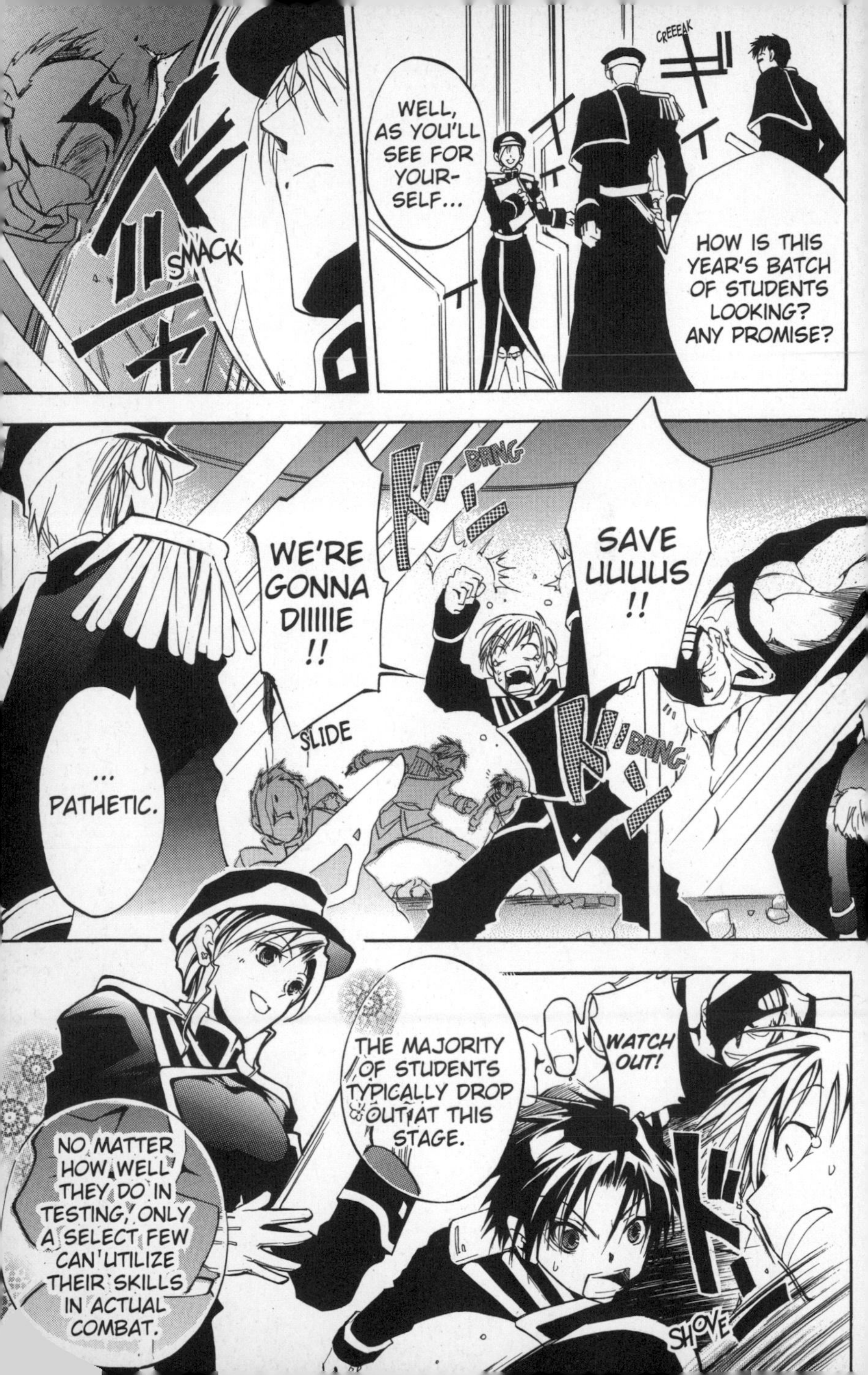
CREEEAK
HOW IS THIS YEAR'S BATCH OF STUDENTS LOOKING? ANY PROMISE?
WELL, AS YOU'LL SEE FOR YOUR-SELF...
SMACK
BANG
SAVE UUUUS!!
WE'RE GONNA DIIIIIE!!
BANG
SLIDE
... PATHETIC.
WATCH OUT!
THE MAJORITY OF STUDENTS TYPICALLY DROP OUT AT THIS STAGE.
SHOVE
NO MATTER HOW WELL THEY DO IN TESTING, ONLY A SELECT FEW CAN UTILIZE THEIR SKILLS IN ACTUAL COMBAT.

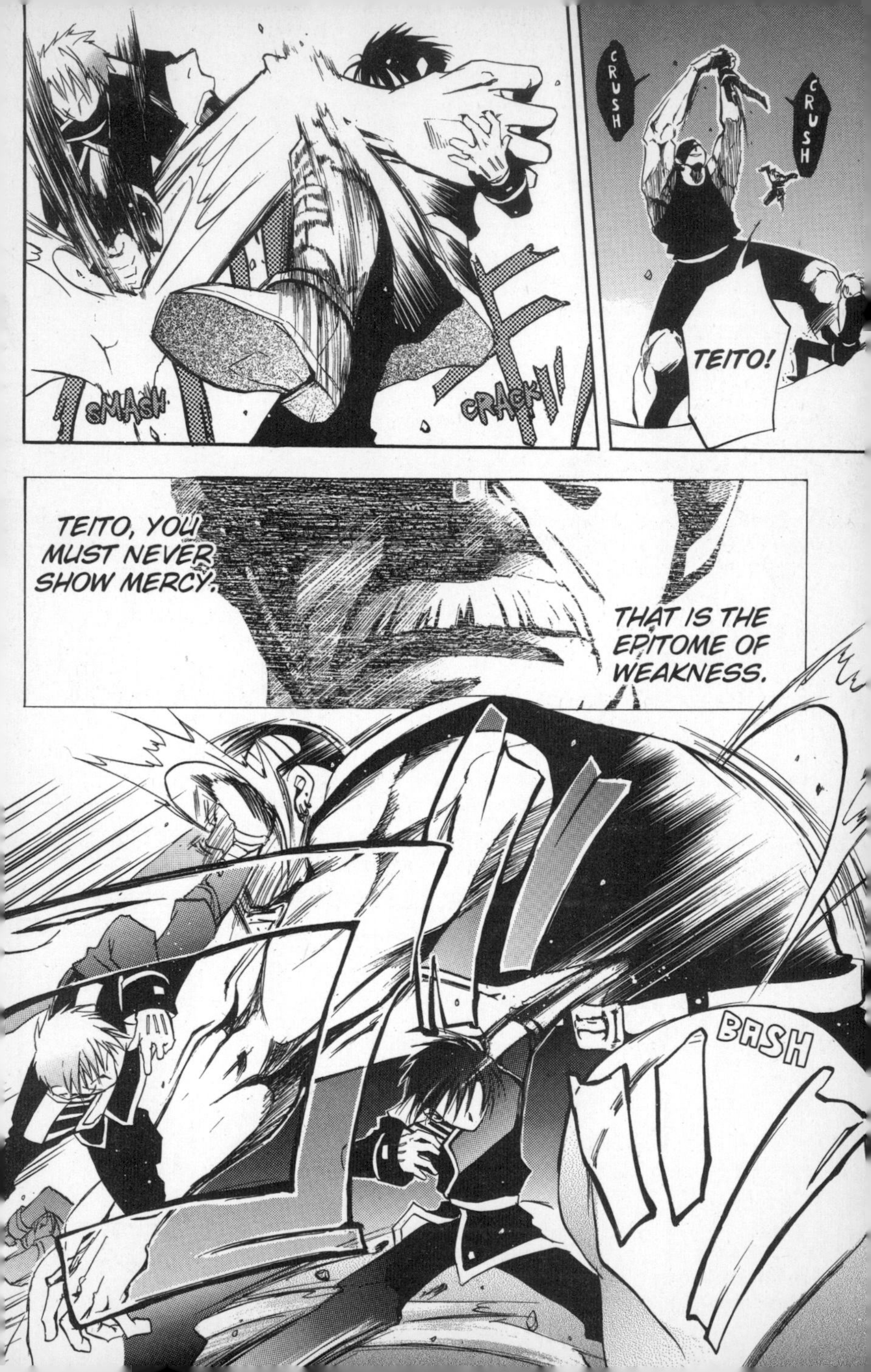
CRUSH
CRUSH
TEITO!
SMASH
CRACK
TEITO, YOU MUST NEVER SHOW MERCY.
THAT IS THE EPITOME OF WEAKNESS.
BASH

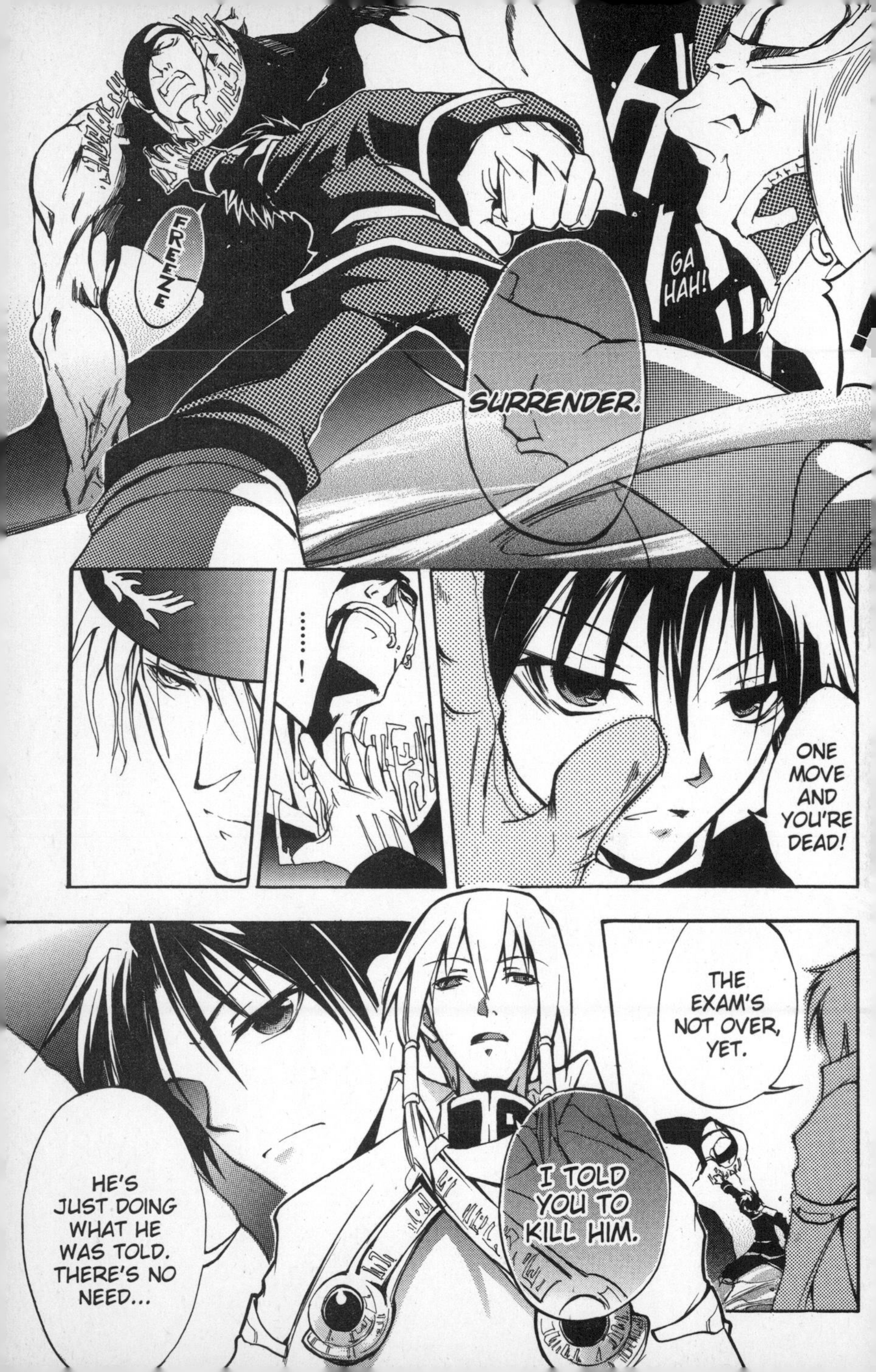
GA HAH!
FREEZE
SURRENDER.
ONE MOVE AND YOU'RE DEAD!
......!
THE EXAM'S NOT OVER, YET.
I TOLD YOU TO KILL HIM.
HE'S JUST DOING WHAT HE WAS TOLD. THERE'S NO NEED...

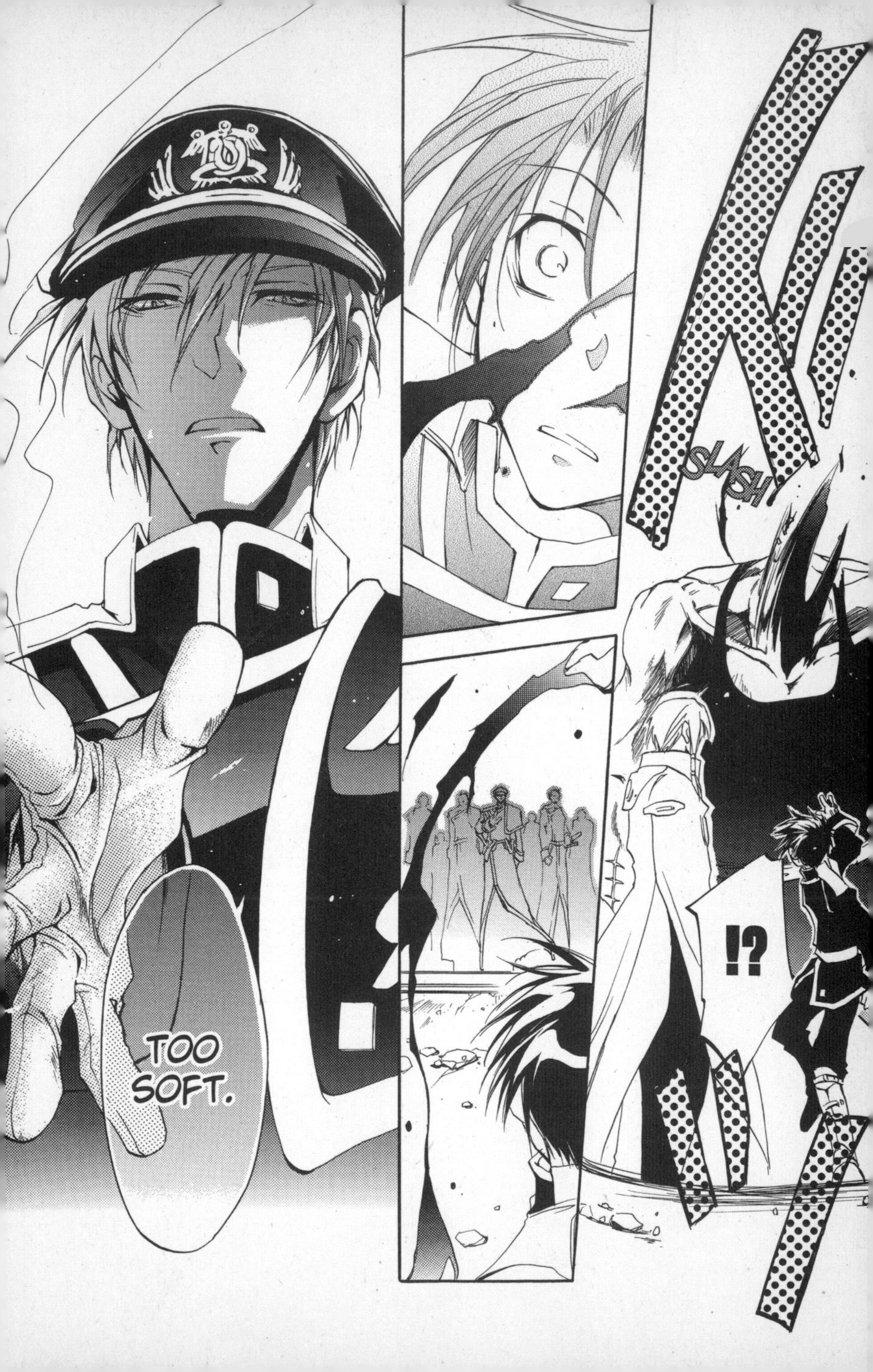
SLASH
!?
TOO SOFT.

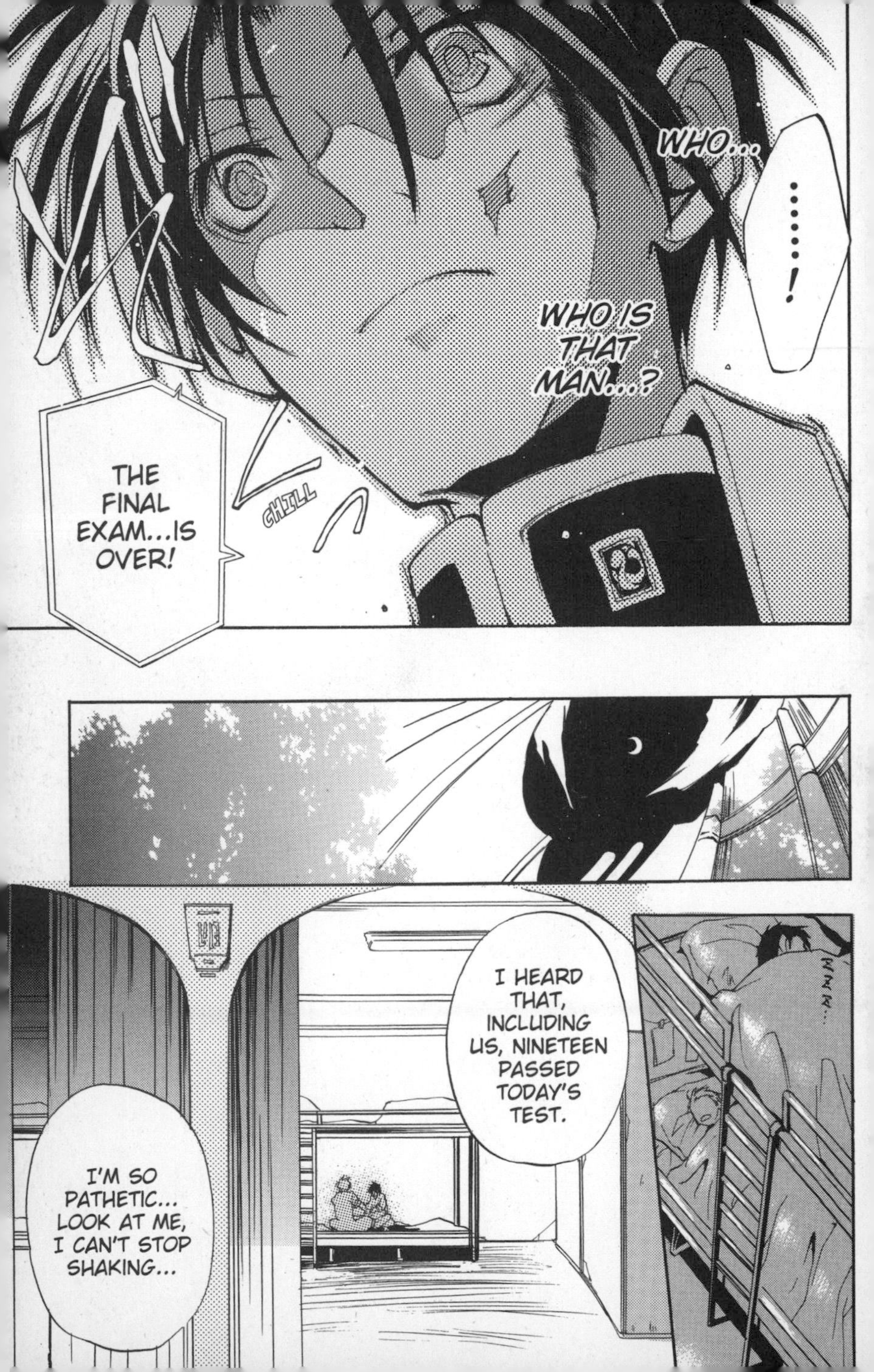
WHO...
......!
WHO IS THAT MAN...?
CHILL
THE FINAL EXAM...IS OVER!
I HEARD THAT, INCLUDING US, NINETEEN PASSED TODAY'S TEST.
I'M SO PATHETIC... LOOK AT ME, I CAN'T STOP SHAKING...

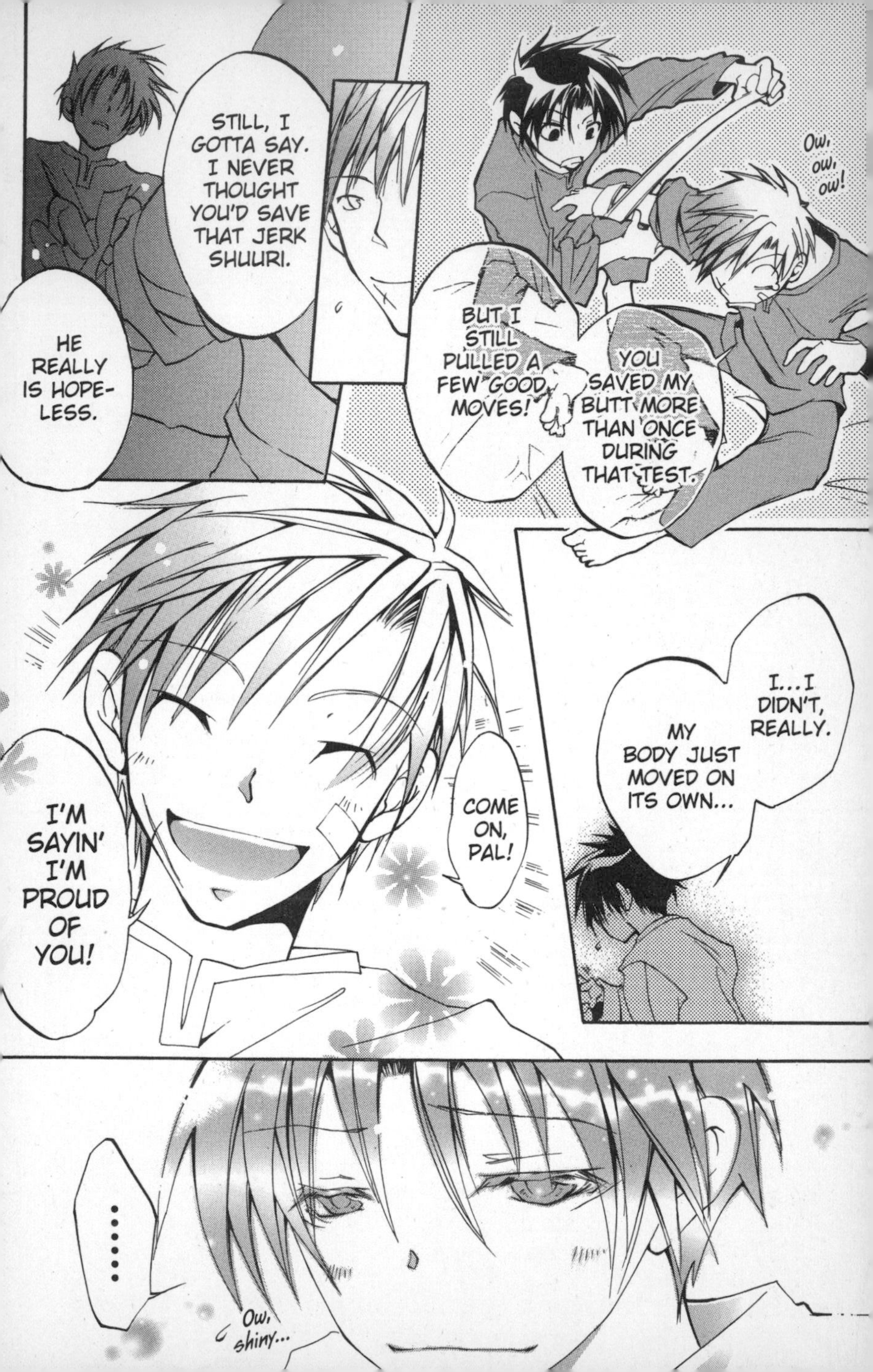
Ow, ow, ow!
YOU SAVED MY BUTT MORE THAN ONCE DURING THAT TEST.
BUT I STILL PULLED A FEW GOOD MOVES!
STILL, I GOTTA SAY. I NEVER THOUGHT YOU'D SAVE THAT JERK SHUURI.
HE REALLY IS HOPE-LESS.
I...I DIDN'T, REALLY.
MY BODY JUST MOVED ON ITS OWN...
COME ON, PAL!
I'M SAYIN' I'M PROUD OF YOU!
......
Ow, shiny...

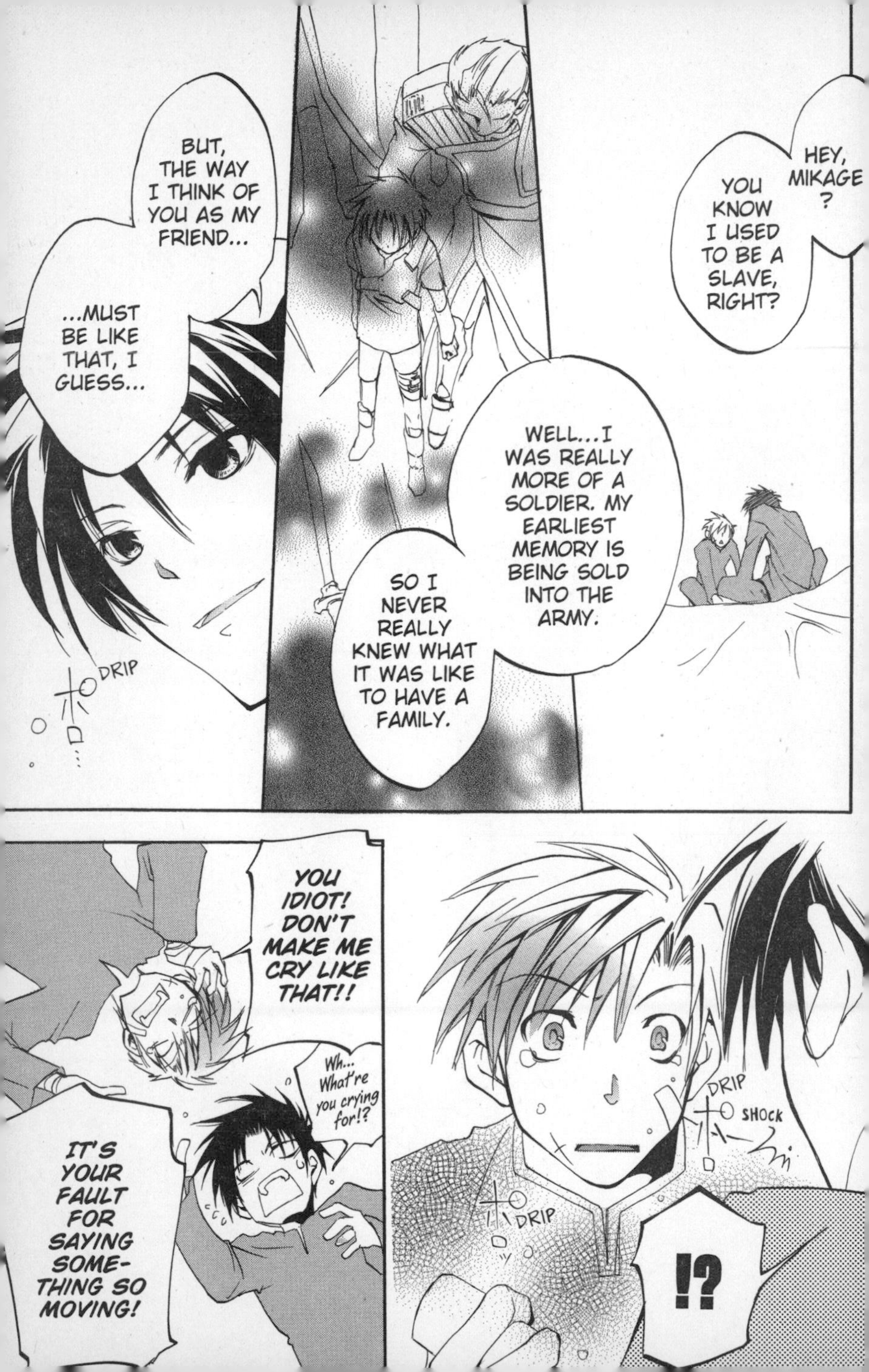
HEY, MIKAGE?
YOU KNOW I USED TO BE A SLAVE, RIGHT?
WELL...I WAS REALLY MORE OF A SOLDIER. MY EARLIEST MEMORY IS BEING SOLD INTO THE ARMY.
SO I NEVER REALLY KNEW WHAT IT WAS LIKE TO HAVE A FAMILY.
BUT, THE WAY I THINK OF YOU AS MY FRIEND...
...MUST BE LIKE THAT, I GUESS...
DRIP
DRIP
SHOCK
DRIP
!?
YOU IDIOT! DON'T MAKE ME CRY LIKE THAT!!
Wh... What're you crying for!?
IT'S YOUR FAULT FOR SAYING SOME-THING SO MOVING!

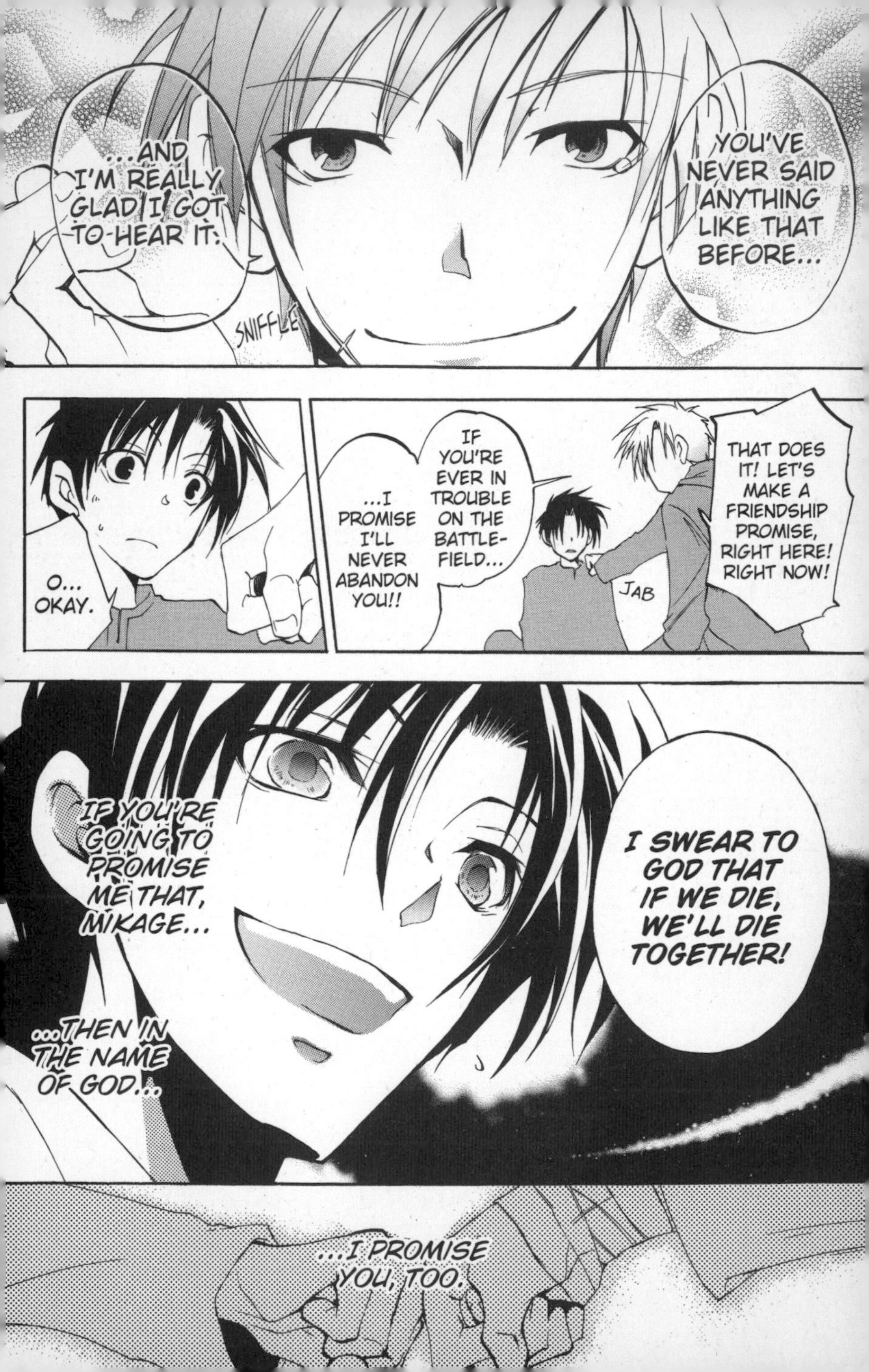
YOU'VE NEVER SAID ANYTHING LIKE THAT BEFORE...
...AND I'M REALLY GLAD I GOT TO HEAR IT.
SNIFFLE
THAT DOES IT! LET'S MAKE A FRIENDSHIP PROMISE, RIGHT HERE! RIGHT NOW!
JAB
IF YOU'RE EVER IN TROUBLE ON THE BATTLE-FIELD...
...I PROMISE I'LL NEVER ABANDON YOU!!
O... OKAY.
IF YOU'RE GOING TO PROMISE ME THAT, MIKAGE...
...THEN IN THE NAME OF GOD...
I SWEAR TO GOD THAT IF WE DIE, WE'LL DIE TOGETHER!
...I PROMISE YOU, TOO.

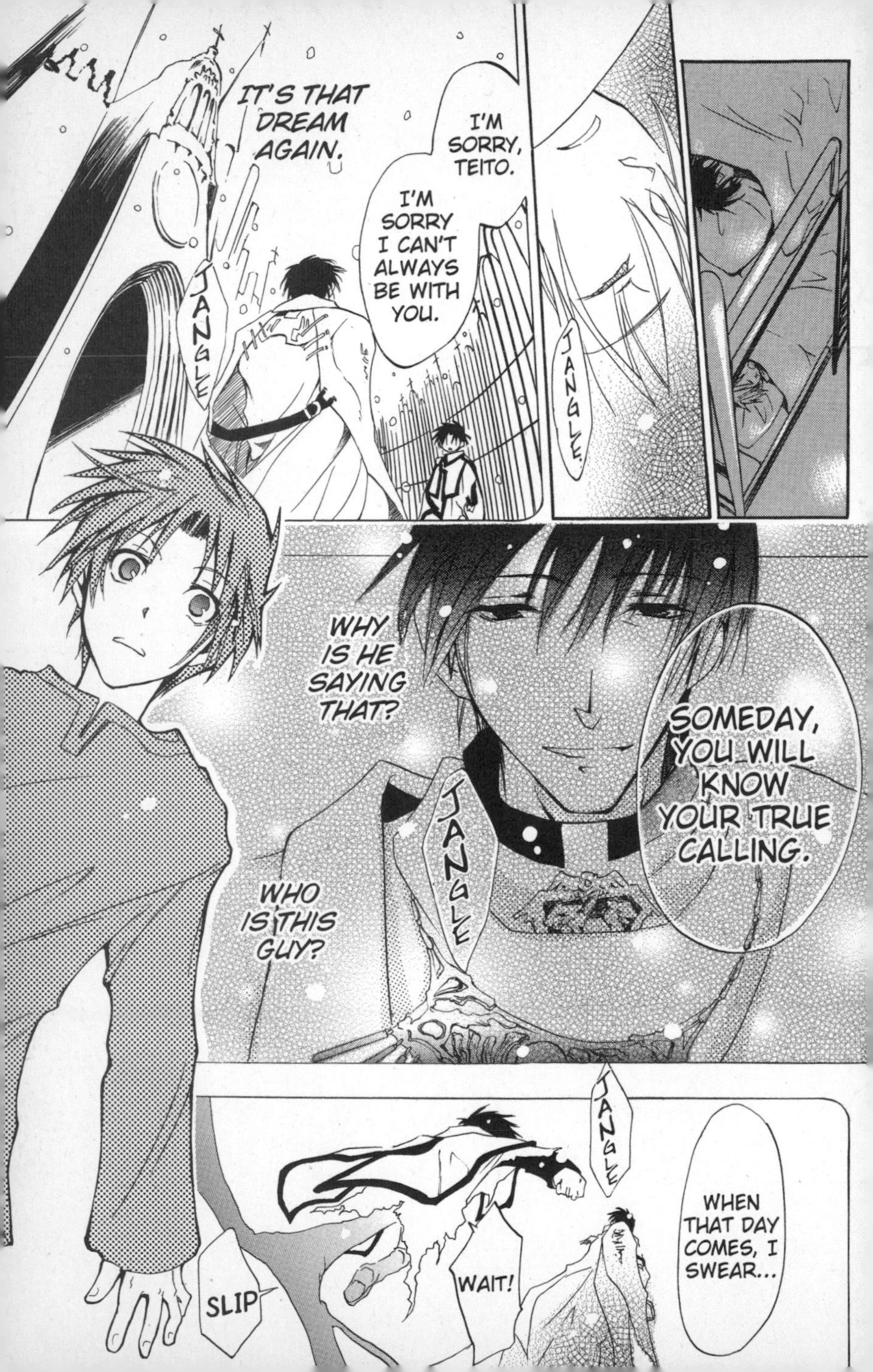
JANGLE
IT'S THAT DREAM AGAIN.
I'M SORRY, TEITO.
I'M SORRY I CAN'T ALWAYS BE WITH YOU.
JANGLE
SOMEDAY, YOU WILL KNOW YOUR TRUE CALLING.
JANGLE
WHY IS HE SAYING THAT?
WHO IS THIS GUY?
JANGLE
WHEN THAT DAY COMES, I SWEAR...
WAIT!
SLIP

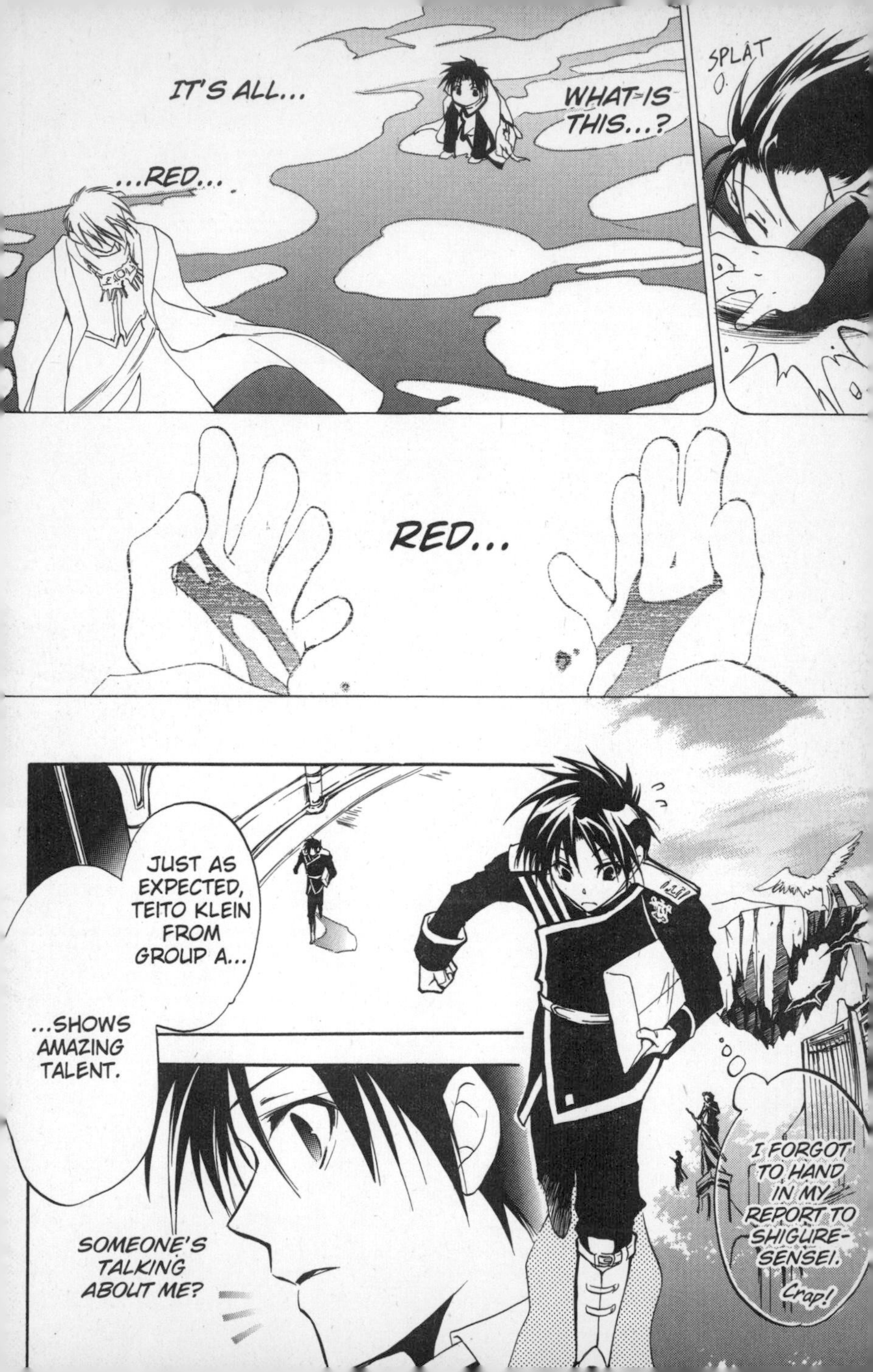
SPLAT
WHAT IS THIS...?
IT'S ALL...
...RED...
RED...
I FORGOT TO HAND IN MY REPORT TO SHIGURE-SENSEI.
Crap!
JUST AS EXPECTED, TEITO KLEIN FROM GROUP A...
...SHOWS AMAZING TALENT.
SOMEONE'S TALKING ABOUT ME?

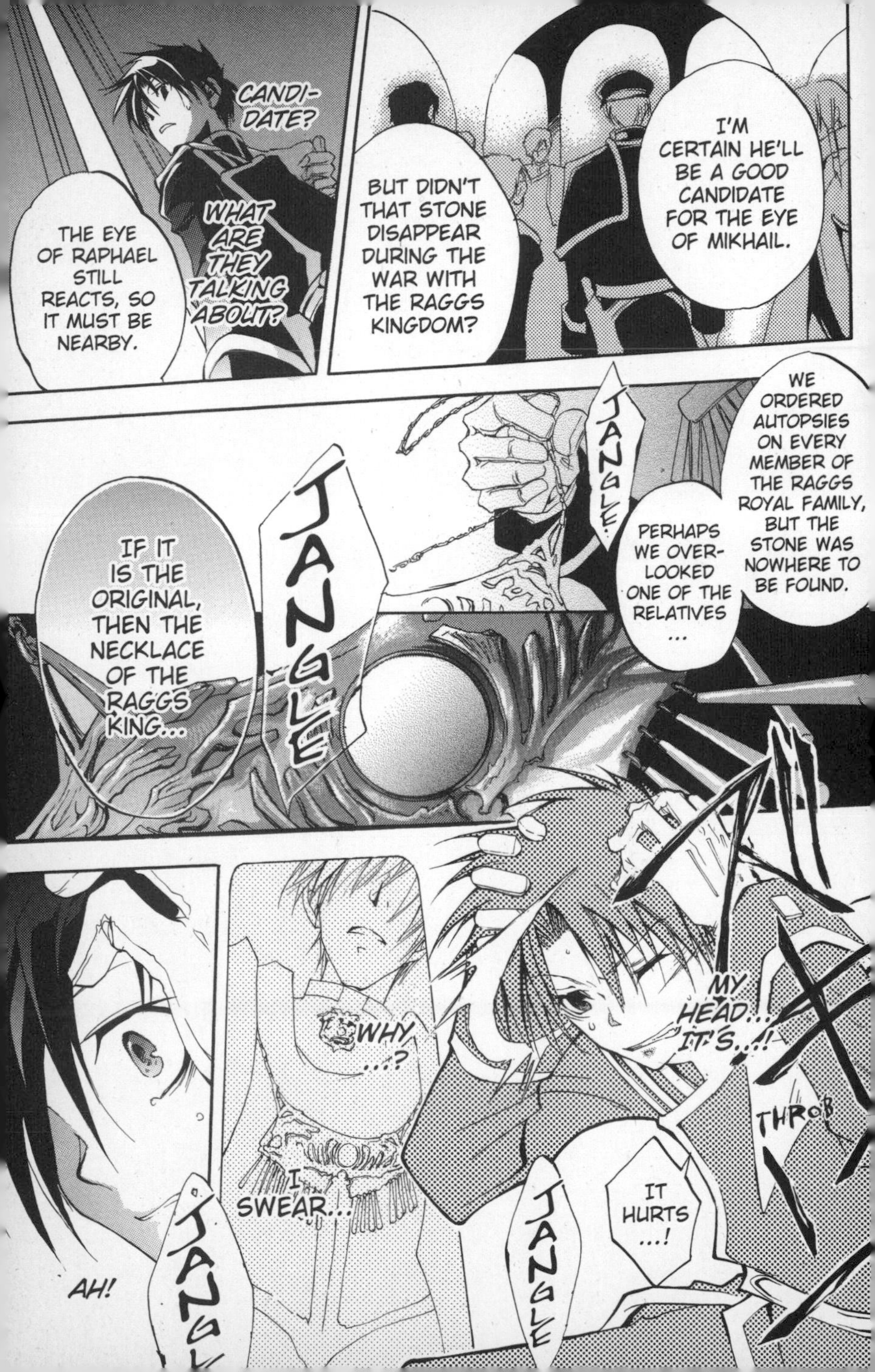
I'M CERTAIN HE'LL BE A GOOD CANDIDATE FOR THE EYE OF MIKHAIL.
BUT DIDN'T THAT STONE DISAPPEAR DURING THE WAR WITH THE RAGGS KINGDOM?
CANDI-DATE?
WHAT ARE THEY TALKING ABOUT?
THE EYE OF RAPHAEL STILL REACTS, SO IT MUST BE NEARBY.
WE ORDERED AUTOPSIES ON EVERY MEMBER OF THE RAGGS ROYAL FAMILY, BUT THE STONE WAS NOWHERE TO BE FOUND.
PERHAPS WE OVER-LOOKED ONE OF THE RELATIVES ...
JANGLE.
JANGLE
IF IT IS THE ORIGINAL, THEN THE NECKLACE OF THE RAGGS KING...
MY HEAD... IT'S...!
THROB
IT HURTS ...!
JANGLE
WHY ...?
I SWEAR...
AH!
JANGL

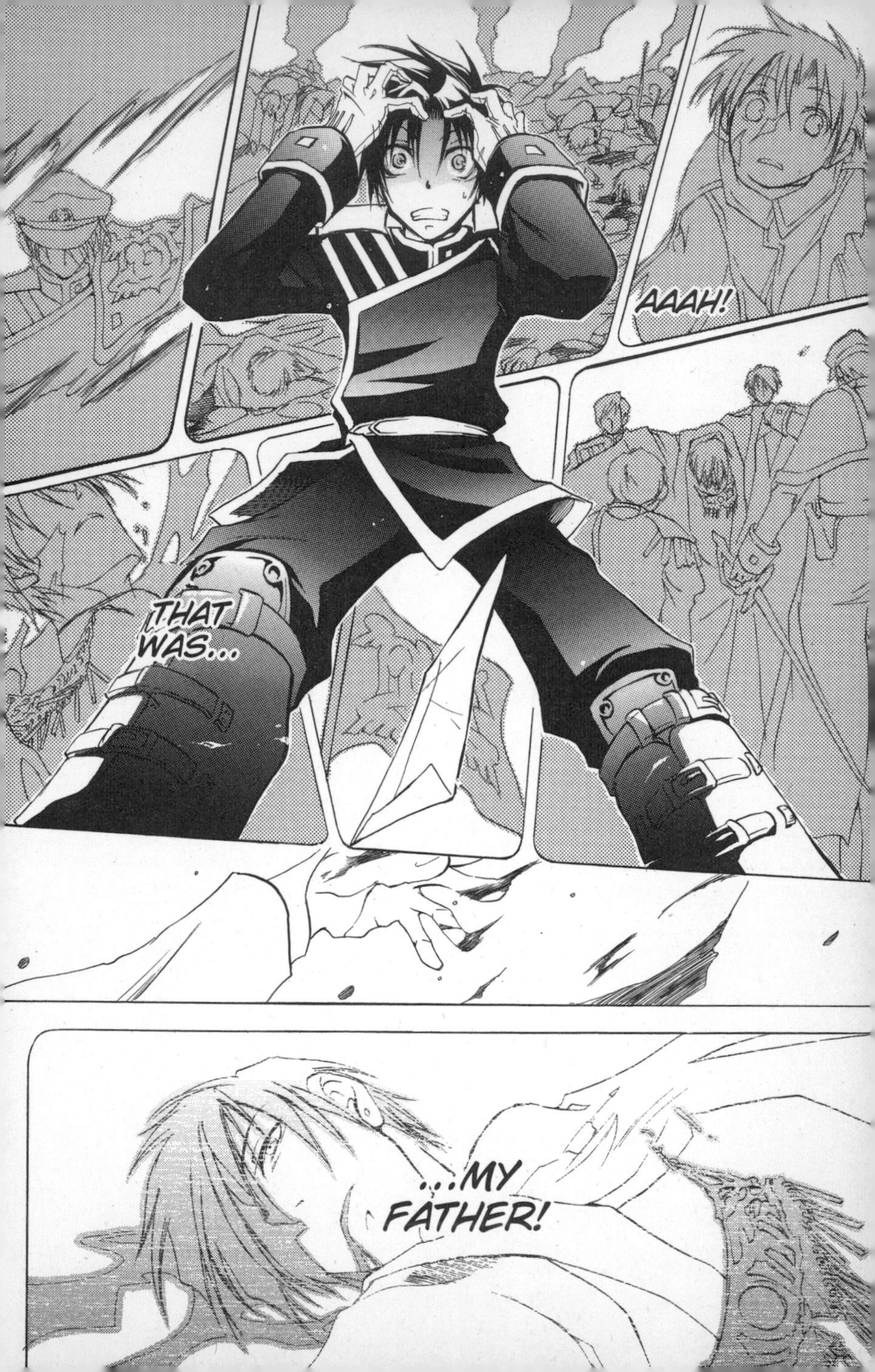
AAAH!
THAT WAS...
...MY FATHER!

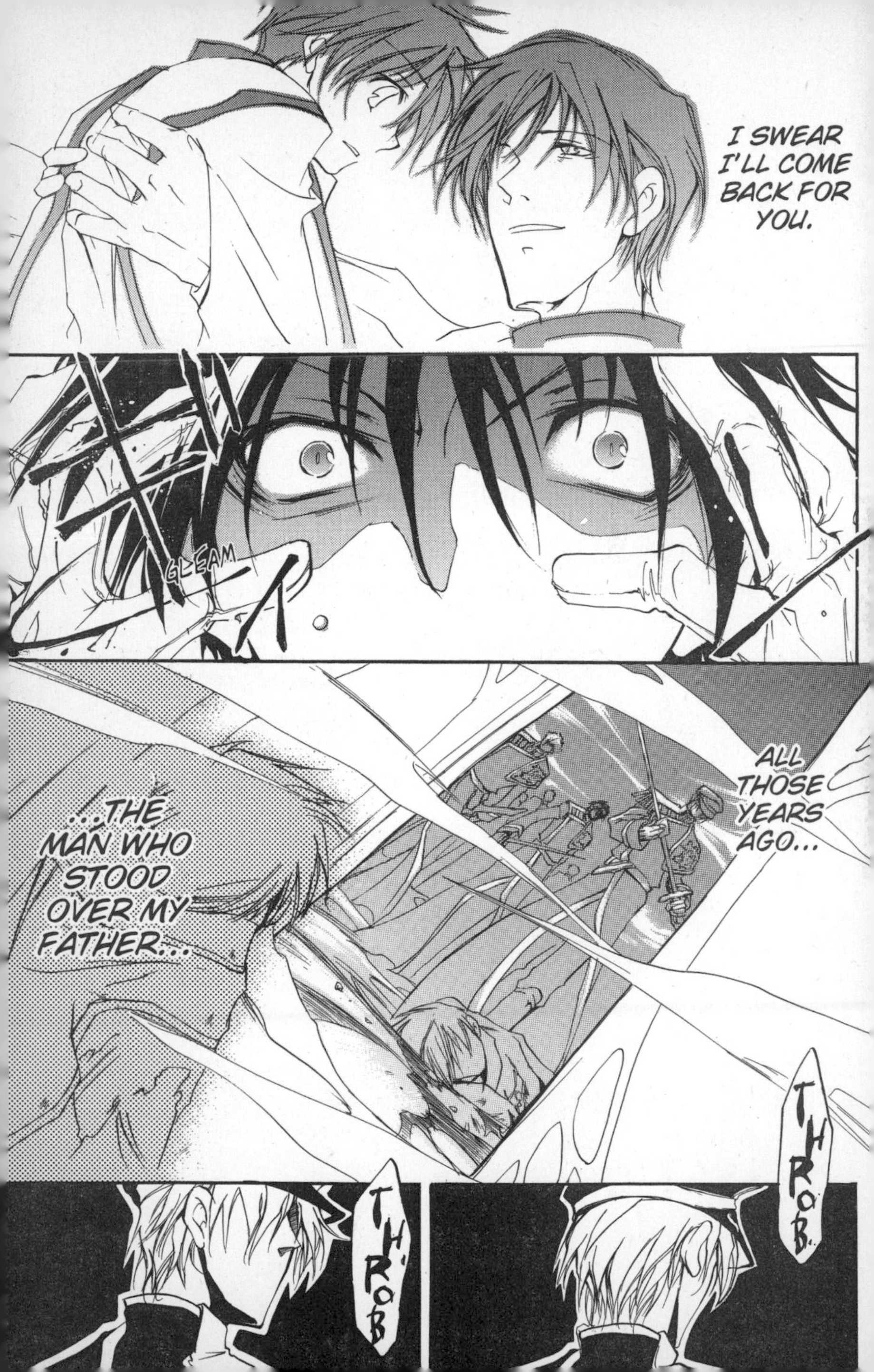
I SWEAR I'LL COME BACK FOR YOU.
GLEAM
ALL THOSE YEARS AGO...
...THE MAN WHO STOOD OVER MY FATHER...
THROB.
THROB

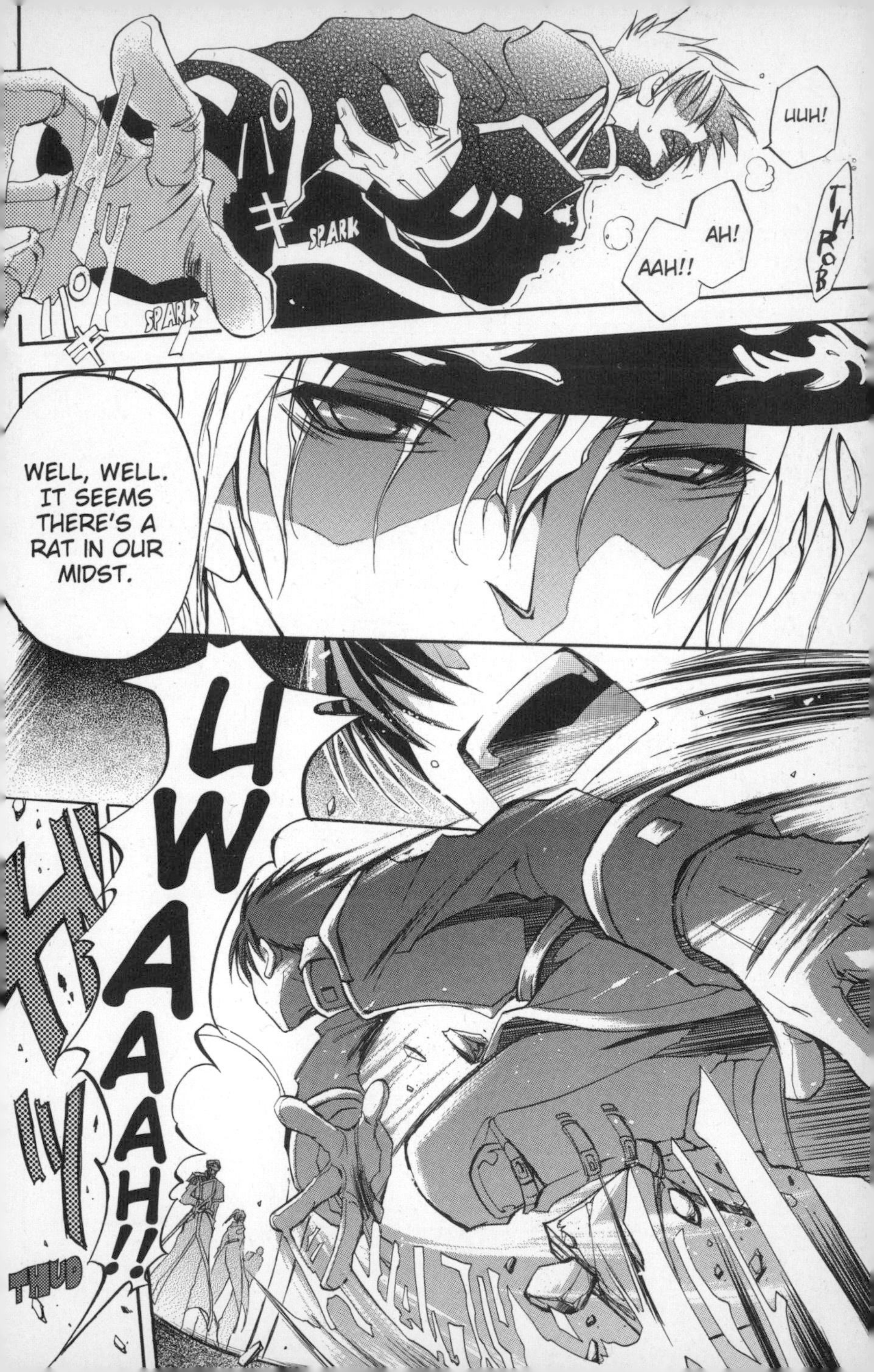
UUH!
THROB
AH!
AAH!!
SPARK
SPARK
WELL, WELL. IT SEEMS THERE'S A RAT IN OUR MIDST.
UWAAAAH!!
THUD

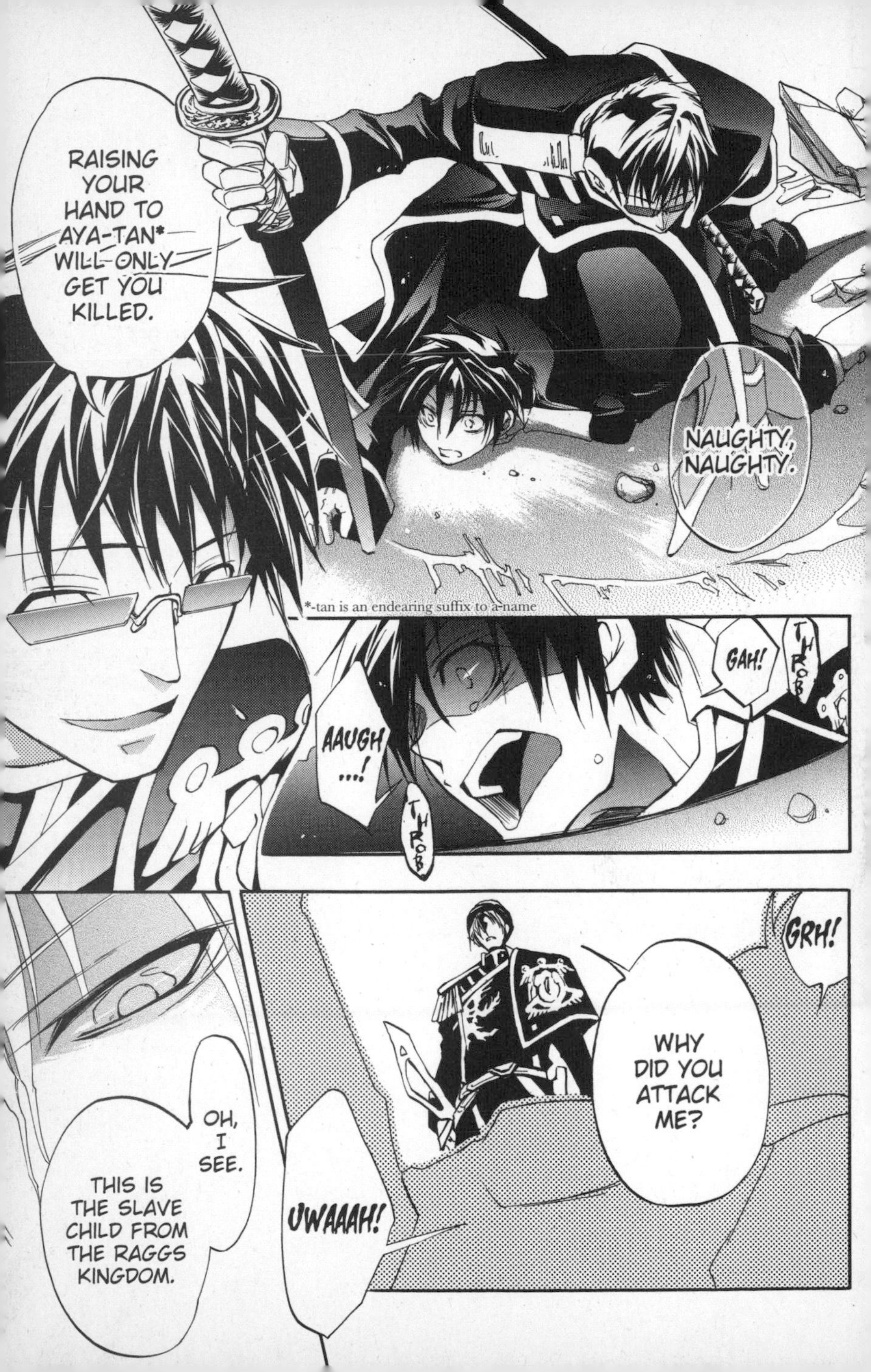
NAUGHTY, NAUGHTY.
RAISING YOUR HAND TO AYA-TAN* WILL ONLY GET YOU KILLED.
*-tan is an endearing suffix to a name
GAH!
THROB
AAUGH ...!
THROB
GRH!
WHY DID YOU ATTACK ME?
UWAAAH!
OH, I SEE.
THIS IS THE SLAVE CHILD FROM THE RAGGS KINGDOM.

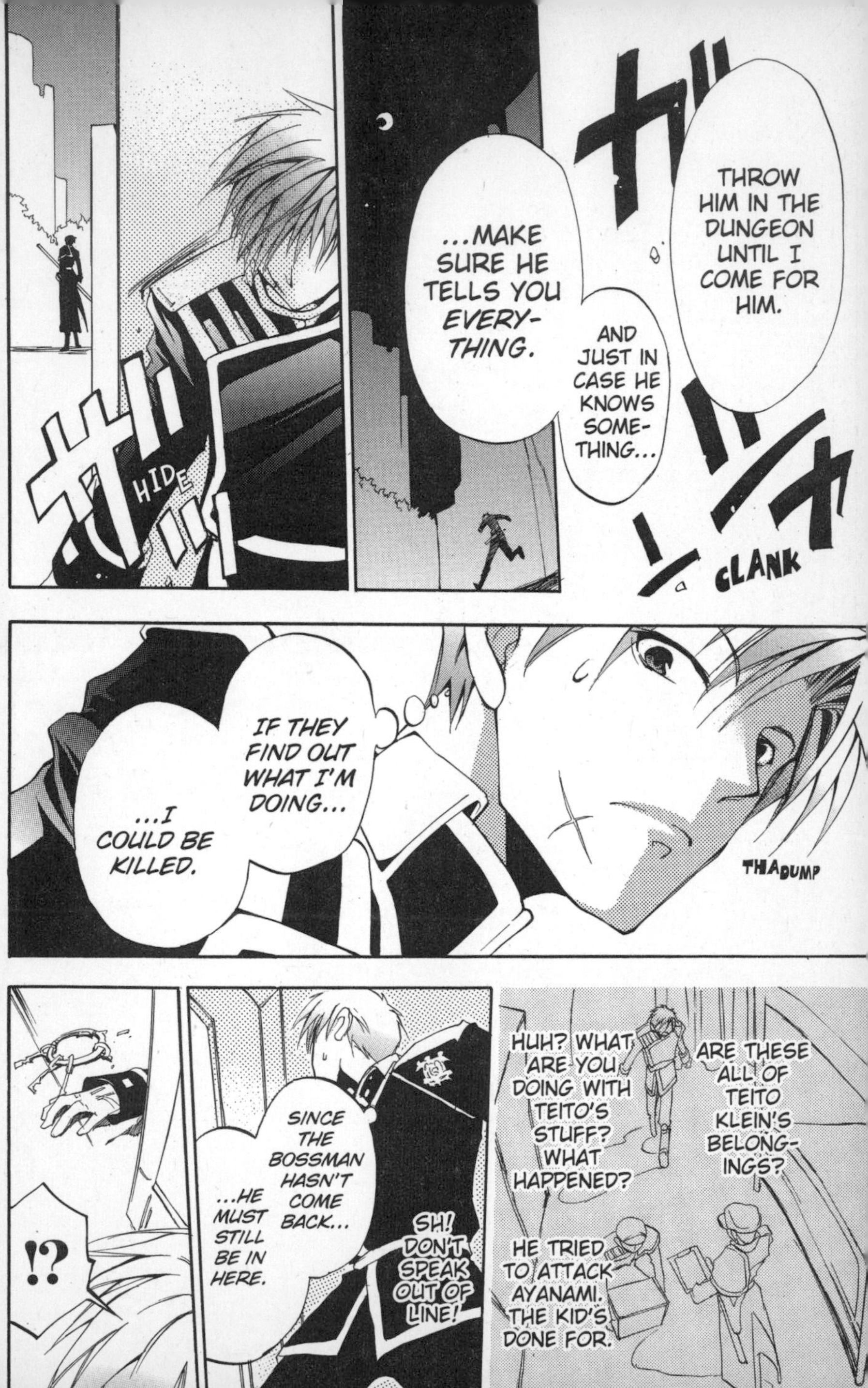
THROW HIM IN THE DUNGEON UNTIL I COME FOR HIM.
AND JUST IN CASE HE KNOWS SOME-THING...
...MAKE SURE HE TELLS YOU EVERY-THING.
CLANK
HIDE
THADUMP
IF THEY FIND OUT WHAT I'M DOING...
...I COULD BE KILLED.
ARE THESE ALL OF TEITO KLEIN'S BELONG-INGS?
HUH? WHAT ARE YOU DOING WITH TEITO'S STUFF? WHAT HAPPENED?
HE TRIED TO ATTACK AYANAMI. THE KID'S DONE FOR.
SH! DON'T SPEAK OUT OF LINE!
SINCE THE BOSSMAN HASN'T COME BACK...
...HE MUST STILL BE IN HERE.
!?

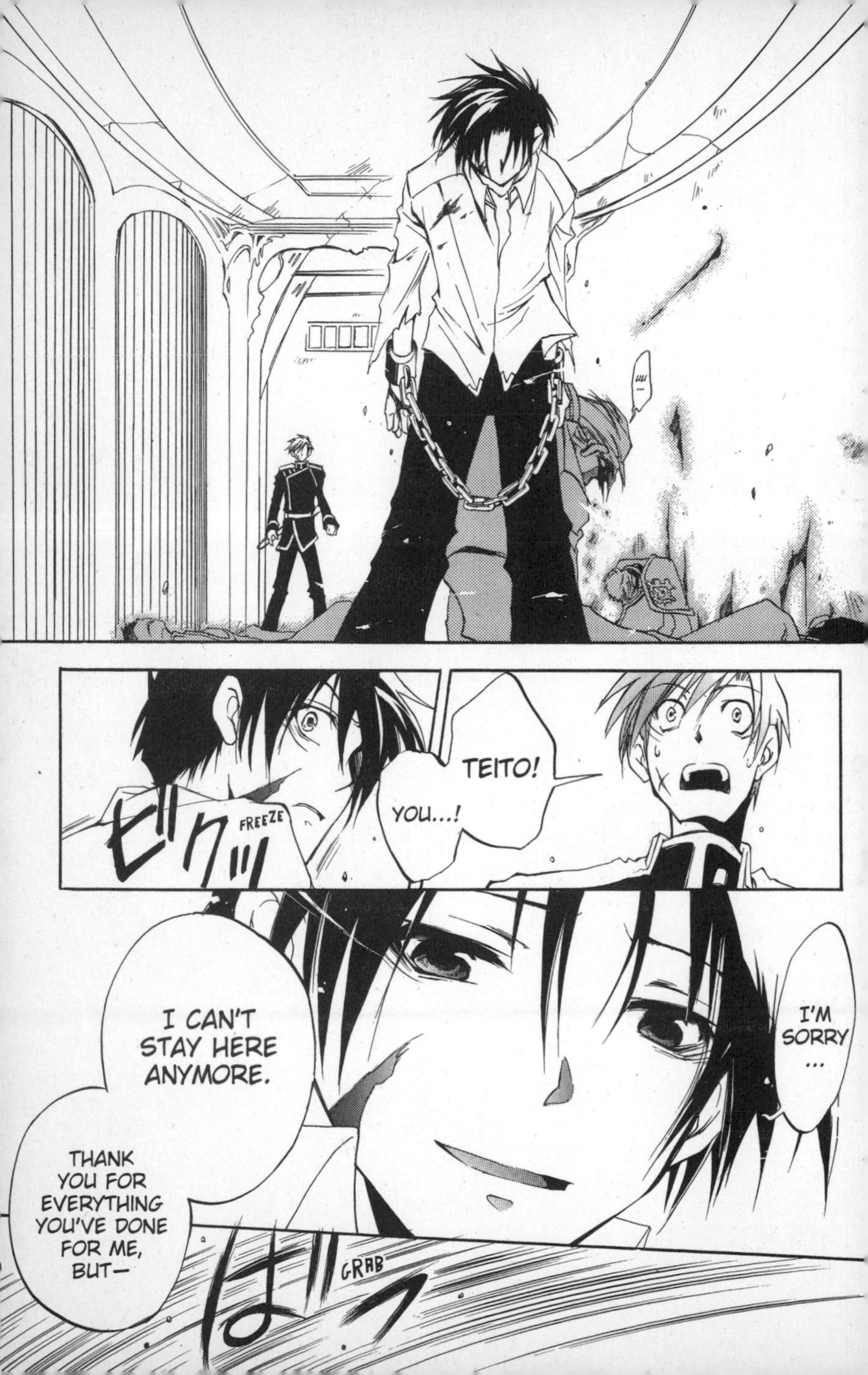
UU...
TEITO!
YOU...!
FREEZE
I'M SORRY...
I CAN'T STAY HERE ANYMORE.
THANK YOU FOR EVERYTHING YOU'VE DONE FOR ME, BUT—
GRAB

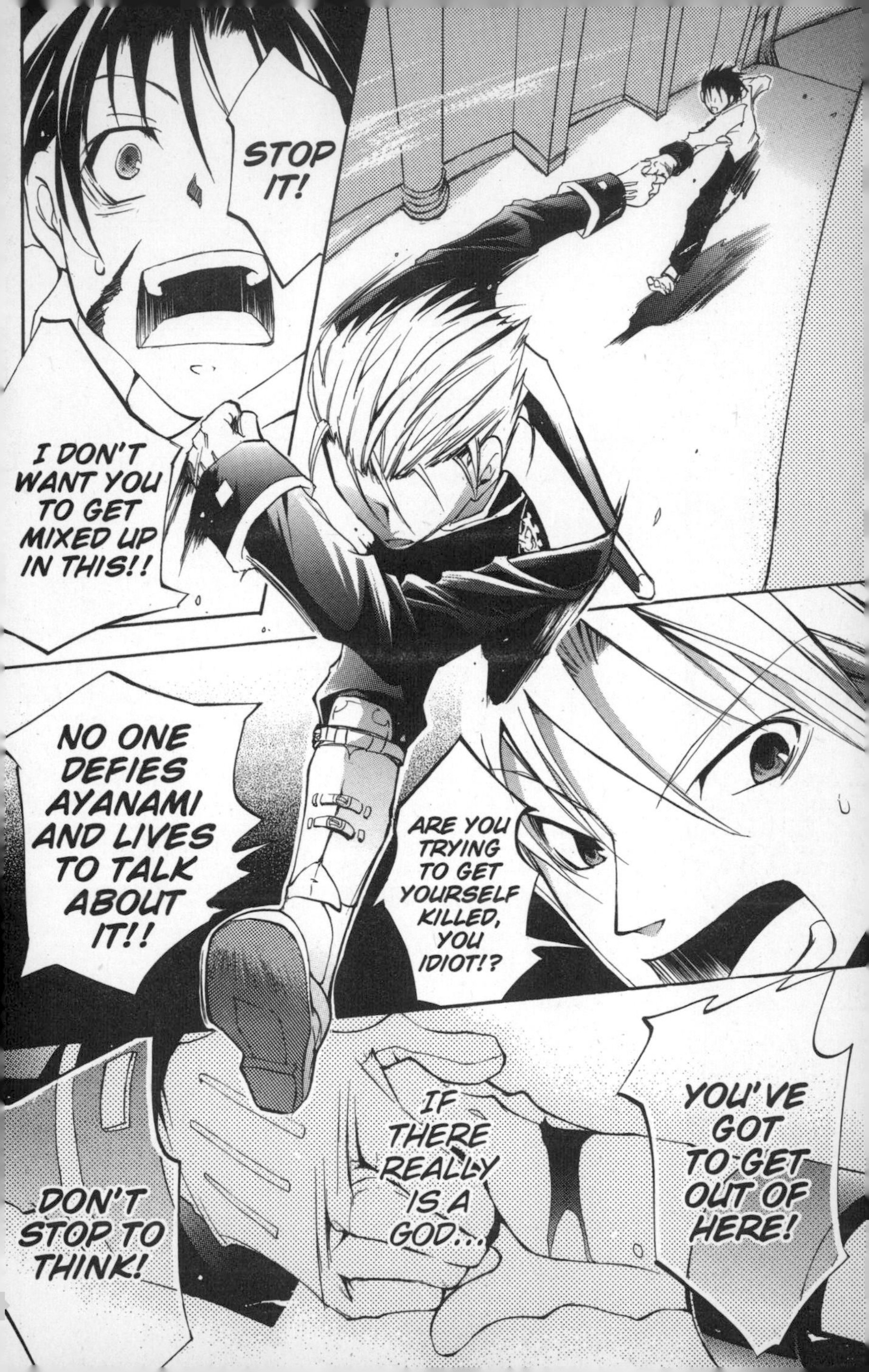
STOP IT!
I DON'T WANT YOU TO GET MIXED UP IN THIS!!
ARE YOU TRYING TO GET YOURSELF KILLED, YOU IDIOT!?
NO ONE DEFIES AYANAMI AND LIVES TO TALK ABOUT IT!!
YOU'VE GOT TO GET OUT OF HERE!
IF THERE REALLY IS A GOD...
DON'T STOP TO THINK!

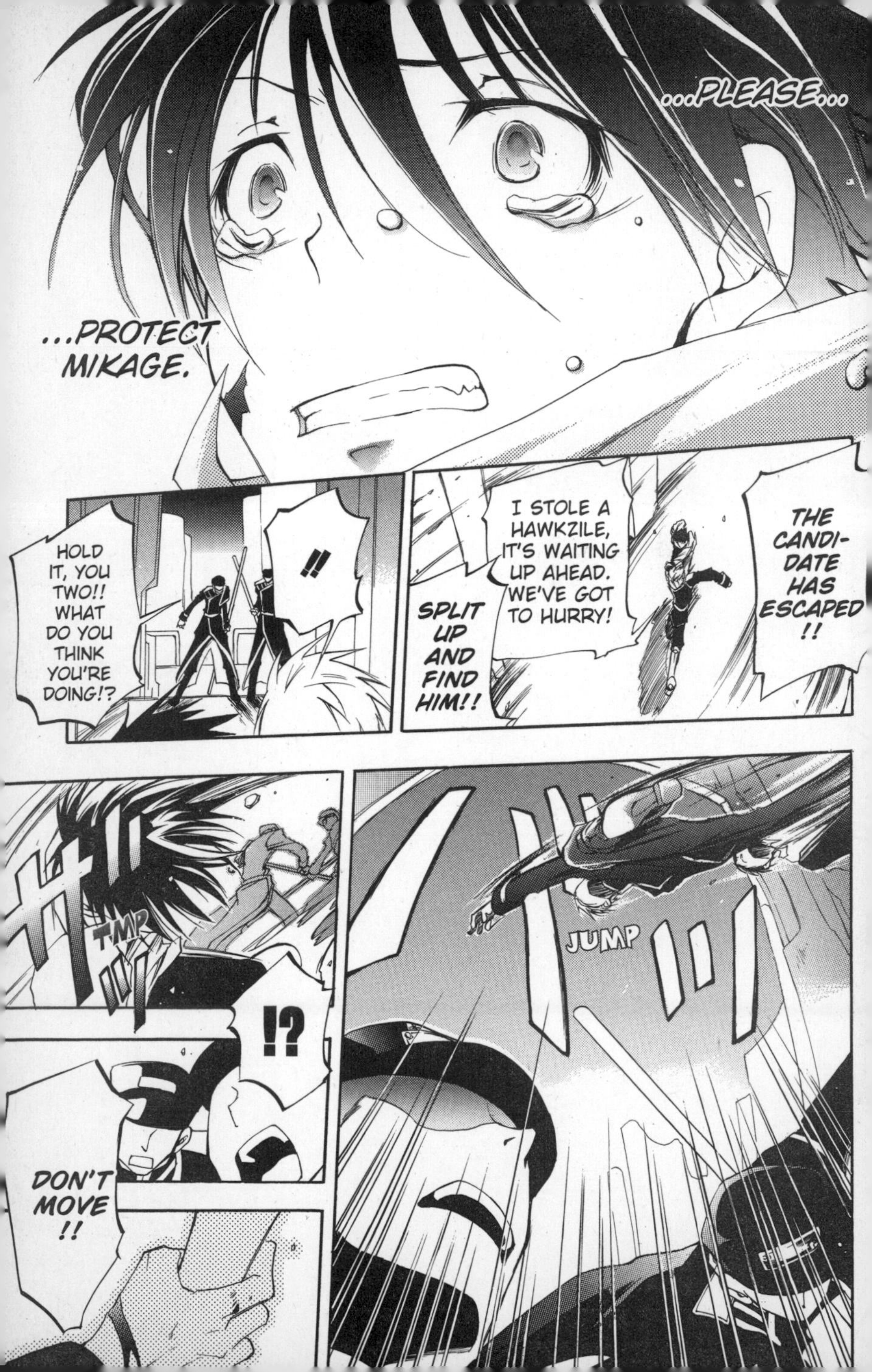
...PLEASE...
...PROTECT MIKAGE.
THE CANDIDATE HAS ESCAPED!!
I STOLE A HAWKZILE, IT'S WAITING UP AHEAD. WE'VE GOT TO HURRY!
SPLIT UP AND FIND HIM!!
!!
HOLD IT, YOU TWO!! WHAT DO YOU THINK YOU'RE DOING!?
JUMP
TMP
!?
DON'T MOVE!!

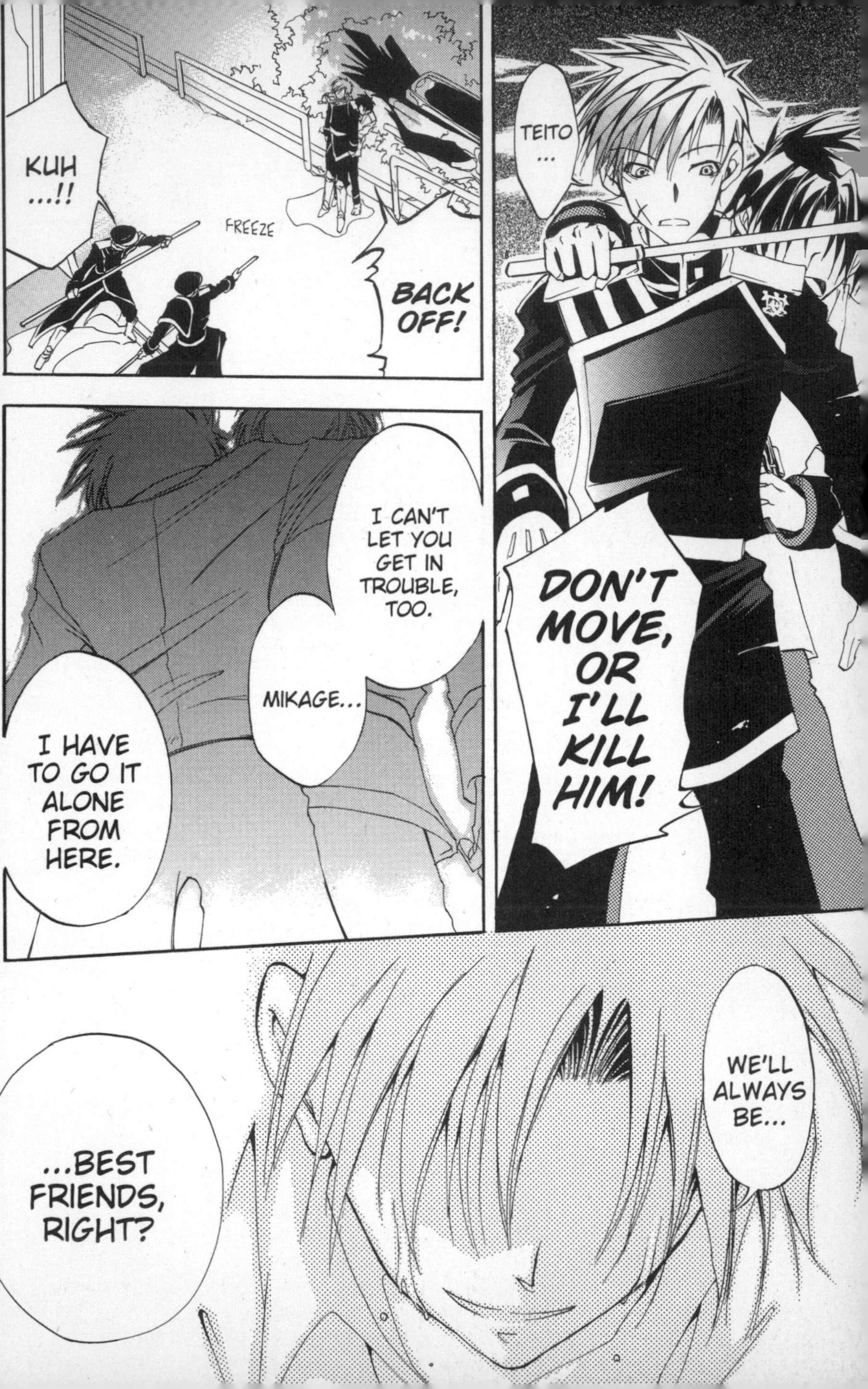
TEITO ...
DON'T MOVE, OR I'LL KILL HIM!
BACK OFF!
FREEZE
KUH ...!!
I CAN'T LET YOU GET IN TROUBLE, TOO.
MIKAGE...
I HAVE TO GO IT ALONE FROM HERE.
WE'LL ALWAYS BE...
...BEST FRIENDS, RIGHT?

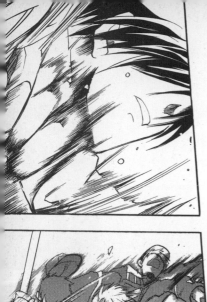

OF COURSE.

GO, TEITO!!

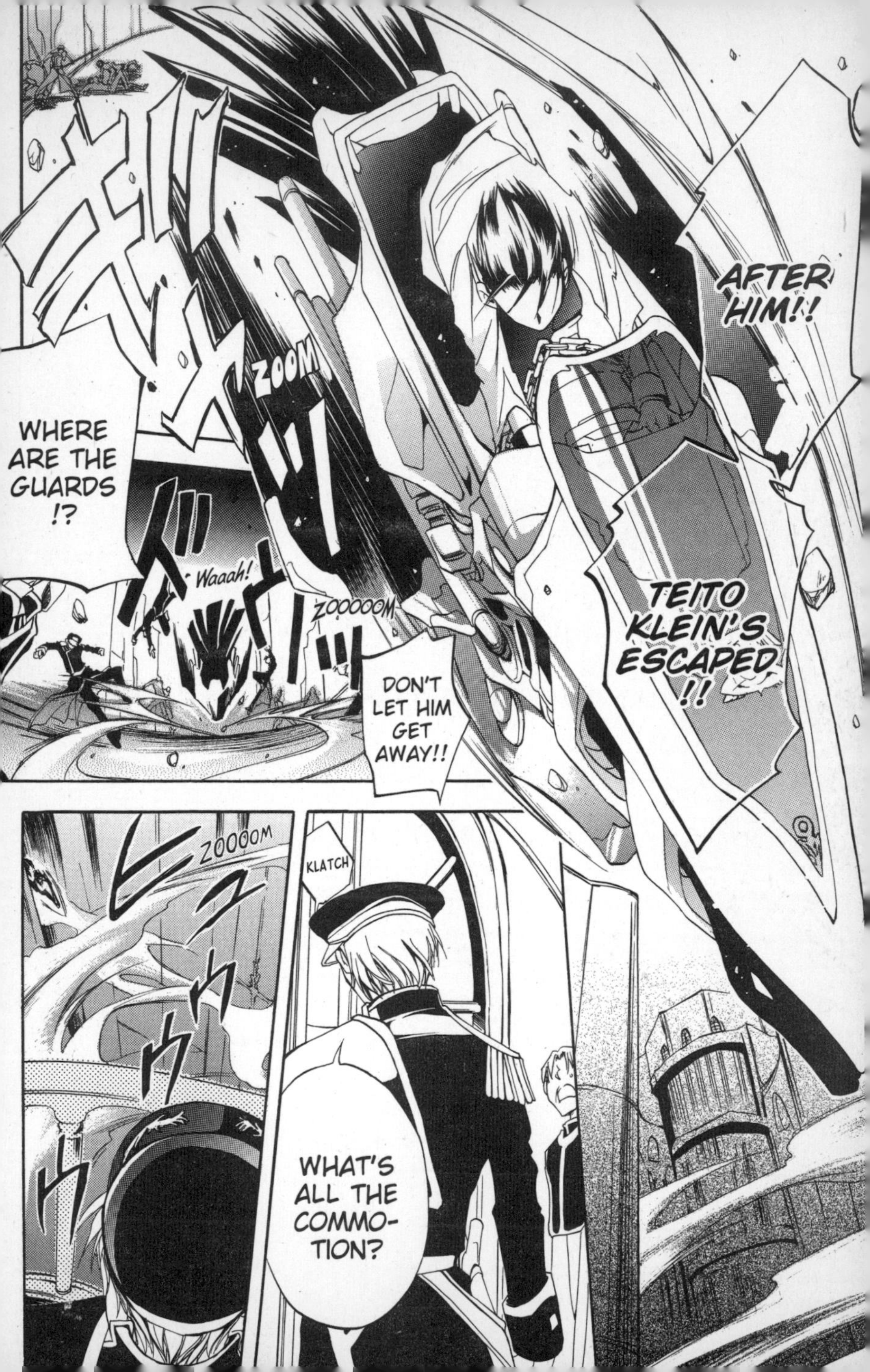
AFTER HIM!!
TEITO KLEIN'S ESCAPED!!
ZOOM
WHERE ARE THE GUARDS !?
Waaah!
ZOOOOOM
DON'T LET HIM GET AWAY!!
KLATCH
WHAT'S ALL THE COMMOTION?
ZOOOOM

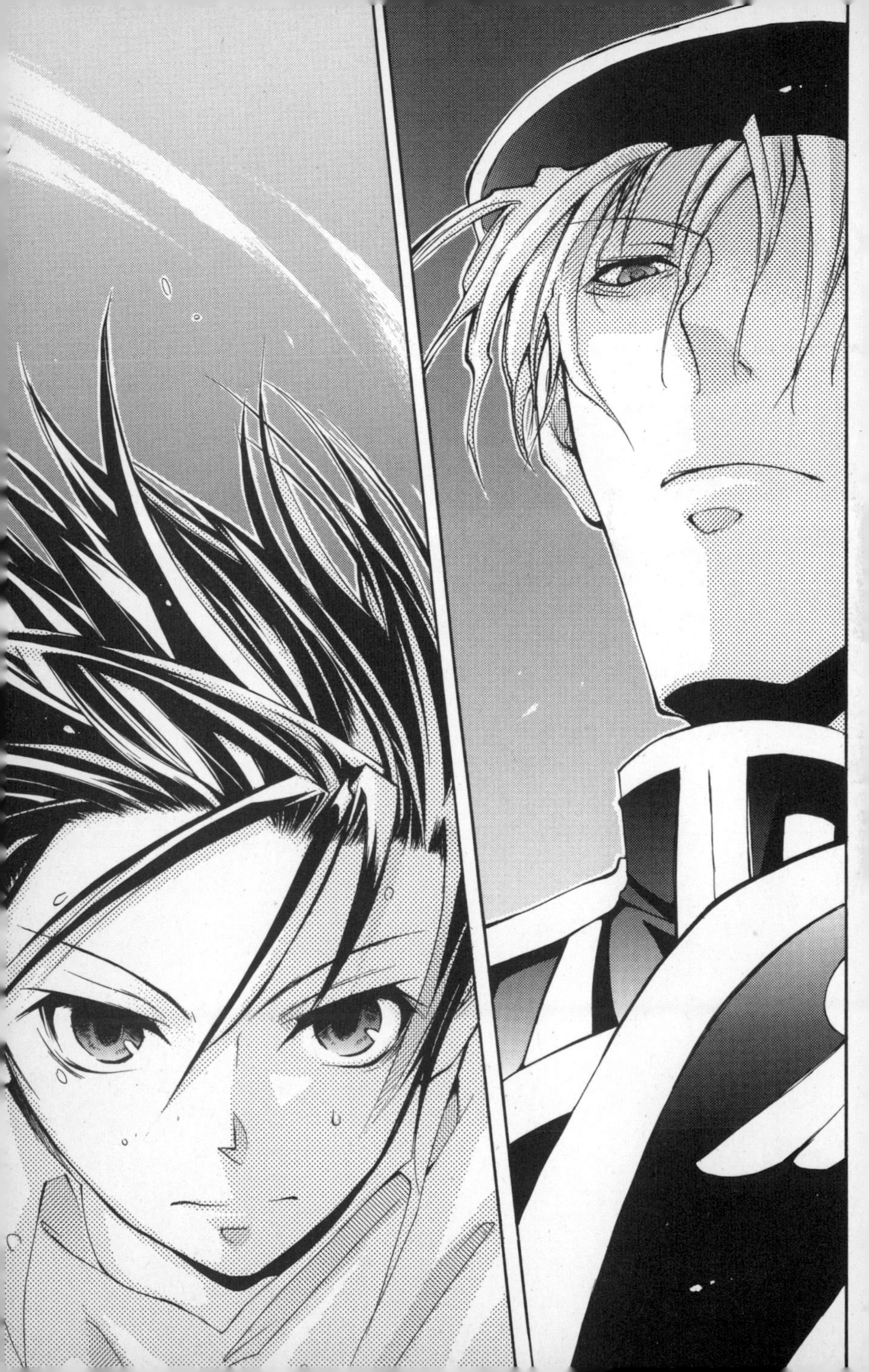

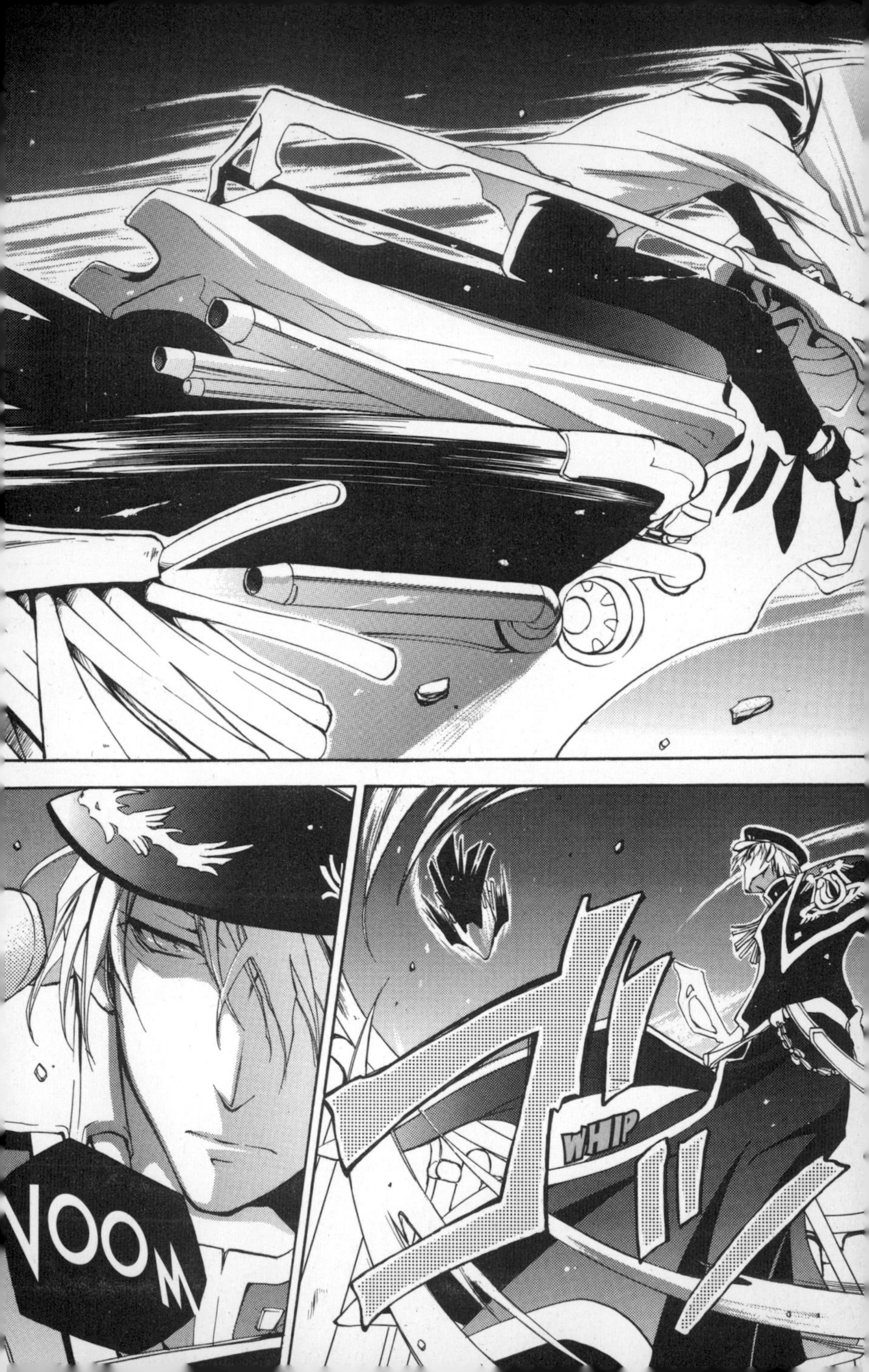
WHIP
VOOM

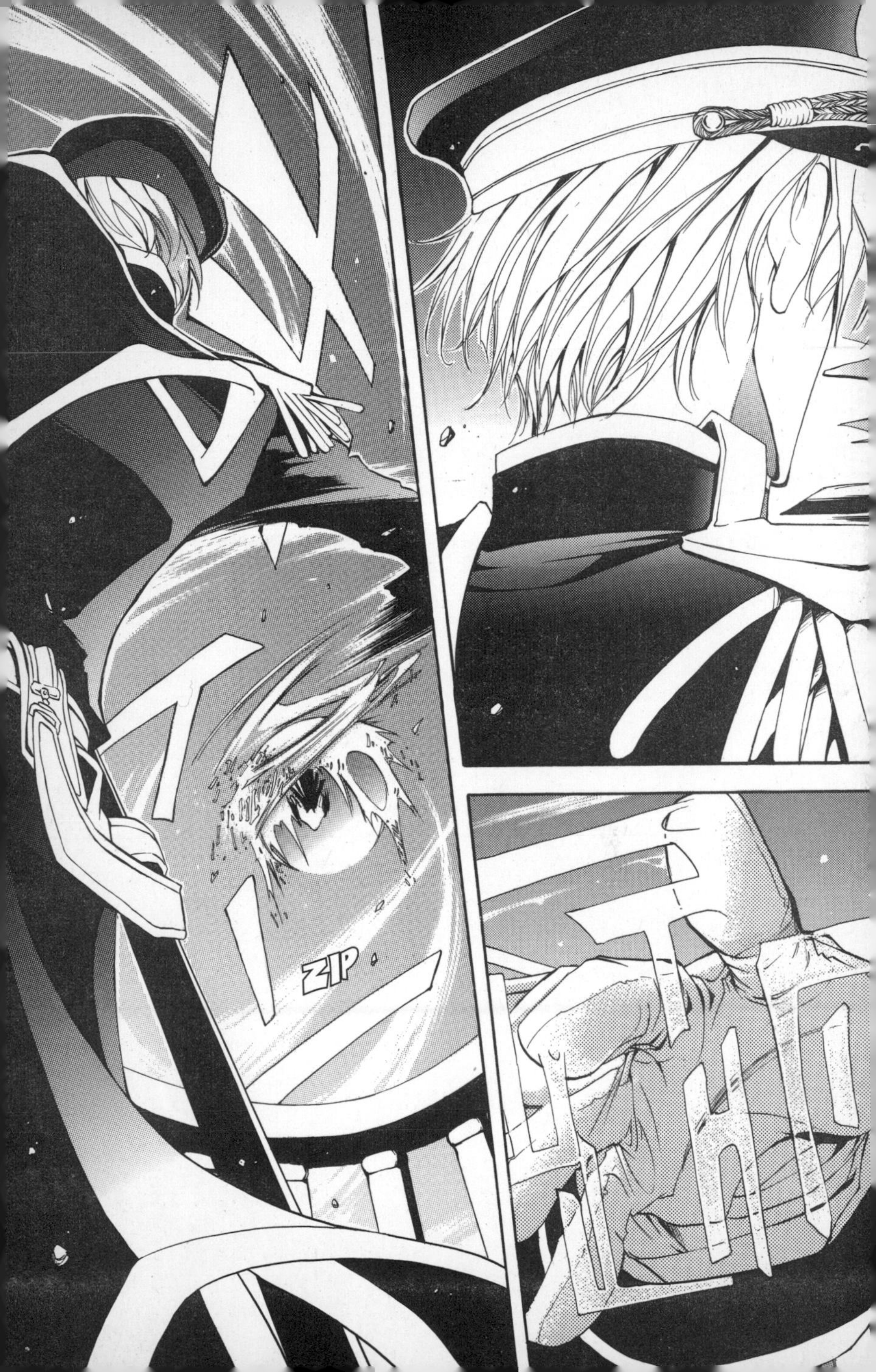
ZIP

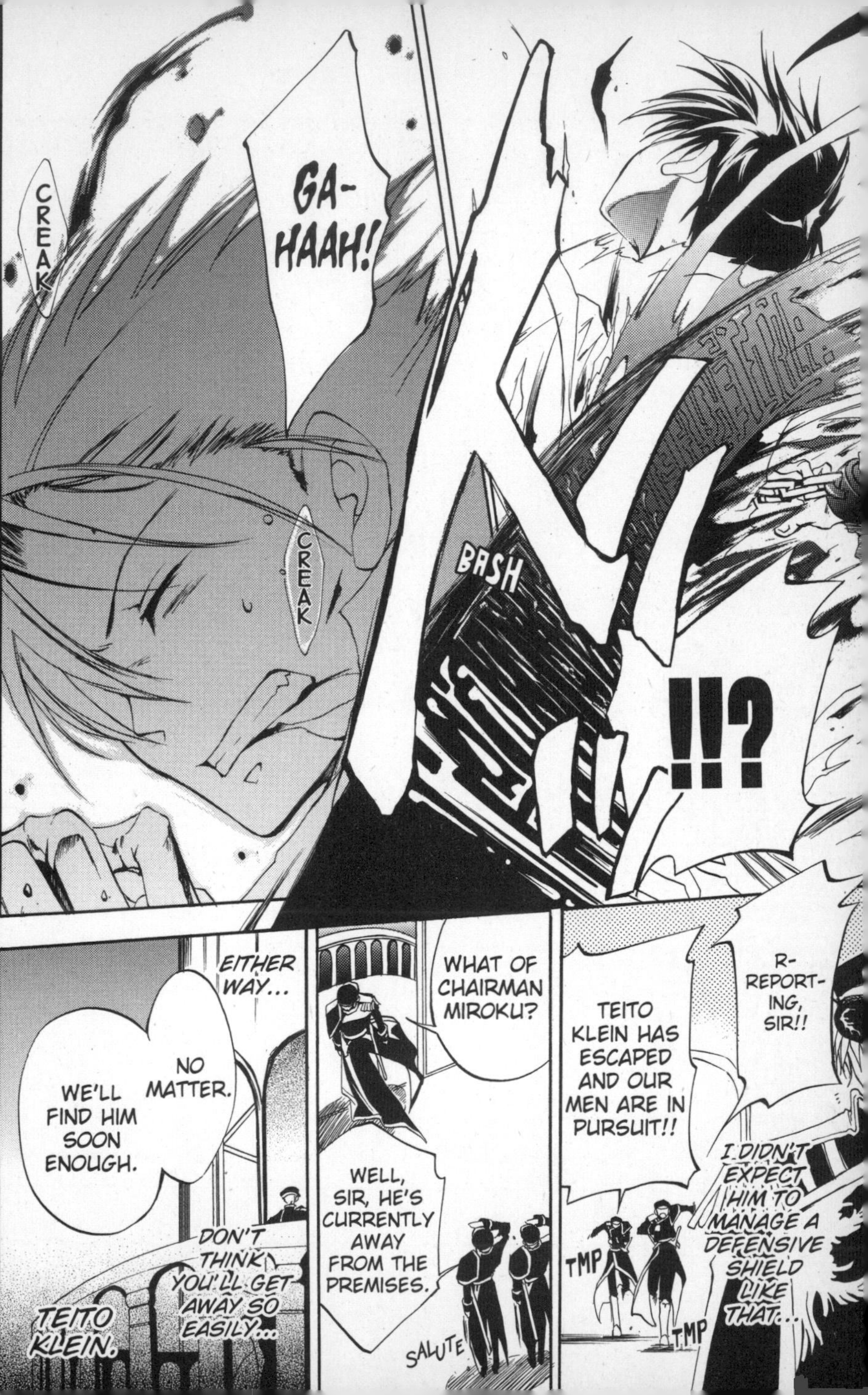
GA-HAAH!
CREAK
CREAK
BASH
!!?
R-REPORTING, SIR!!
TEITO KLEIN HAS ESCAPED AND OUR MEN ARE IN PURSUIT!!
I DIDN'T EXPECT HIM TO MANAGE A DEFENSIVE SHIELD LIKE THAT...
TMP
TMP
WHAT OF CHAIRMAN MIROKU?
WELL, SIR, HE'S CURRENTLY AWAY FROM THE PREMISES.
SALUTE
EITHER WAY...
NO MATTER.
WE'LL FIND HIM SOON ENOUGH.
DON'T THINK YOU'LL GET AWAY SO EASILY...
TEITO KLEIN.

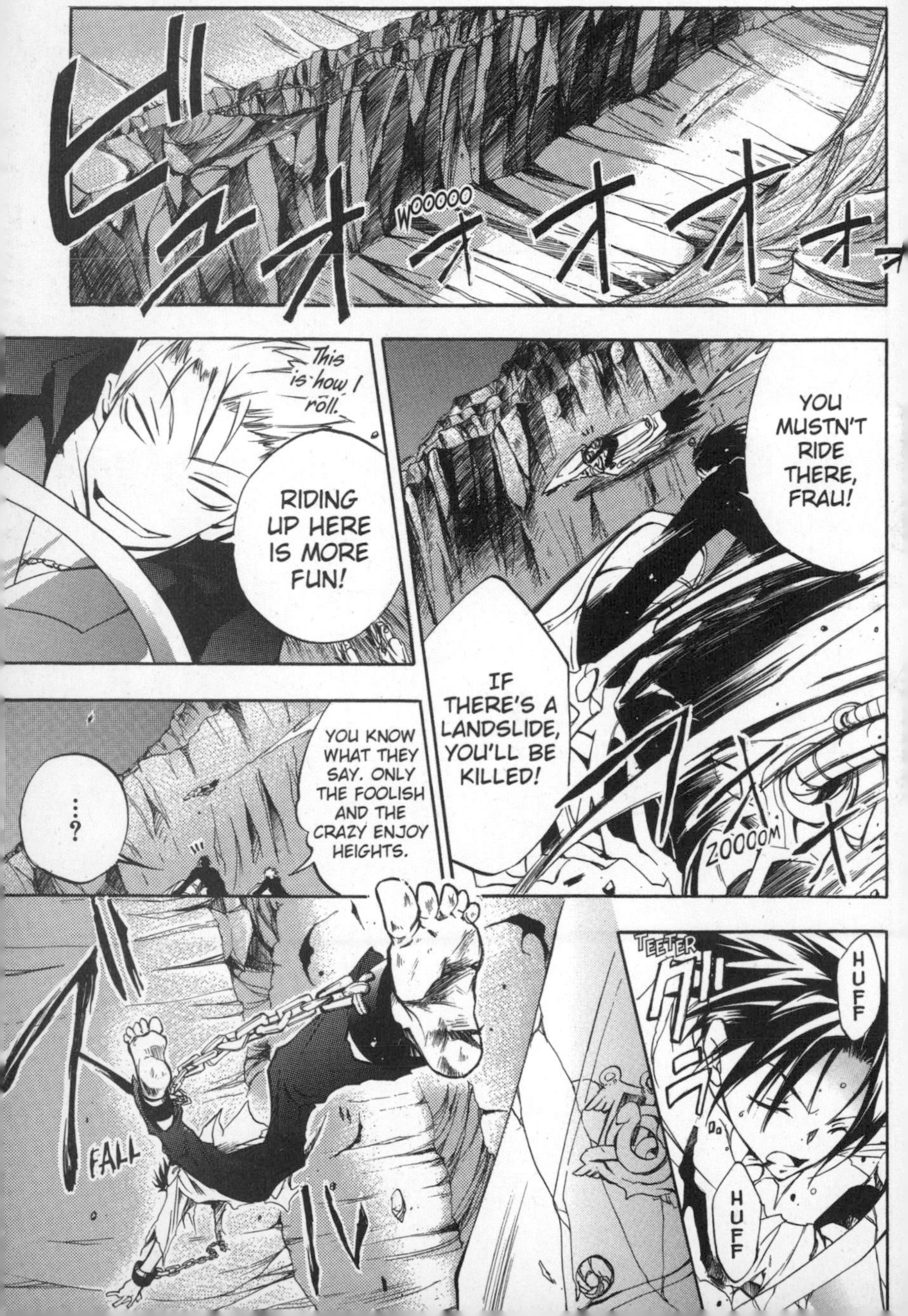
WOOOOO
YOU MUSTN'T RIDE THERE, FRAU!
RIDING UP HERE IS MORE FUN!
This is how I roll.
IF THERE'S A LANDSLIDE, YOU'LL BE KILLED!
ZOOOOM
YOU KNOW WHAT THEY SAY. ONLY THE FOOLISH AND THE CRAZY ENJOY HEIGHTS.
...?
TEETER
HUFF
HUFF
FALL

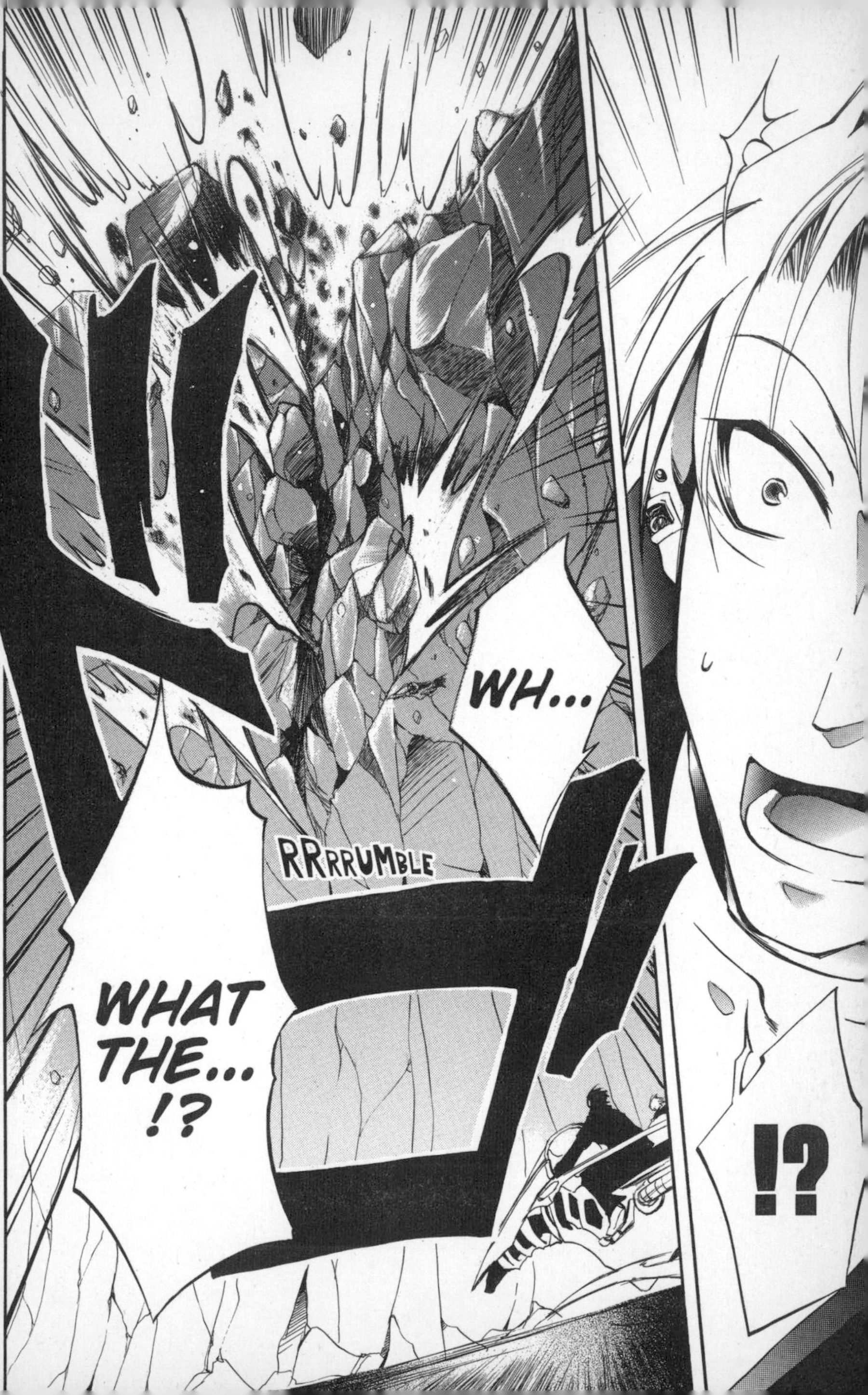
!?
WH...
RRRRUMBLE
WHAT THE... !?

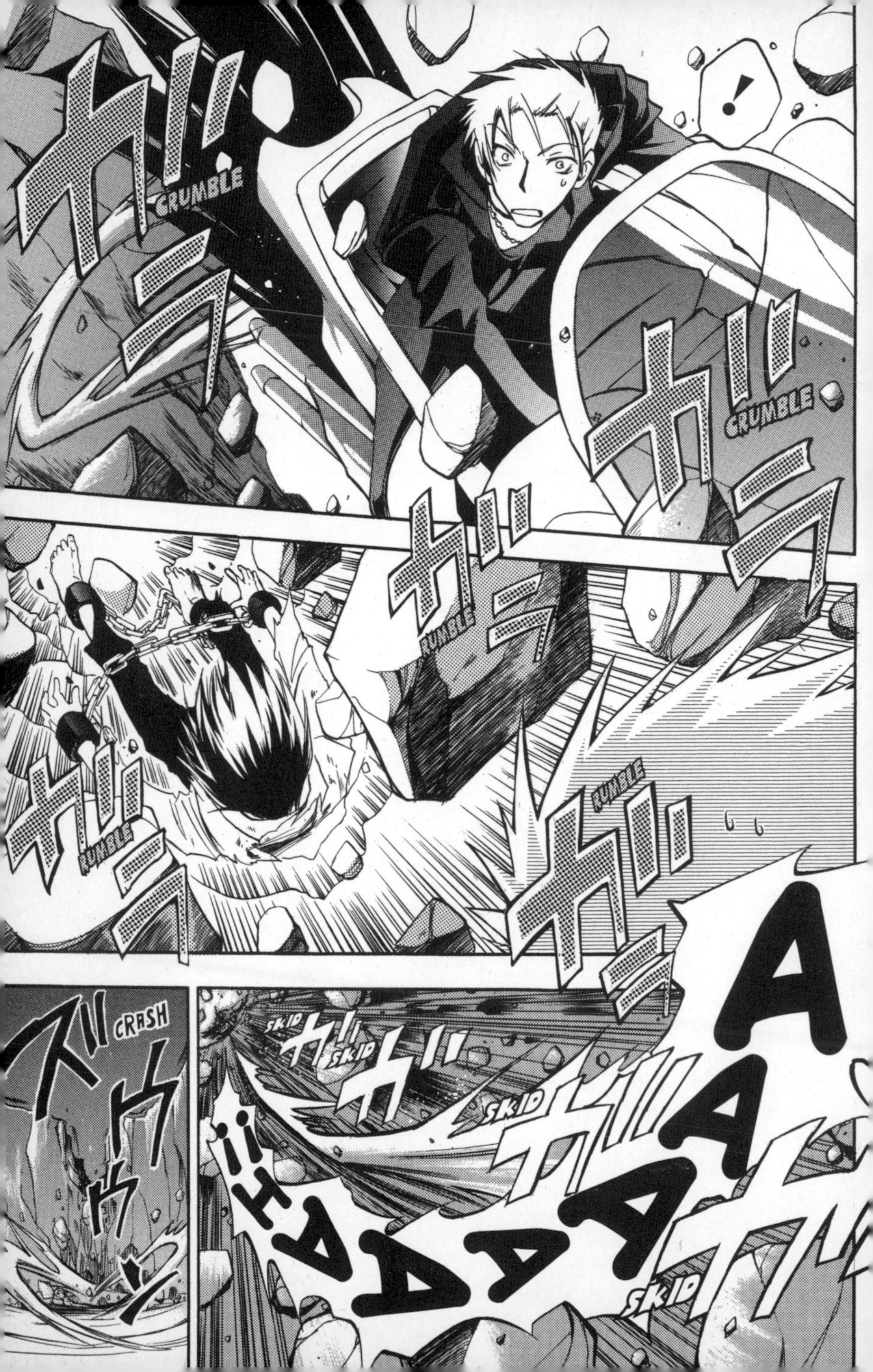
!
CRUMBLE
CRUMBLE
RUMBLE
RUMBLE
RUMBLE
SKID
SKID
SKID
SKID
AAAAAAAH!!
CRASH

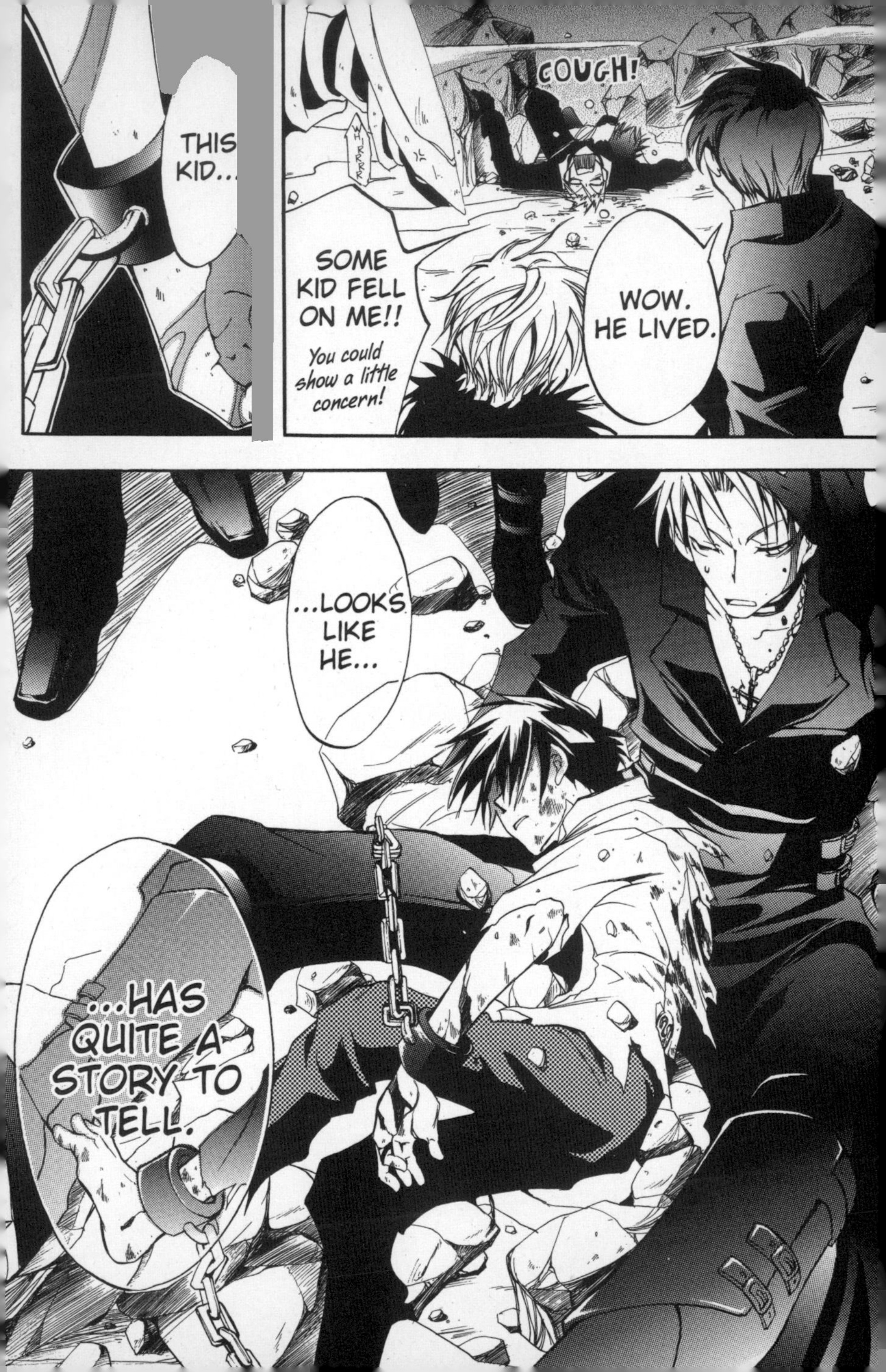
COUGH!
WHIRRR
WOW. HE LIVED.
SOME KID FELL ON ME!!
You could show a little concern!
THIS KID...
...LOOKS LIKE HE...
...HAS QUITE A STORY TO TELL.

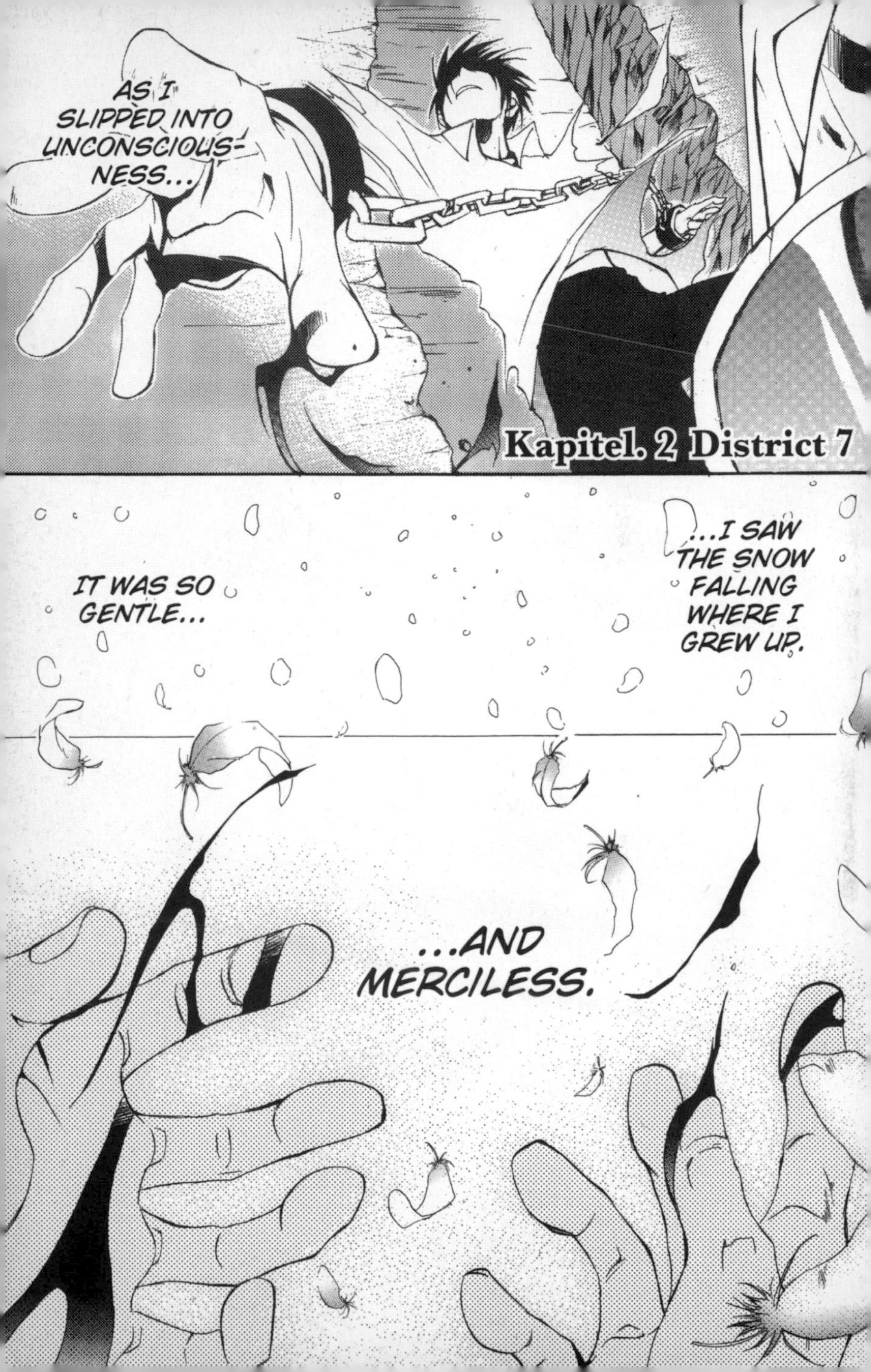
AS I SLIPPED INTO UNCONSCIOUS-NESS...
Kapitel. 2 District 7
...I SAW THE SNOW FALLING WHERE I GREW UP.
IT WAS SO GENTLE...
...AND MERCILESS.

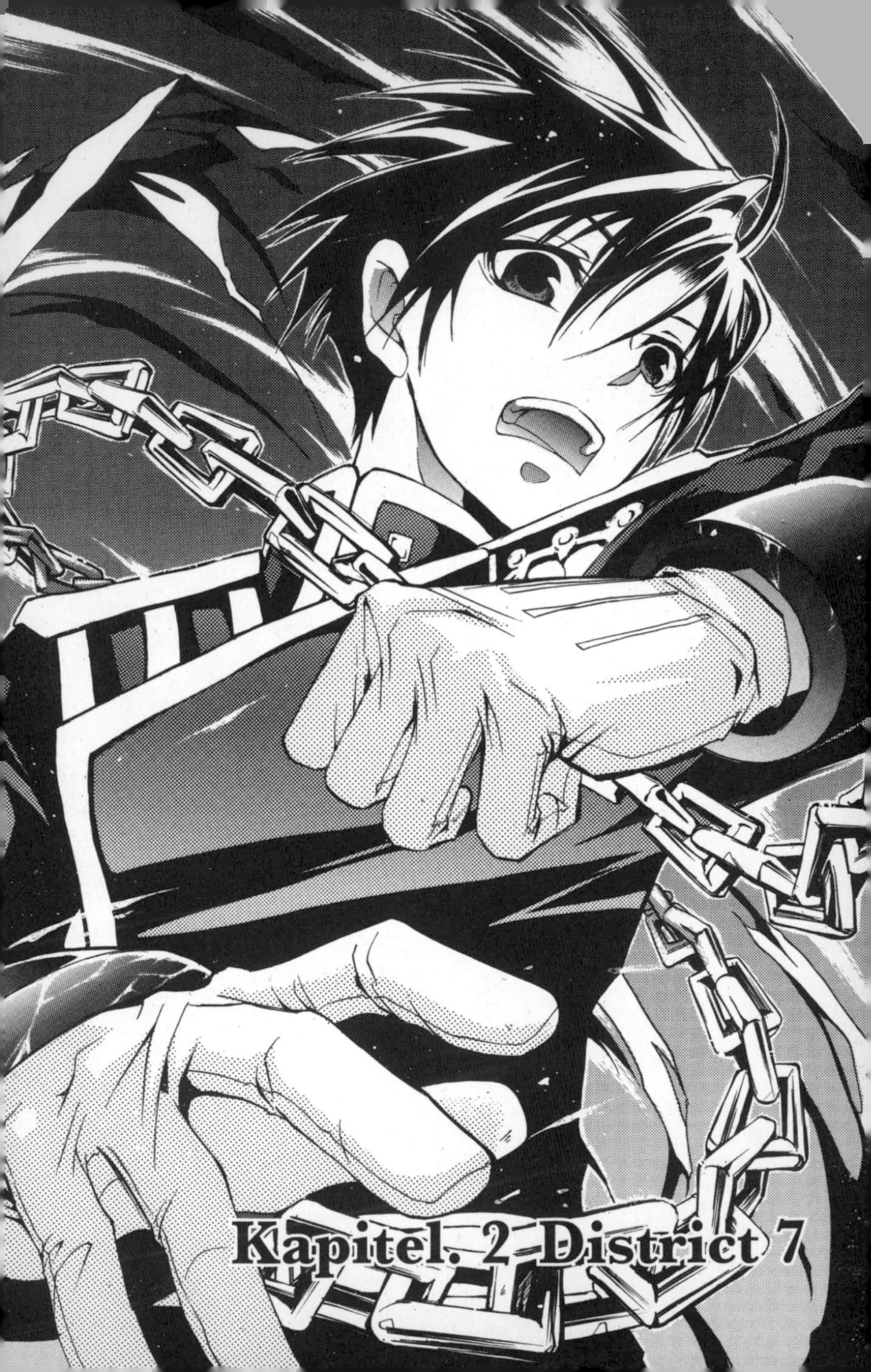
Kapitel. 2 District 7

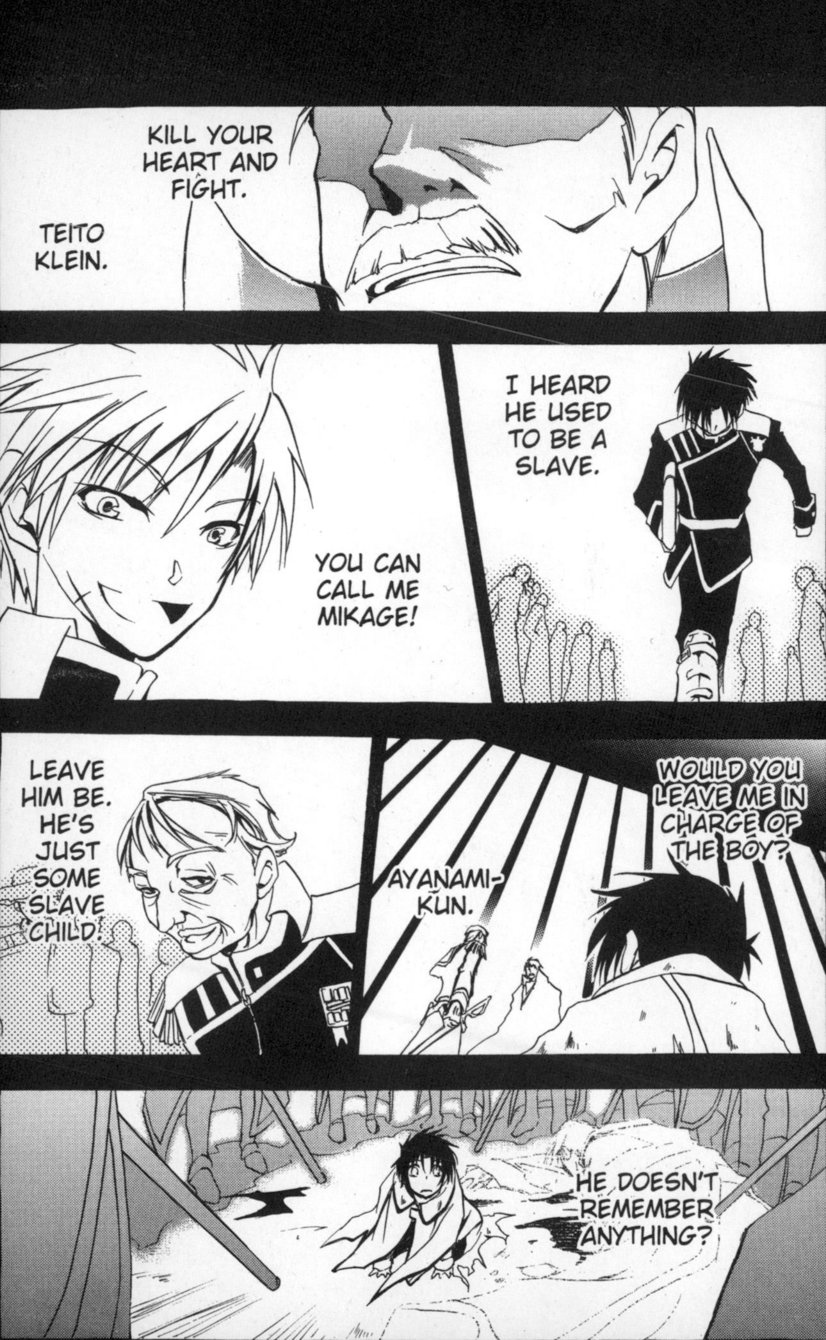
KILL YOUR HEART AND FIGHT.
TEITO KLEIN.
I HEARD HE USED TO BE A SLAVE.
YOU CAN CALL ME MIKAGE!
WOULD YOU LEAVE ME IN CHARGE OF THE BOY?
AYANAMI-KUN.
LEAVE HIM BE. HE'S JUST SOME SLAVE CHILD.
HE DOESN'T REMEMBER ANYTHING?

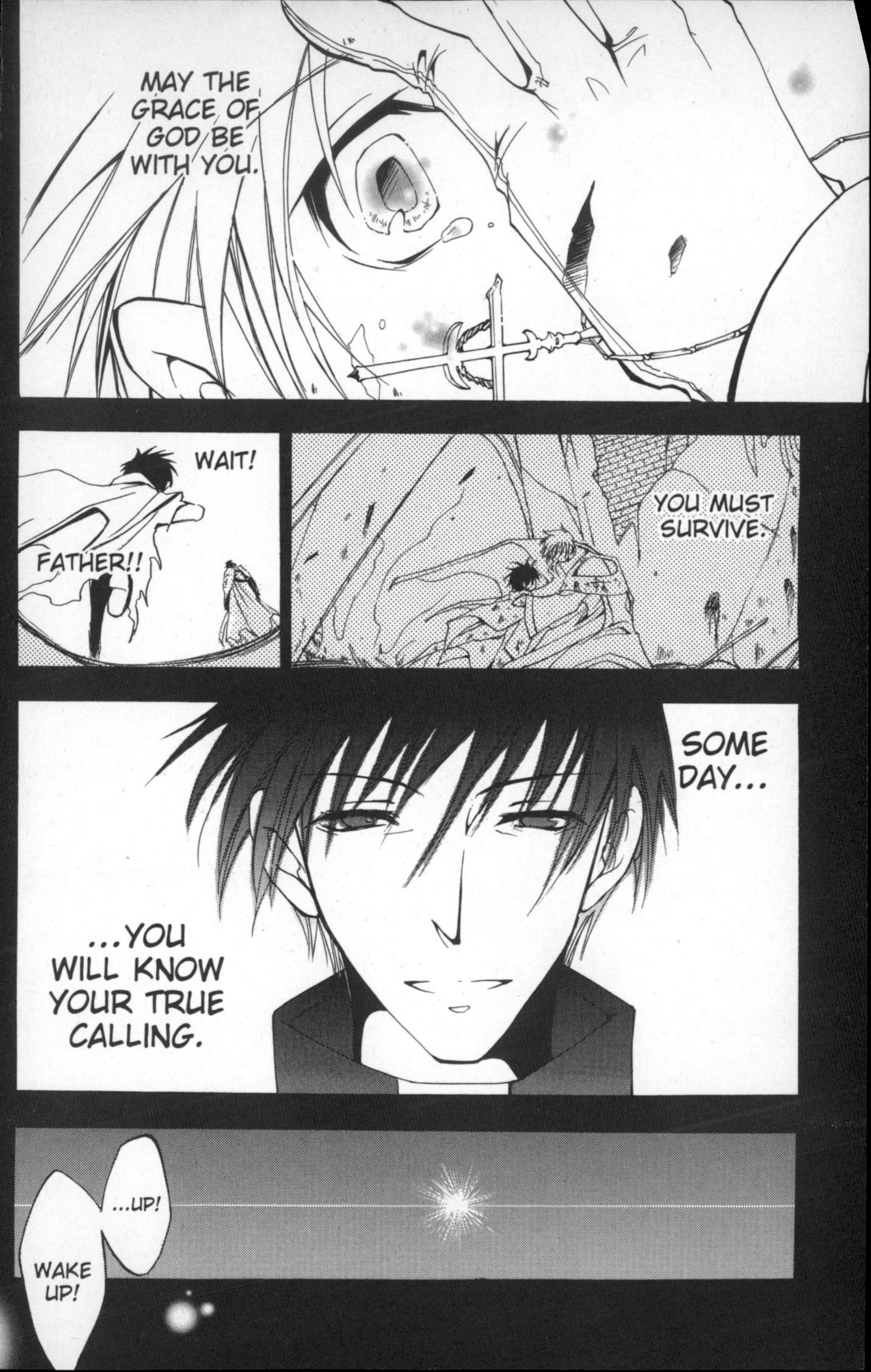
MAY THE GRACE OF GOD BE WITH YOU.
YOU MUST SURVIVE.
WAIT!
FATHER!!
SOME DAY...
...YOU WILL KNOW YOUR TRUE CALLING.
...UP!
WAKE UP!

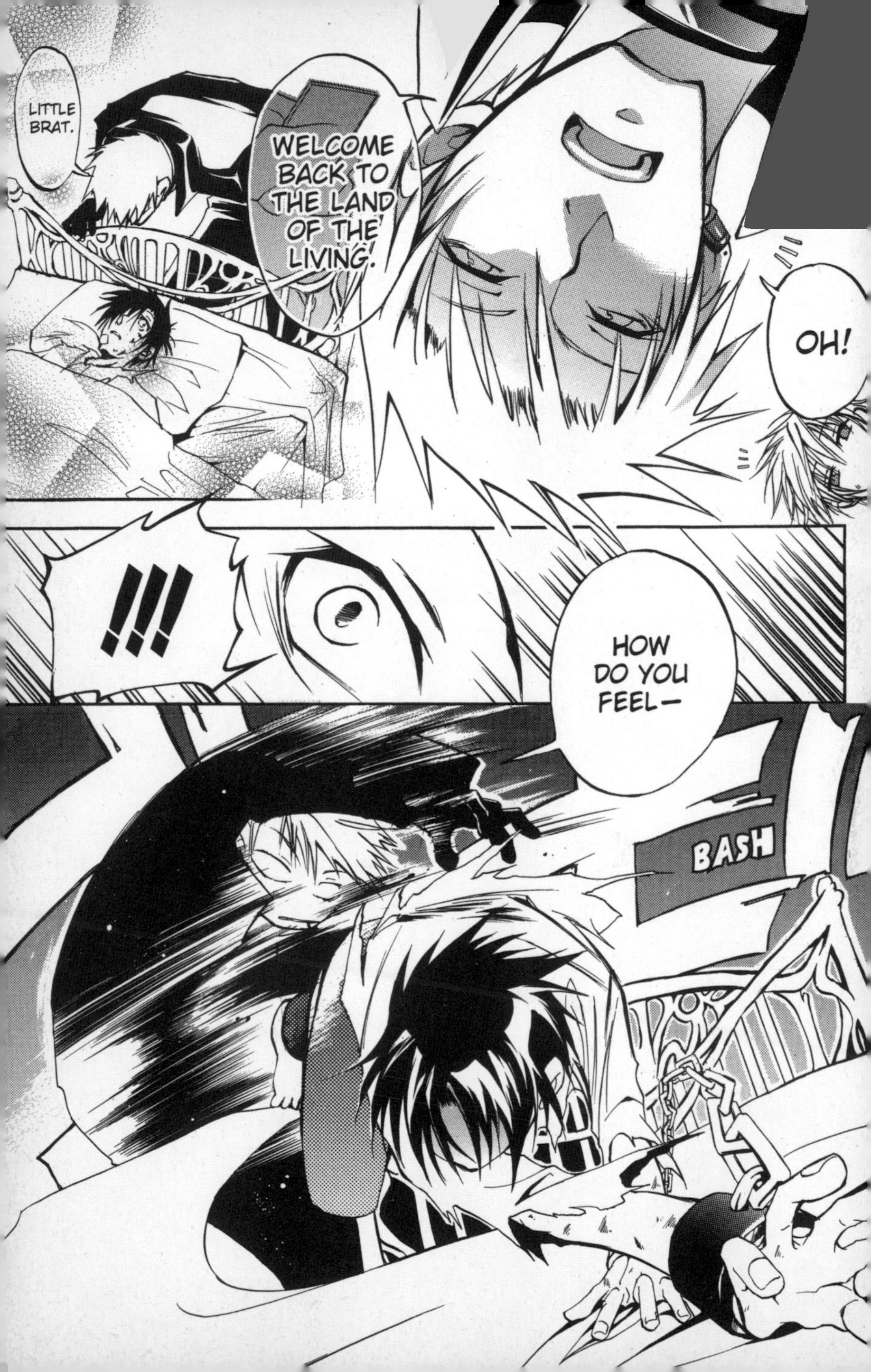
OH!
WELCOME BACK TO THE LAND OF THE LIVING!
LITTLE BRAT.
HOW DO YOU FEEL—
!!!!
BASH

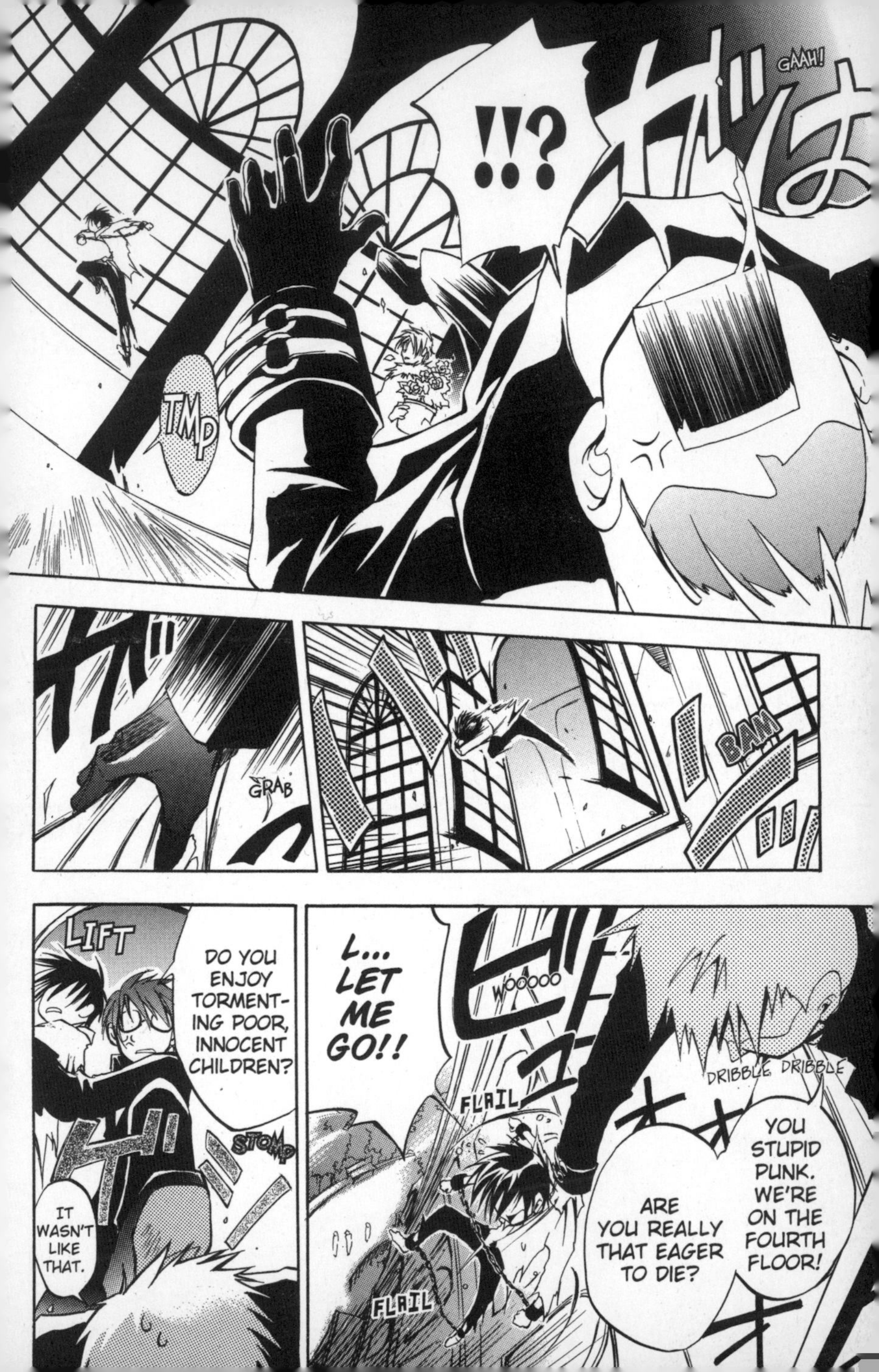
GAAH!
!!?
TMP
BAM
GRAB
L... LET ME GO!!
WOOOOO
FLAIL
DRIBBLE DRIBBLE
YOU STUPID PUNK. WE'RE ON THE FOURTH FLOOR!
ARE YOU REALLY THAT EAGER TO DIE?
FLAIL
LIFT
DO YOU ENJOY TORMENT-ING POOR, INNOCENT CHILDREN?
STOMP
IT WASN'T LIKE THAT.

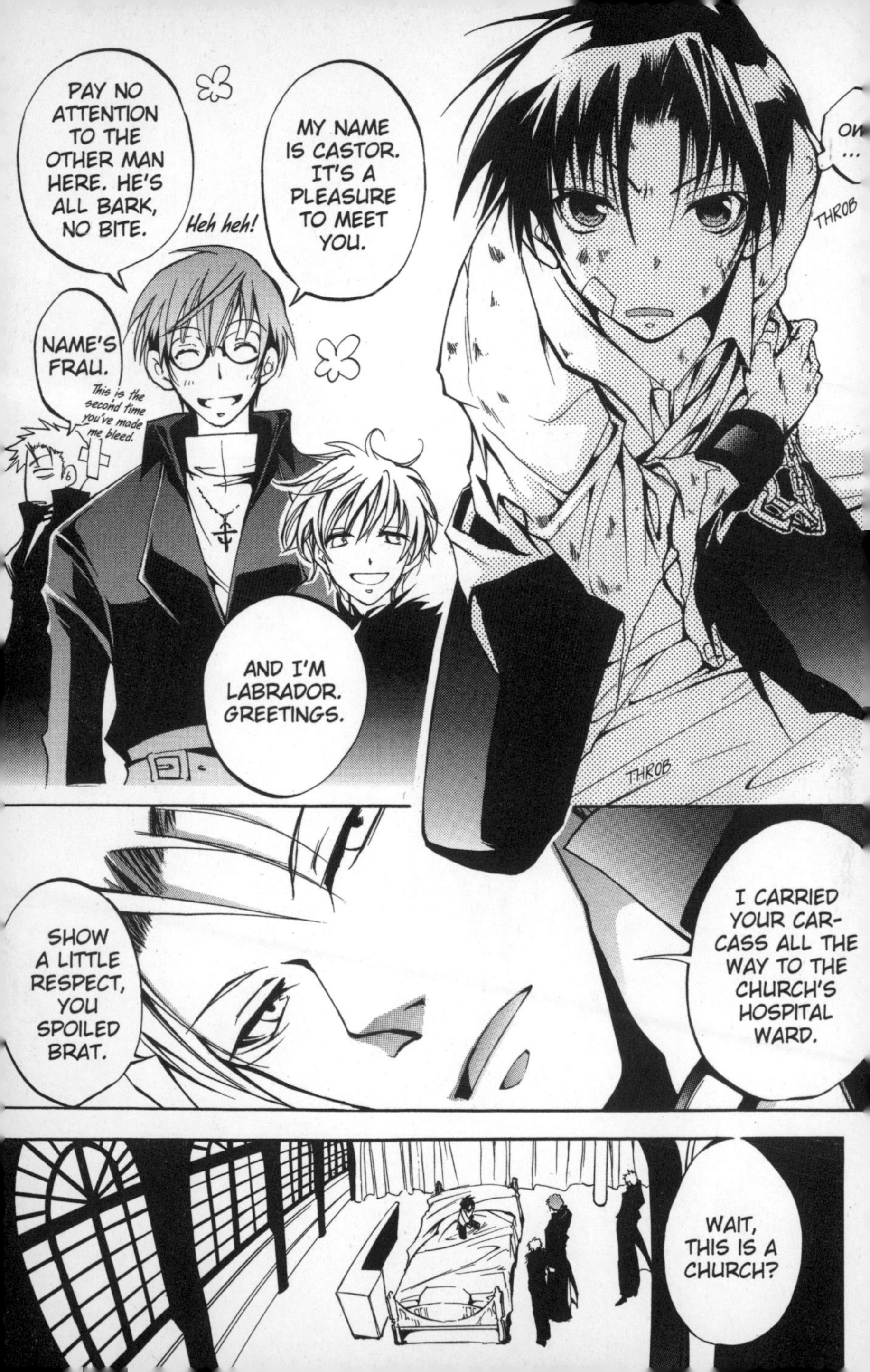
OW ...
THROB
THROB
MY NAME IS CASTOR. IT'S A PLEASURE TO MEET YOU.
Heh heh!
PAY NO ATTENTION TO THE OTHER MAN HERE. HE'S ALL BARK, NO BITE.
NAME'S FRAU.
This is the second time you've made me bleed.
AND I'M LABRADOR. GREETINGS.
I CARRIED YOUR CAR-CASS ALL THE WAY TO THE CHURCH'S HOSPITAL WARD.
SHOW A LITTLE RESPECT, YOU SPOILED BRAT.
WAIT, THIS IS A CHURCH?

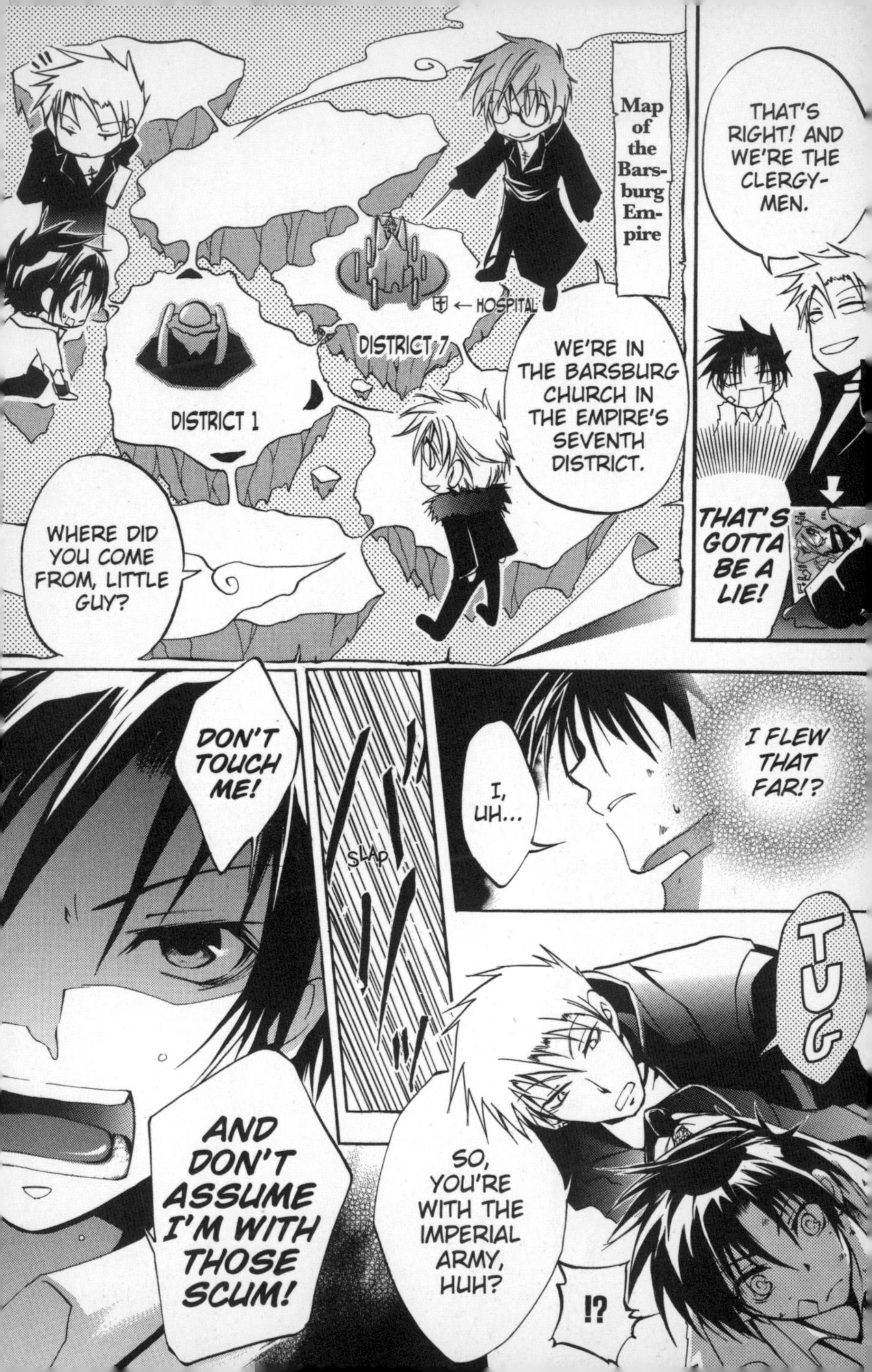
THAT'S RIGHT! AND WE'RE THE CLERGYMEN.
THAT'S GOTTA BE A LIE!
Map of the Barsburg Empire
HOSPITAL
DISTRICT 7
WE'RE IN THE BARSBURG CHURCH IN THE EMPIRE'S SEVENTH DISTRICT.
DISTRICT 1
WHERE DID YOU COME FROM, LITTLE GUY?
I FLEW THAT FAR!?
I, UH...
TUG
SO, YOU'RE WITH THE IMPERIAL ARMY, HUH?
!?
SLAP
DON'T TOUCH ME!
AND DON'T ASSUME I'M WITH THOSE SCUM!

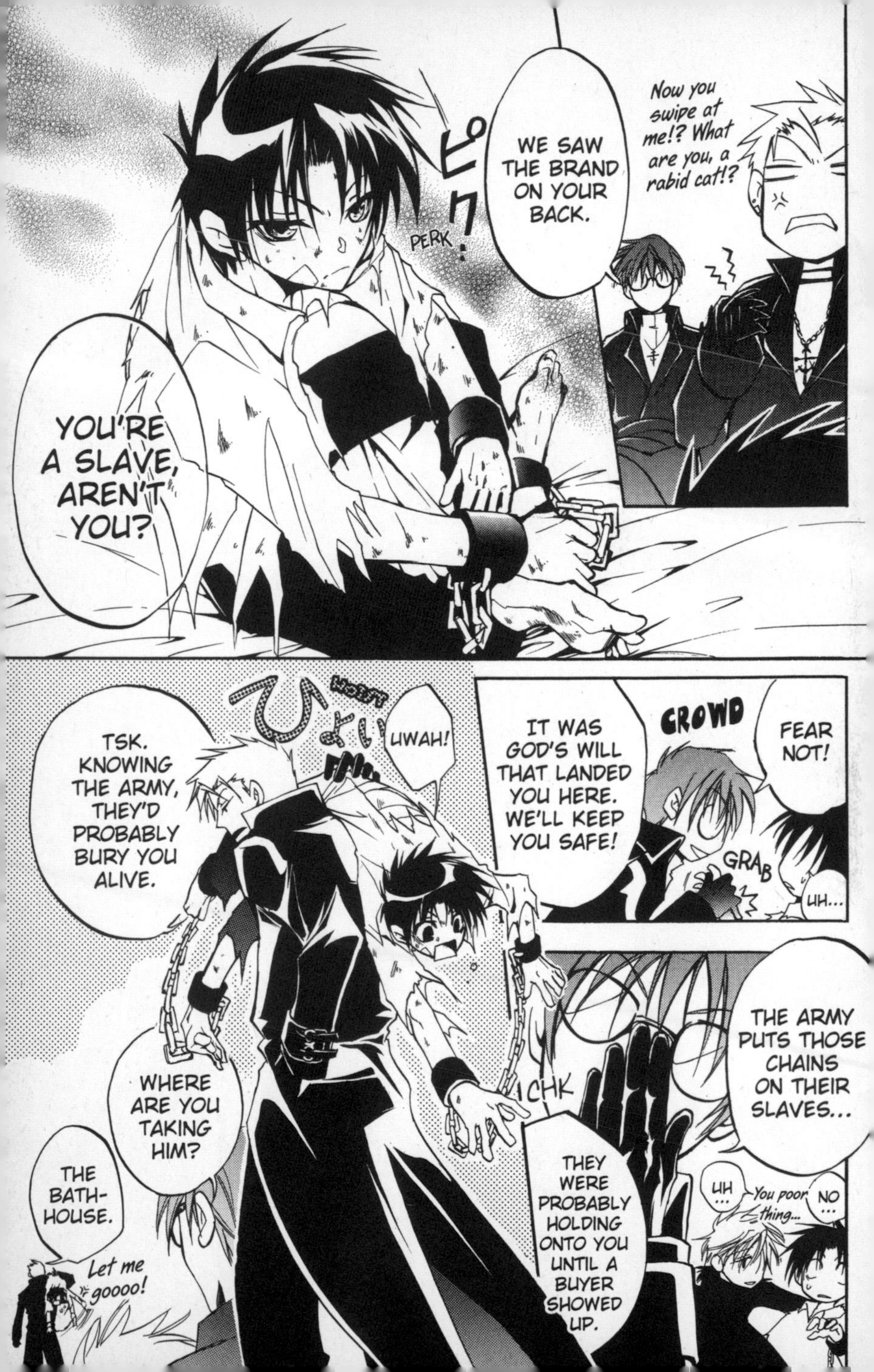
Now you swipe at me!? What are you, a rabid cat!?
WE SAW THE BRAND ON YOUR BACK.
ピク
PERK
YOU'RE A SLAVE, AREN'T YOU?
FEAR NOT!
CROWD
IT WAS GOD'S WILL THAT LANDED YOU HERE. WE'LL KEEP YOU SAFE!
GRAB
UH...
THE ARMY PUTS THOSE CHAINS ON THEIR SLAVES...
NO...
You poor thing...
UH...
THEY WERE PROBABLY HOLDING ONTO YOU UNTIL A BUYER SHOWED UP.
CHK
HOIST
ひょい
UWAH!
TSK. KNOWING THE ARMY, THEY'D PROBABLY BURY YOU ALIVE.
WHERE ARE YOU TAKING HIM?
THE BATH-HOUSE.
Let me goooo!

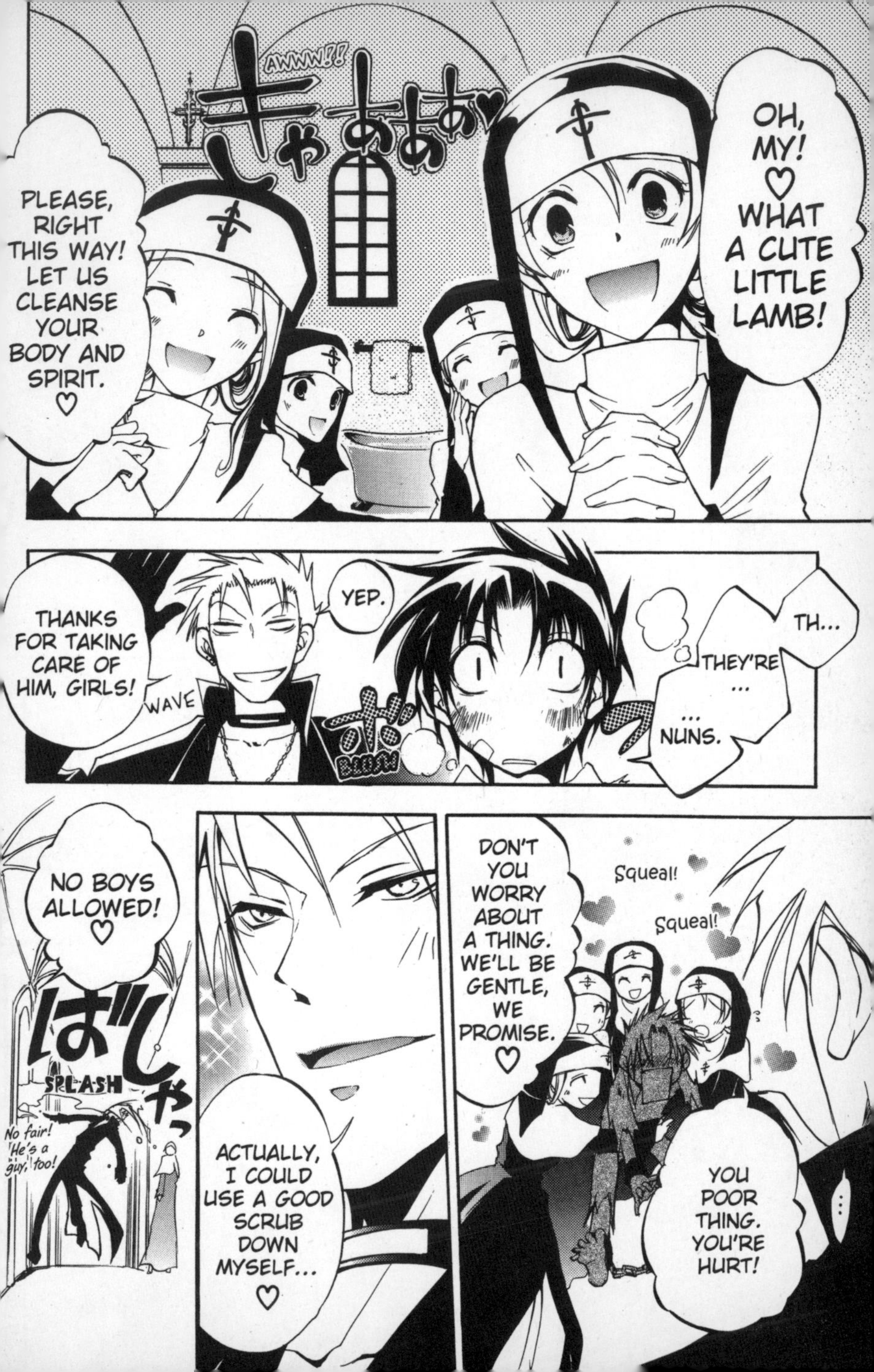
OH, MY! ♡ WHAT A CUTE LITTLE LAMB!
AWWW?!
PLEASE, RIGHT THIS WAY! LET US CLEANSE YOUR BODY AND SPIRIT. ♡
TH...
THEY'RE ...
... NUNS.
BLUSH
YEP.
THANKS FOR TAKING CARE OF HIM, GIRLS!
WAVE
Squeal!
Squeal!
DON'T YOU WORRY ABOUT A THING. WE'LL BE GENTLE, WE PROMISE. ♡
...
YOU POOR THING. YOU'RE HURT!
ACTUALLY, I COULD USE A GOOD SCRUB DOWN MYSELF... ♡
NO BOYS ALLOWED! ♡
SPLASH
No fair! He's a guy, too!

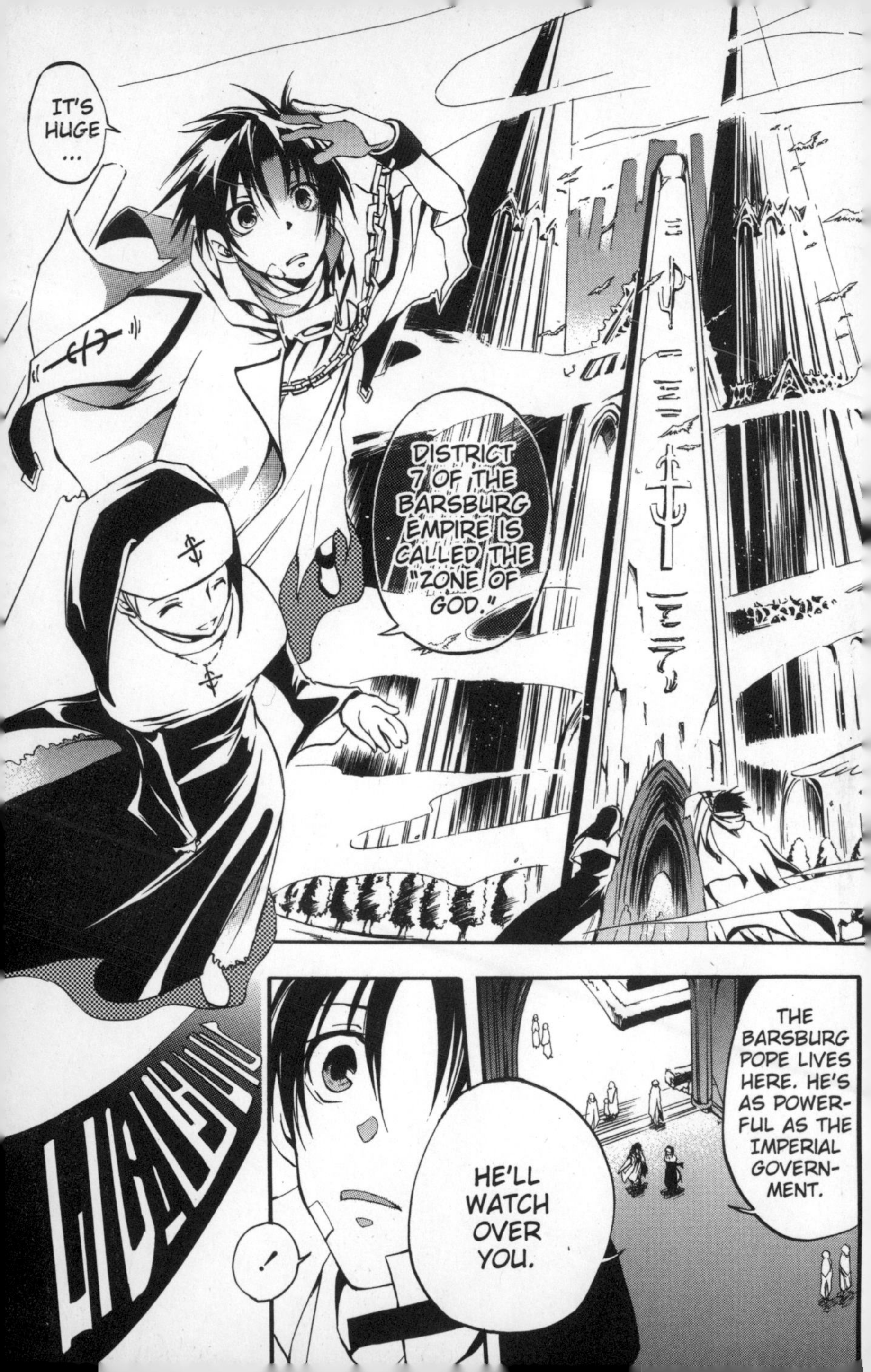
IT'S HUGE ...
DISTRICT 7 OF THE BARSBURG EMPIRE IS CALLED THE "ZONE OF GOD."
THE BARSBURG POPE LIVES HERE. HE'S AS POWERFUL AS THE IMPERIAL GOVERNMENT.
HE'LL WATCH OVER YOU.
!

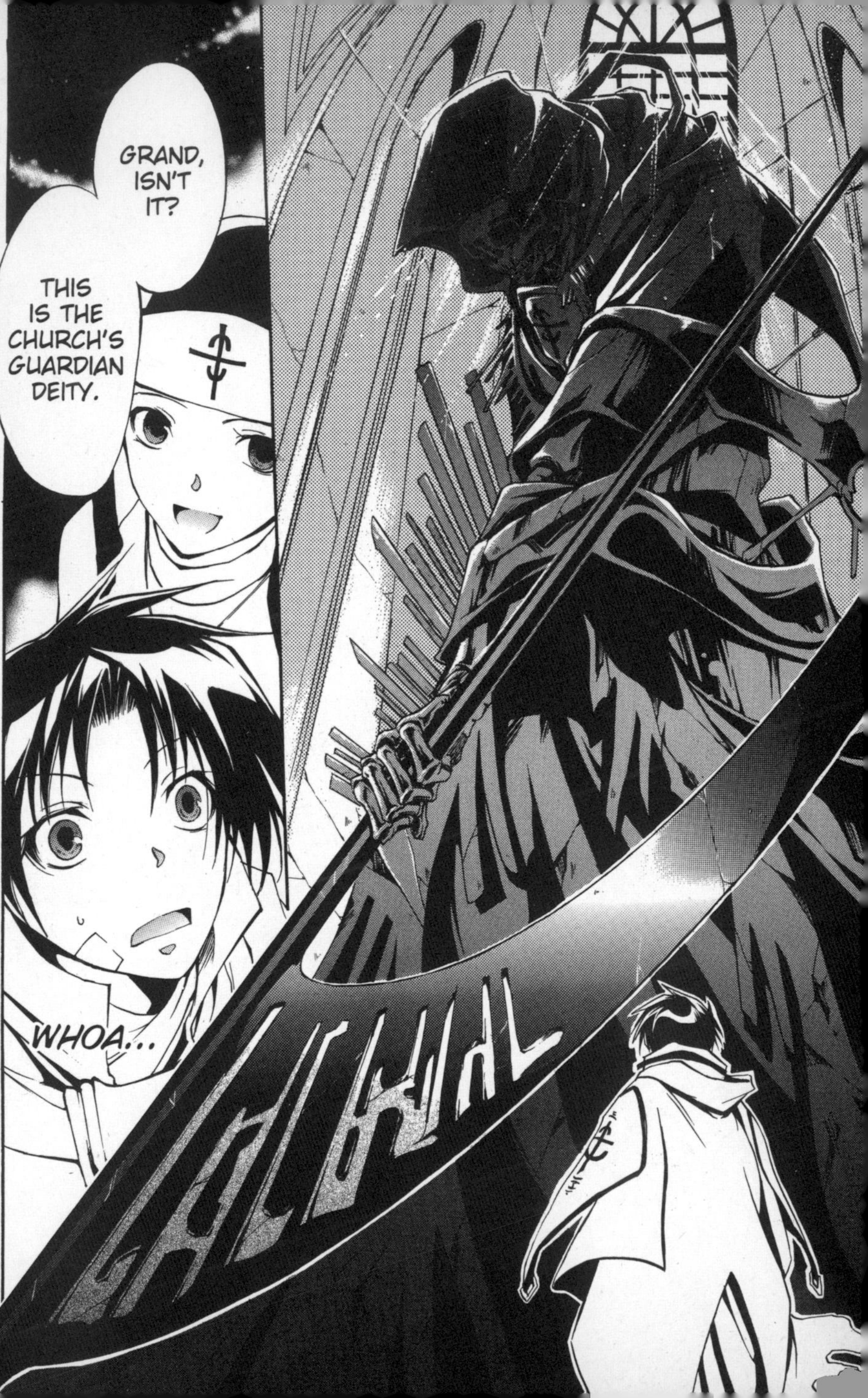
GRAND, ISN'T IT?
THIS IS THE CHURCH'S GUARDIAN DEITY.
WHOA...

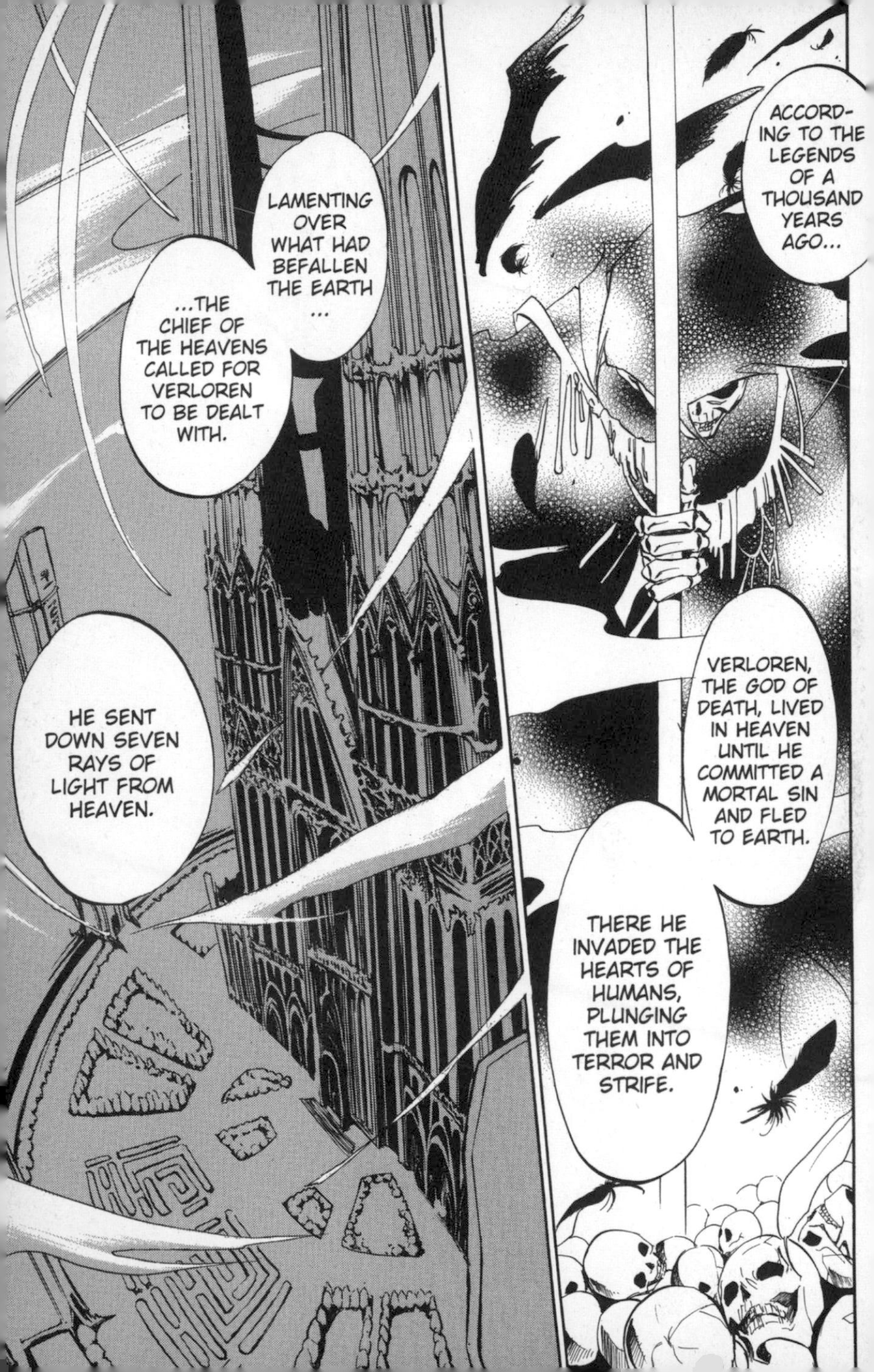
ACCORD-ING TO THE LEGENDS OF A THOUSAND YEARS AGO...
VERLOREN, THE GOD OF DEATH, LIVED IN HEAVEN UNTIL HE COMMITTED A MORTAL SIN AND FLED TO EARTH.
THERE HE INVADED THE HEARTS OF HUMANS, PLUNGING THEM INTO TERROR AND STRIFE.
LAMENTING OVER WHAT HAD BEFALLEN THE EARTH ...
...THE CHIEF OF THE HEAVENS CALLED FOR VERLOREN TO BE DEALT WITH.
HE SENT DOWN SEVEN RAYS OF LIGHT FROM HEAVEN.

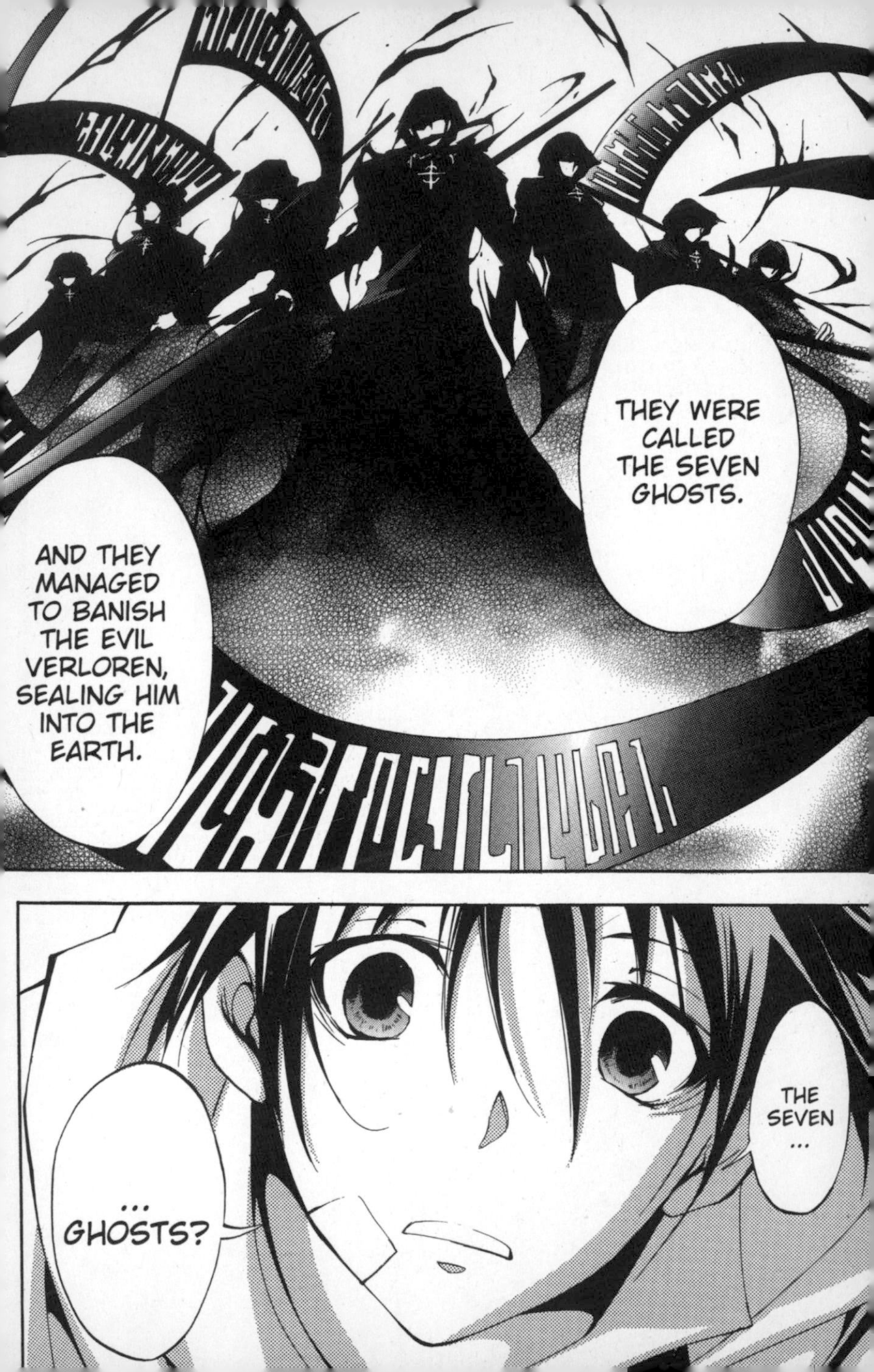
THEY WERE CALLED THE SEVEN GHOSTS.
AND THEY MANAGED TO BANISH THE EVIL VERLOREN, SEALING HIM INTO THE EARTH.
THE SEVEN ...
... GHOSTS?

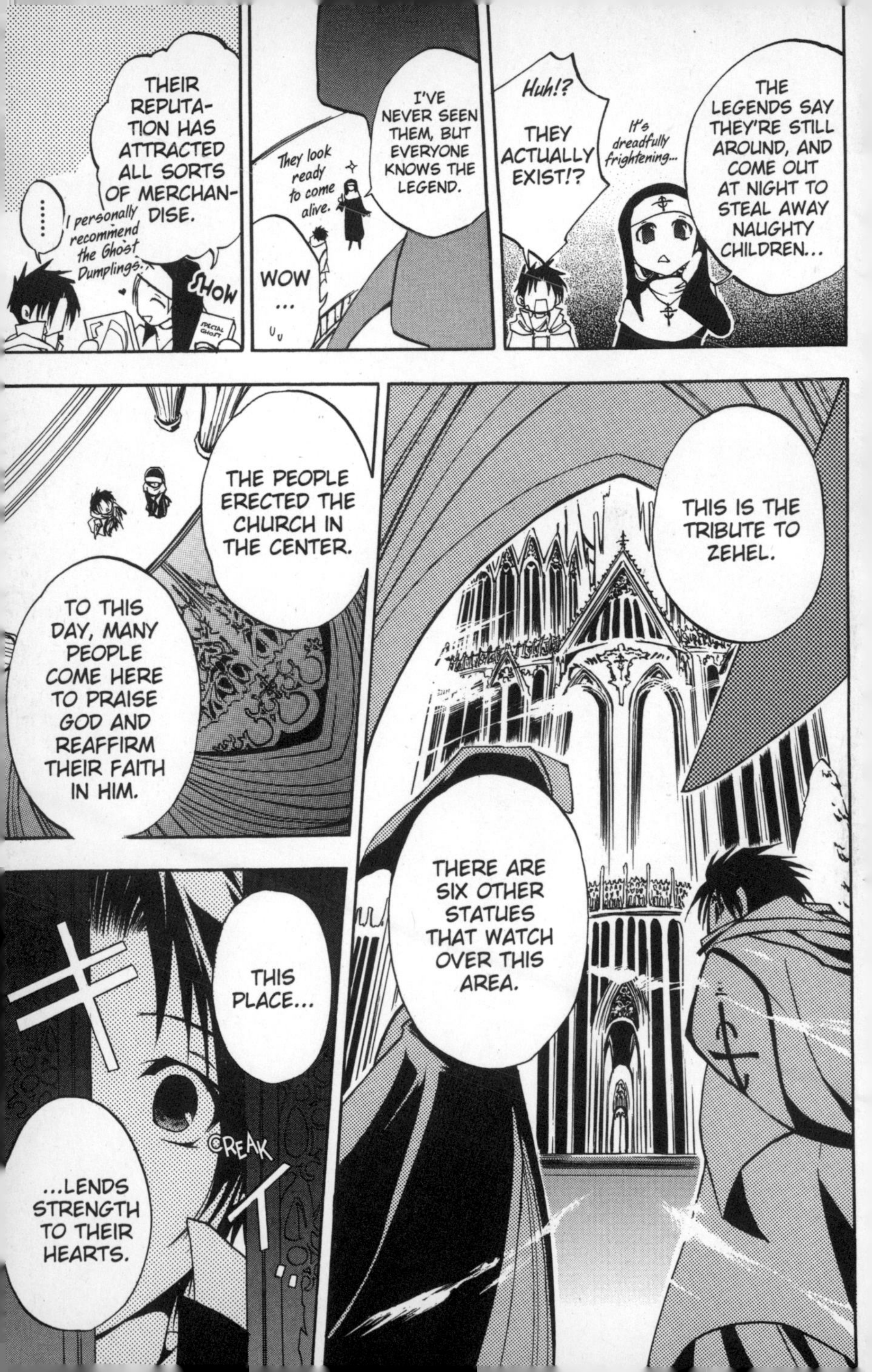
THE LEGENDS SAY THEY'RE STILL AROUND, AND COME OUT AT NIGHT TO STEAL AWAY NAUGHTY CHILDREN...
It's dreadfully frightening...
Huh!?
THEY ACTUALLY EXIST!?
I'VE NEVER SEEN THEM, BUT EVERYONE KNOWS THE LEGEND.
They look ready to come alive.
WOW ...
THEIR REPUTATION HAS ATTRACTED ALL SORTS OF MERCHANDISE.
I personally recommend the Ghost Dumplings.
SHOW
SPECIAL GHOST
......
THIS IS THE TRIBUTE TO ZEHEL.
THERE ARE SIX OTHER STATUES THAT WATCH OVER THIS AREA.
THE PEOPLE ERECTED THE CHURCH IN THE CENTER.
TO THIS DAY, MANY PEOPLE COME HERE TO PRAISE GOD AND REAFFIRM THEIR FAITH IN HIM.
THIS PLACE...
CREAK
...LENDS STRENGTH TO THEIR HEARTS.

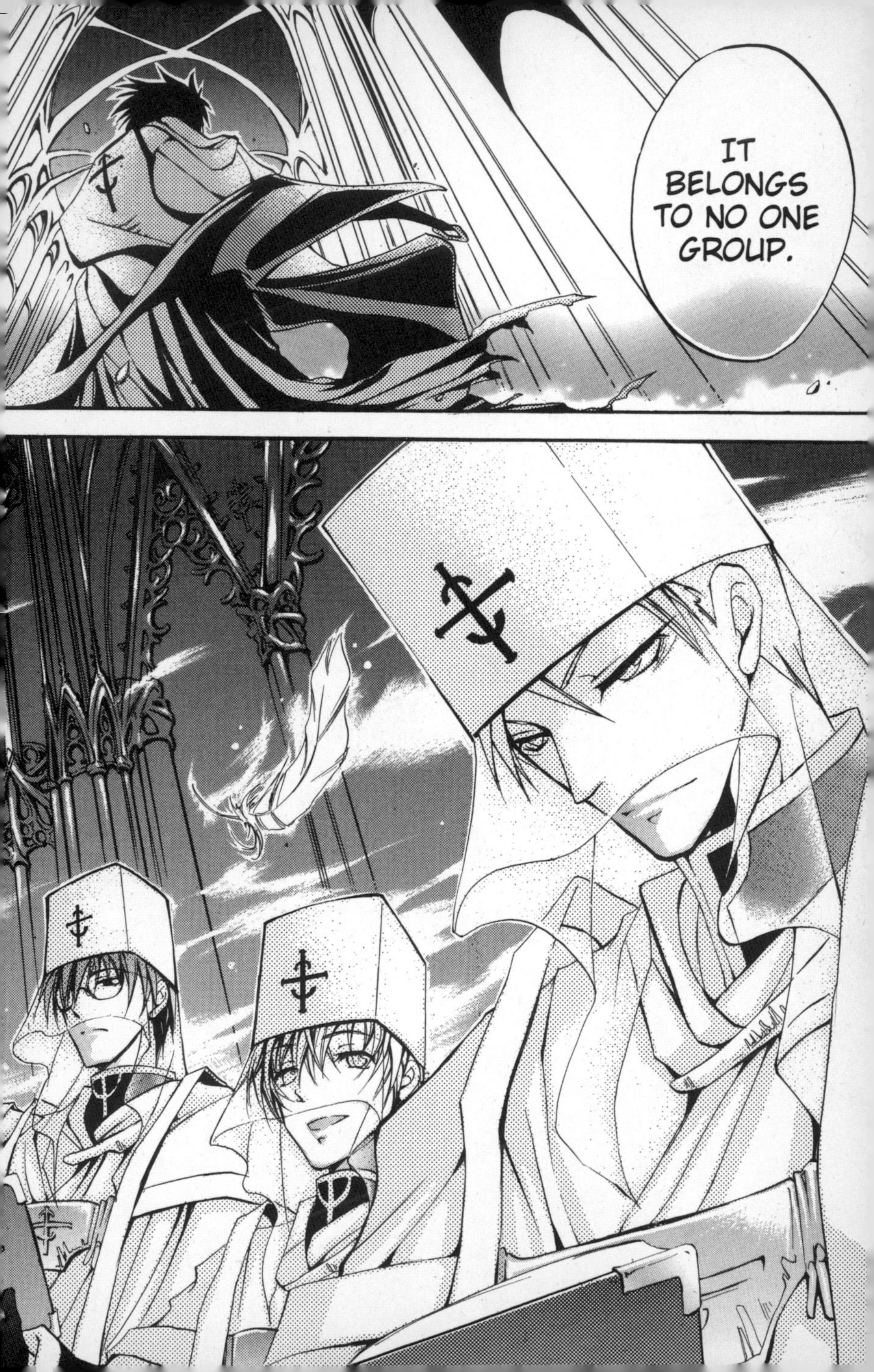
IT BELONGS TO NO ONE GROUP.

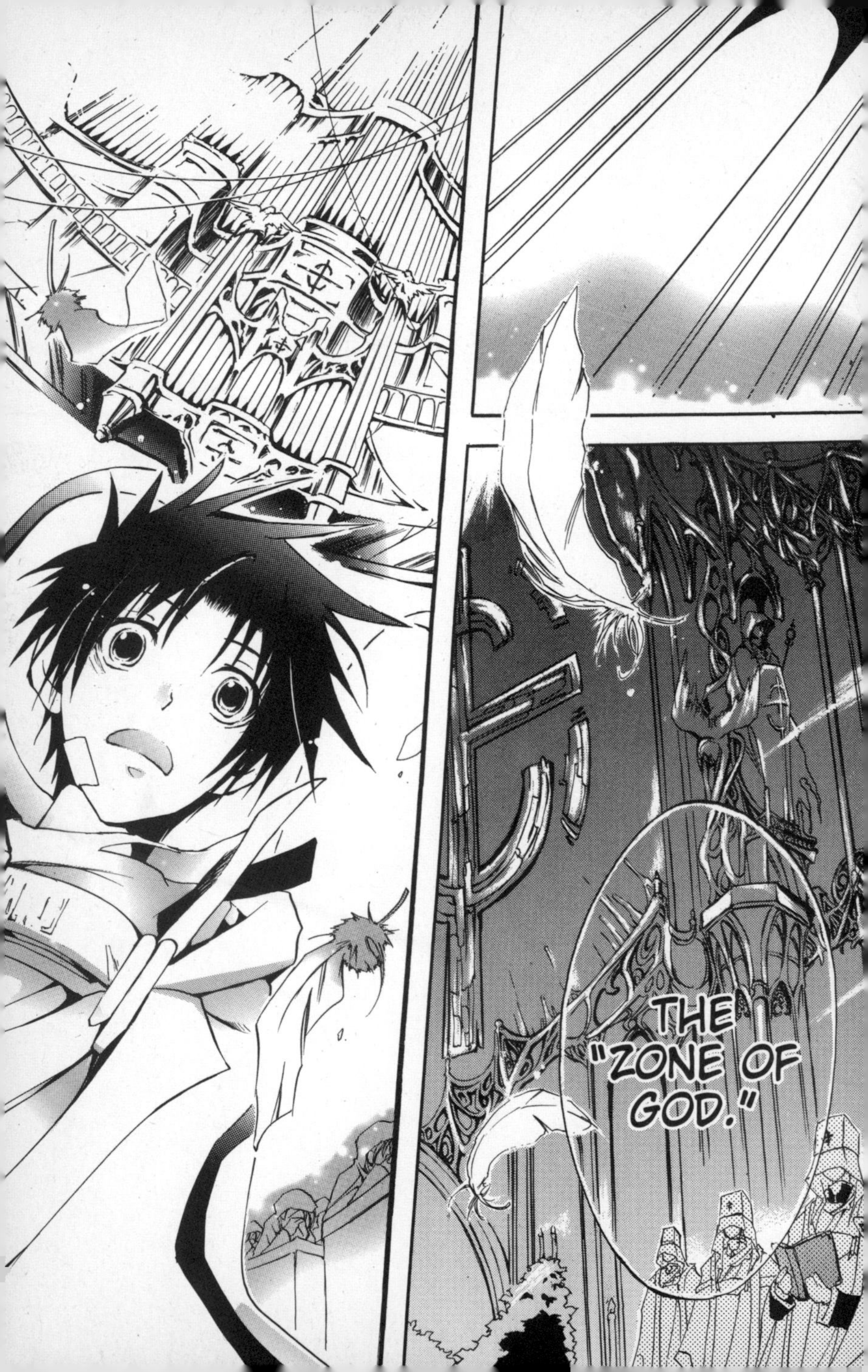
THE "ZONE OF GOD."

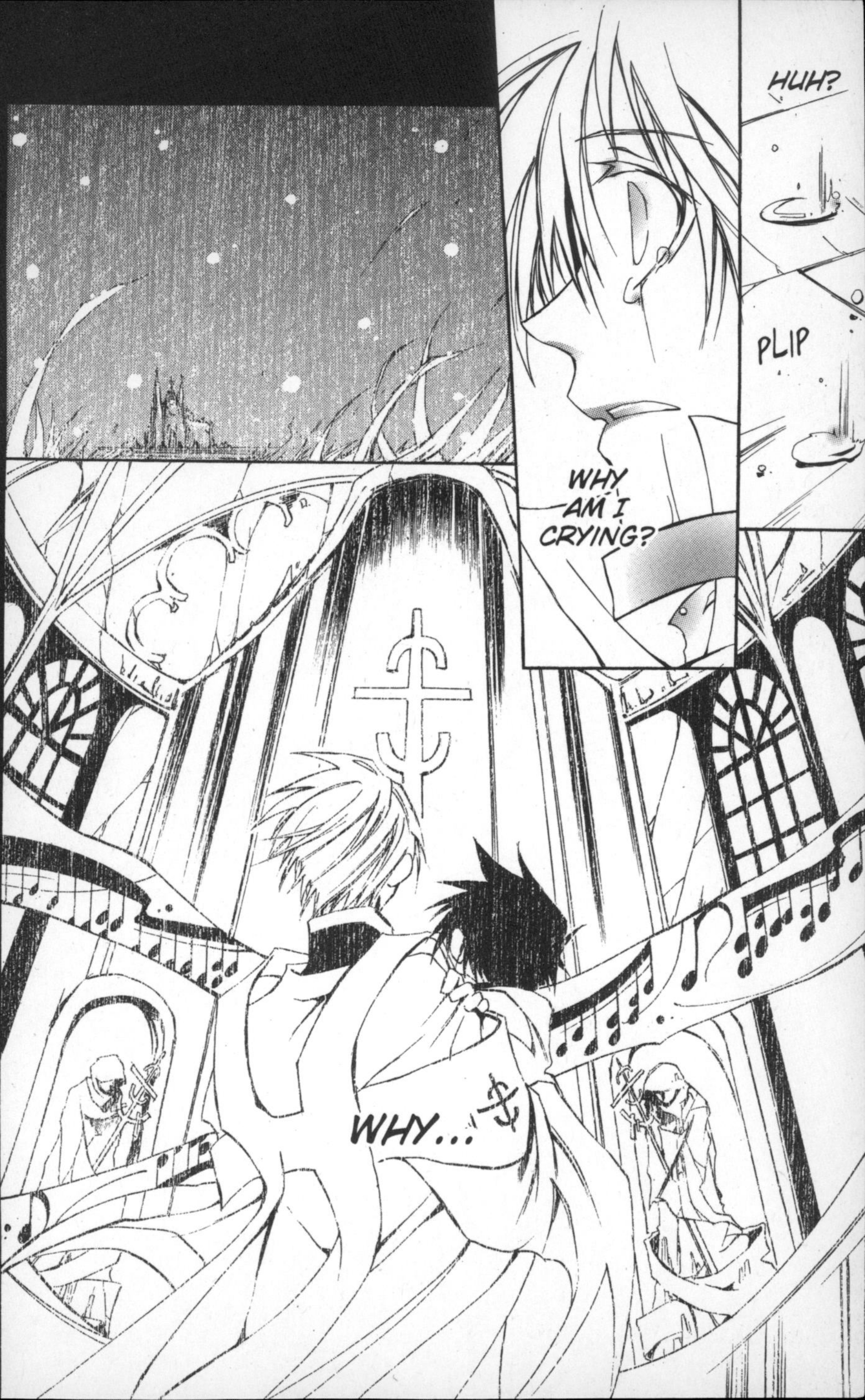
HUH?
PLIP
WHY AM I CRYING?
WHY...

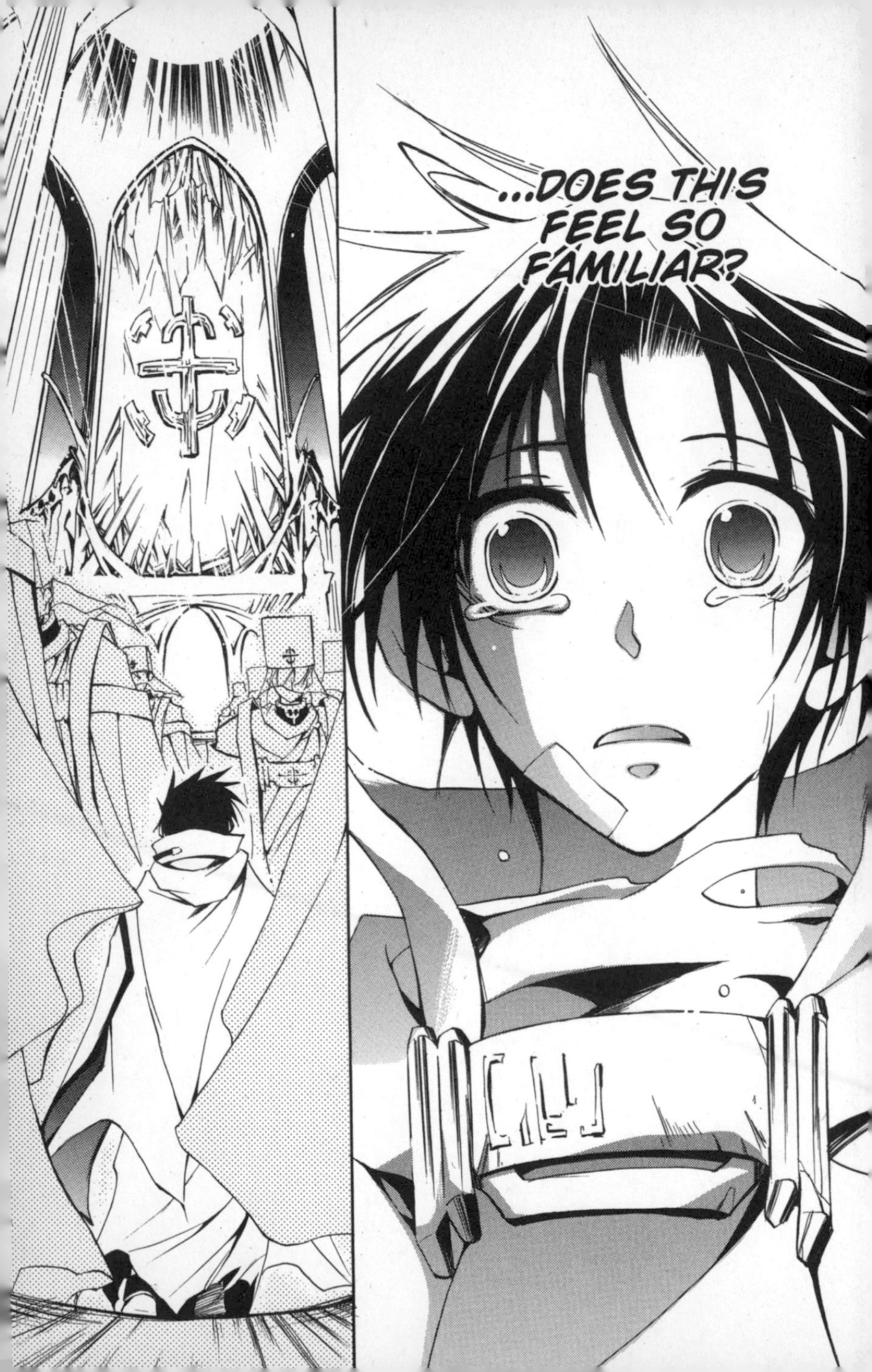
...DOES THIS FEEL SO FAMILIAR?

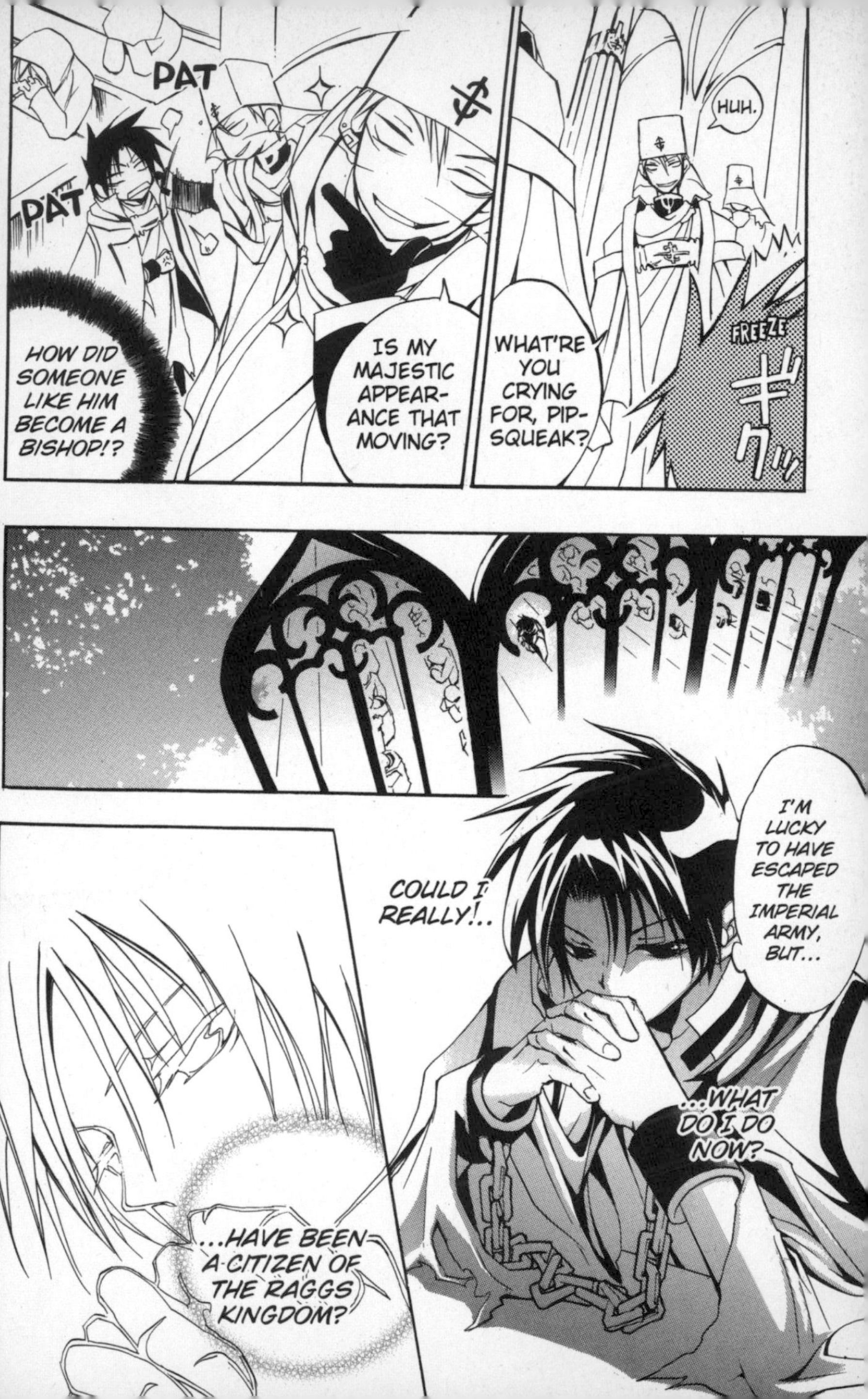
HUH.
WHAT'RE YOU CRYING FOR, PIP-SQUEAK?
FREEZE
ギクッ
PAT
PAT
IS MY MAJESTIC APPEAR-ANCE THAT MOVING?
HOW DID SOMEONE LIKE HIM BECOME A BISHOP!?
I'M LUCKY TO HAVE ESCAPED THE IMPERIAL ARMY, BUT...
...WHAT DO I DO NOW?
COULD I REALLY!...
...HAVE BEEN A CITIZEN OF THE RAGGS KINGDOM?

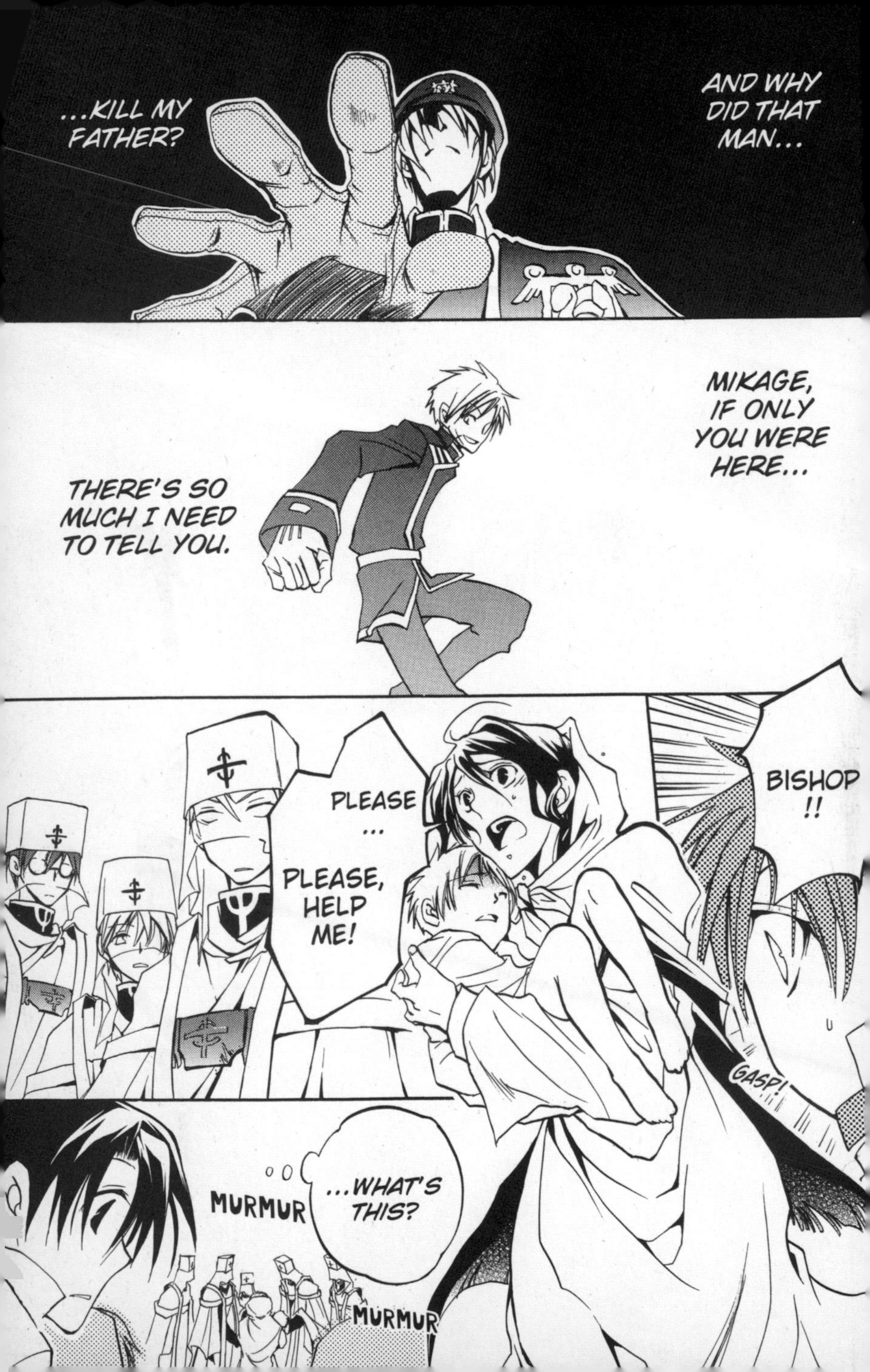
AND WHY DID THAT MAN...
...KILL MY FATHER?
MIKAGE, IF ONLY YOU WERE HERE...
THERE'S SO MUCH I NEED TO TELL YOU.
BISHOP!!
GASP!
PLEASE...
PLEASE, HELP ME!
...WHAT'S THIS?
MURMUR
MURMUR

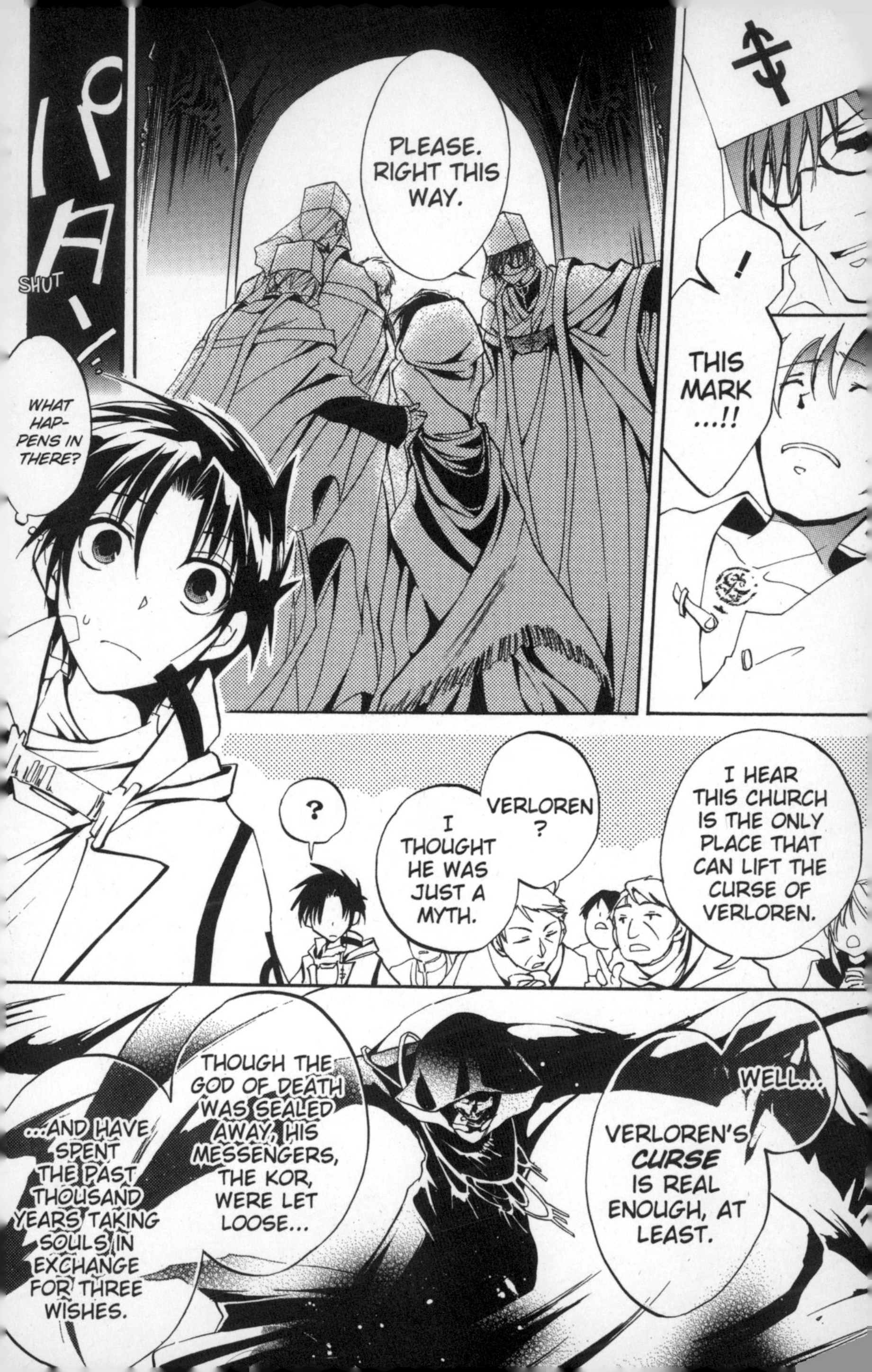
!
THIS MARK ...!!
PLEASE. RIGHT THIS WAY.
SHUT
WHAT HAPPENS IN THERE?
I HEAR THIS CHURCH IS THE ONLY PLACE THAT CAN LIFT THE CURSE OF VERLOREN.
VERLOREN?
I THOUGHT HE WAS JUST A MYTH.
?
WELL...
VERLOREN'S CURSE IS REAL ENOUGH, AT LEAST.
THOUGH THE GOD OF DEATH WAS SEALED AWAY, HIS MESSENGERS, THE KOR, WERE LET LOOSE...
...AND HAVE SPENT THE PAST THOUSAND YEARS TAKING SOULS IN EXCHANGE FOR THREE WISHES.

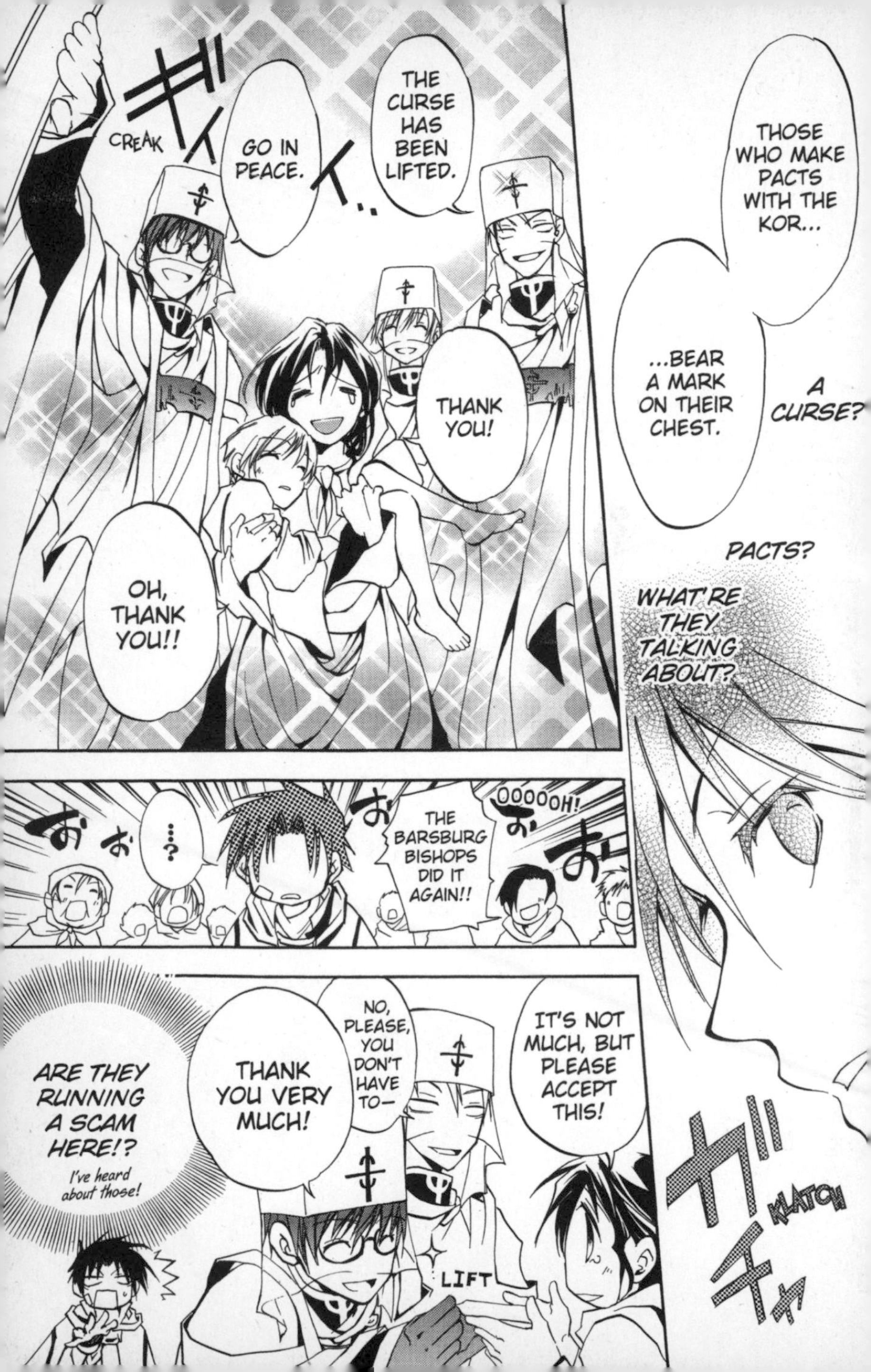
THOSE WHO MAKE PACTS WITH THE KOR...
...BEAR A MARK ON THEIR CHEST.
A CURSE?
PACTS?
WHAT'RE THEY TALKING ABOUT?
KLATCH
THE CURSE HAS BEEN LIFTED.
GO IN PEACE.
CREAK
THANK YOU!
OH, THANK YOU!!
OOOOOH!
THE BARSBURG BISHOPS DID IT AGAIN!!
...?
IT'S NOT MUCH, BUT PLEASE ACCEPT THIS!
NO, PLEASE, YOU DON'T HAVE TO—
THANK YOU VERY MUCH!
LIFT
ARE THEY RUNNING A SCAM HERE!?
I've heard about those!

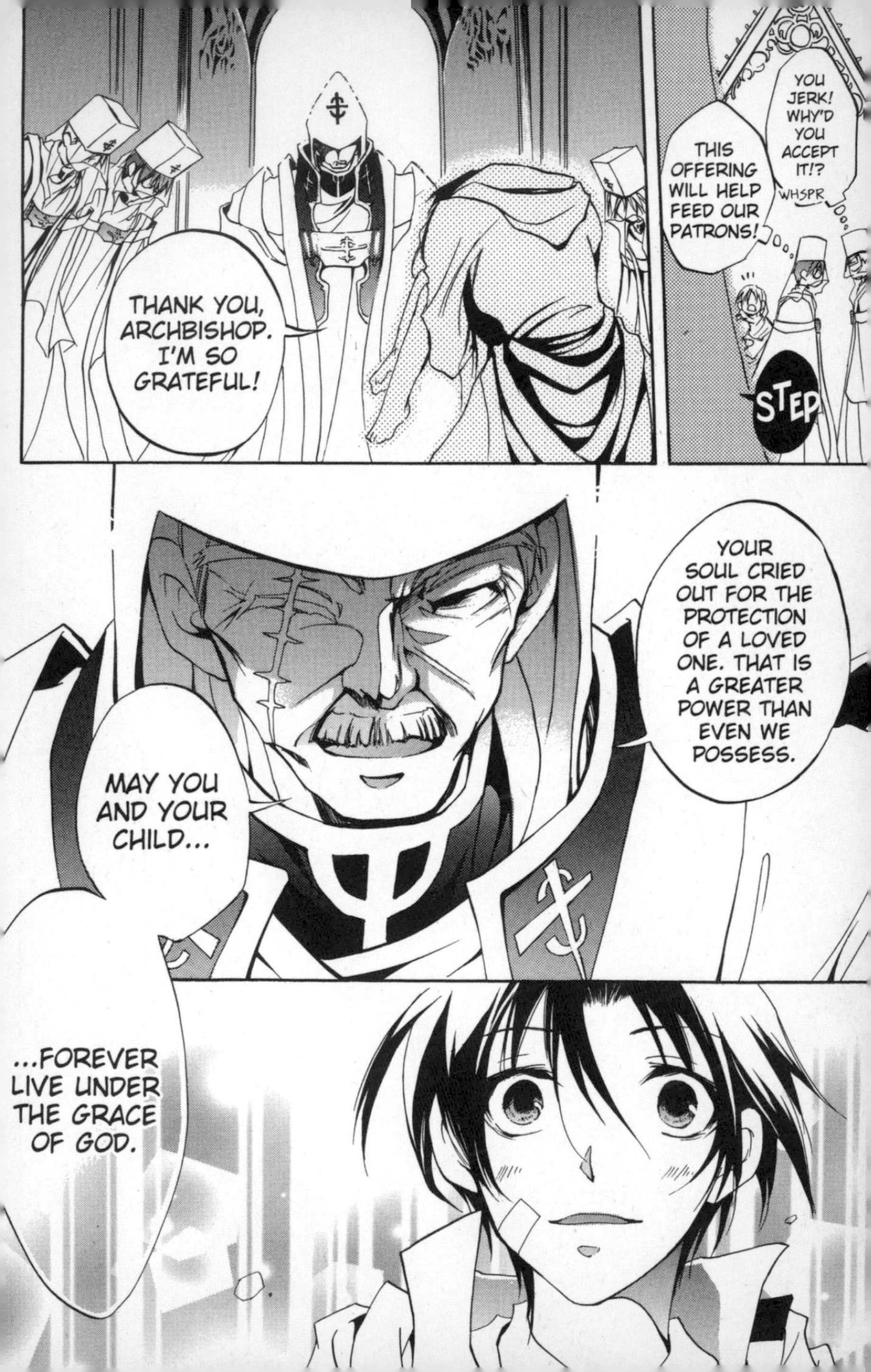
YOU JERK! WHY'D YOU ACCEPT IT!?
WHSPR
THIS OFFERING WILL HELP FEED OUR PATRONS!
STEP
THANK YOU, ARCHBISHOP. I'M SO GRATEFUL!
YOUR SOUL CRIED OUT FOR THE PROTECTION OF A LOVED ONE. THAT IS A GREATER POWER THAN EVEN WE POSSESS.
MAY YOU AND YOUR CHILD...
...FOREVER LIVE UNDER THE GRACE OF GOD.

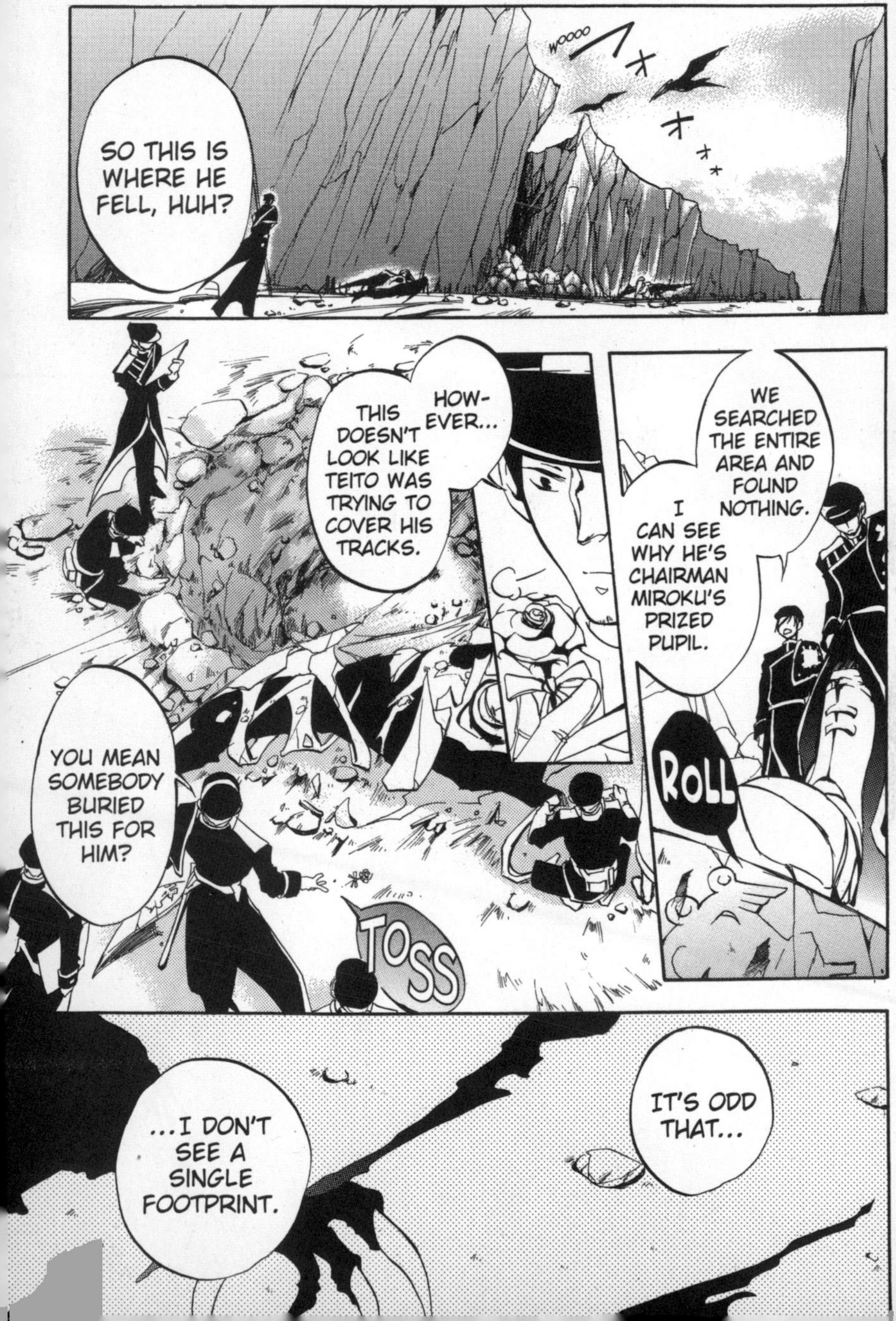
WOOOO
SO THIS IS WHERE HE FELL, HUH?
WE SEARCHED THE ENTIRE AREA AND FOUND NOTHING.
I CAN SEE WHY HE'S CHAIRMAN MIROKU'S PRIZED PUPIL.
ROLL
HOW-EVER...
THIS DOESN'T LOOK LIKE TEITO WAS TRYING TO COVER HIS TRACKS.
YOU MEAN SOMEBODY BURIED THIS FOR HIM?
TOSS
IT'S ODD THAT...
...I DON'T SEE A SINGLE FOOTPRINT.

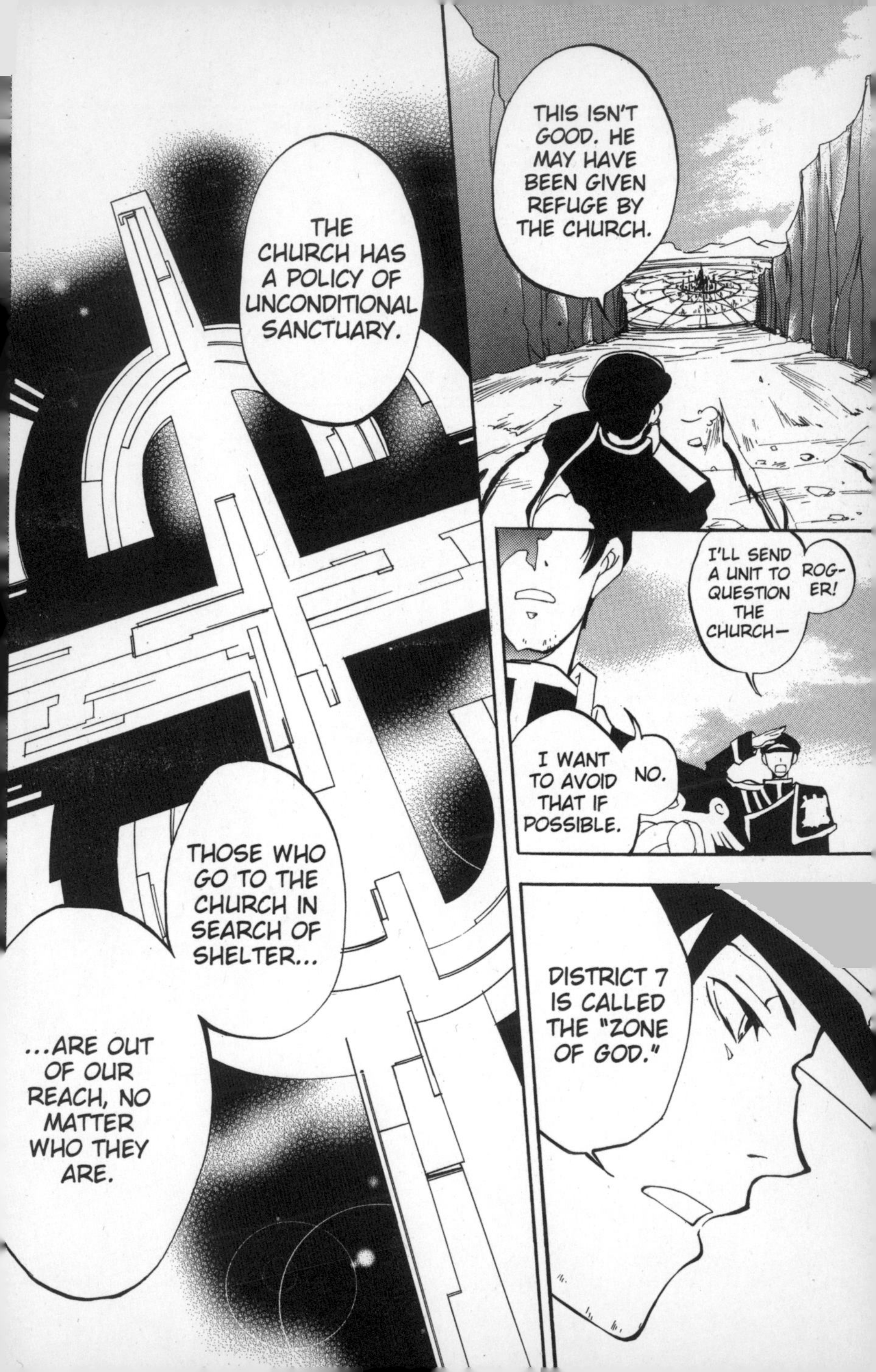
THIS ISN'T GOOD. HE MAY HAVE BEEN GIVEN REFUGE BY THE CHURCH.
ROG-ER!
I'LL SEND A UNIT TO QUESTION THE CHURCH—
NO.
I WANT TO AVOID THAT IF POSSIBLE.
DISTRICT 7 IS CALLED THE "ZONE OF GOD."
THE CHURCH HAS A POLICY OF UNCONDITIONAL SANCTUARY.
THOSE WHO GO TO THE CHURCH IN SEARCH OF SHELTER...
...ARE OUT OF OUR REACH, NO MATTER WHO THEY ARE.

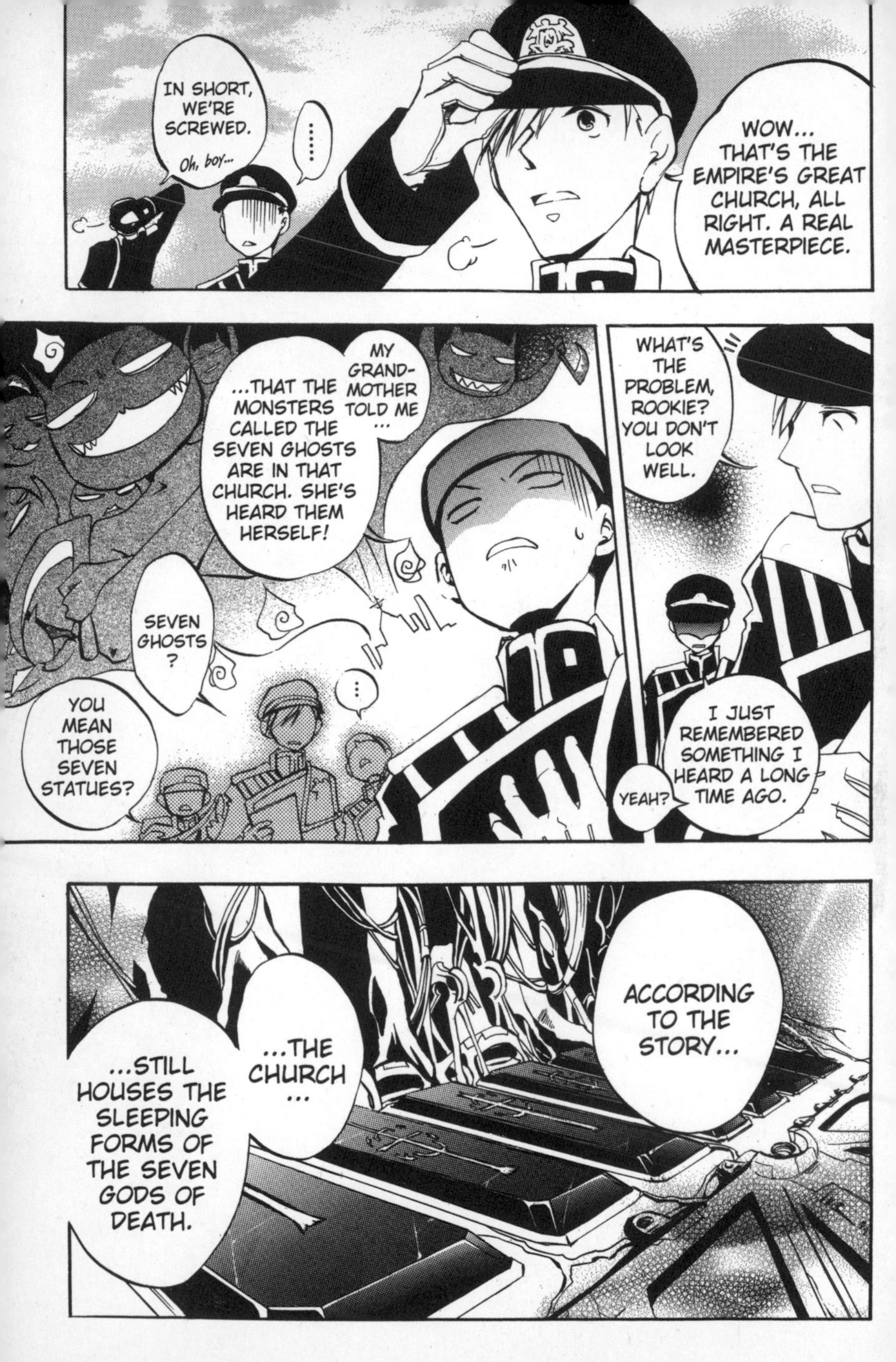
WOW... THAT'S THE EMPIRE'S GREAT CHURCH, ALL RIGHT. A REAL MASTERPIECE.
......
IN SHORT, WE'RE SCREWED.
Oh, boy...
WHAT'S THE PROBLEM, ROOKIE? YOU DON'T LOOK WELL.
I JUST REMEMBERED SOMETHING I HEARD A LONG TIME AGO.
YEAH?
MY GRAND-MOTHER TOLD ME...
...THAT THE MONSTERS CALLED THE SEVEN GHOSTS ARE IN THAT CHURCH. SHE'S HEARD THEM HERSELF!
...
SEVEN GHOSTS?
YOU MEAN THOSE SEVEN STATUES?
ACCORDING TO THE STORY...
...THE CHURCH...
...STILL HOUSES THE SLEEPING FORMS OF THE SEVEN GODS OF DEATH.

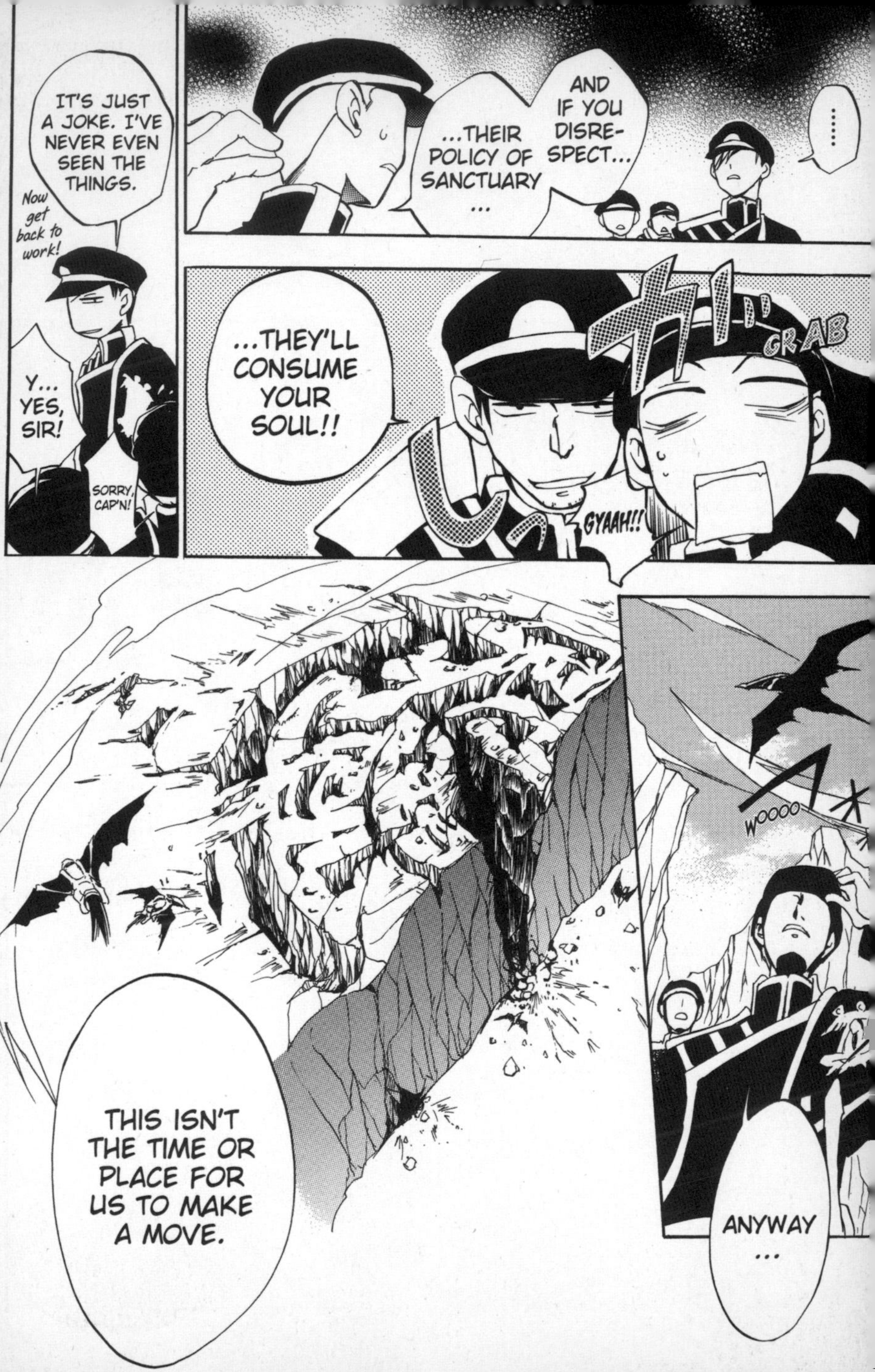
......
AND IF YOU DISRE-SPECT...
...THEIR POLICY OF SANCTUARY ...
...THEY'LL CONSUME YOUR SOUL!!
GRAB
GYAAH!!
IT'S JUST A JOKE. I'VE NEVER EVEN SEEN THE THINGS.
Now get back to work!
Y... YES, SIR!
SORRY, CAP'N!
WOOOO
ANYWAY ...
THIS ISN'T THE TIME OR PLACE FOR US TO MAKE A MOVE.

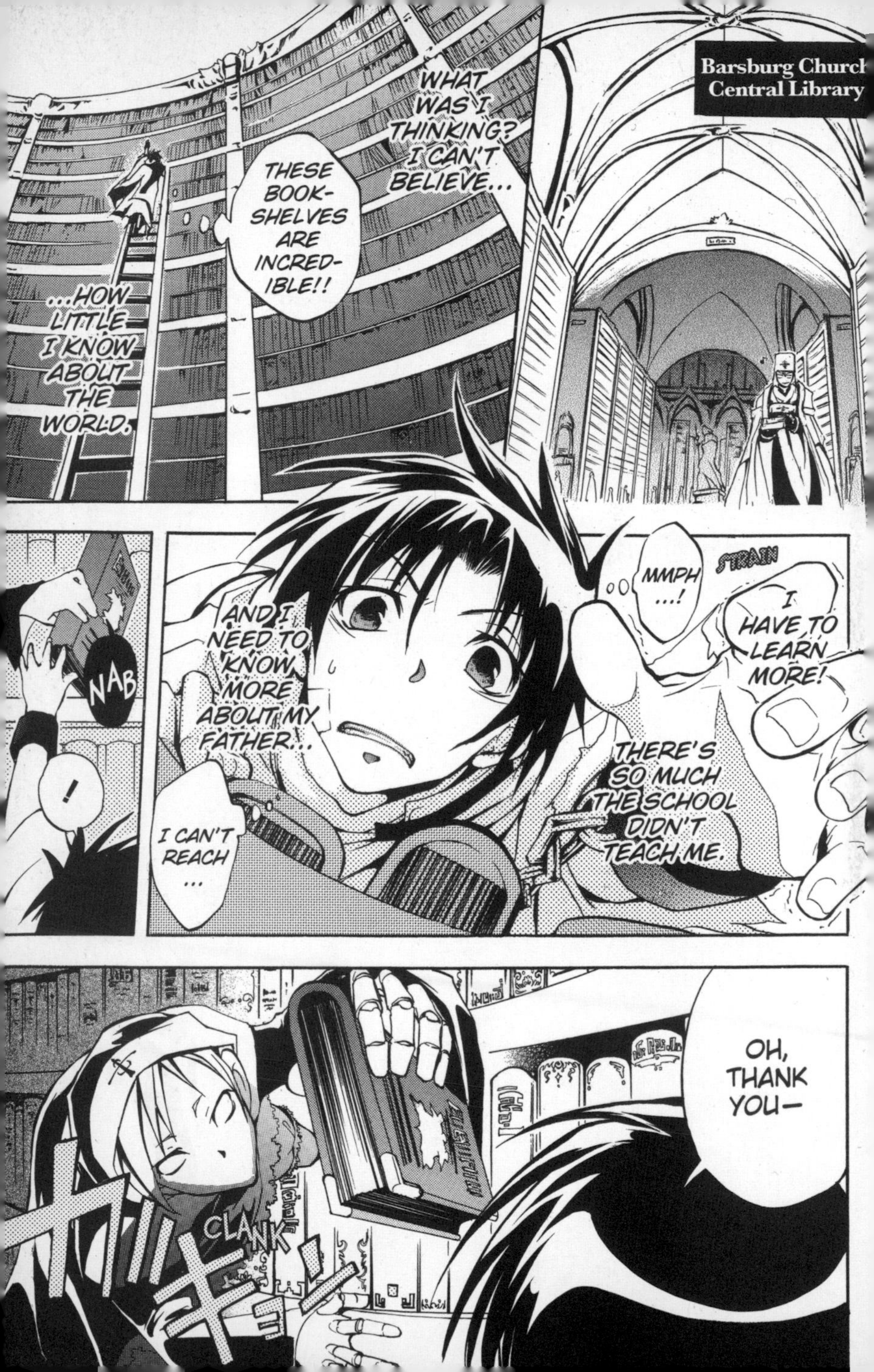

Barsburg Church Central Library
WHAT WAS I THINKING? I CAN'T BELIEVE...
THESE BOOK-SHELVES ARE INCRED-IBLE!!
...HOW LITTLE I KNOW ABOUT THE WORLD.
MMPH ...!
STRAIN
I HAVE TO LEARN MORE!
AND I NEED TO KNOW MORE ABOUT MY FATHER...
THERE'S SO MUCH THE SCHOOL DIDN'T TEACH ME.
I CAN'T REACH ...
NAB
!
OH, THANK YOU—
CLANK

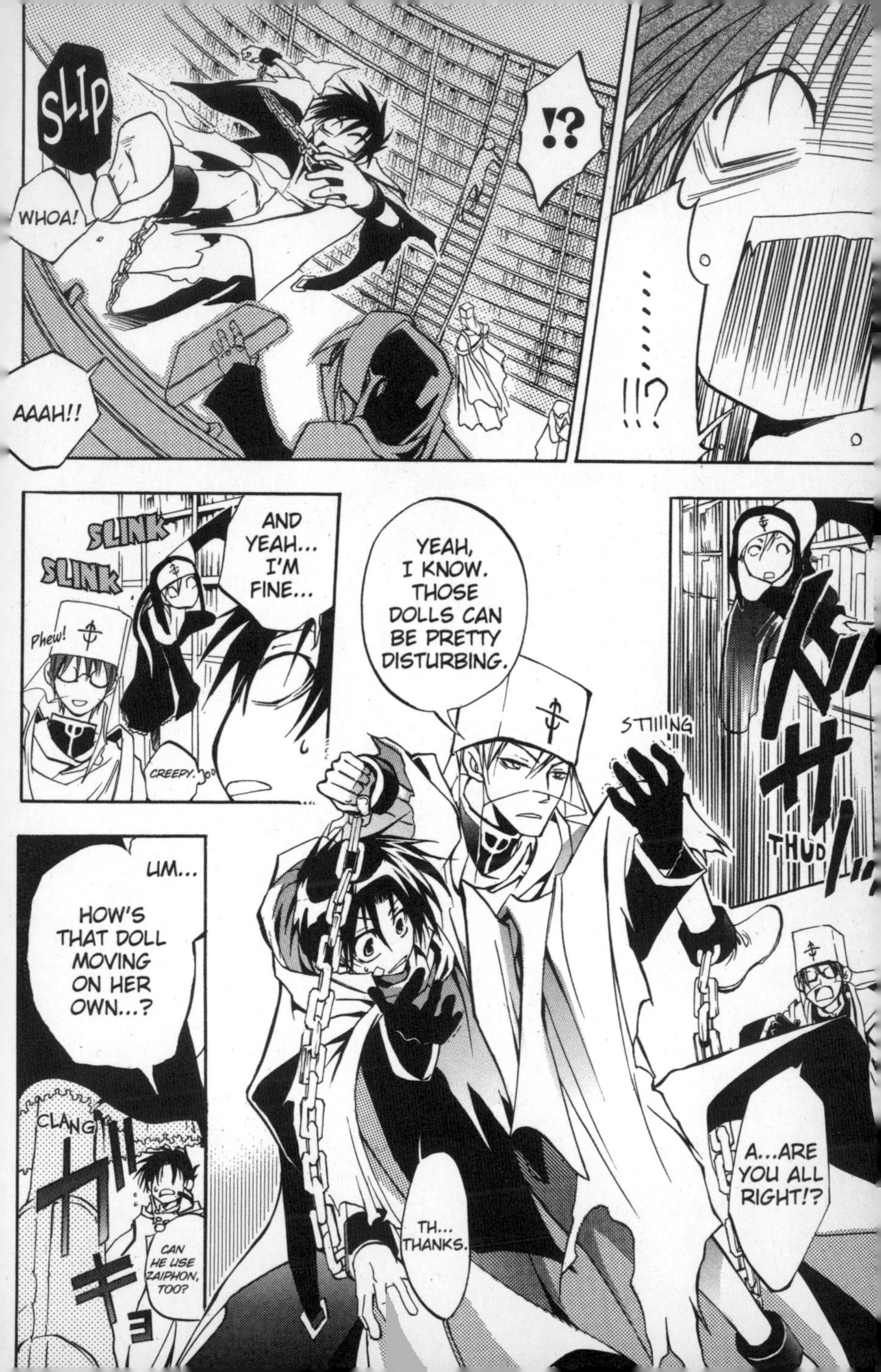
!?
......
!!?
SLIP
WHOA!
AAAH!!
THUD
A...ARE YOU ALL RIGHT!?
STIIING
YEAH, I KNOW. THOSE DOLLS CAN BE PRETTY DISTURBING.
TH... THANKS.
AND YEAH... I'M FINE...
SLINK
SLINK
Phew!
CREEPY.
UM...
HOW'S THAT DOLL MOVING ON HER OWN...?
CLANG
CAN HE USE ZAIPHON, TOO?

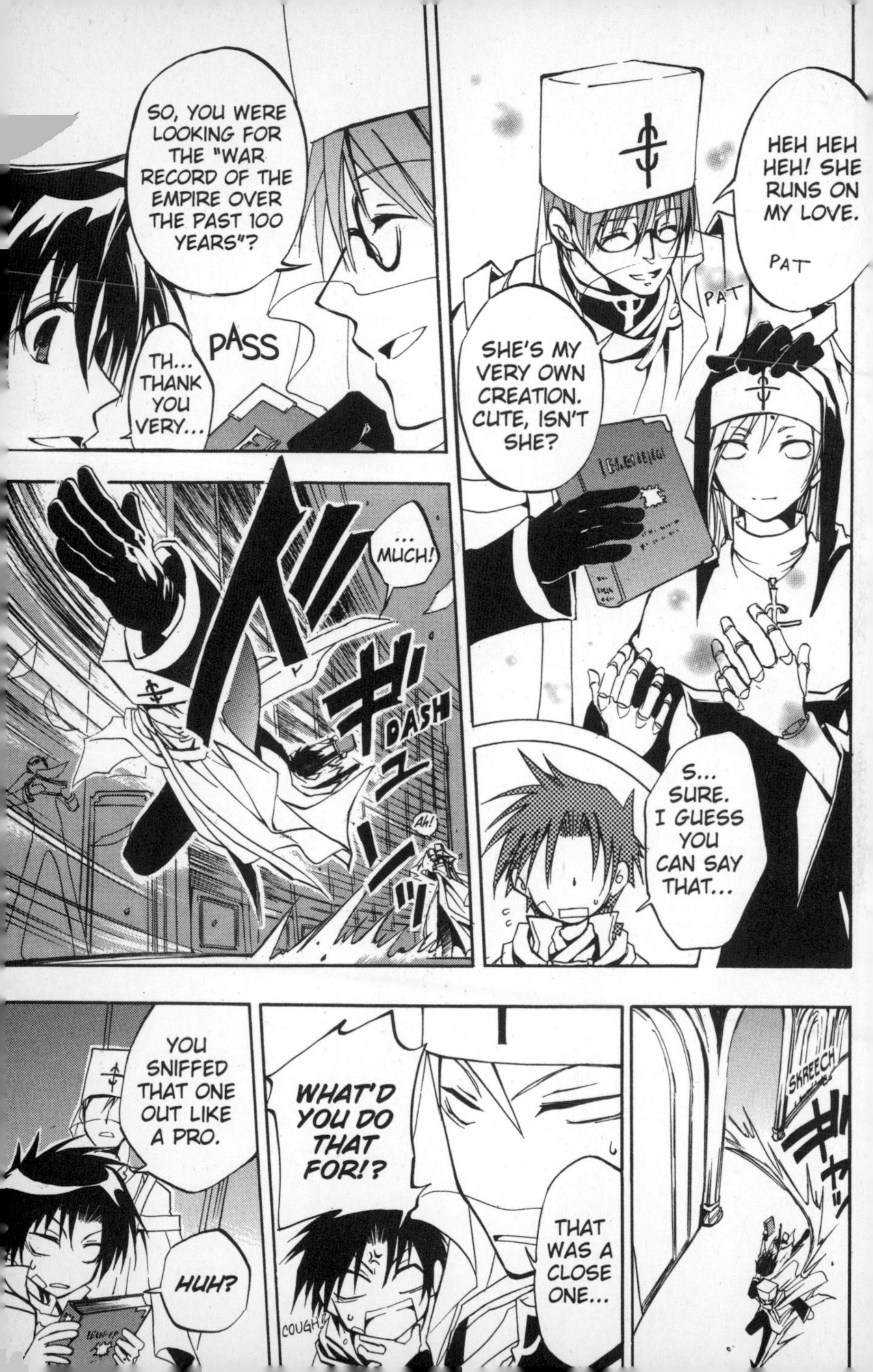
HEH HEH HEH! SHE RUNS ON MY LOVE.
PAT
PAT
SHE'S MY VERY OWN CREATION. CUTE, ISN'T SHE?
S... SURE. I GUESS YOU CAN SAY THAT...
SO, YOU WERE LOOKING FOR THE "WAR RECORD OF THE EMPIRE OVER THE PAST 100 YEARS"?
PASS
TH... THANK YOU VERY...
...MUCH!
DASH
Ah!
SKREECH
WHAT'D YOU DO THAT FOR!?
THAT WAS A CLOSE ONE...
COUGH
YOU SNIFFED THAT ONE OUT LIKE A PRO.
HUH?

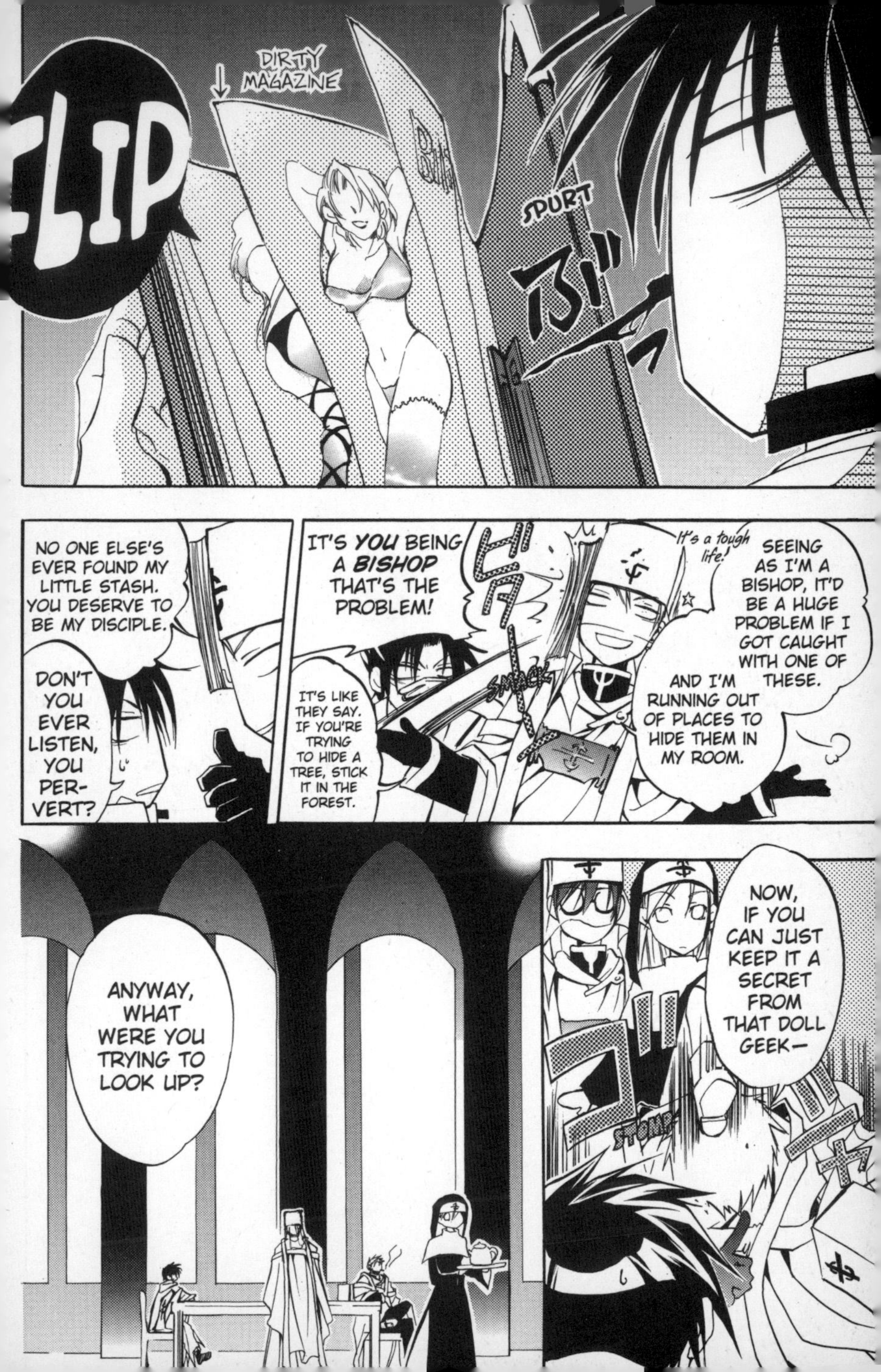
DIRTY MAGAZINE
LIP
SPURT
It's a tough life!
SEEING AS I'M A BISHOP, IT'D BE A HUGE PROBLEM IF I GOT CAUGHT WITH ONE OF THESE.
AND I'M RUNNING OUT OF PLACES TO HIDE THEM IN MY ROOM.
IT'S YOU BEING A BISHOP THAT'S THE PROBLEM!
SMACK
IT'S LIKE THEY SAY. IF YOU'RE TRYING TO HIDE A TREE, STICK IT IN THE FOREST.
NO ONE ELSE'S EVER FOUND MY LITTLE STASH. YOU DESERVE TO BE MY DISCIPLE.
DON'T YOU EVER LISTEN, YOU PER-VERT?
NOW, IF YOU CAN JUST KEEP IT A SECRET FROM THAT DOLL GEEK—
STOMP
ANYWAY, WHAT WERE YOU TRYING TO LOOK UP?

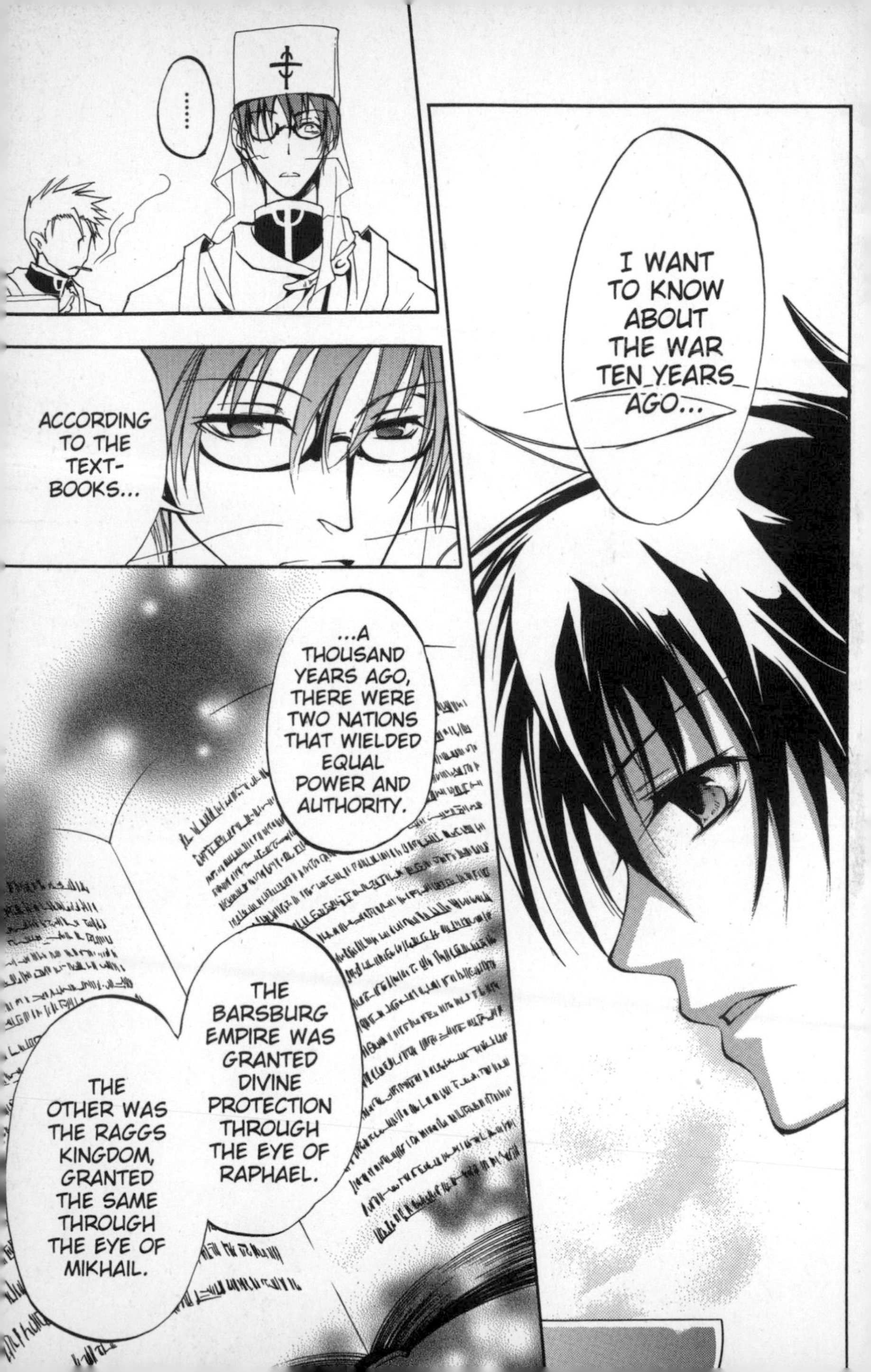
I WANT TO KNOW ABOUT THE WAR TEN YEARS AGO...
......
ACCORDING TO THE TEXT-BOOKS...
...A THOUSAND YEARS AGO, THERE WERE TWO NATIONS THAT WIELDED EQUAL POWER AND AUTHORITY.
THE BARSBURG EMPIRE WAS GRANTED DIVINE PROTECTION THROUGH THE EYE OF RAPHAEL.
THE OTHER WAS THE RAGGS KINGDOM, GRANTED THE SAME THROUGH THE EYE OF MIKHAIL.

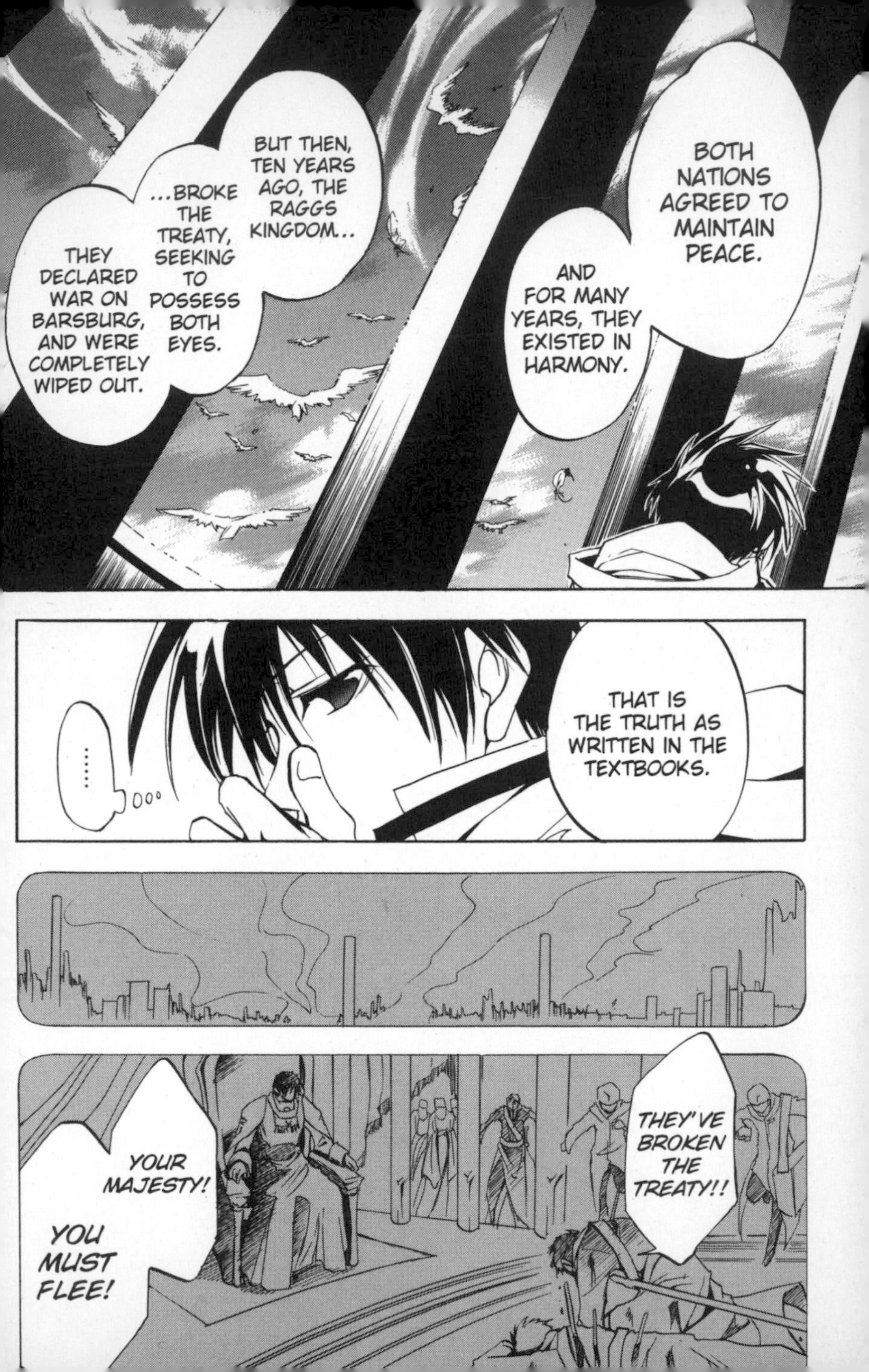
BOTH NATIONS AGREED TO MAINTAIN PEACE.
AND FOR MANY YEARS, THEY EXISTED IN HARMONY.
BUT THEN, TEN YEARS AGO, THE RAGGS KINGDOM...
...BROKE THE TREATY, SEEKING TO POSSESS BOTH EYES.
THEY DECLARED WAR ON BARSBURG, AND WERE COMPLETELY WIPED OUT.
THAT IS THE TRUTH AS WRITTEN IN THE TEXTBOOKS.
......
THEY'VE BROKEN THE TREATY!!
YOUR MAJESTY!
YOU MUST FLEE!

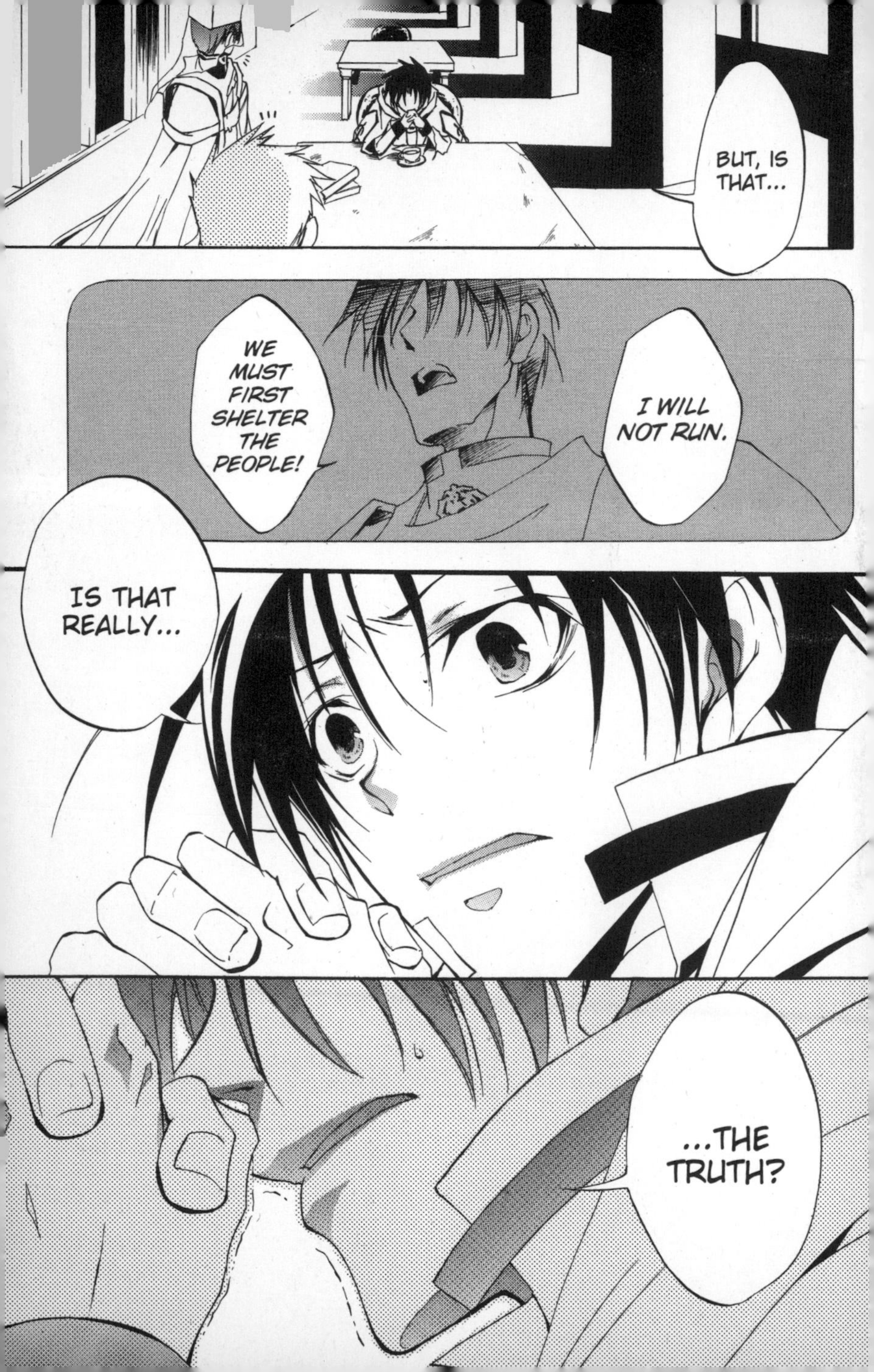
BUT, IS THAT...
I WILL NOT RUN.
WE MUST FIRST SHELTER THE PEOPLE!
IS THAT REALLY...
...THE TRUTH?

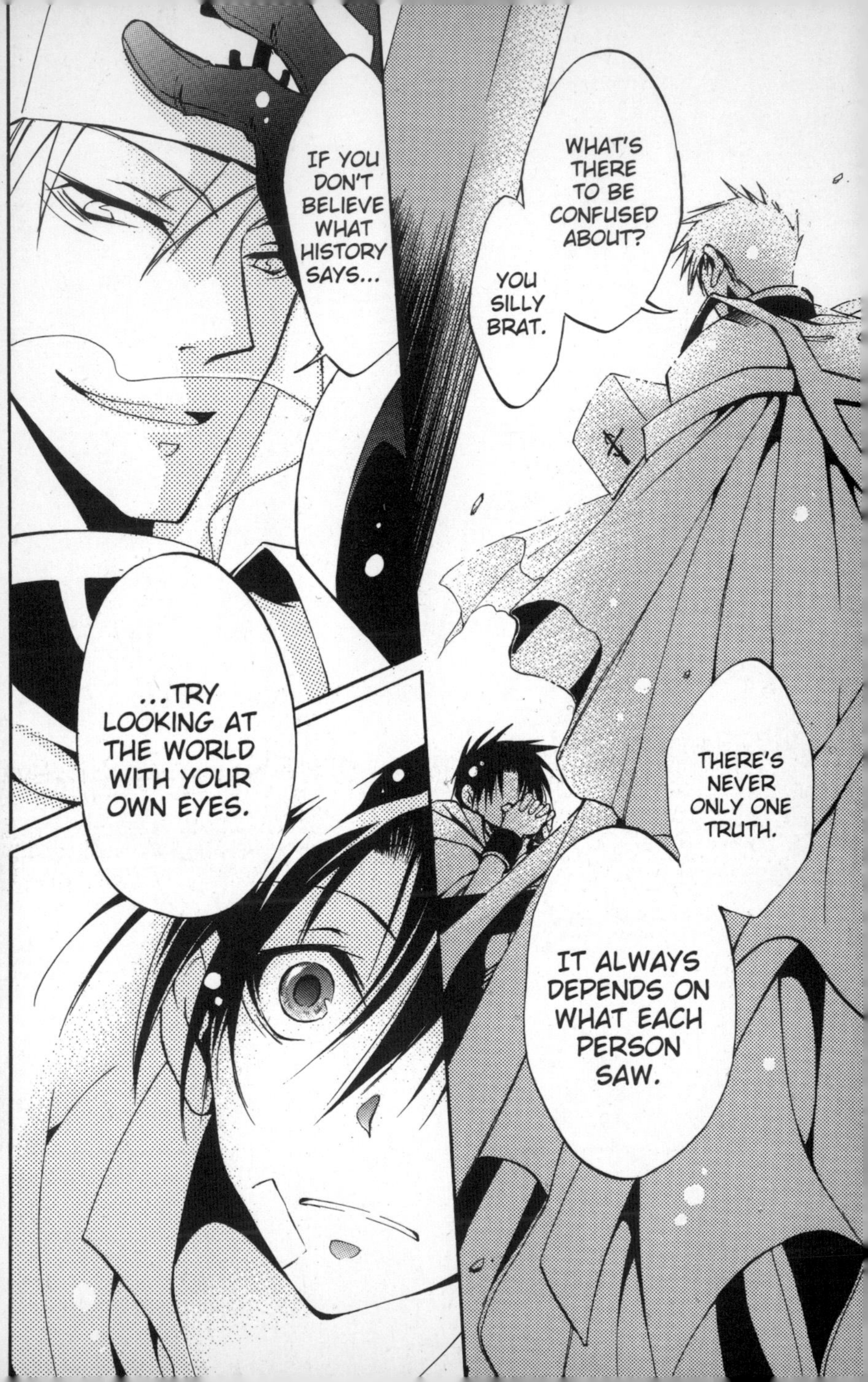
WHAT'S THERE TO BE CONFUSED ABOUT?
YOU SILLY BRAT.
THERE'S NEVER ONLY ONE TRUTH.
IT ALWAYS DEPENDS ON WHAT EACH PERSON SAW.
IF YOU DON'T BELIEVE WHAT HISTORY SAYS...
...TRY LOOKING AT THE WORLD WITH YOUR OWN EYES.

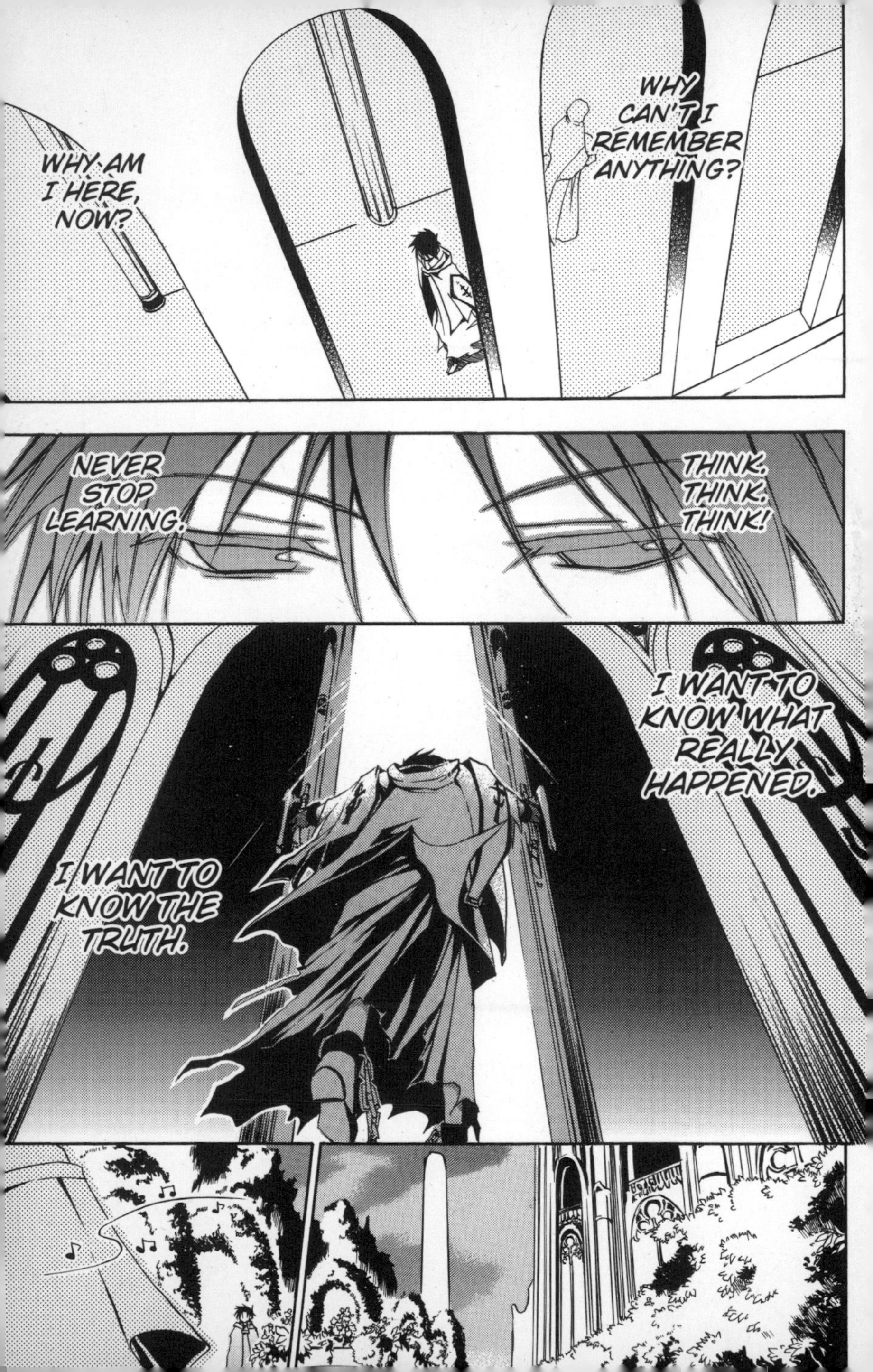
WHY CAN'T I REMEMBER ANYTHING?
WHY AM I HERE, NOW?
THINK. THINK. THINK!
NEVER STOP LEARNING.
I WANT TO KNOW WHAT REALLY HAPPENED.
I WANT TO KNOW THE TRUTH.

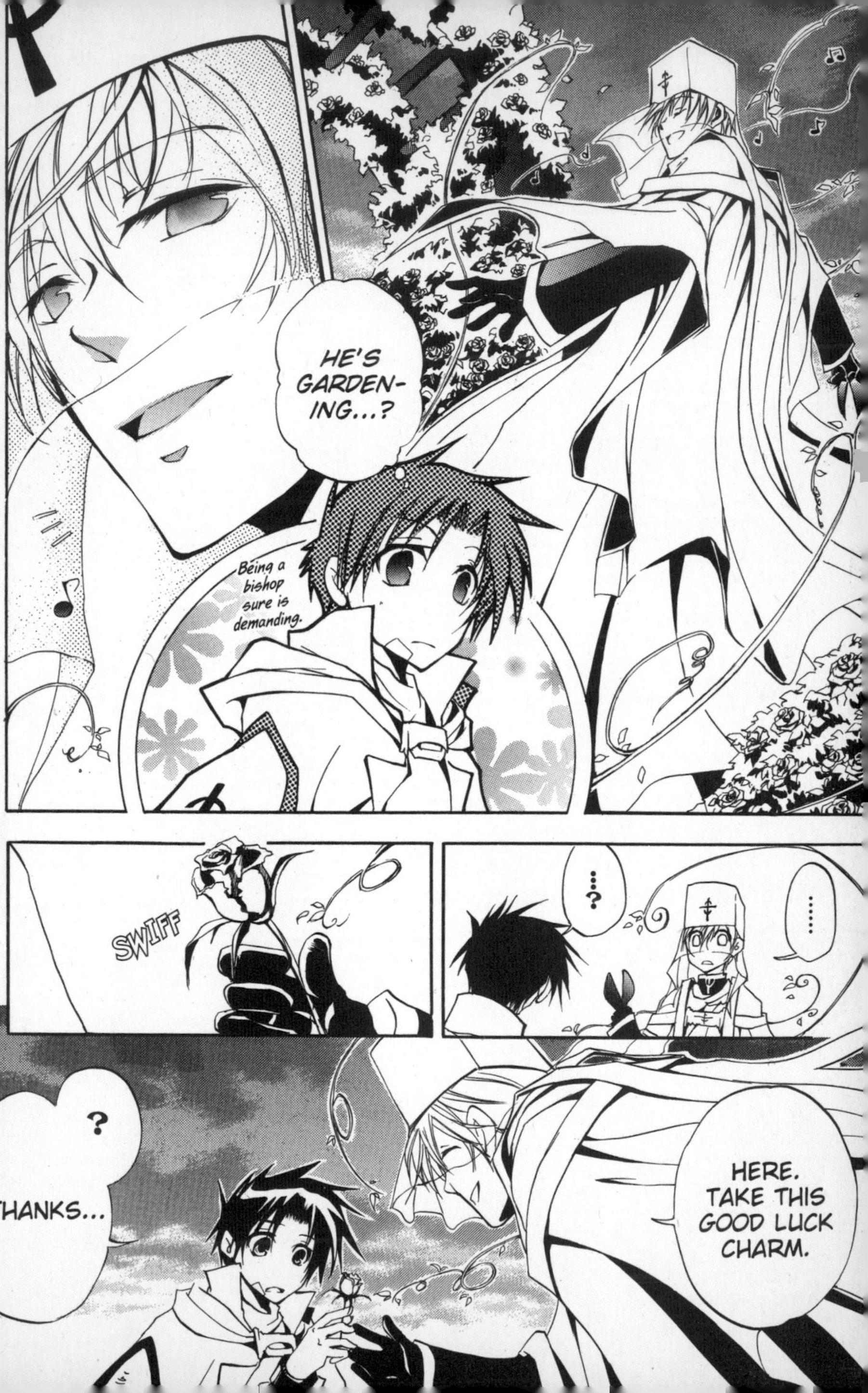
HE'S GARDEN-ING...?
Being a bishop sure is demanding.
......
...?
SWIFF
HERE. TAKE THIS GOOD LUCK CHARM.
?
THANKS...

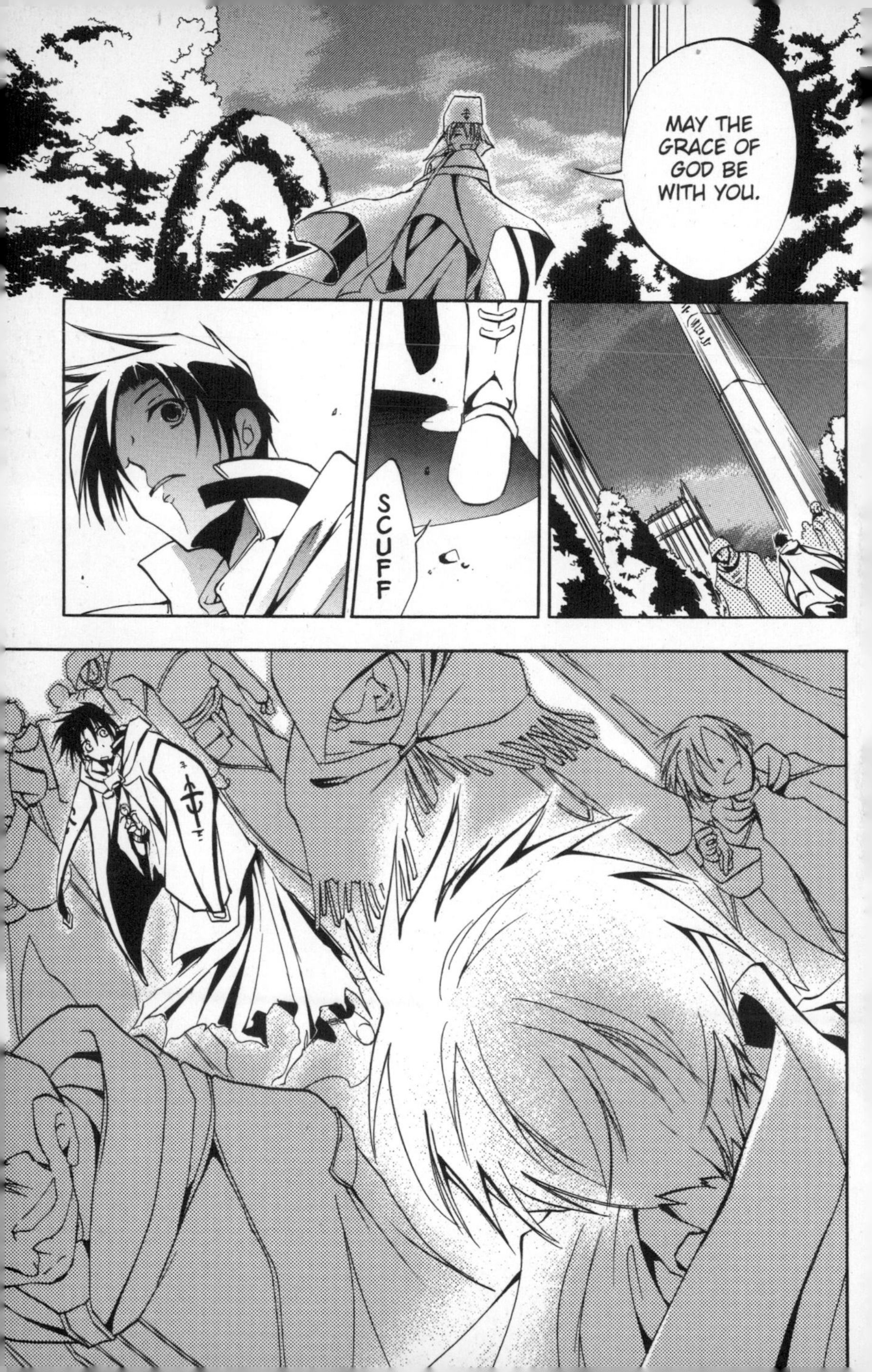
MAY THE GRACE OF GOD BE WITH YOU.
SCUFF

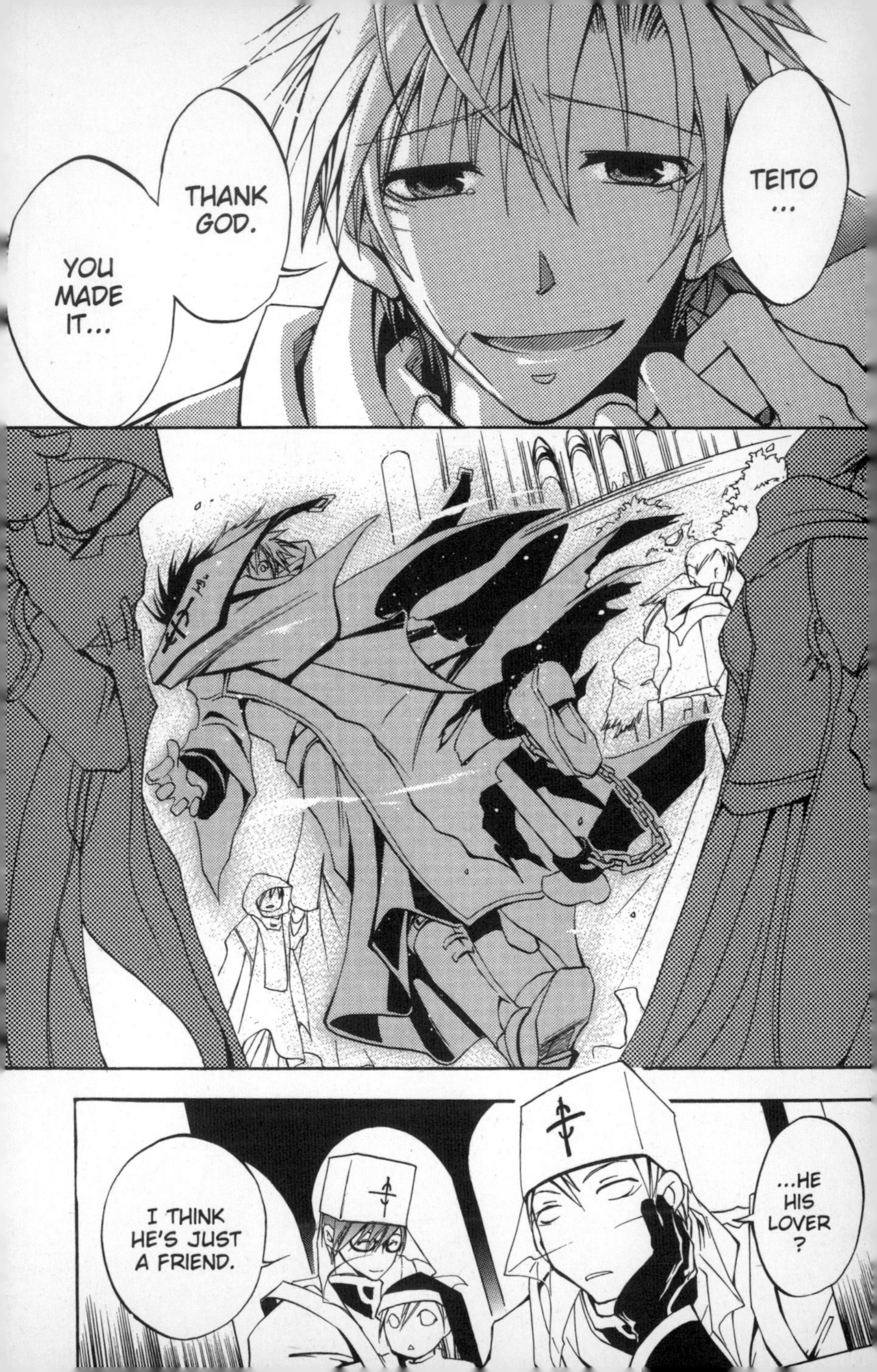
TEITO ...
THANK GOD.
YOU MADE IT...
...HE HIS LOVER ?
I THINK HE'S JUST A FRIEND.

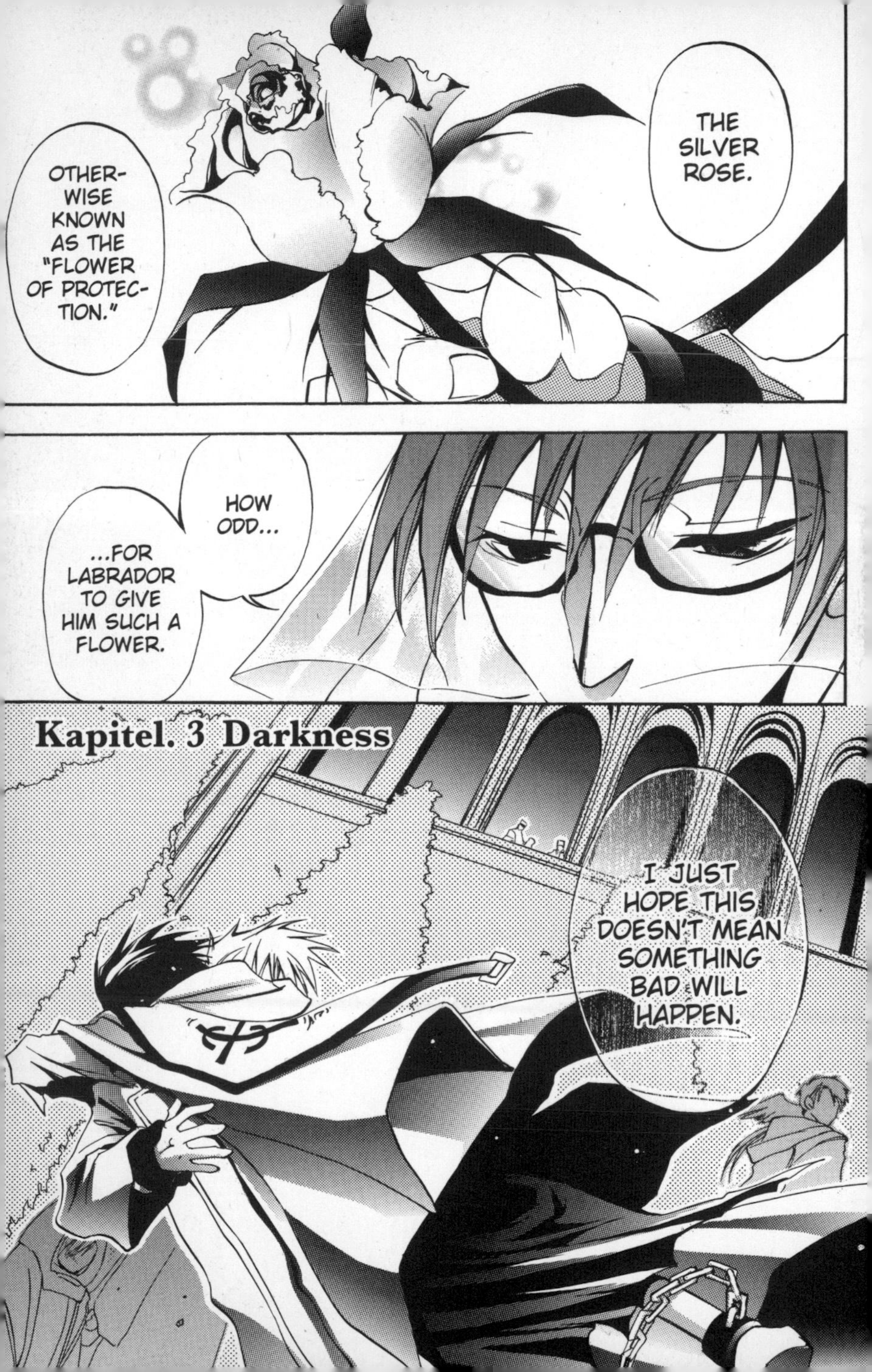
THE SILVER ROSE.
OTHER-WISE KNOWN AS THE "FLOWER OF PROTECTION."
HOW ODD...
...FOR LABRADOR TO GIVE HIM SUCH A FLOWER.
Kapitel. 3 Darkness
I JUST HOPE THIS DOESN'T MEAN SOMETHING BAD WILL HAPPEN.

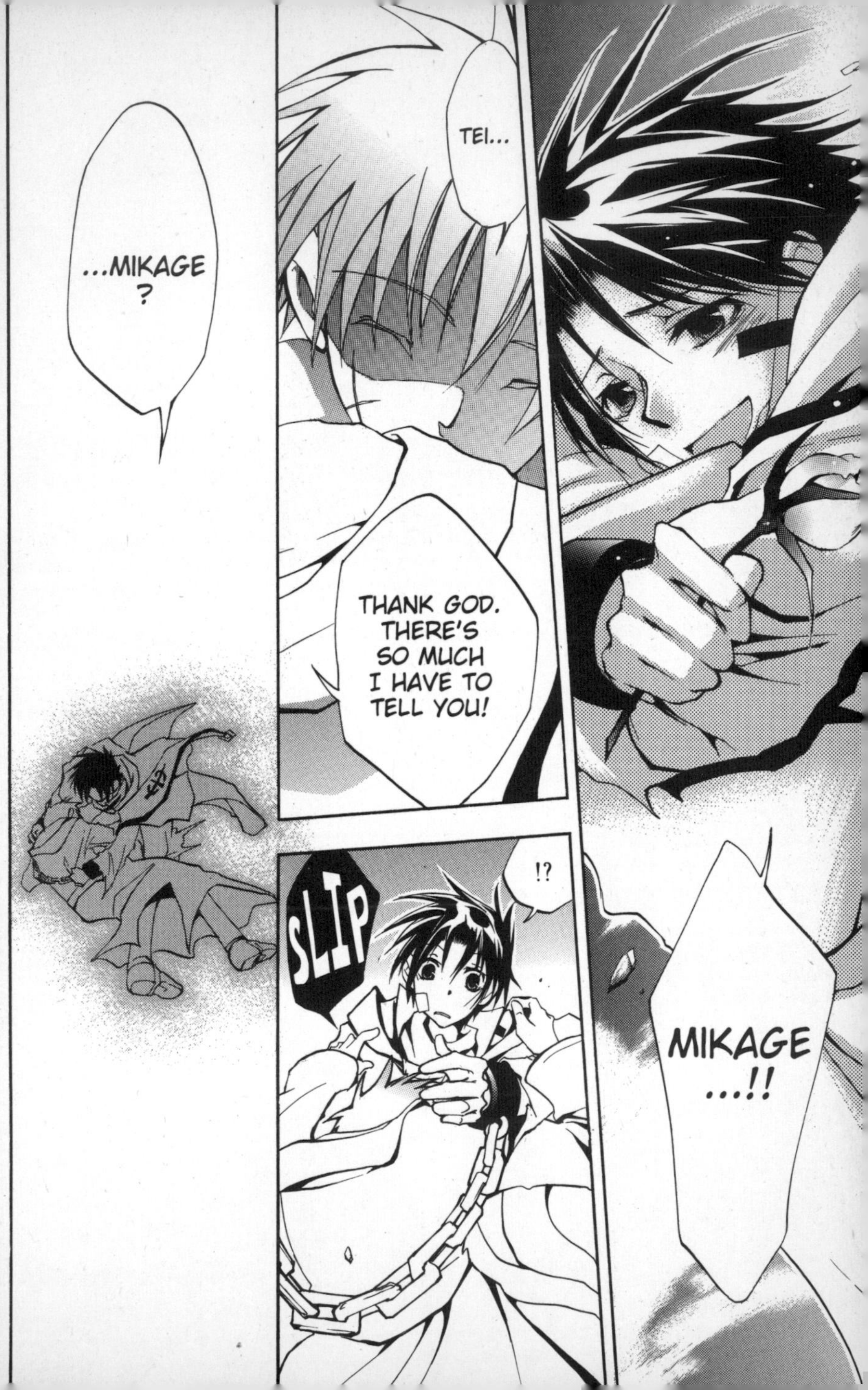
TEI...
THANK GOD. THERE'S SO MUCH I HAVE TO TELL YOU!
MIKAGE ...!!
SLIP
!?
...MIKAGE ?

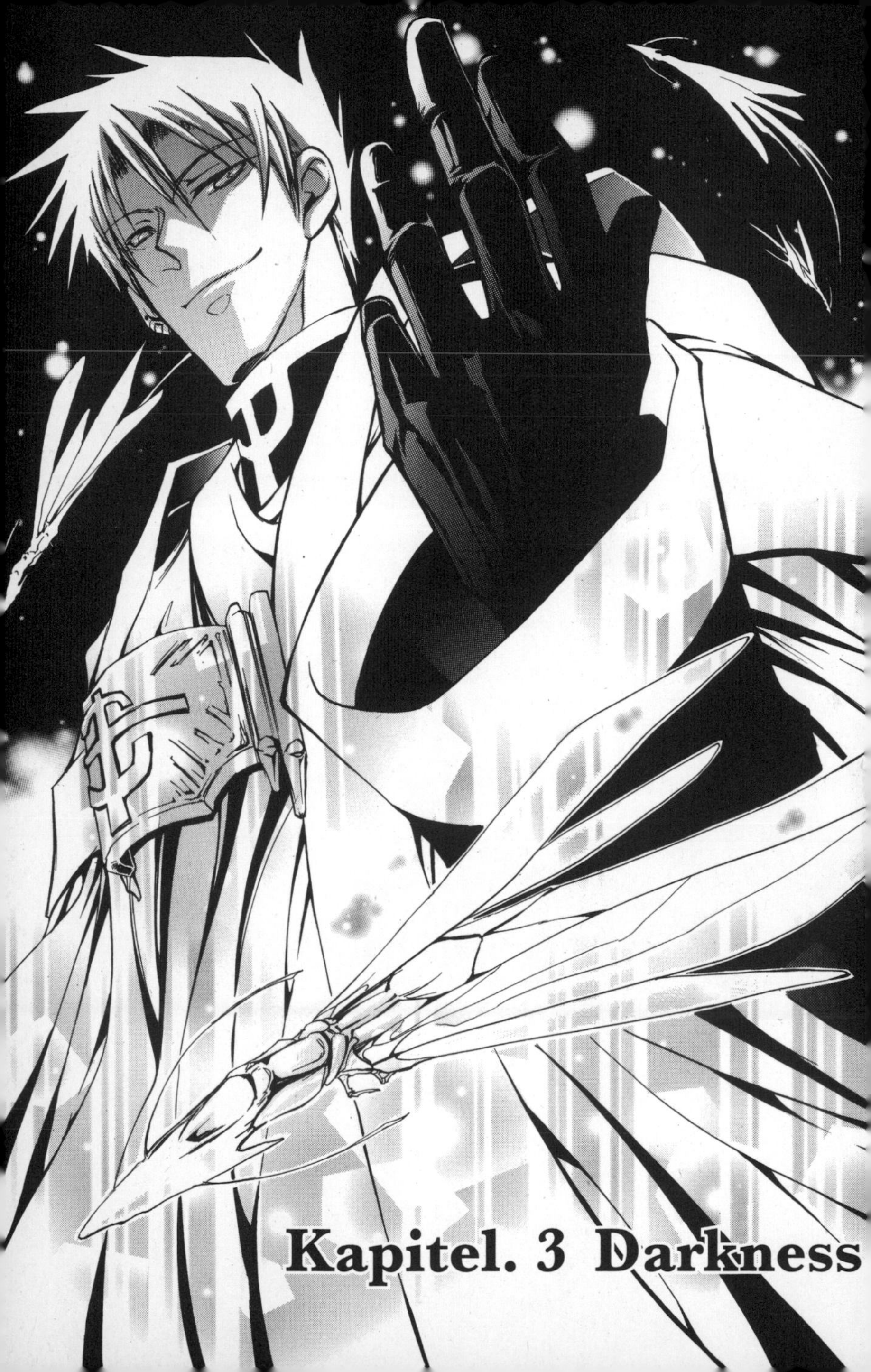
Kapitel. 3 Darkness

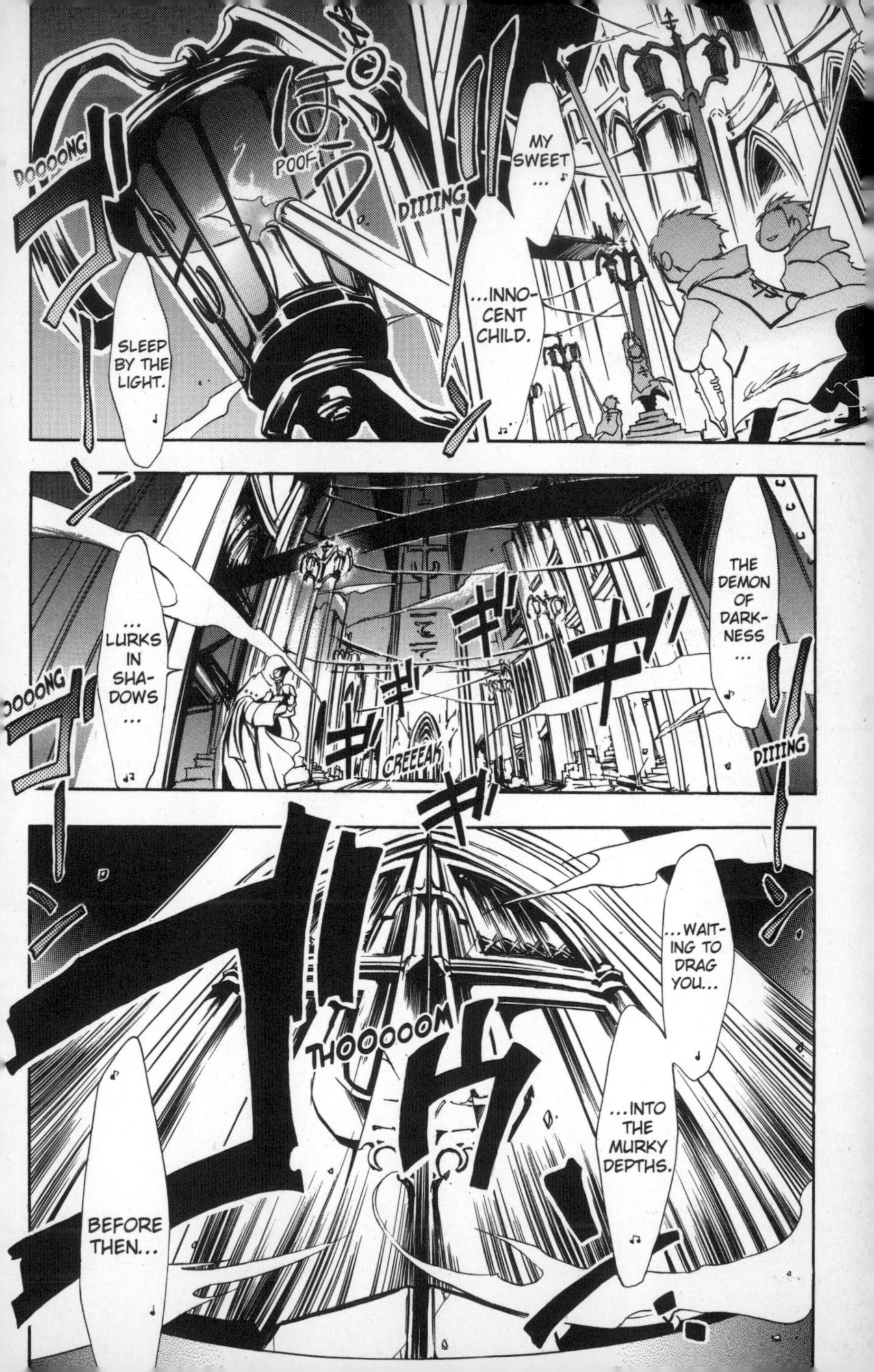
MY SWEET ...
...INNO-CENT CHILD.
DIIIING
POOF
DOOOONG
SLEEP BY THE LIGHT.
THE DEMON OF DARK-NESS ...
DIIIING
CREEEAK
... LURKS IN SHA-DOWS ...
OOOONG
...WAIT-ING TO DRAG YOU...
...INTO THE MURKY DEPTHS.
THOOOOOM
BEFORE THEN...

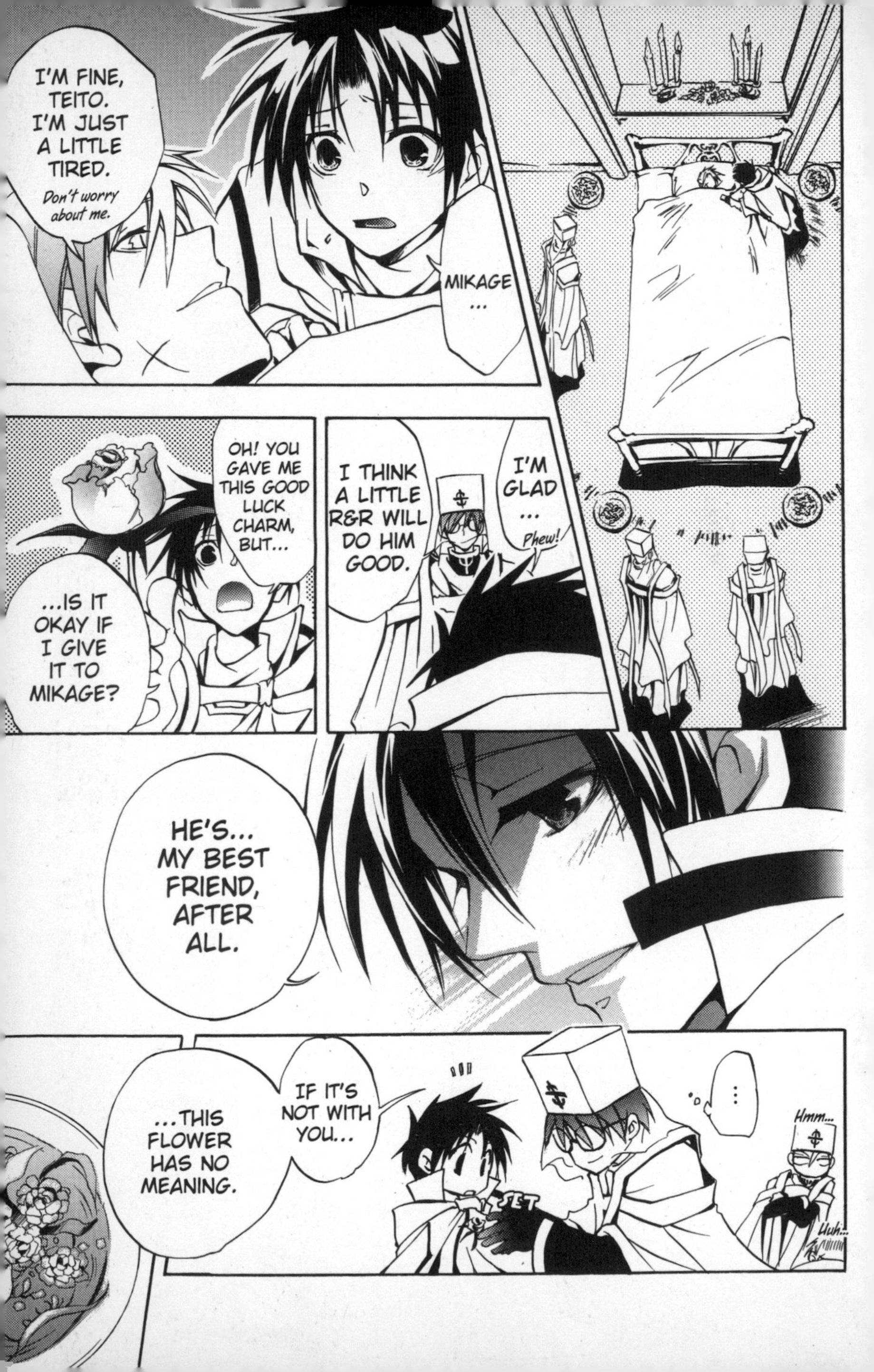
I'M FINE, TEITO. I'M JUST A LITTLE TIRED.
Don't worry about me.
MIKAGE...
I'M GLAD...
Phew!
I THINK A LITTLE R&R WILL DO HIM GOOD.
OH! YOU GAVE ME THIS GOOD LUCK CHARM, BUT...
...IS IT OKAY IF I GIVE IT TO MIKAGE?
HE'S... MY BEST FRIEND, AFTER ALL.
Hmm...
Huh...
...
IF IT'S NOT WITH YOU...
...THIS FLOWER HAS NO MEANING.

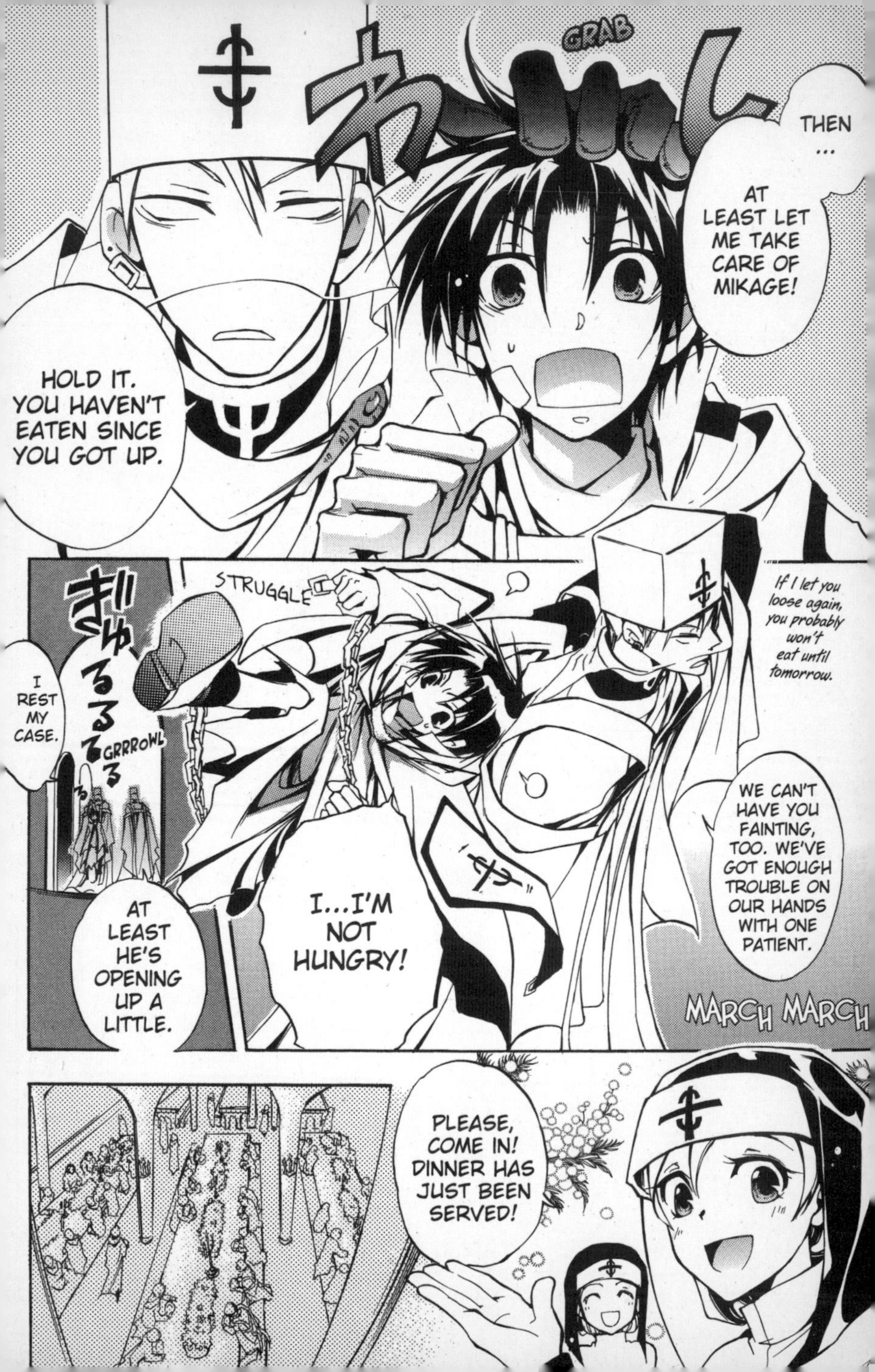
GRAB
THEN ...
AT LEAST LET ME TAKE CARE OF MIKAGE!
HOLD IT. YOU HAVEN'T EATEN SINCE YOU GOT UP.
If I let you loose again, you probably won't eat until tomorrow.
WE CAN'T HAVE YOU FAINTING, TOO. WE'VE GOT ENOUGH TROUBLE ON OUR HANDS WITH ONE PATIENT.
MARCH MARCH
STRUGGLE
I...I'M NOT HUNGRY!
GRRROWL
I REST MY CASE.
AT LEAST HE'S OPENING UP A LITTLE.
PLEASE, COME IN! DINNER HAS JUST BEEN SERVED!

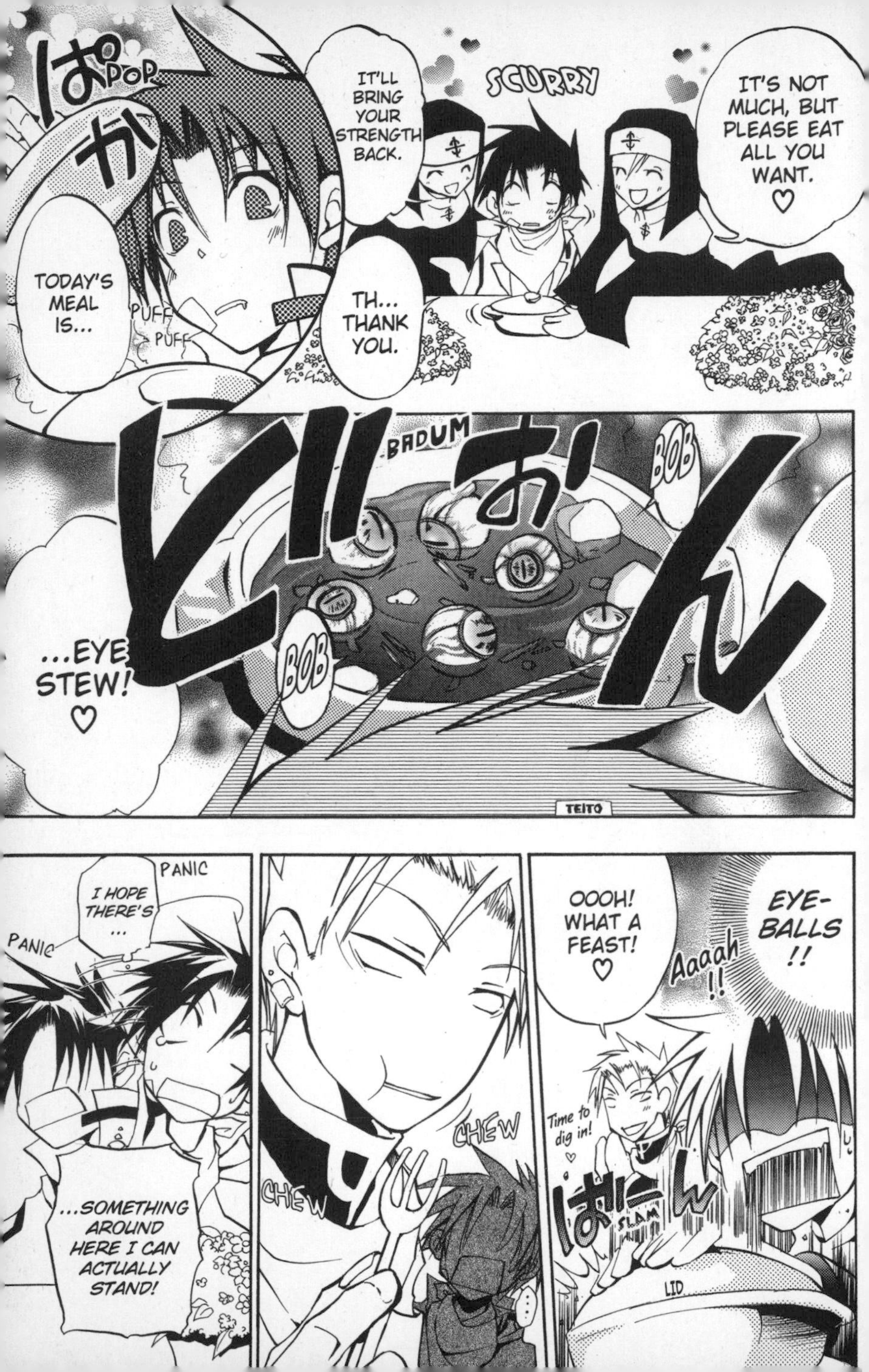
IT'S NOT MUCH, BUT PLEASE EAT ALL YOU WANT. ♡
SCURRY
IT'LL BRING YOUR STRENGTH BACK.
TH... THANK YOU.
ぱか
POP
TODAY'S MEAL IS...
PUFF
PUFF
BOB
BADUM
BOB
...EYE STEW! ♡
TEITO
EYE-BALLS!!
OOOH! WHAT A FEAST! ♡
Aaaah!!
Time to dig in! ♡
SLAM
LID
CHEW
CHEW
PANIC
I HOPE THERE'S...
PANIC
...SOMETHING AROUND HERE I CAN ACTUALLY STAND!

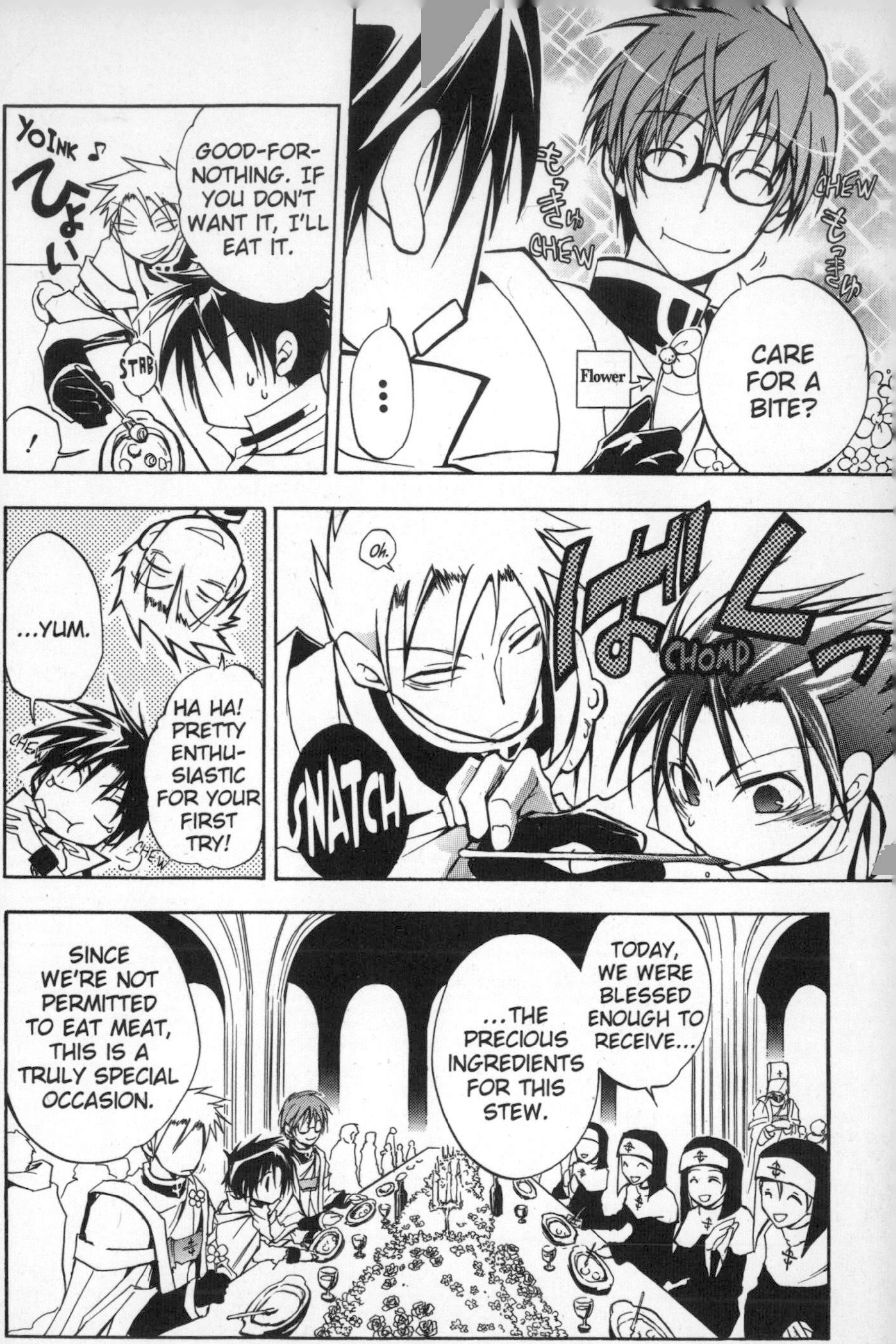
もっきゅ
CHEW
CHEW
もっきゅ
CARE FOR A BITE?
Flower
...
GOOD-FOR-NOTHING. IF YOU DON'T WANT IT, I'LL EAT IT.
YOINK ♪
ひょい
STAB
!
Oh.
ぱくっ
CHOMP
SNATCH
...YUM.
HA HA! PRETTY ENTHUSIASTIC FOR YOUR FIRST TRY!
CHEW
CHEW
TODAY, WE WERE BLESSED ENOUGH TO RECEIVE...
...THE PRECIOUS INGREDIENTS FOR THIS STEW.
SINCE WE'RE NOT PERMITTED TO EAT MEAT, THIS IS A TRULY SPECIAL OCCASION.

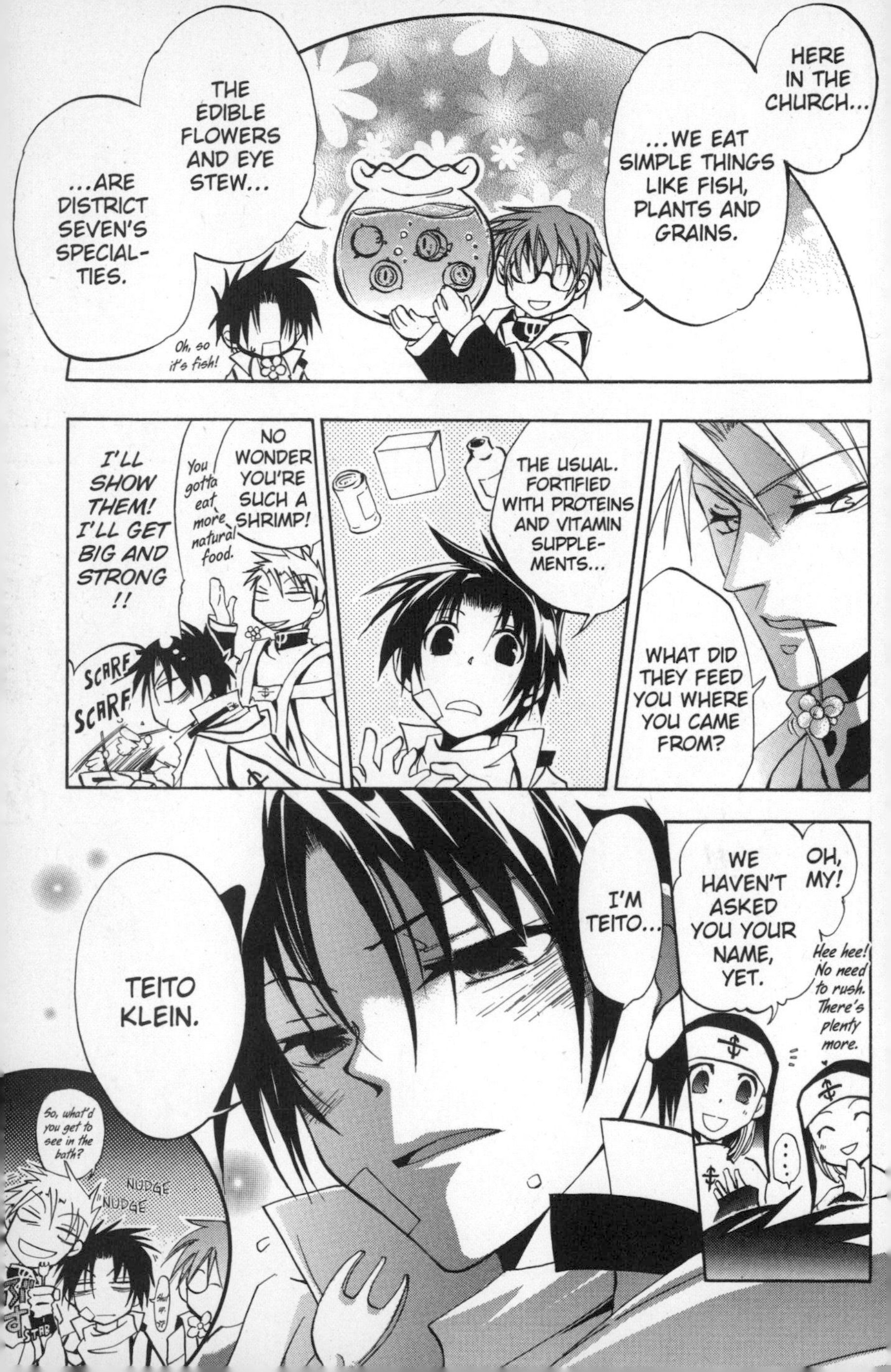
HERE IN THE CHURCH...
...WE EAT SIMPLE THINGS LIKE FISH, PLANTS AND GRAINS.
THE EDIBLE FLOWERS AND EYE STEW...
...ARE DISTRICT SEVEN'S SPECIAL-TIES.
Oh, so it's fish!
WHAT DID THEY FEED YOU WHERE YOU CAME FROM?
THE USUAL. FORTIFIED WITH PROTEINS AND VITAMIN SUPPLE-MENTS...
NO WONDER YOU'RE SUCH A SHRIMP!
You gotta eat more natural food.
I'LL SHOW THEM! I'LL GET BIG AND STRONG!!
SCARF
SCARF
OH, MY!
WE HAVEN'T ASKED YOU YOUR NAME, YET.
Hee hee! No need to rush. There's plenty more.
....
I'M TEITO...
TEITO KLEIN.
So, what'd you get to see in the bath?
NUDGE
NUDGE
STAB

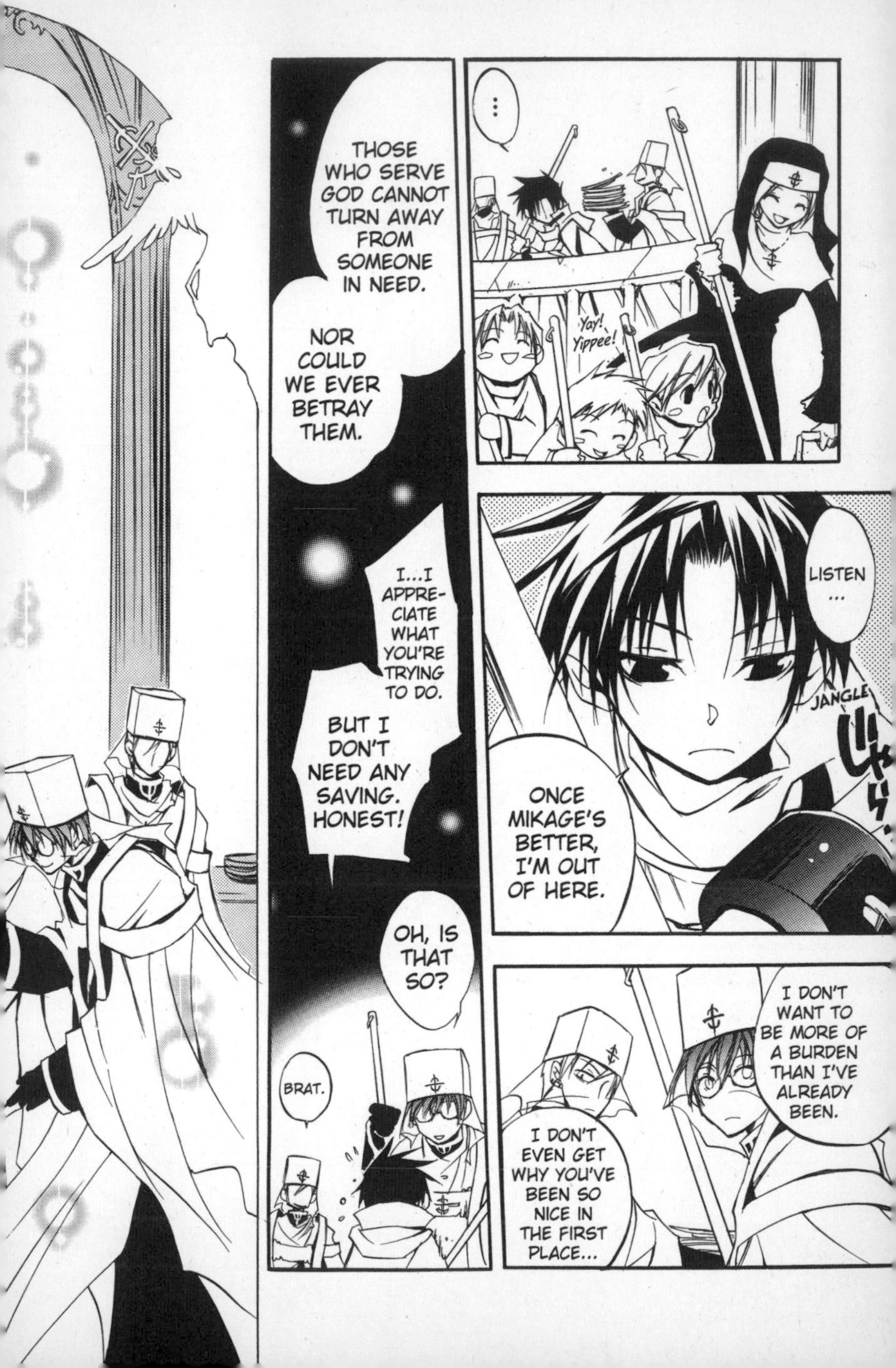
...
Yay! Yippee!
LISTEN...
JANGLE
ONCE MIKAGE'S BETTER, I'M OUT OF HERE.
I DON'T WANT TO BE MORE OF A BURDEN THAN I'VE ALREADY BEEN.
I DON'T EVEN GET WHY YOU'VE BEEN SO NICE IN THE FIRST PLACE...
THOSE WHO SERVE GOD CANNOT TURN AWAY FROM SOMEONE IN NEED.
NOR COULD WE EVER BETRAY THEM.
I...I APPRECIATE WHAT YOU'RE TRYING TO DO.
BUT I DON'T NEED ANY SAVING. HONEST!
OH, IS THAT SO?
BRAT.

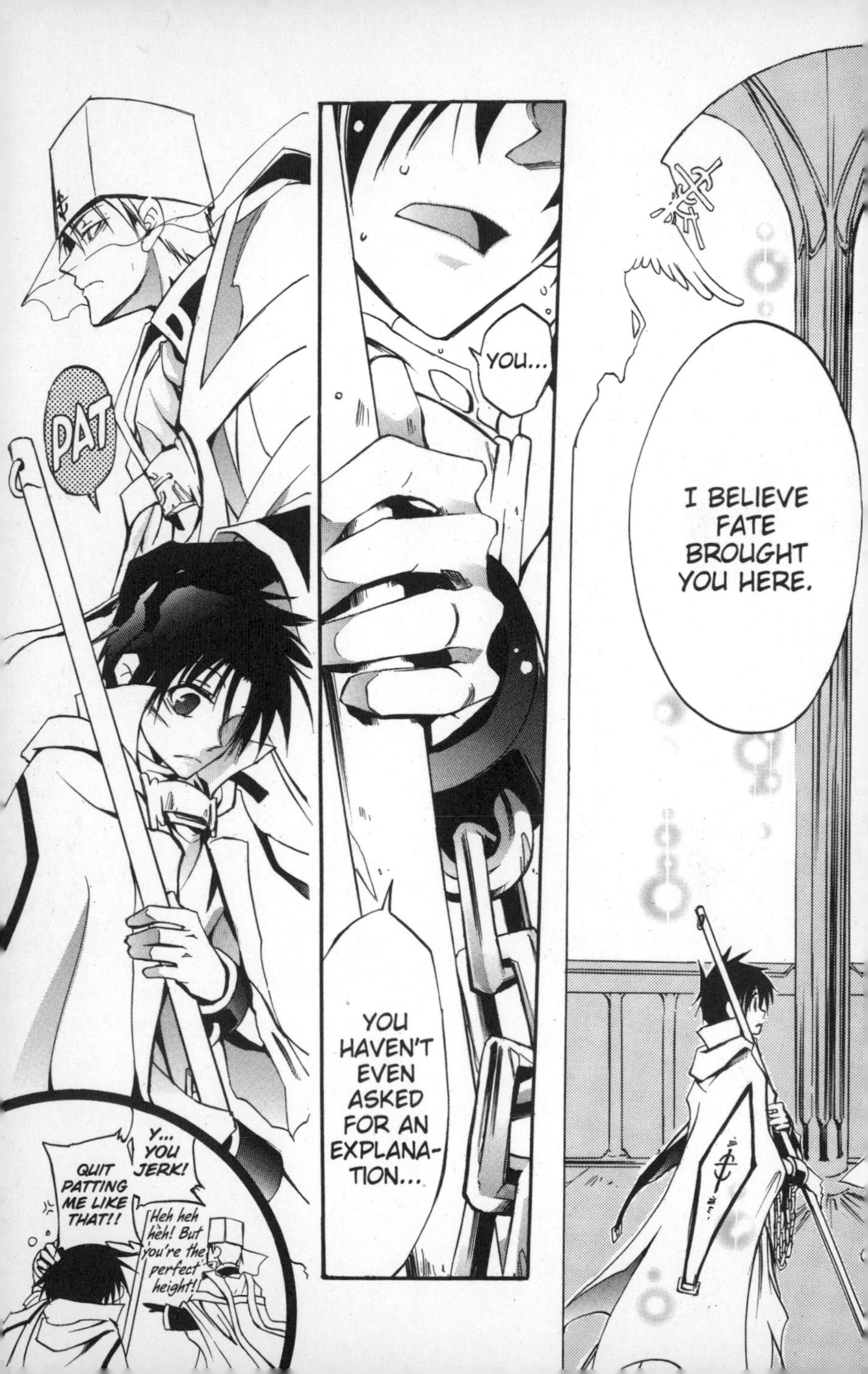
I BELIEVE FATE BROUGHT YOU HERE.
YOU...
YOU HAVEN'T EVEN ASKED FOR AN EXPLANATION...
PAT
Y... YOU JERK!
QUIT PATTING ME LIKE THAT!!
Heh heh heh! But you're the perfect height!

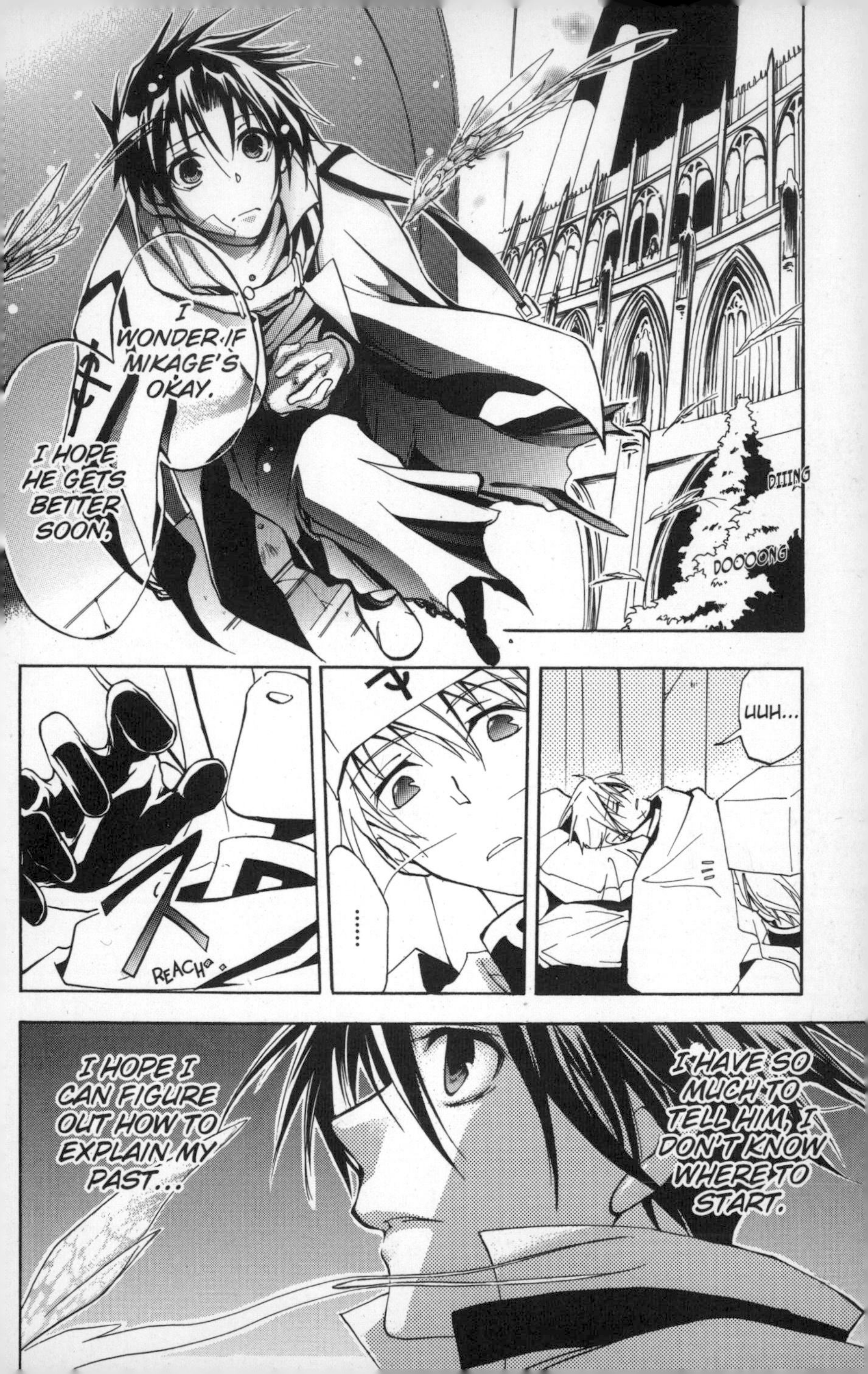
DIIING
DOOOONG
I WONDER IF MIKAGE'S OKAY.
I HOPE HE GETS BETTER SOON.
UUH...
......
REACH
I HAVE SO MUCH TO TELL HIM, I DON'T KNOW WHERE TO START.
I HOPE I CAN FIGURE OUT HOW TO EXPLAIN MY PAST...

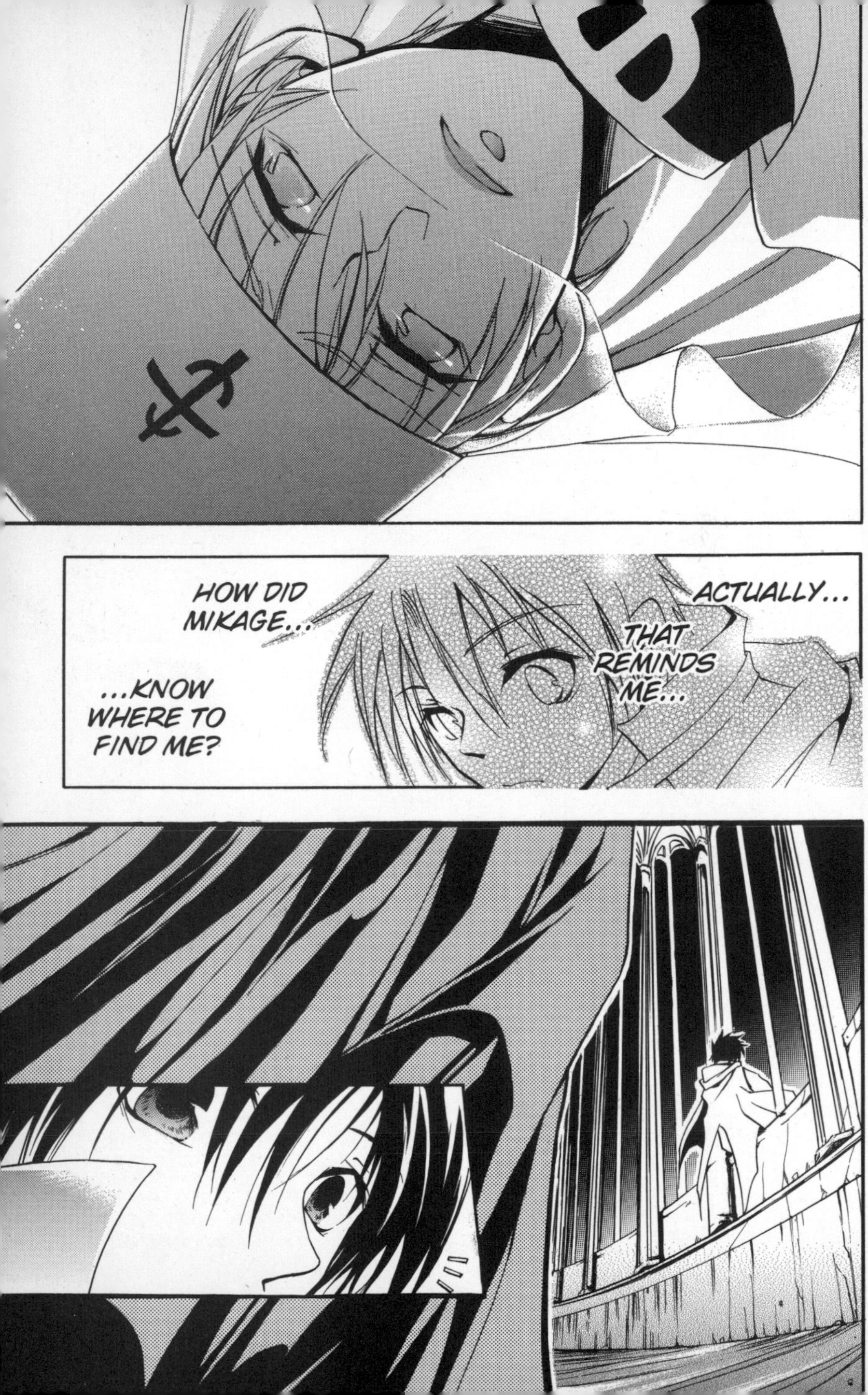
ACTUALLY...
THAT REMINDS ME...
HOW DID MIKAGE...
...KNOW WHERE TO FIND ME?

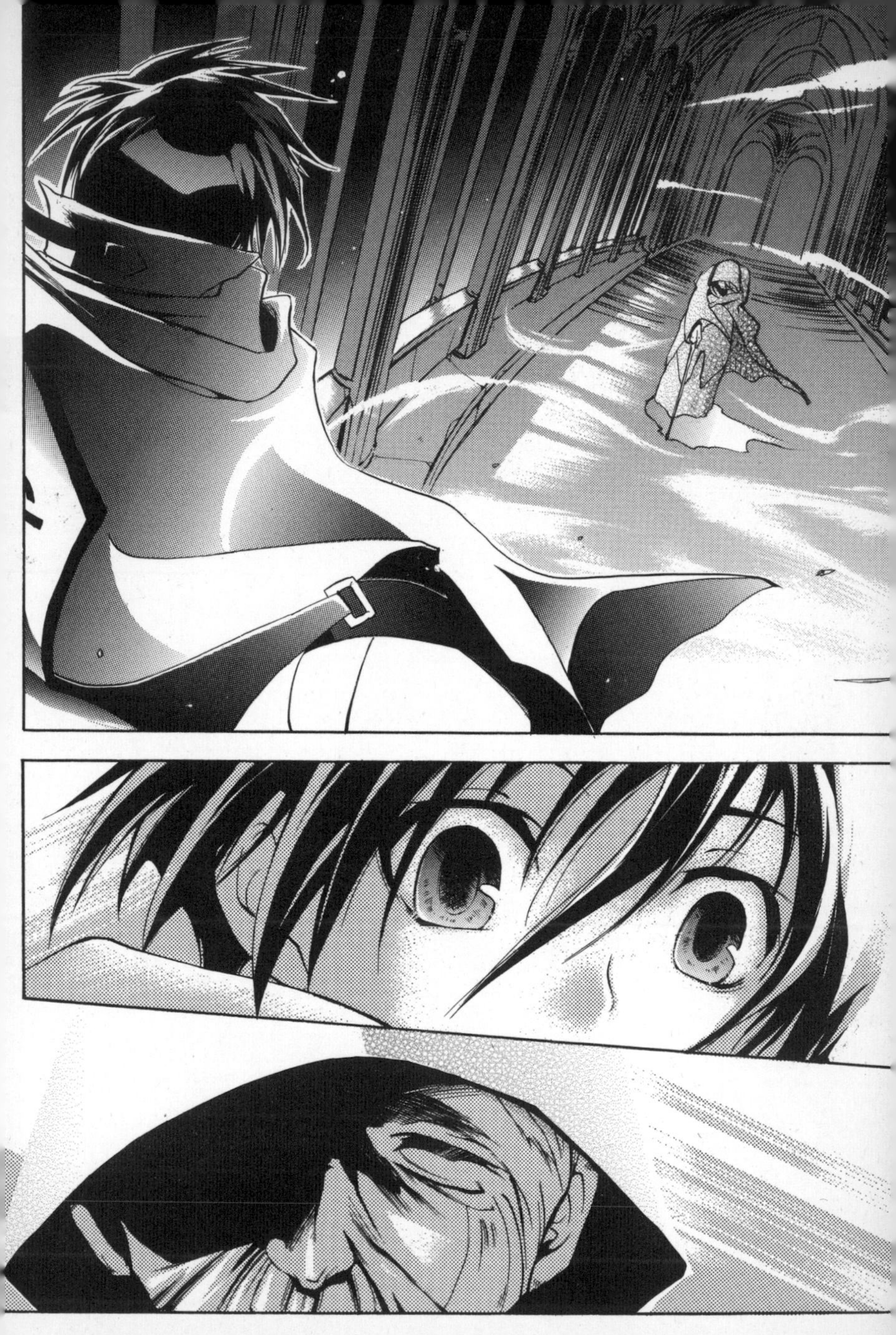

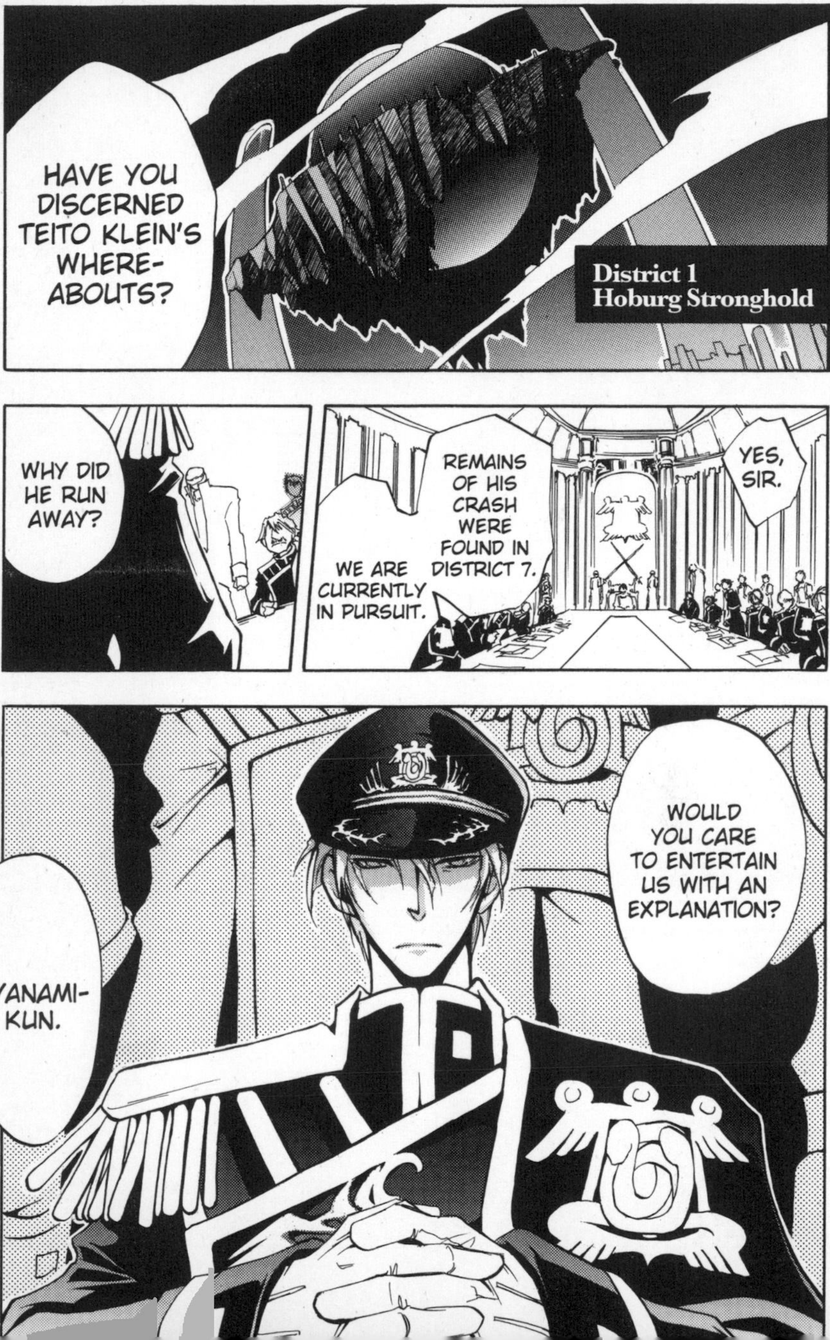
District 1
Hoburg Stronghold
HAVE YOU DISCERNED TEITO KLEIN'S WHERE-ABOUTS?
YES, SIR.
REMAINS OF HIS CRASH WERE FOUND IN DISTRICT 7.
WE ARE CURRENTLY IN PURSUIT.
WHY DID HE RUN AWAY?
WOULD YOU CARE TO ENTERTAIN US WITH AN EXPLANATION?
AYANAMI-KUN.

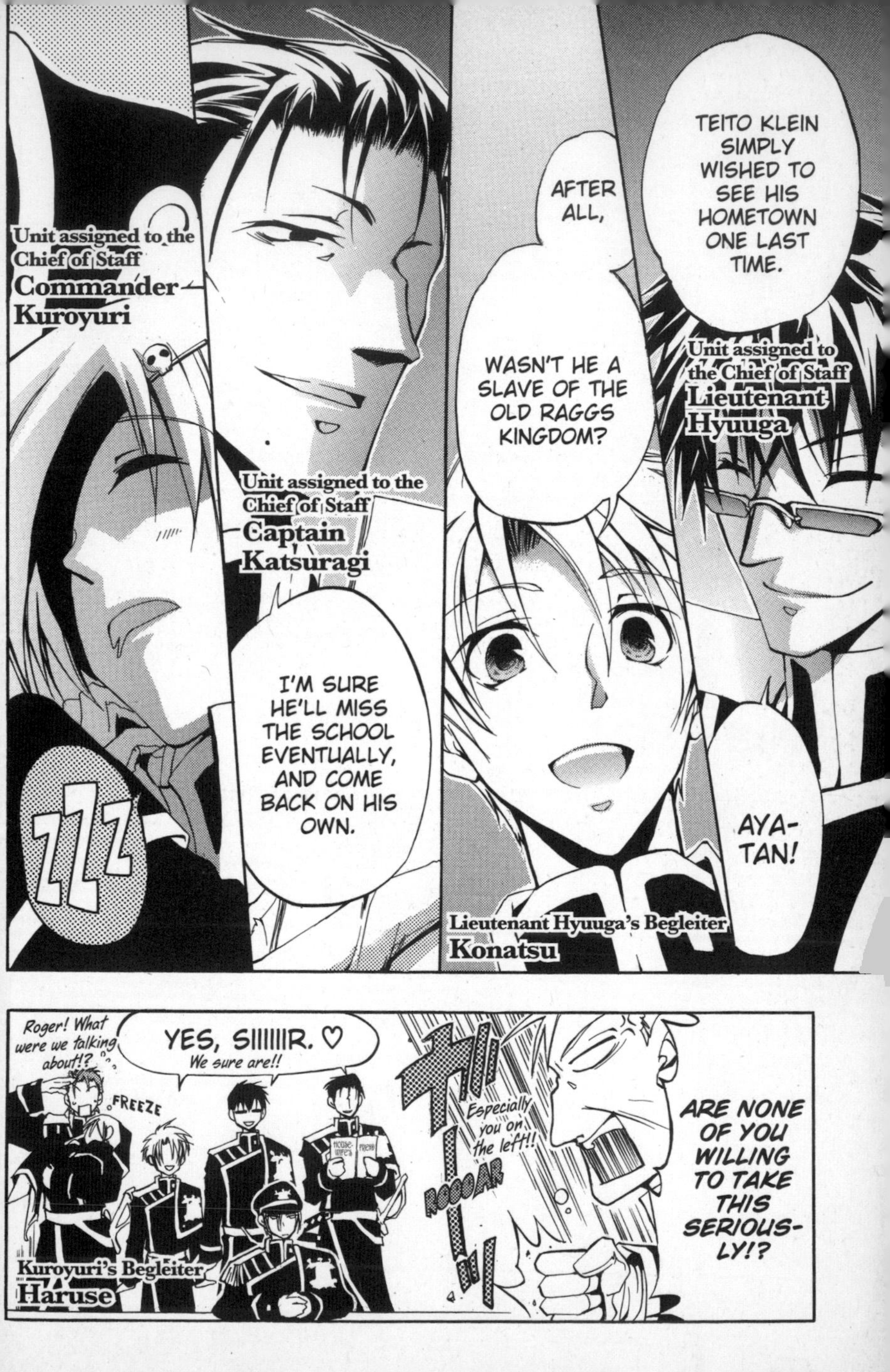
TEITO KLEIN SIMPLY WISHED TO SEE HIS HOMETOWN ONE LAST TIME.
Unit assigned to the Chief of Staff Lieutenant Hyuuga
AFTER ALL,
WASN'T HE A SLAVE OF THE OLD RAGGS KINGDOM?
AYA-TAN!
Lieutenant Hyuuga's Begleiter Konatsu
Unit assigned to the Chief of Staff Commander Kuroyuri
Unit assigned to the Chief of Staff Captain Katsuragi
I'M SURE HE'LL MISS THE SCHOOL EVENTUALLY, AND COME BACK ON HIS OWN.
ZZZ
ARE NONE OF YOU WILLING TO TAKE THIS SERIOUSLY!?
ROOOAR
Especially you on the left!!
YES, SIIIIIR. ♡
We sure are!!
Roger! What were we talking about!?
FREEZE
Kuroyuri's Begleiter Haruse

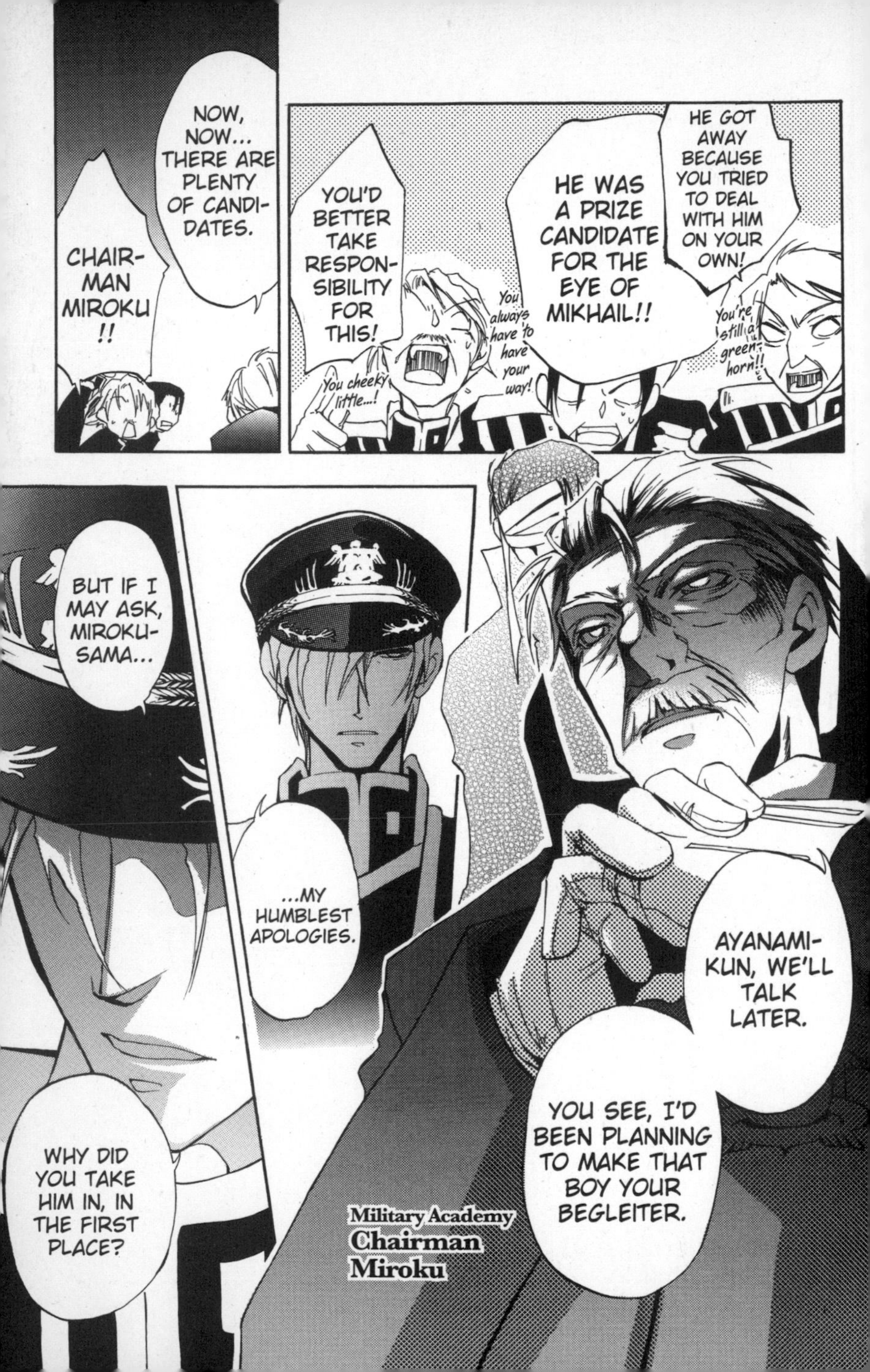
HE GOT AWAY BECAUSE YOU TRIED TO DEAL WITH HIM ON YOUR OWN!
You're still a greenhorn!!
HE WAS A PRIZE CANDIDATE FOR THE EYE OF MIKHAIL!!
You always have to have your way!
YOU'D BETTER TAKE RESPONSIBILITY FOR THIS!
You cheeky little...!
NOW, NOW... THERE ARE PLENTY OF CANDIDATES.
CHAIRMAN MIROKU!!
AYANAMI-KUN, WE'LL TALK LATER.
YOU SEE, I'D BEEN PLANNING TO MAKE THAT BOY YOUR BEGLEITER.
Military Academy Chairman Miroku
...MY HUMBLEST APOLOGIES.
BUT IF I MAY ASK, MIROKU-SAMA...
WHY DID YOU TAKE HIM IN, IN THE FIRST PLACE?

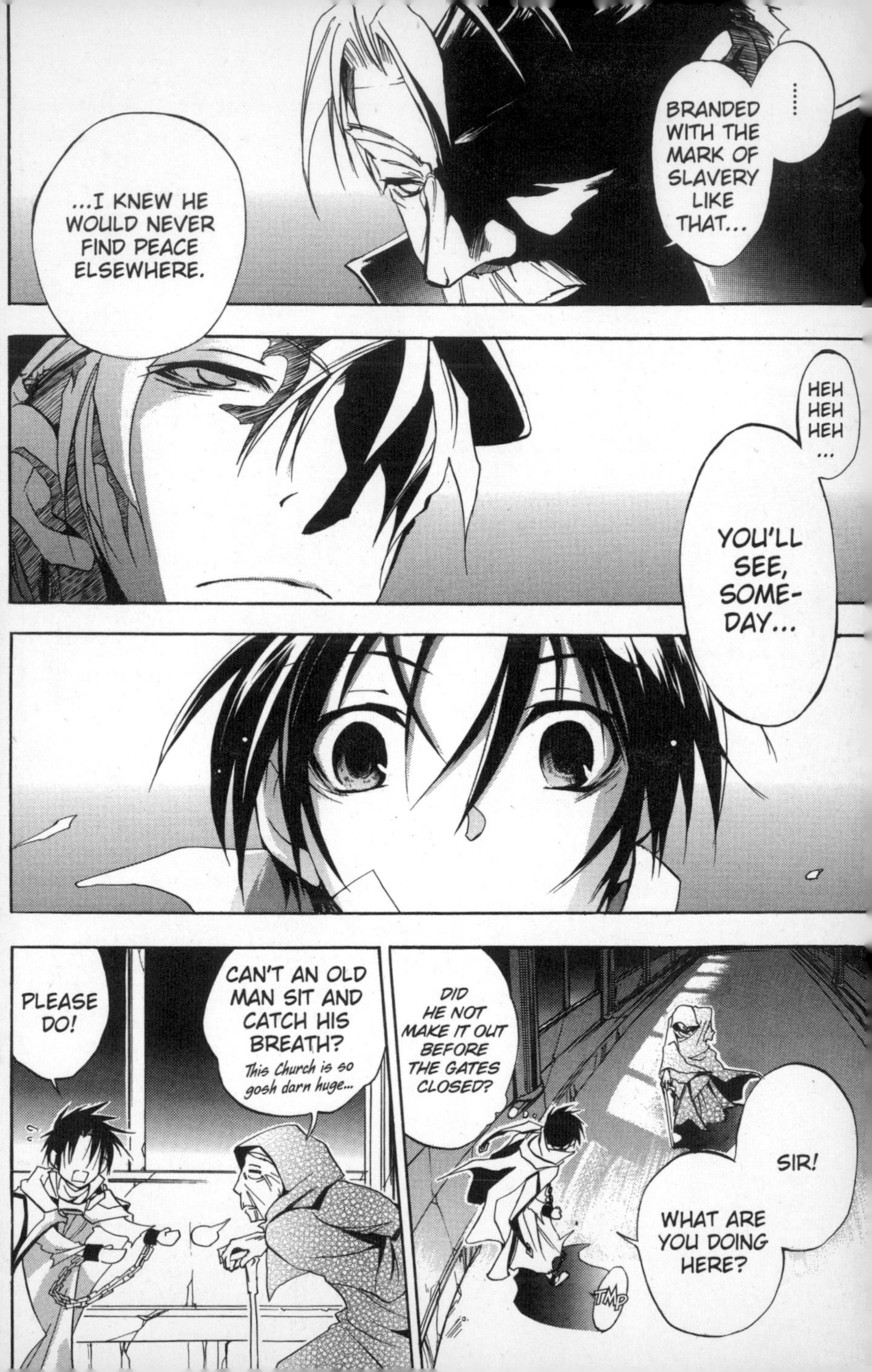
......
BRANDED WITH THE MARK OF SLAVERY LIKE THAT...
...I KNEW HE WOULD NEVER FIND PEACE ELSEWHERE.
HEH HEH HEH ...
YOU'LL SEE, SOME-DAY...
SIR!
WHAT ARE YOU DOING HERE?
TMP
DID HE NOT MAKE IT OUT BEFORE THE GATES CLOSED?
CAN'T AN OLD MAN SIT AND CATCH HIS BREATH?
This Church is so gosh darn huge...
PLEASE DO!

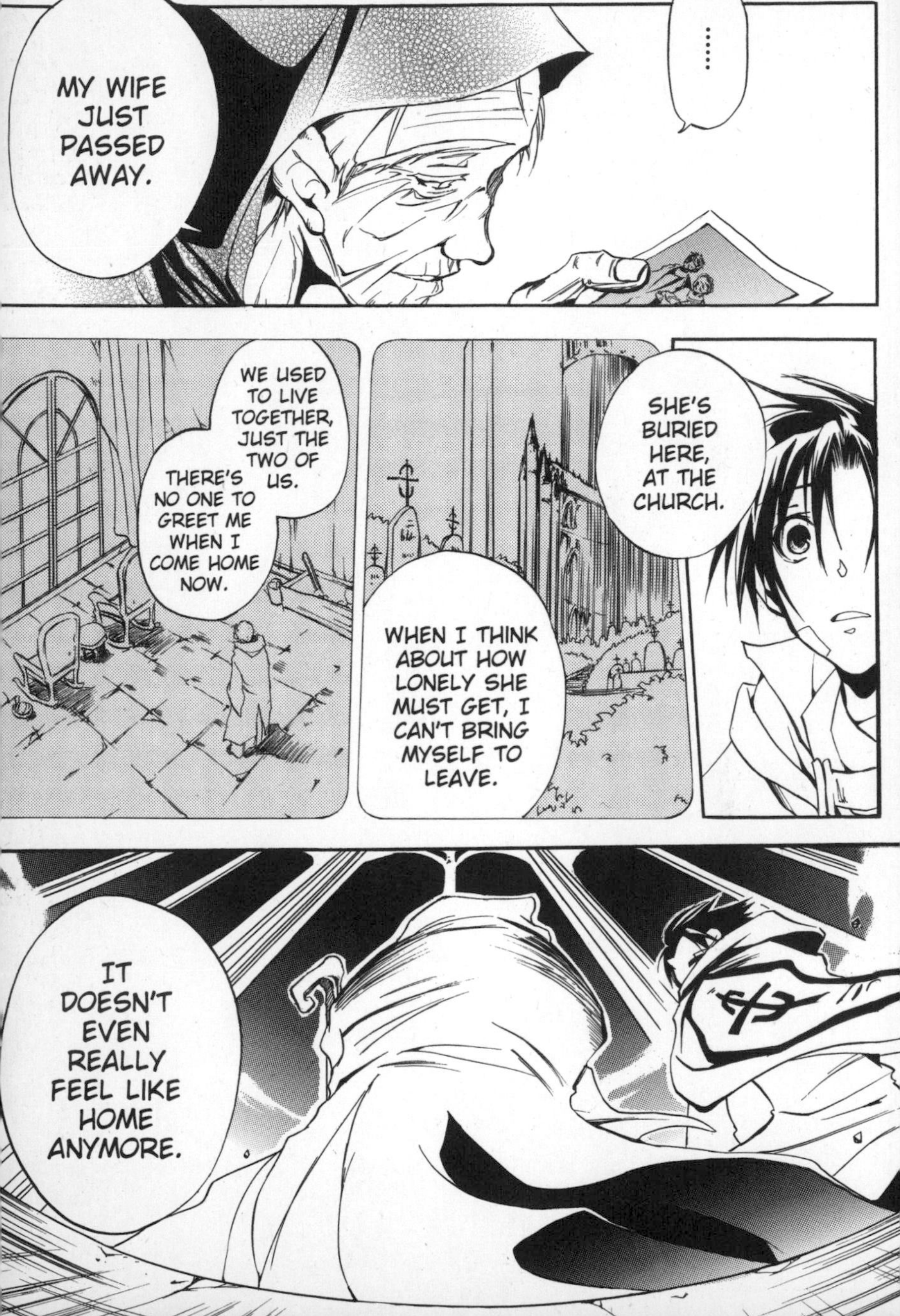
......
MY WIFE JUST PASSED AWAY.
SHE'S BURIED HERE, AT THE CHURCH.
WHEN I THINK ABOUT HOW LONELY SHE MUST GET, I CAN'T BRING MYSELF TO LEAVE.
WE USED TO LIVE TOGETHER, JUST THE TWO OF US.
THERE'S NO ONE TO GREET ME WHEN I COME HOME NOW.
IT DOESN'T EVEN REALLY FEEL LIKE HOME ANYMORE.

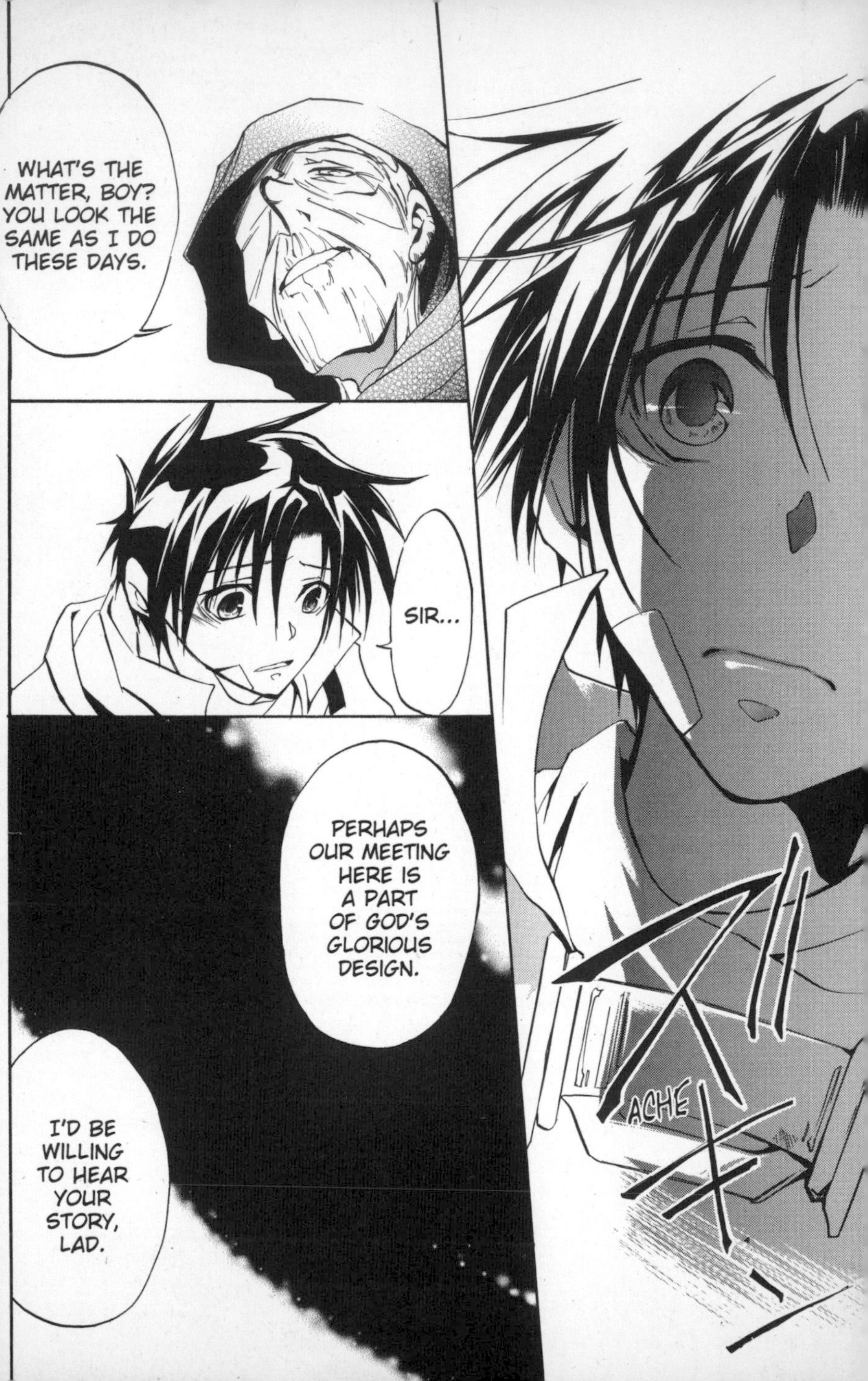
ACHE
WHAT'S THE MATTER, BOY? YOU LOOK THE SAME AS I DO THESE DAYS.
SIR...
PERHAPS OUR MEETING HERE IS A PART OF GOD'S GLORIOUS DESIGN.
I'D BE WILLING TO HEAR YOUR STORY, LAD.

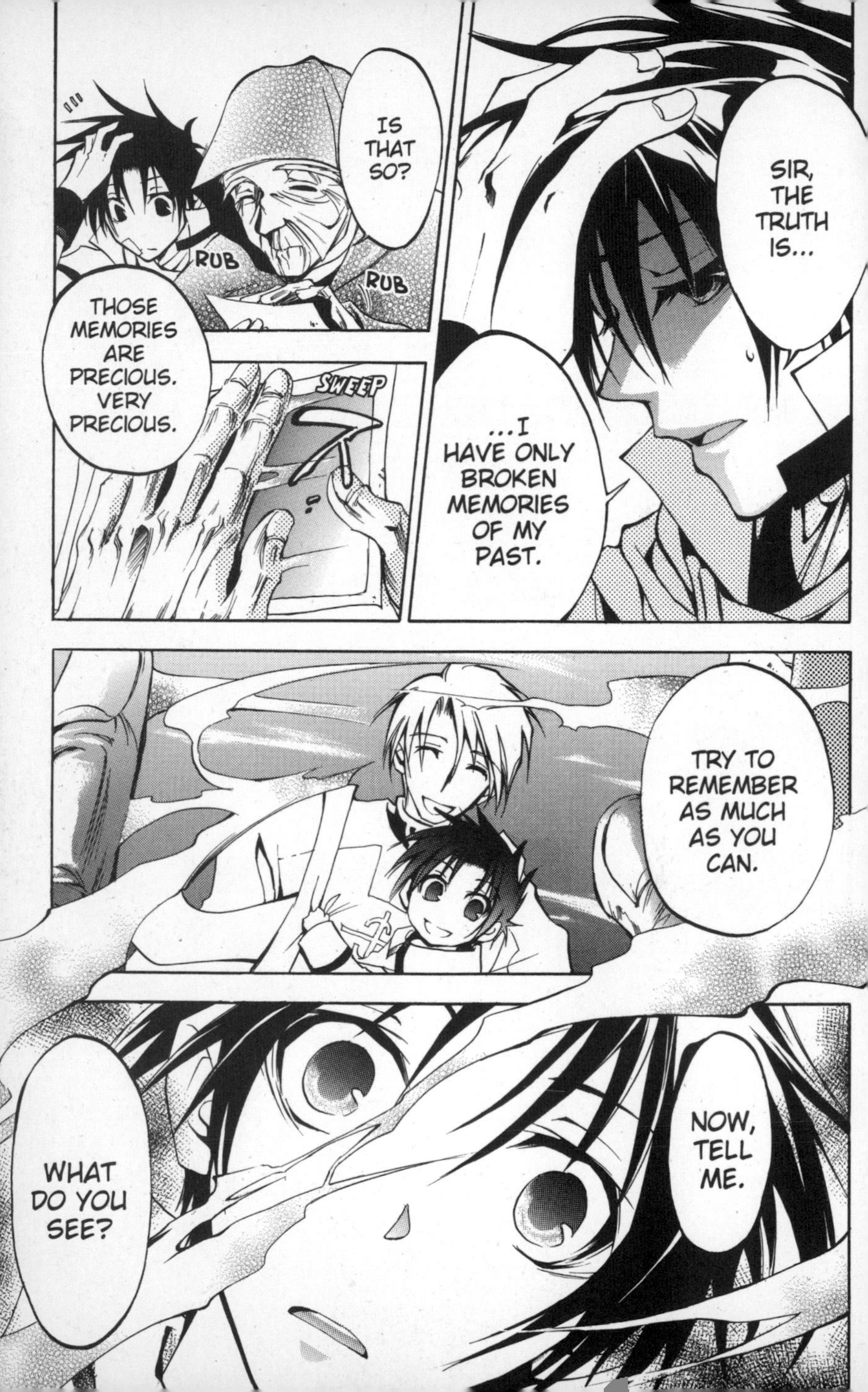
SIR, THE TRUTH IS...
...I HAVE ONLY BROKEN MEMORIES OF MY PAST.
IS THAT SO?
RUB
RUB
THOSE MEMORIES ARE PRECIOUS. VERY PRECIOUS.
SWEEP
TRY TO REMEMBER AS MUCH AS YOU CAN.
NOW, TELL ME.
WHAT DO YOU SEE?

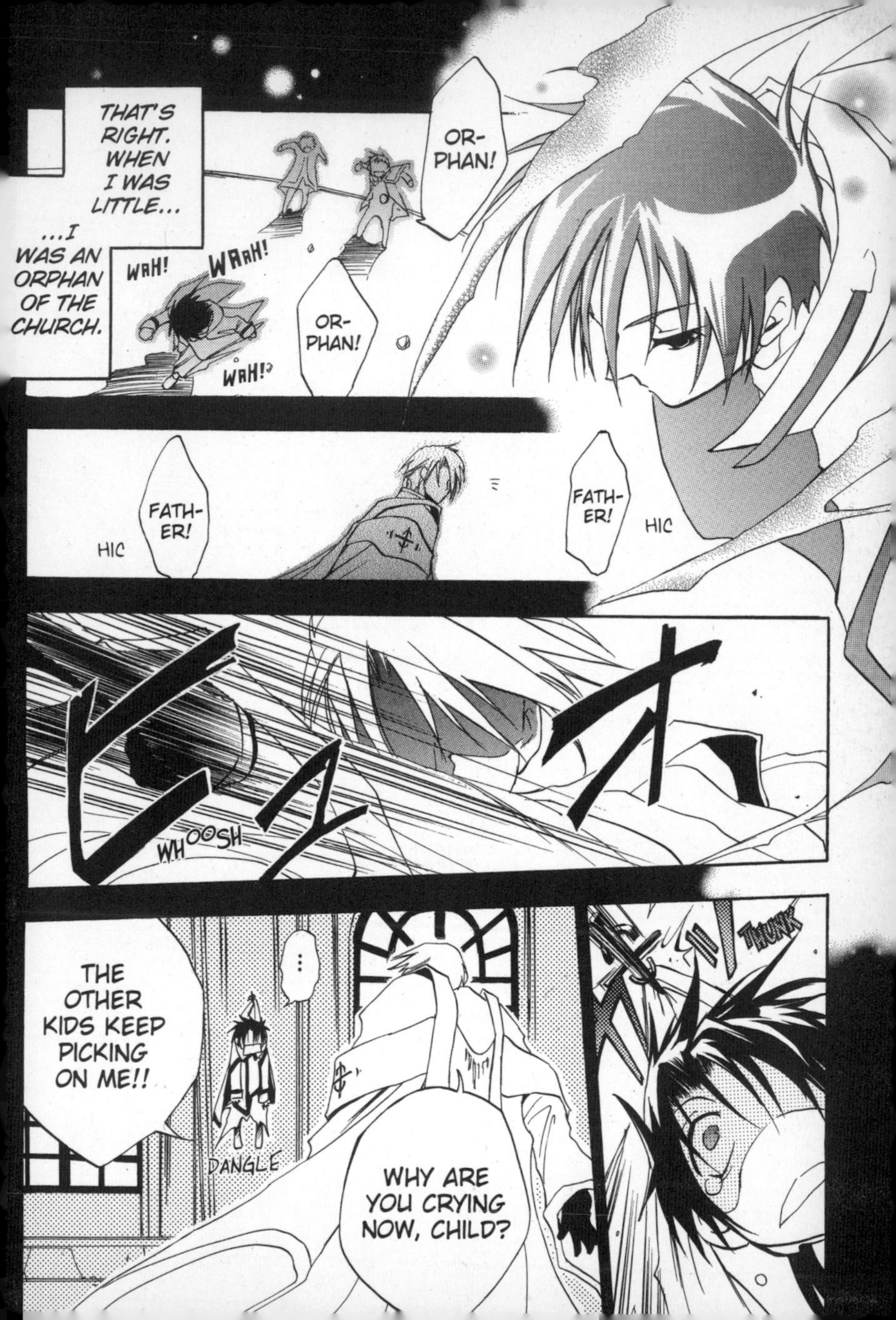
OR-PHAN!
THAT'S RIGHT. WHEN I WAS LITTLE...
...I WAS AN ORPHAN OF THE CHURCH.
WAAH!
WAH!
OR-PHAN!
WAH!?
FATH-ER!
HIC
FATH-ER!
HIC
WHOOSH
THUNK
...
THE OTHER KIDS KEEP PICKING ON ME!!
DANGLE
WHY ARE YOU CRYING NOW, CHILD?

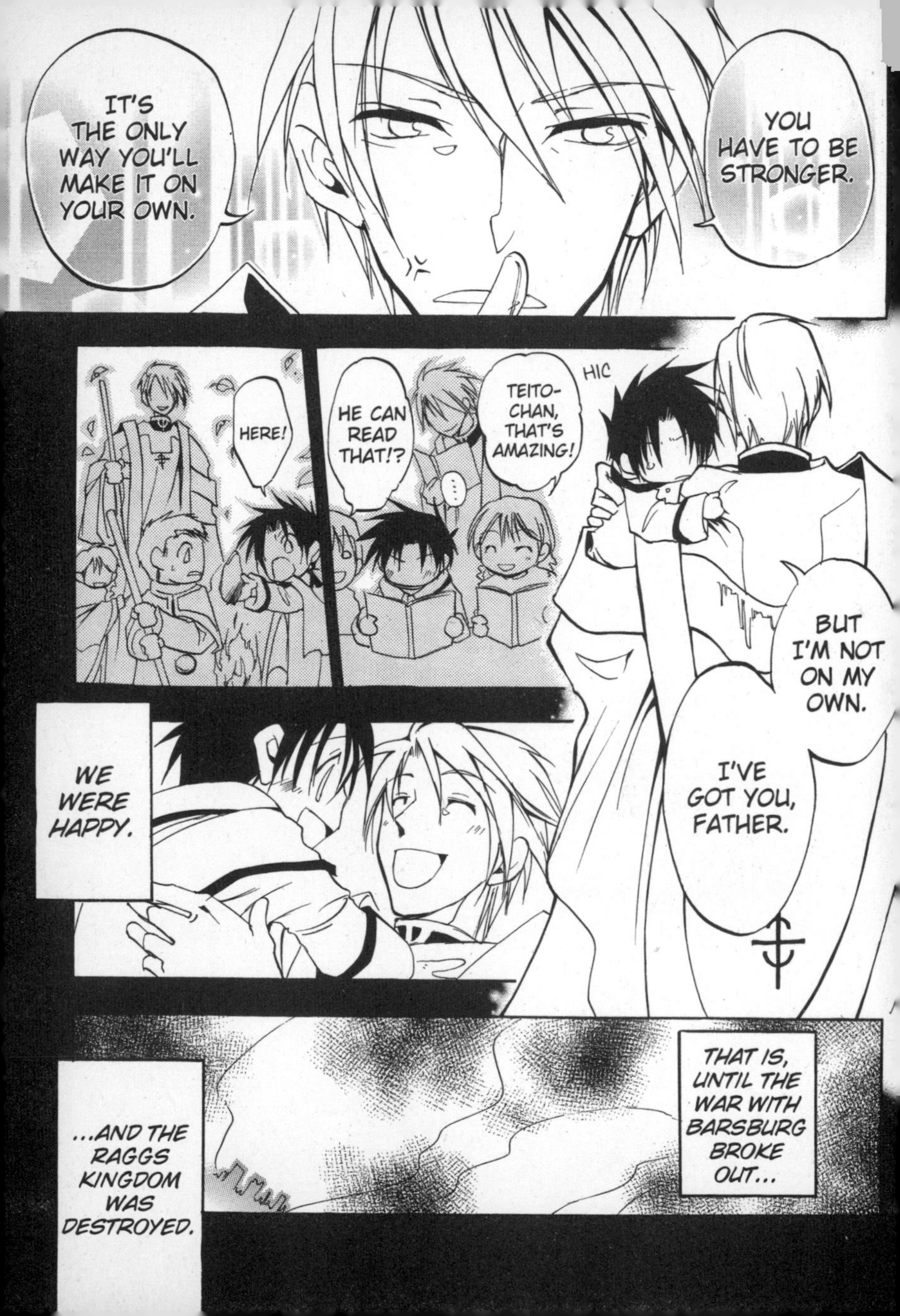
YOU HAVE TO BE STRONGER.
IT'S THE ONLY WAY YOU'LL MAKE IT ON YOUR OWN.
HIC
BUT I'M NOT ON MY OWN.
I'VE GOT YOU, FATHER.
TEITO-CHAN, THAT'S AMAZING!
...
HE CAN READ THAT!?
HERE!
WE WERE HAPPY.
THAT IS, UNTIL THE WAR WITH BARSBURG BROKE OUT...
...AND THE RAGGS KINGDOM WAS DESTROYED.

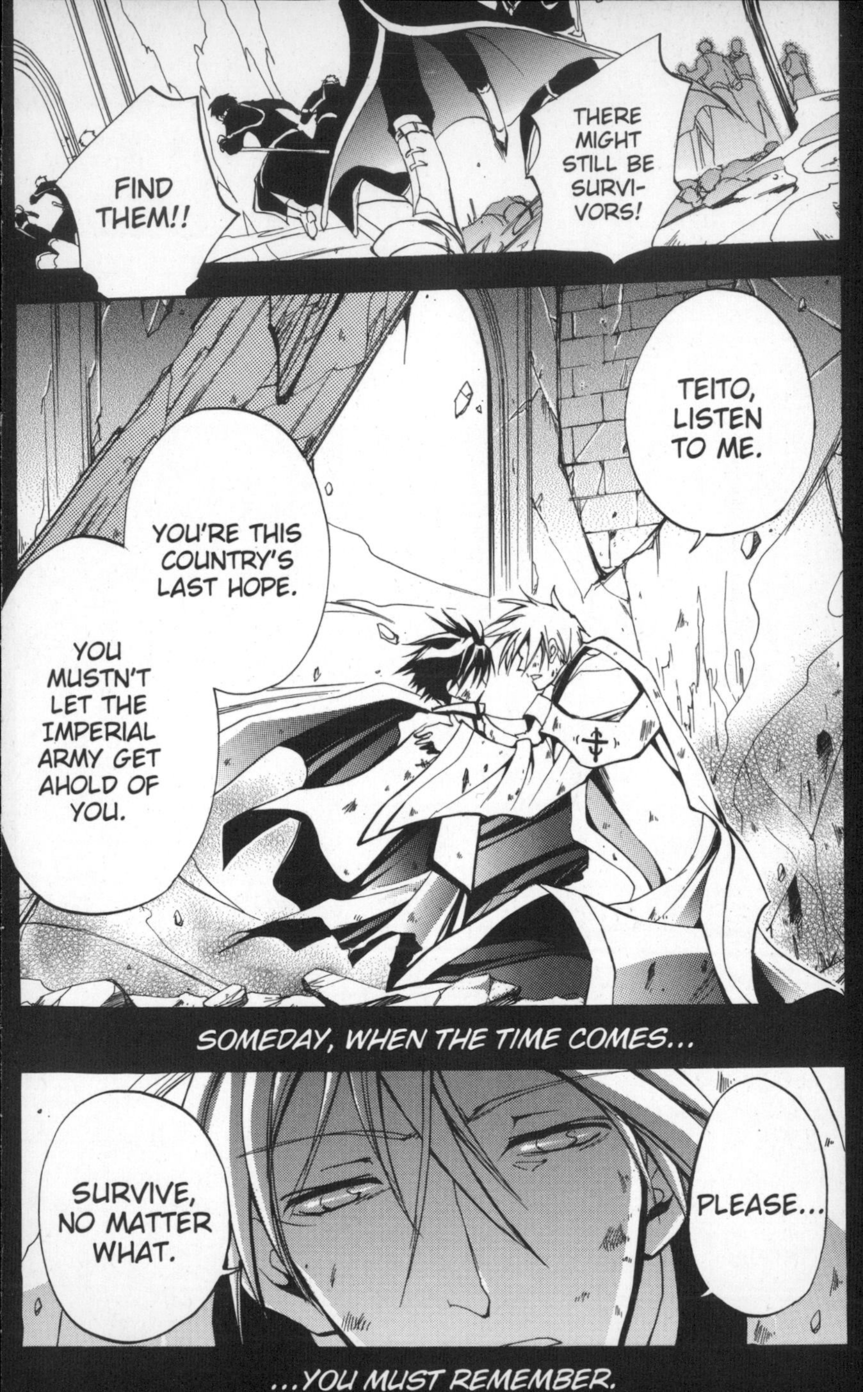
THERE MIGHT STILL BE SURVIVORS!
FIND THEM!!
TEITO, LISTEN TO ME.
YOU'RE THIS COUNTRY'S LAST HOPE.
YOU MUSTN'T LET THE IMPERIAL ARMY GET AHOLD OF YOU.
SOMEDAY, WHEN THE TIME COMES...
PLEASE...
SURVIVE, NO MATTER WHAT.
...YOU MUST REMEMBER.

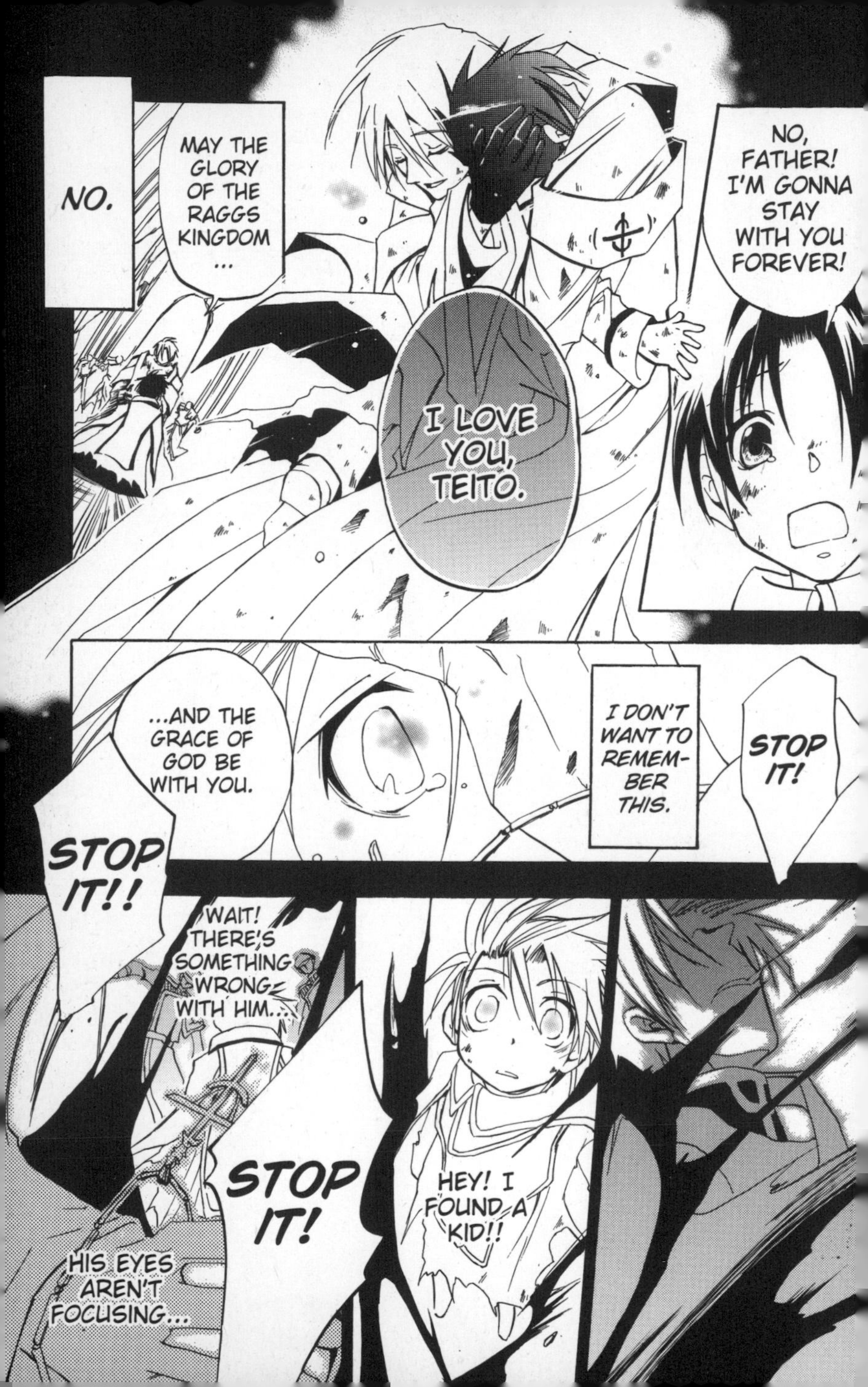
NO, FATHER! I'M GONNA STAY WITH YOU FOREVER!
MAY THE GLORY OF THE RAGGS KINGDOM ...
NO.
I LOVE YOU, TEITO.
STOP IT!
I DON'T WANT TO REMEMBER THIS.
...AND THE GRACE OF GOD BE WITH YOU.
STOP IT!!
HEY! I FOUND A KID!!
STOP IT!
WAIT! THERE'S SOMETHING WRONG WITH HIM...
HIS EYES AREN'T FOCUSING...

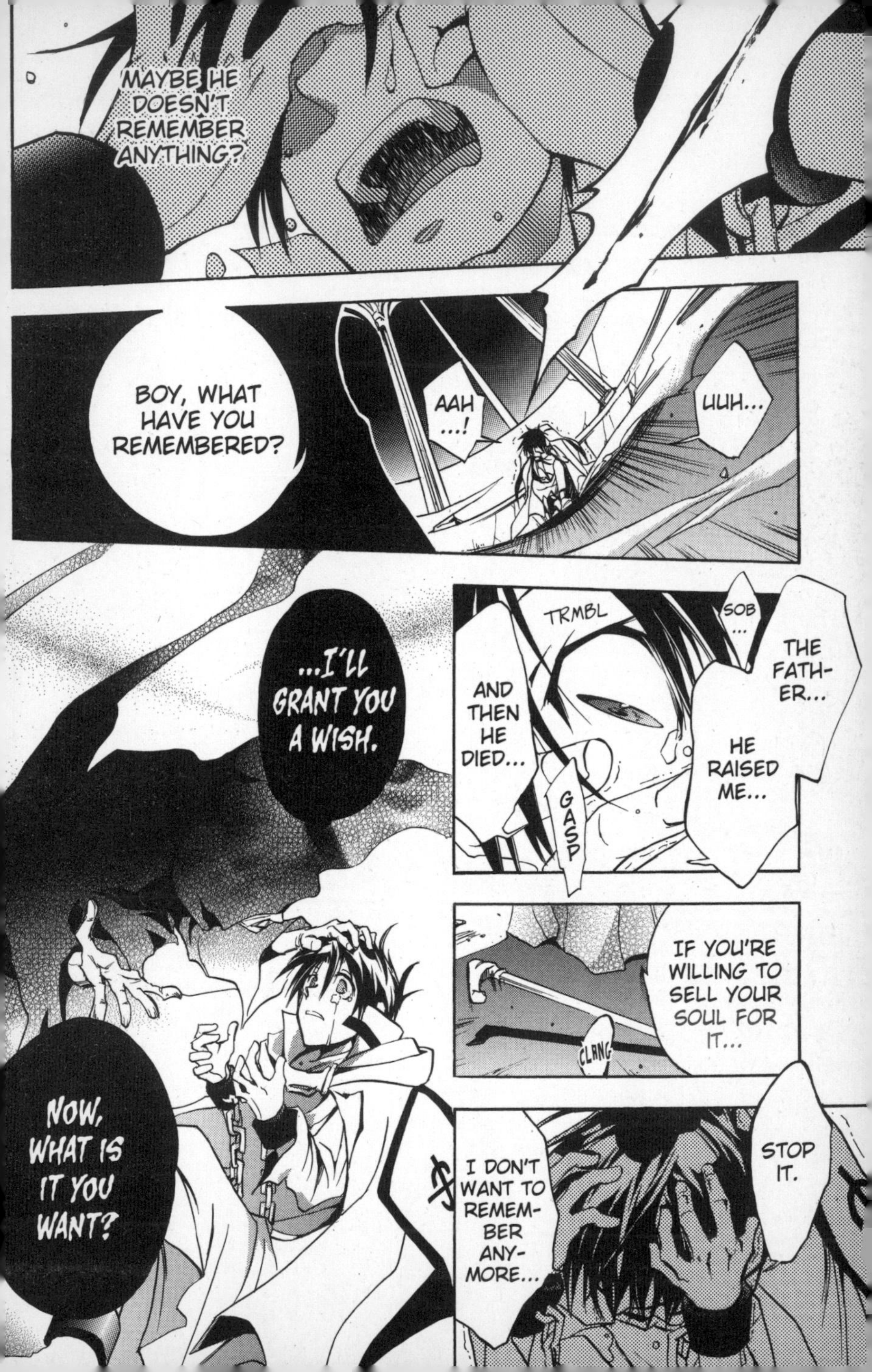
MAYBE HE DOESN'T REMEMBER ANYTHING?
UUH...
AAH ...!
BOY, WHAT HAVE YOU REMEMBERED?
SOB ...
THE FATHER...
HE RAISED ME...
TRMBL
AND THEN HE DIED...
GASP
IF YOU'RE WILLING TO SELL YOUR SOUL FOR IT...
CLANG
STOP IT.
I DON'T WANT TO REMEMBER ANYMORE...
...I'LL GRANT YOU A WISH.
NOW, WHAT IS IT YOU WANT?

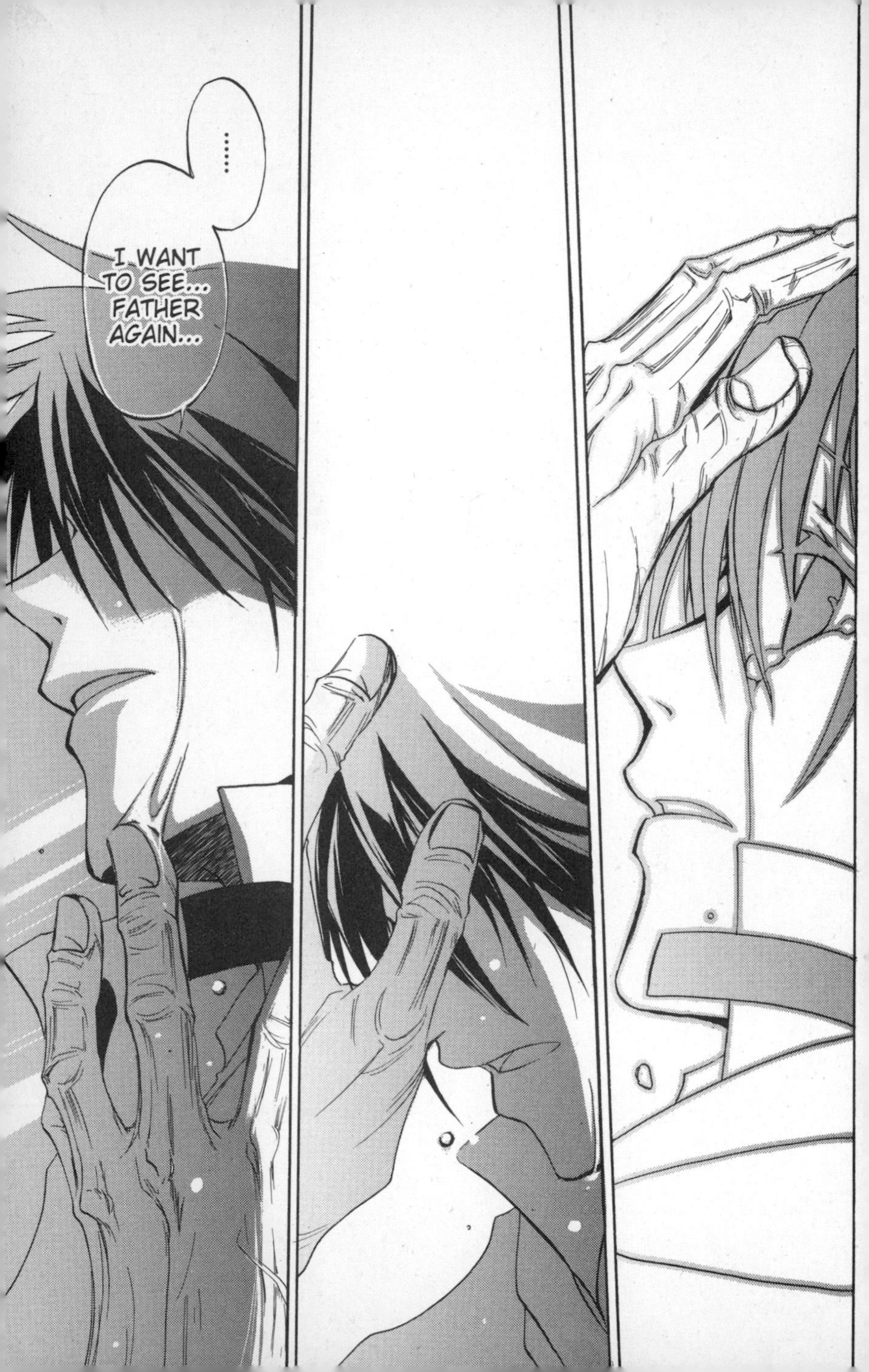

......
I WANT TO SEE... FATHER AGAIN...

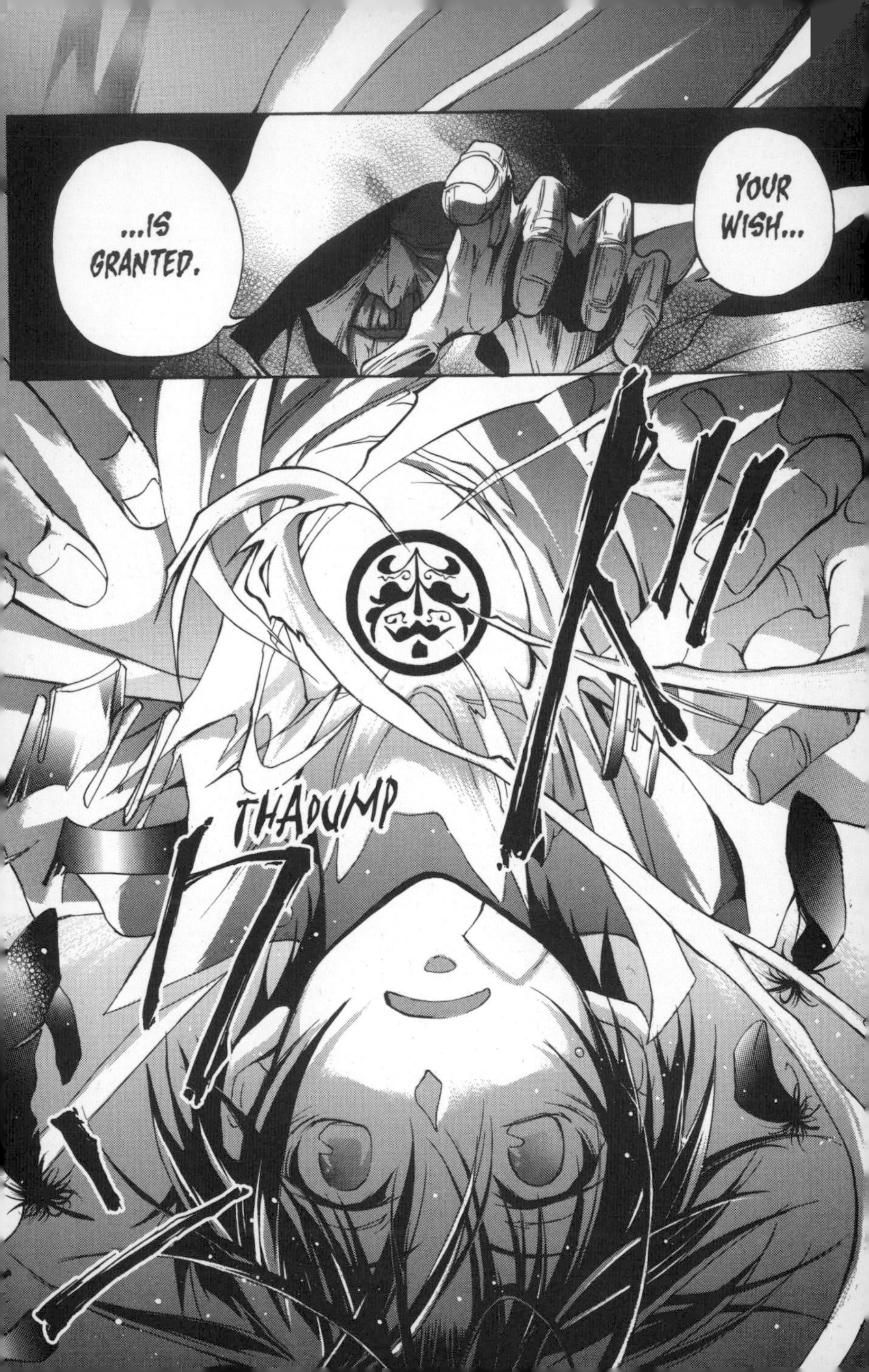
YOUR WISH...
...IS GRANTED.
THADUMP

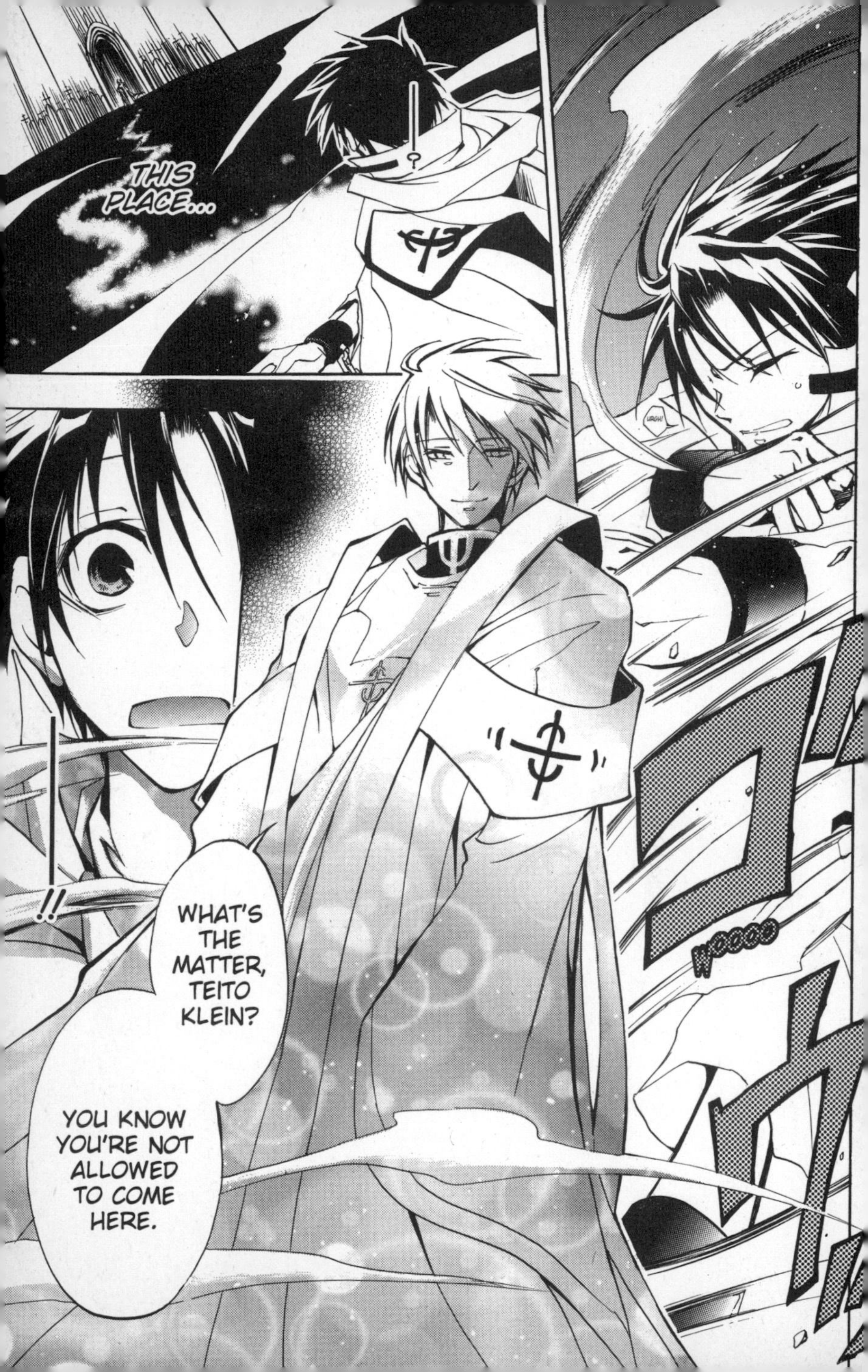
URGH!
WOOOO
THIS PLACE...
!!
WHAT'S THE MATTER, TEITO KLEIN?
YOU KNOW YOU'RE NOT ALLOWED TO COME HERE.

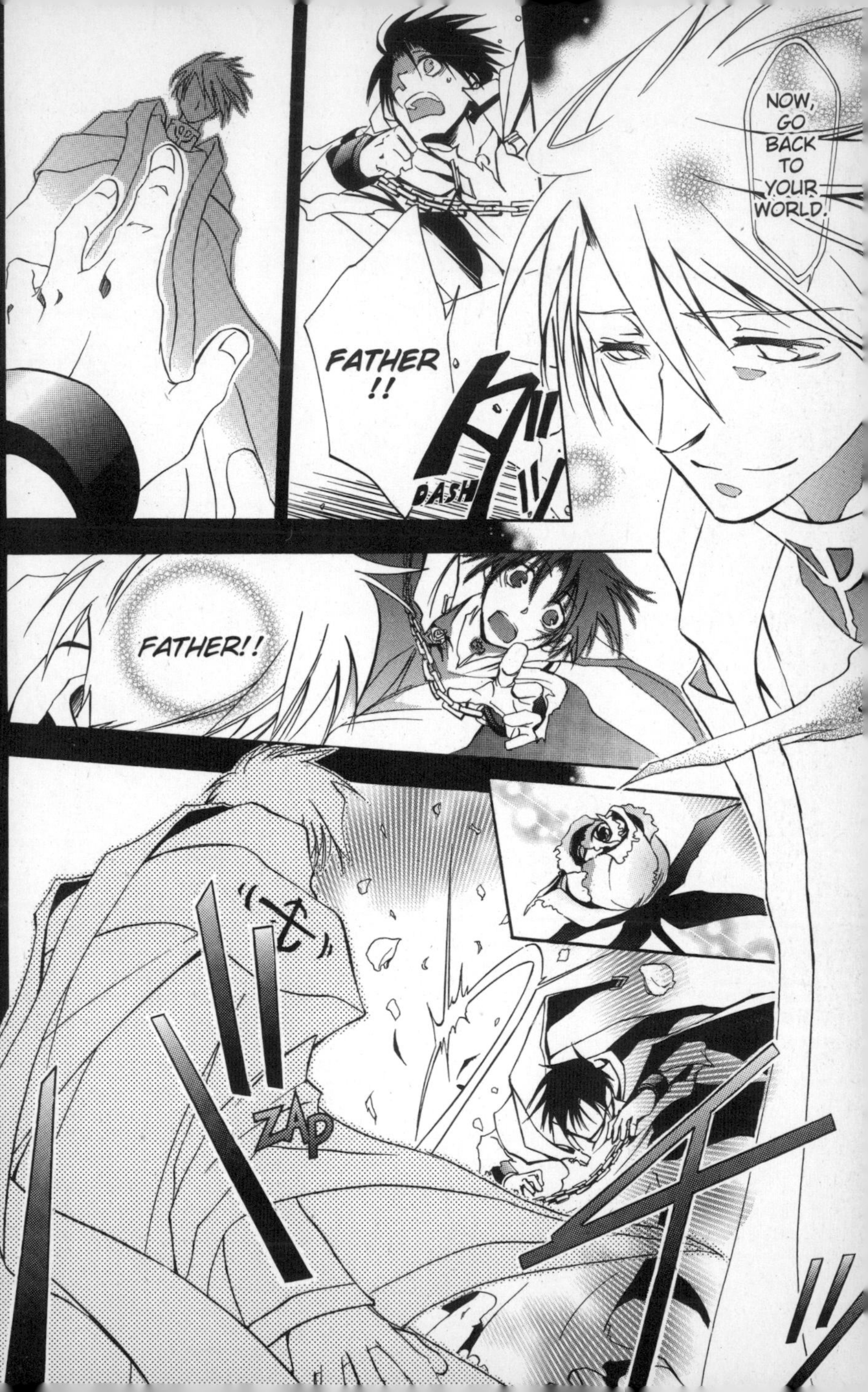
NOW, GO BACK TO YOUR WORLD.
FATHER!!
DASH
FATHER!!
ZAP

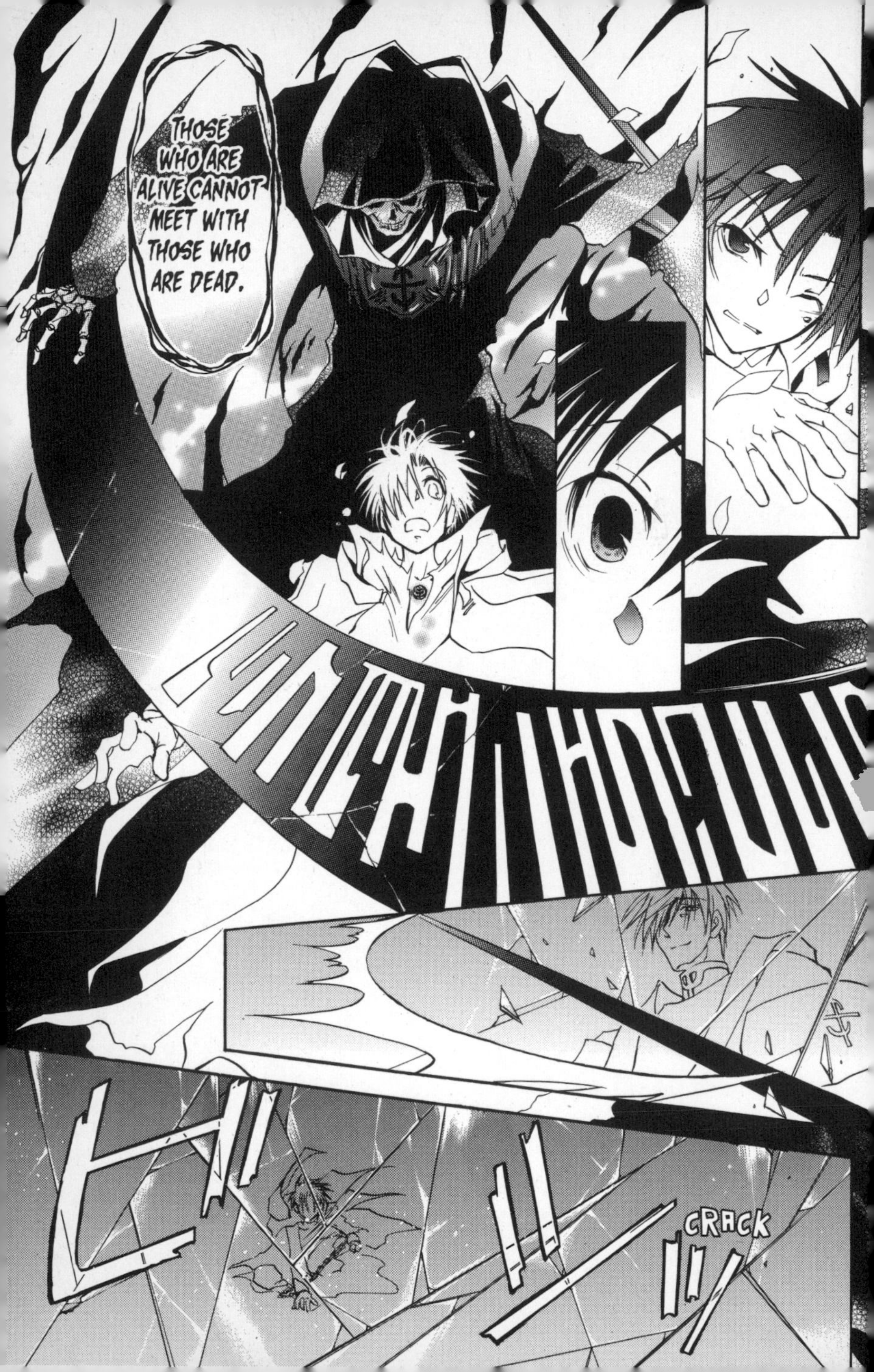
THOSE WHO ARE ALIVE CANNOT MEET WITH THOSE WHO ARE DEAD.
CRACK

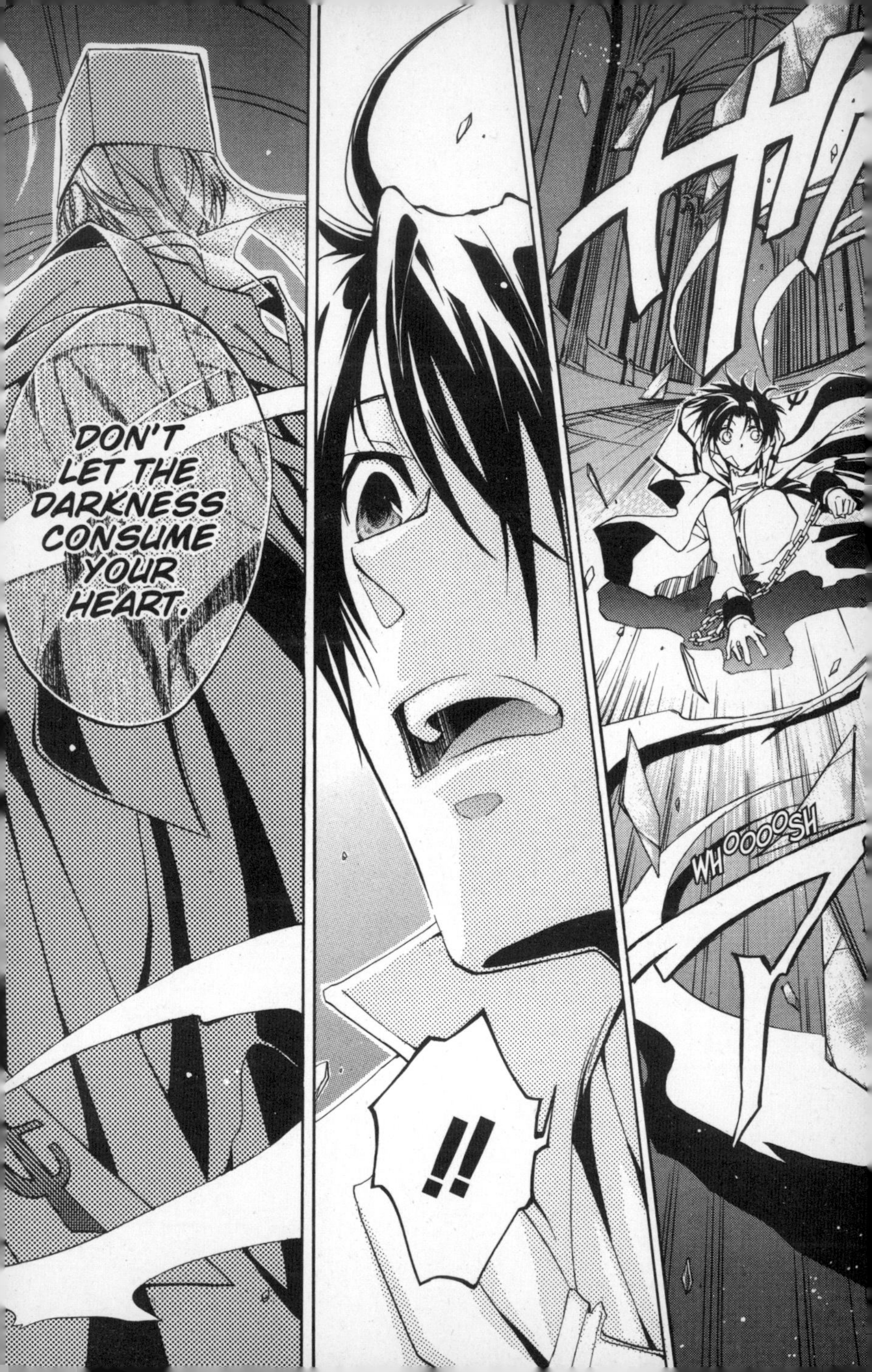
WHOOOOSH
!!
DON'T LET THE DARKNESS CONSUME YOUR HEART.

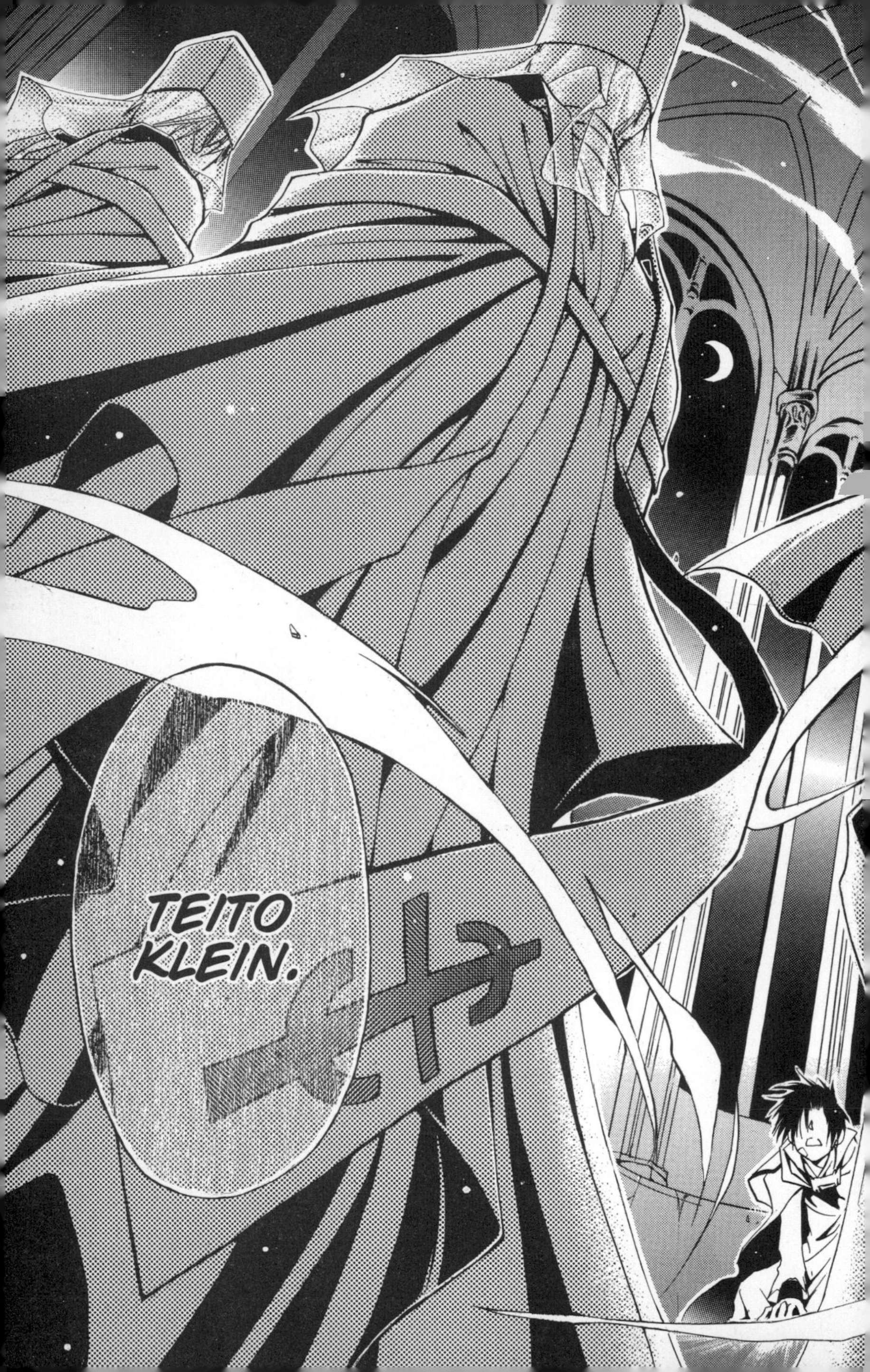
TEITO KLEIN.

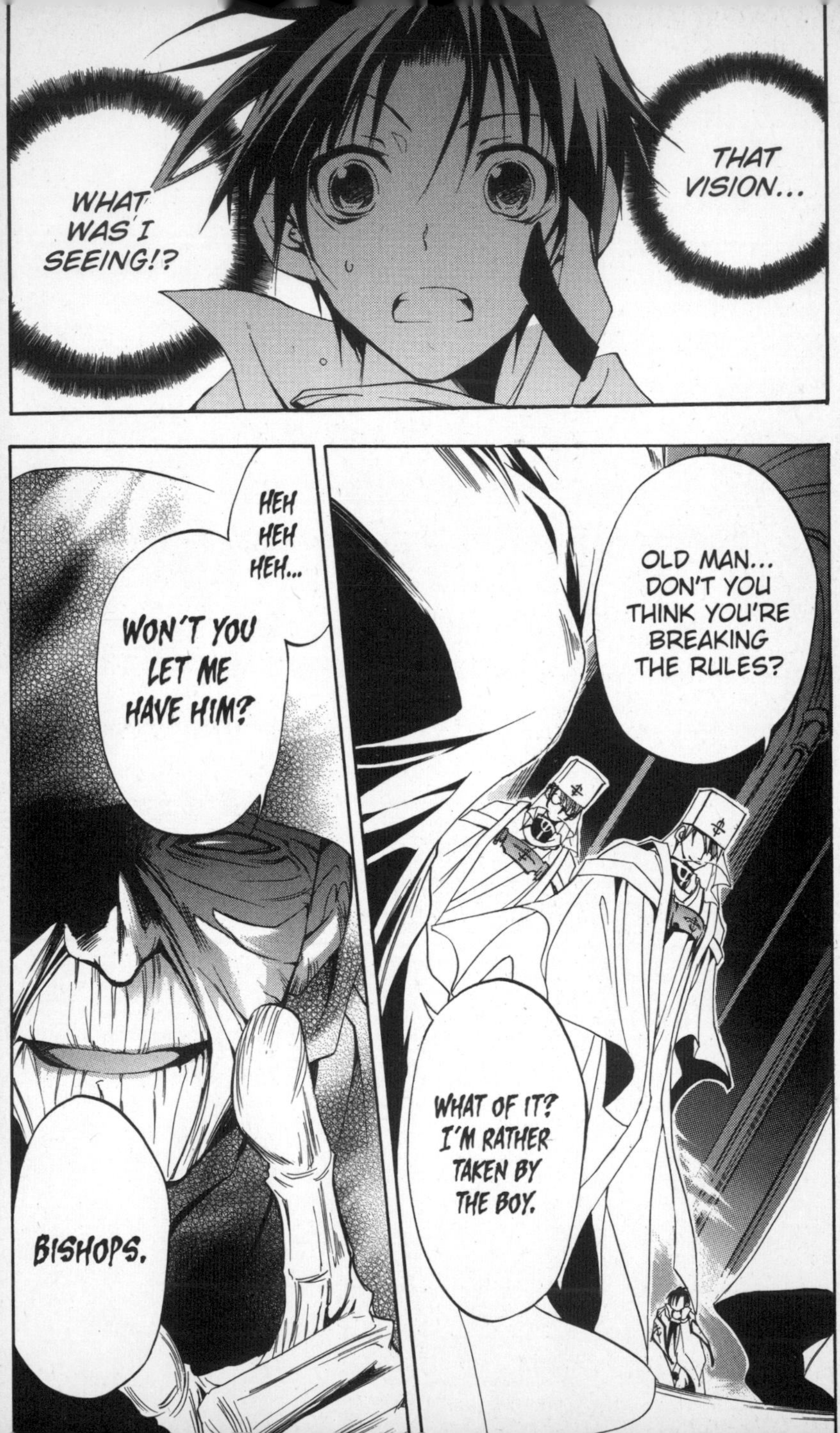
THAT VISION...
WHAT WAS I SEEING!?
OLD MAN... DON'T YOU THINK YOU'RE BREAKING THE RULES?
WHAT OF IT? I'M RATHER TAKEN BY THE BOY.
HEH HEH HEH...
WON'T YOU LET ME HAVE HIM?
BISHOPS.

Kapitel. 4 Kor

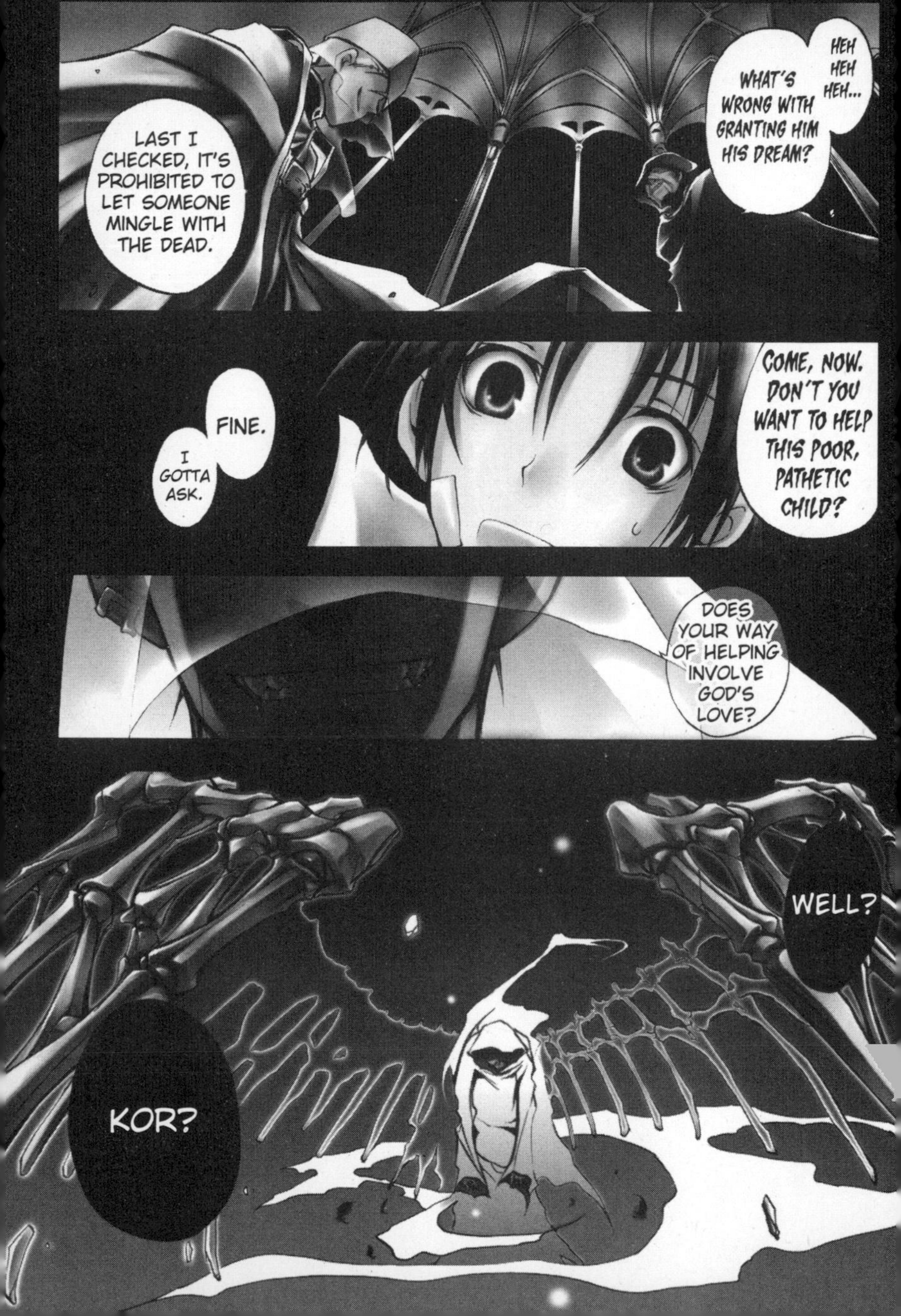
HEH HEH HEH...
WHAT'S WRONG WITH GRANTING HIM HIS DREAM?
LAST I CHECKED, IT'S PROHIBITED TO LET SOMEONE MINGLE WITH THE DEAD.
COME, NOW. DON'T YOU WANT TO HELP THIS POOR, PATHETIC CHILD?
FINE.
I GOTTA ASK.
DOES YOUR WAY OF HELPING INVOLVE GOD'S LOVE?
WELL?
KOR?

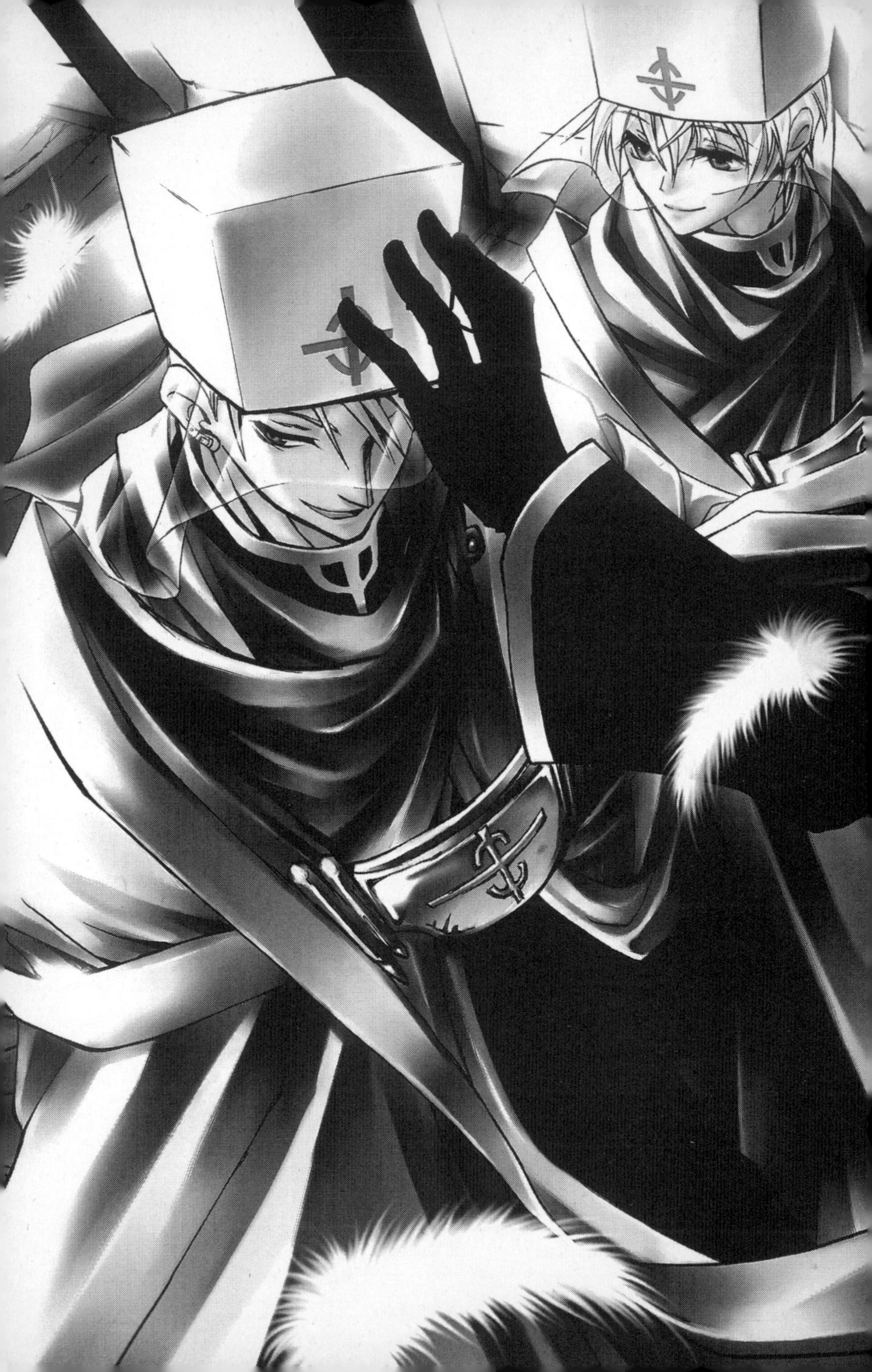

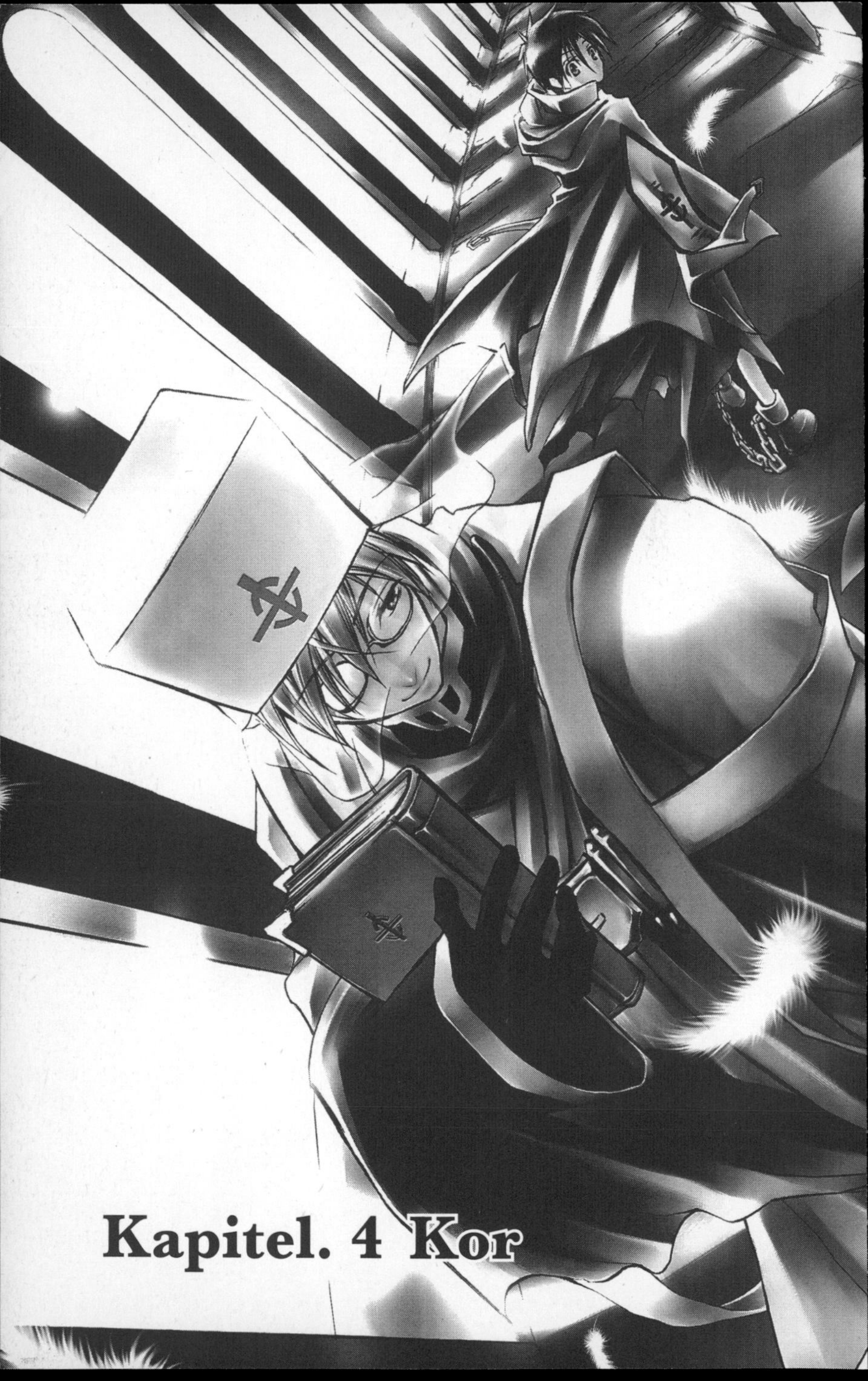
Kapitel. 4 Kor

Only by
devout
prayer
can your
greatest
dreams
come
true.

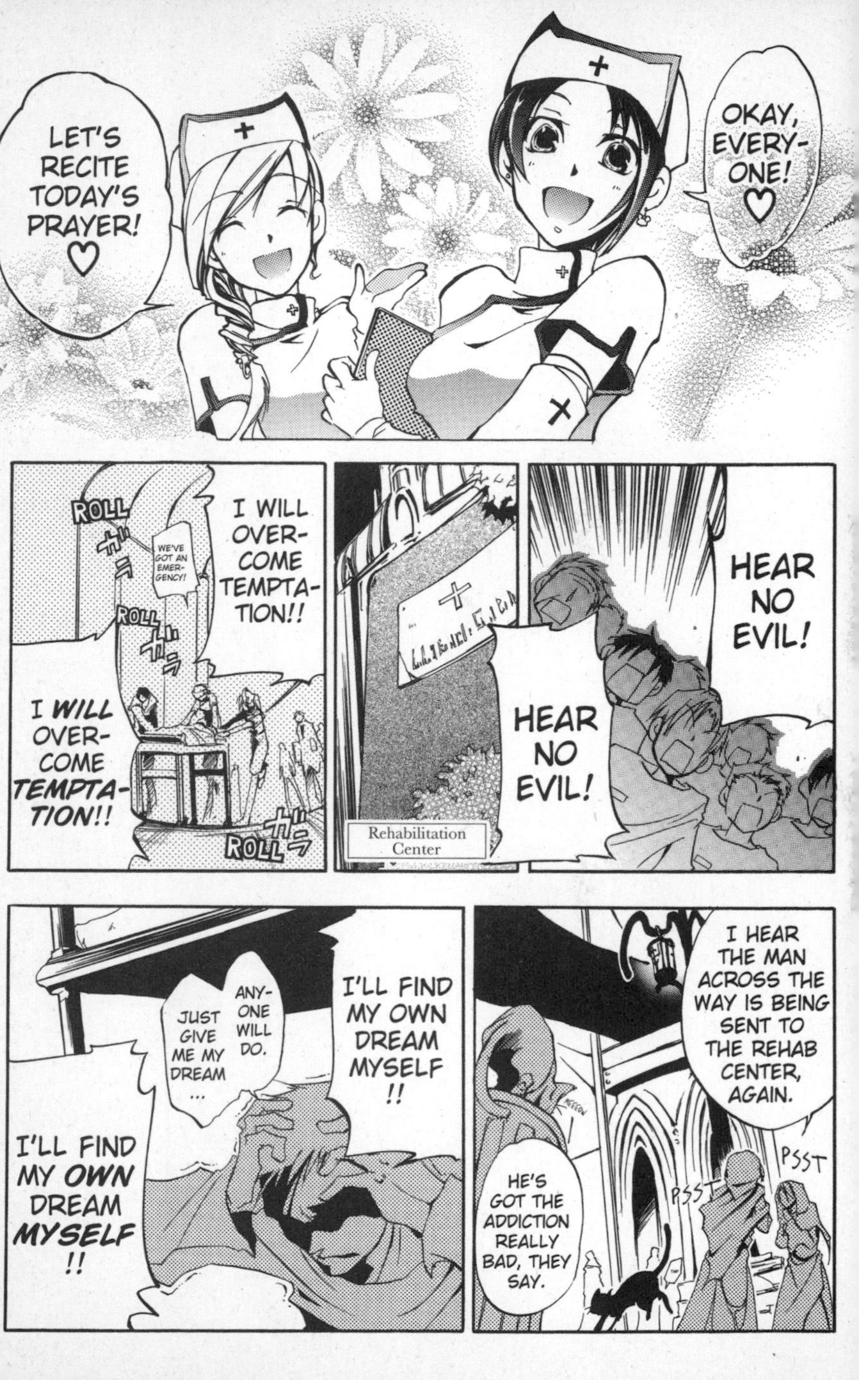
OKAY, EVERY-ONE! ♥
LET'S RECITE TODAY'S PRAYER! ♥
HEAR NO EVIL!
HEAR NO EVIL!
Rehabilitation Center
I WILL OVER-COME TEMPTA-TION!!
ROLL
WE'VE GOT AN EMER-GENCY!
ROLL
I WILL OVER-COME TEMPTA-TION!!
ROLL
I HEAR THE MAN ACROSS THE WAY IS BEING SENT TO THE REHAB CENTER, AGAIN.
PSST
PSST
HE'S GOT THE ADDICTION REALLY BAD, THEY SAY.
I'LL FIND MY OWN DREAM MYSELF!!
ANY-ONE WILL DO.
JUST GIVE ME MY DREAM...
I'LL FIND MY OWN DREAM MYSELF!!

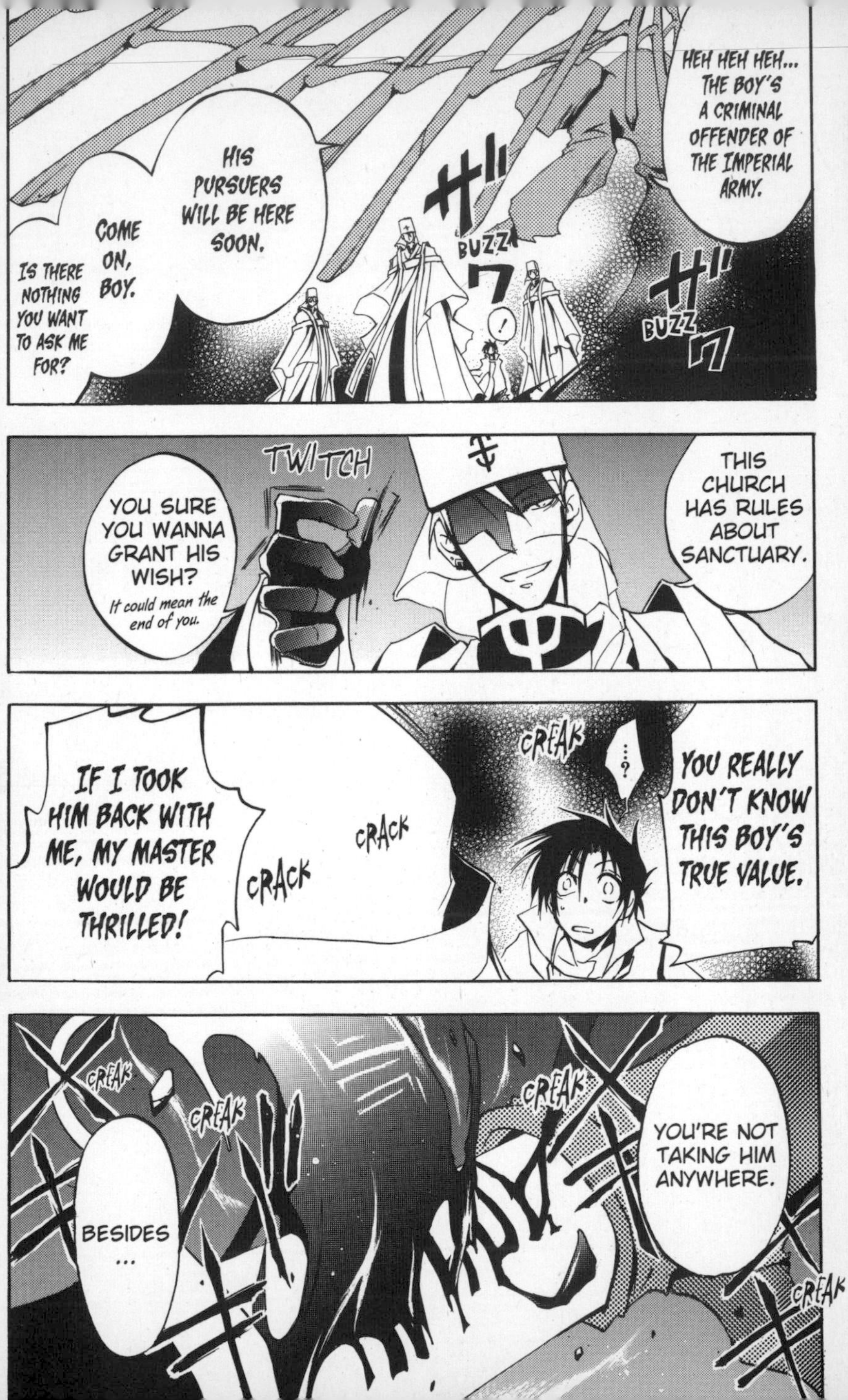
HEH HEH HEH... THE BOY'S A CRIMINAL OFFENDER OF THE IMPERIAL ARMY.
BUZZ
BUZZ
HIS PURSUERS WILL BE HERE SOON.
COME ON, BOY.
IS THERE NOTHING YOU WANT TO ASK ME FOR?
!
THIS CHURCH HAS RULES ABOUT SANCTUARY.
TWITCH
YOU SURE YOU WANNA GRANT HIS WISH? It could mean the end of you.
YOU REALLY DON'T KNOW THIS BOY'S TRUE VALUE.
...?
CREAK
CRACK
CRACK
IF I TOOK HIM BACK WITH ME, MY MASTER WOULD BE THRILLED!
CREAK
YOU'RE NOT TAKING HIM ANYWHERE.
CREAK
CREAK
CREAK
BESIDES ...

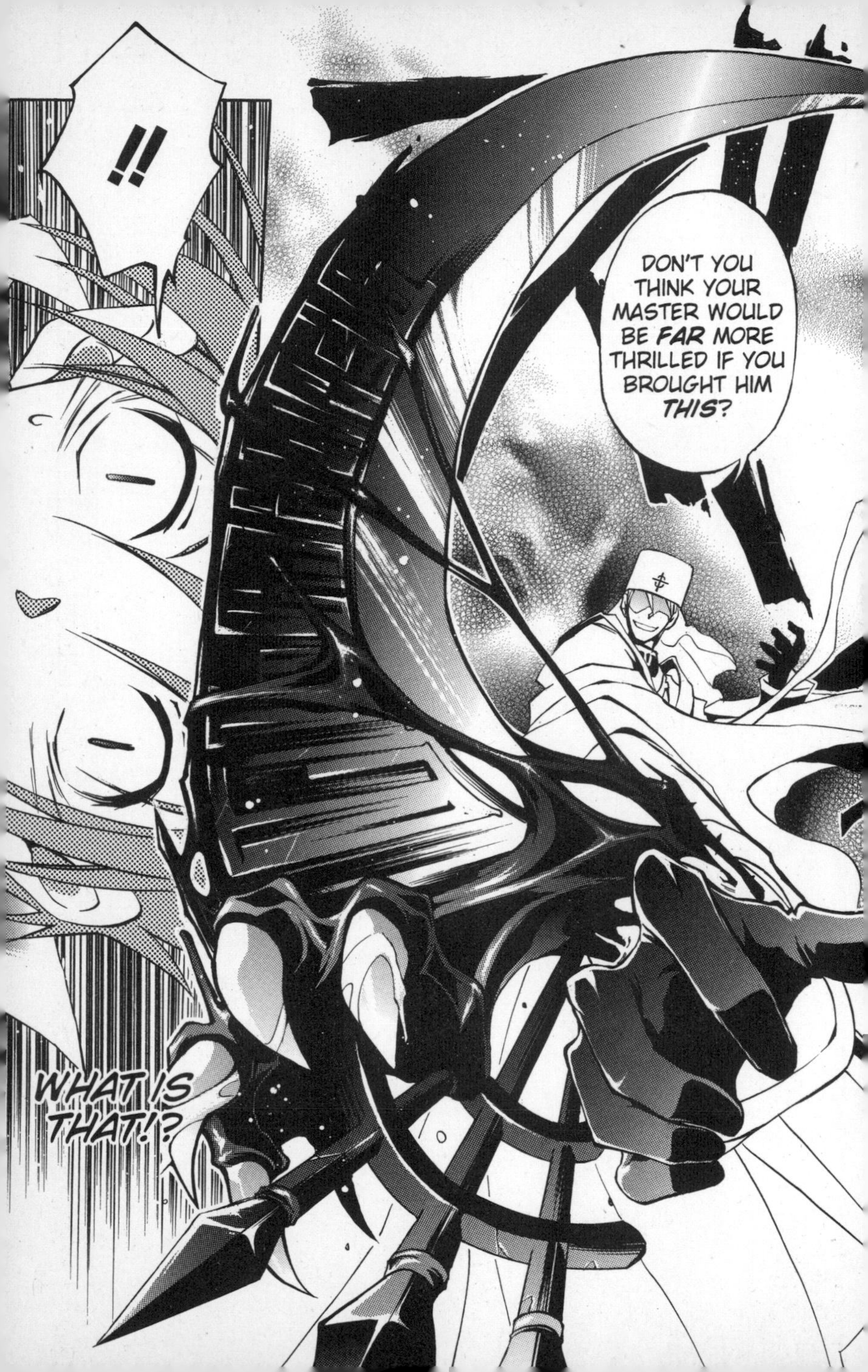
DON'T YOU THINK YOUR MASTER WOULD BE **FAR** MORE THRILLED IF YOU BROUGHT HIM ***THIS***?
!!
WHAT IS THAT!?

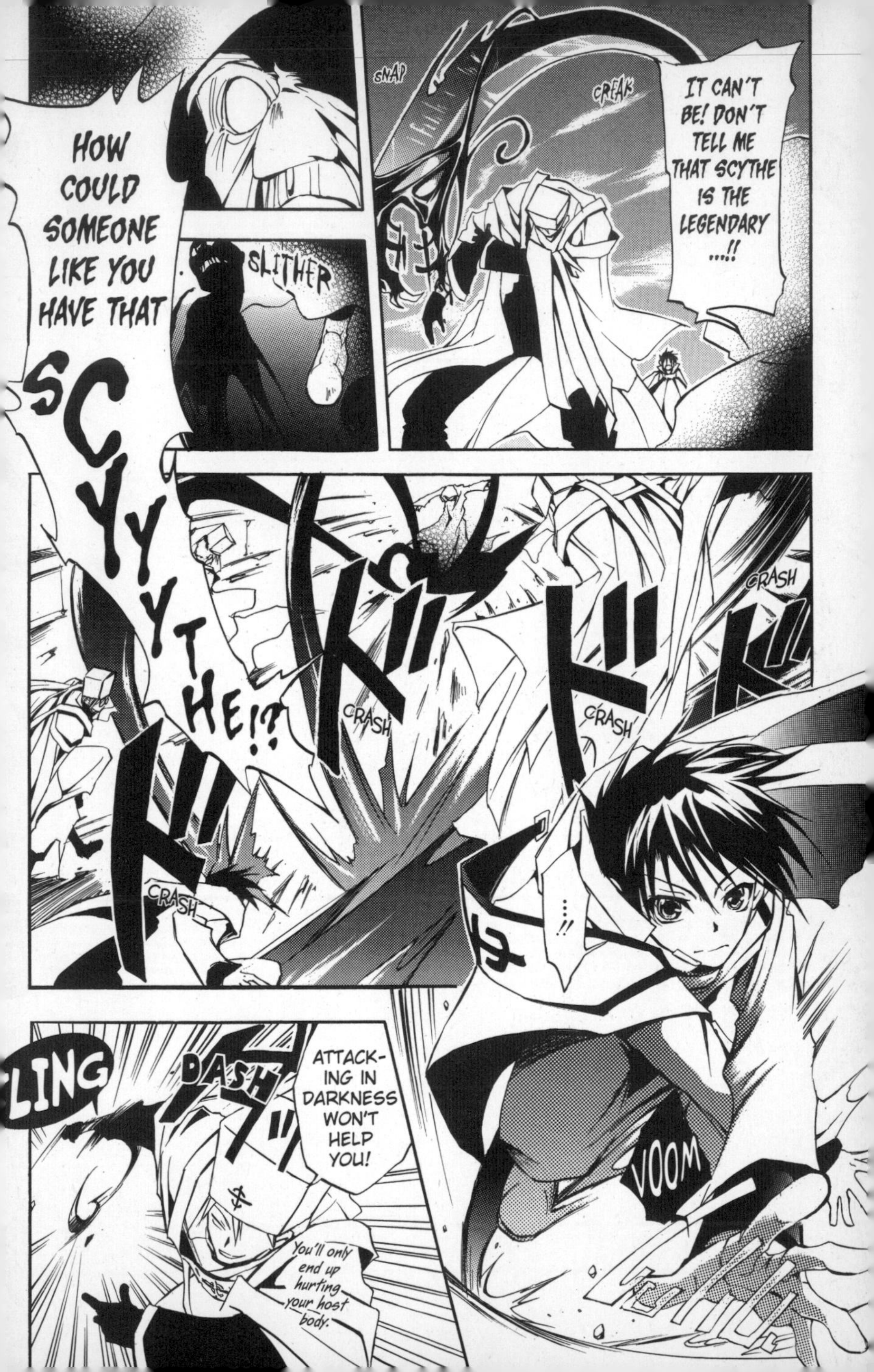
SNAP
CREAK
IT CAN'T BE! DON'T TELL ME THAT SCYTHE IS THE LEGENDARY ...!!
HOW COULD SOMEONE LIKE YOU HAVE THAT SCYYTHE!?
SLITHER
CRASH
CRASH
CRASH
CRASH
...!!
VOOM
DASH
LING
ATTACK-ING IN DARKNESS WON'T HELP YOU!
You'll only end up hurting your host body.

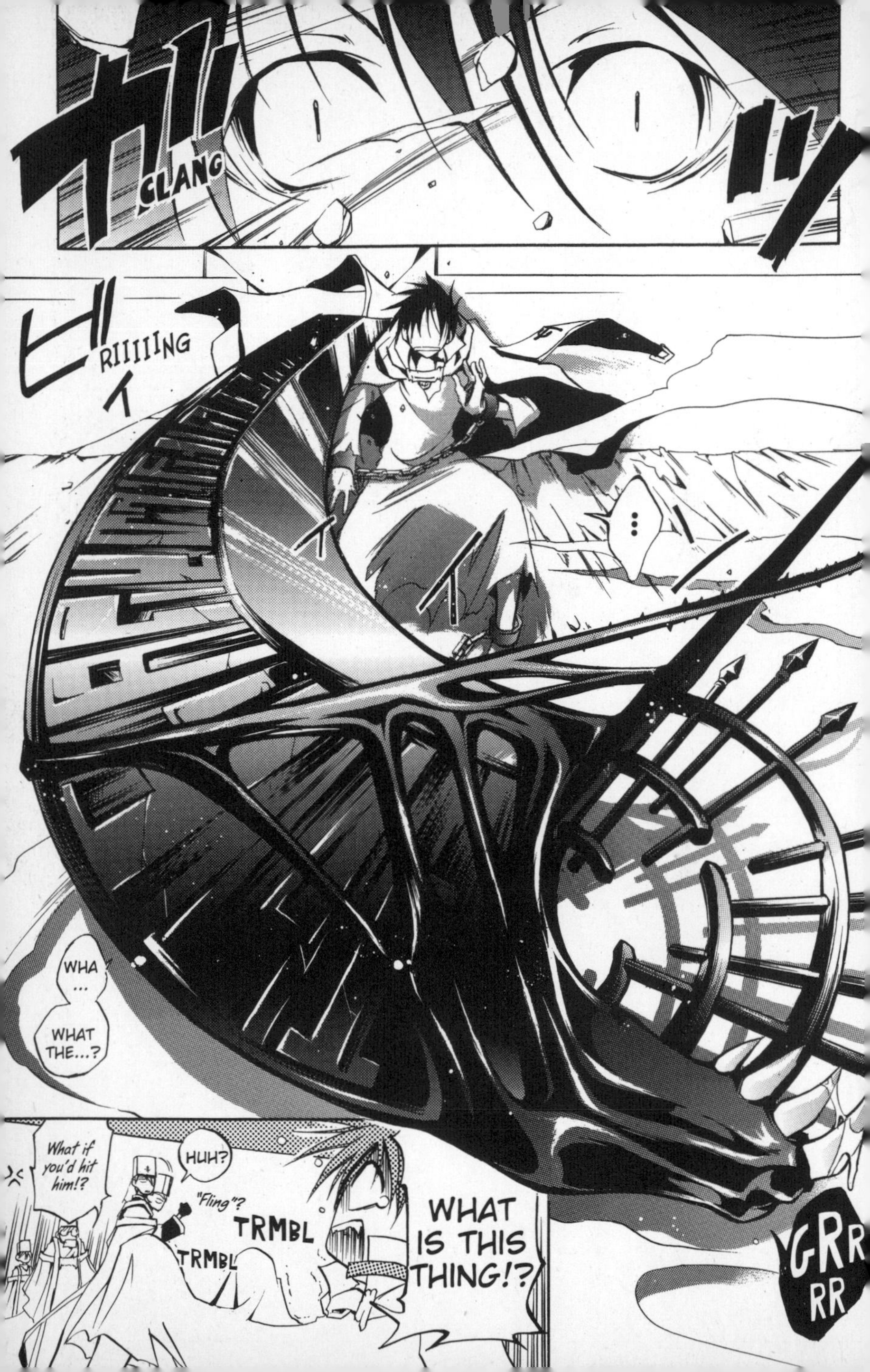

CLANG
RIIIIING
...
GRRRRR
WHA... WHAT THE...?
WHAT IS THIS THING!?
TRMBL TRMBL
HUH?
"Fling"?
What if you'd hit him!?

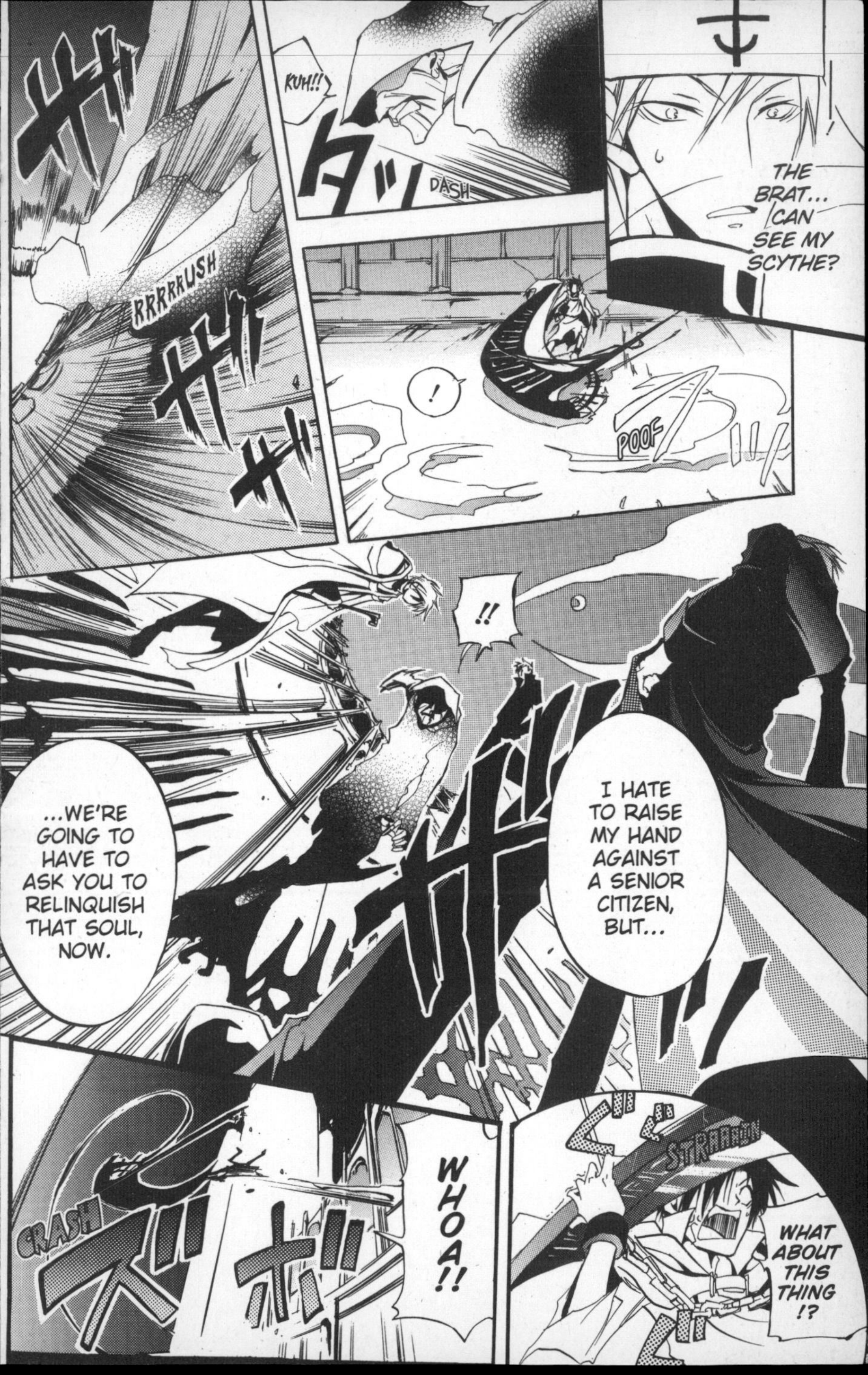
THE BRAT... CAN SEE MY SCYTHE?
KUH!!
DASH
!
POOF
RRRRRUSH
!!
I HATE TO RAISE MY HAND AGAINST A SENIOR CITIZEN, BUT...
...WE'RE GOING TO HAVE TO ASK YOU TO RELINQUISH THAT SOUL, NOW.
STRAAAIN
WHAT ABOUT THIS THING!?
WHOA!!
CRASH

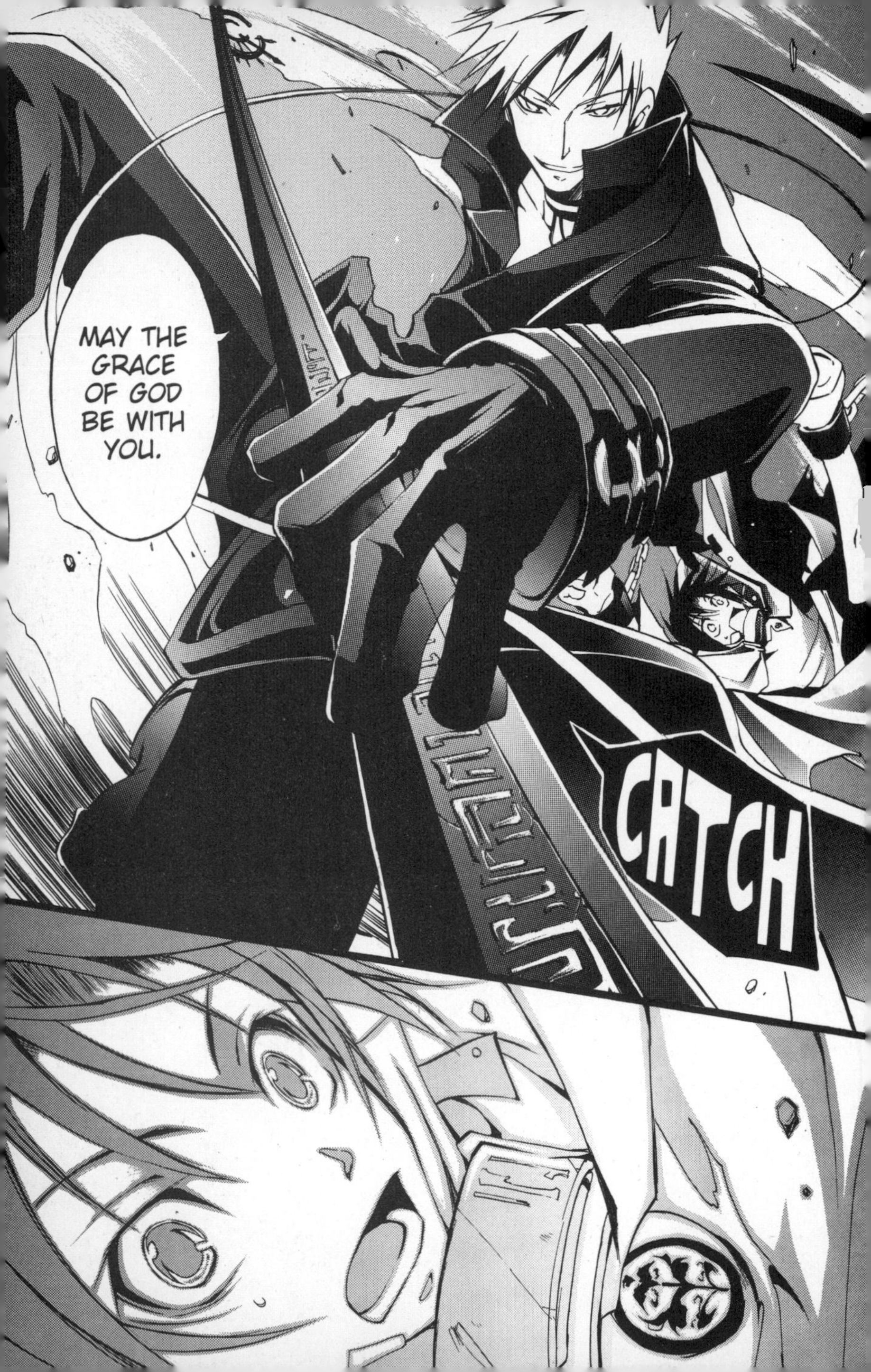
MAY THE GRACE OF GOD BE WITH YOU.
CATCH

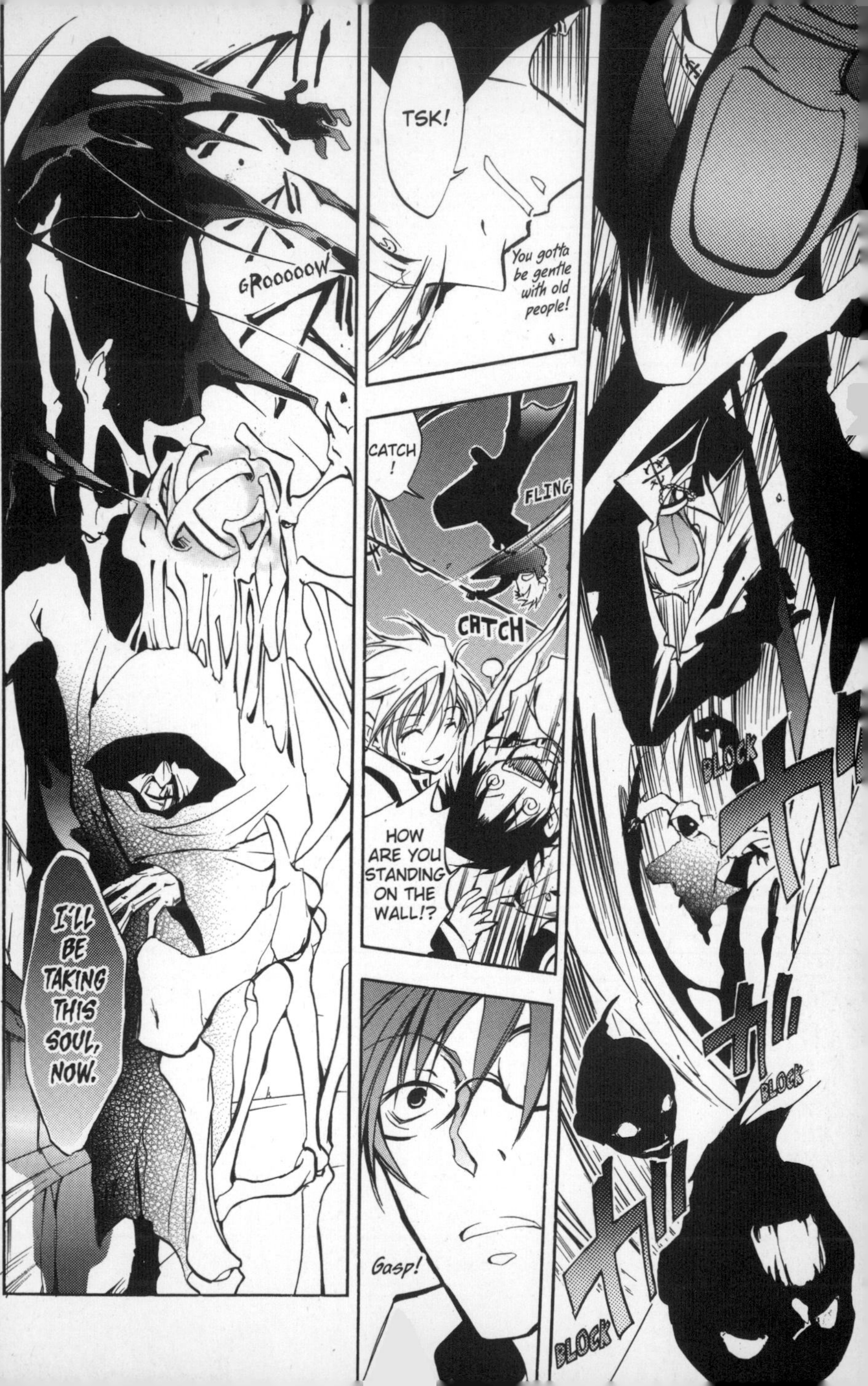
BLOCK
BLOCK
BLOCK
TSK!
You gotta be gentle with old people!
CATCH!
FLING
CATCH
HOW ARE YOU STANDING ON THE WALL!?
Gasp!
GROOOOOW
I'LL BE TAKING THIS SOUL, NOW.

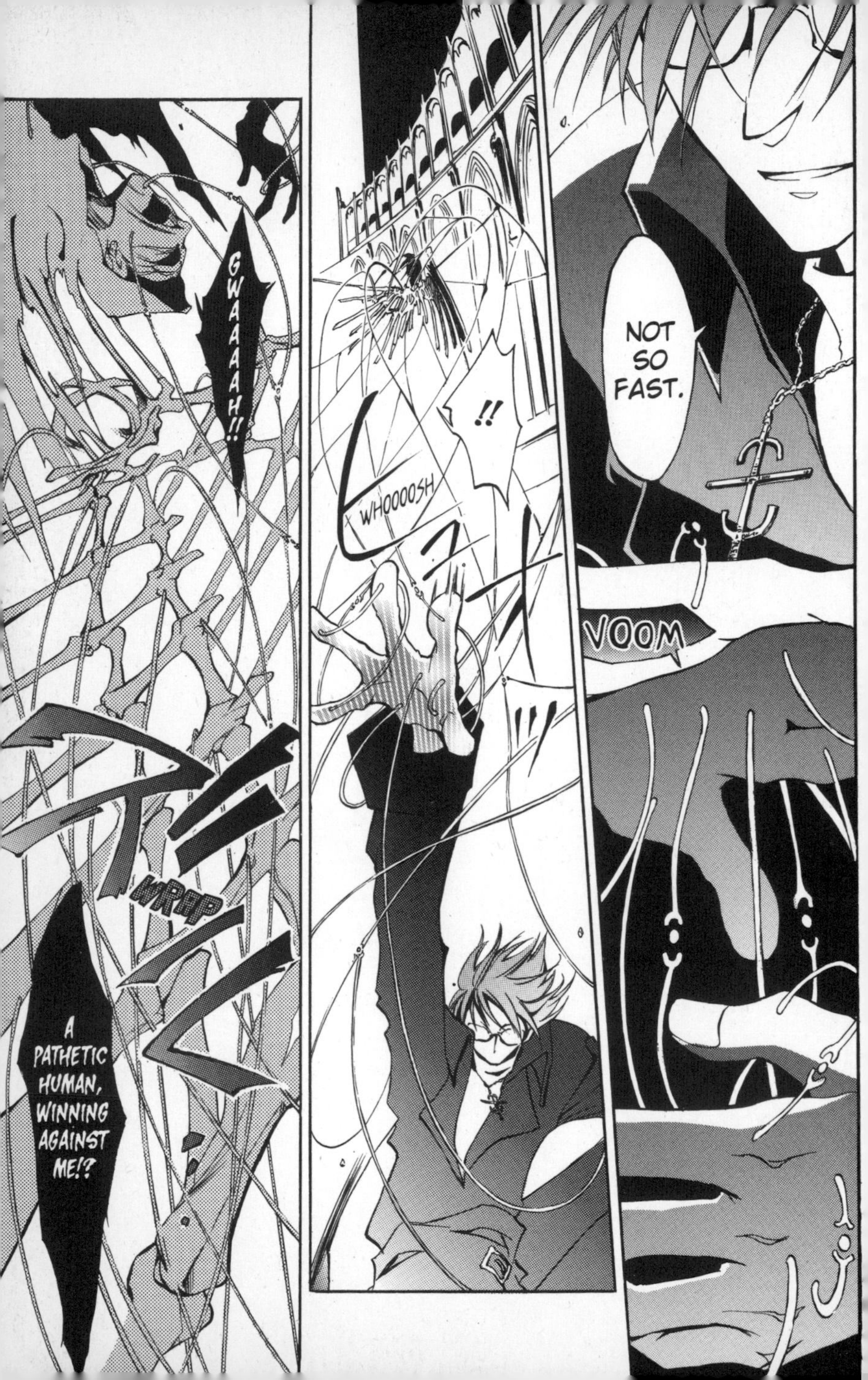
NOT SO FAST.
VOOM
!!
WHOOOOSH
GWAAAAAH!!
WRAP
A PATHETIC HUMAN, WINNING AGAINST ME!?

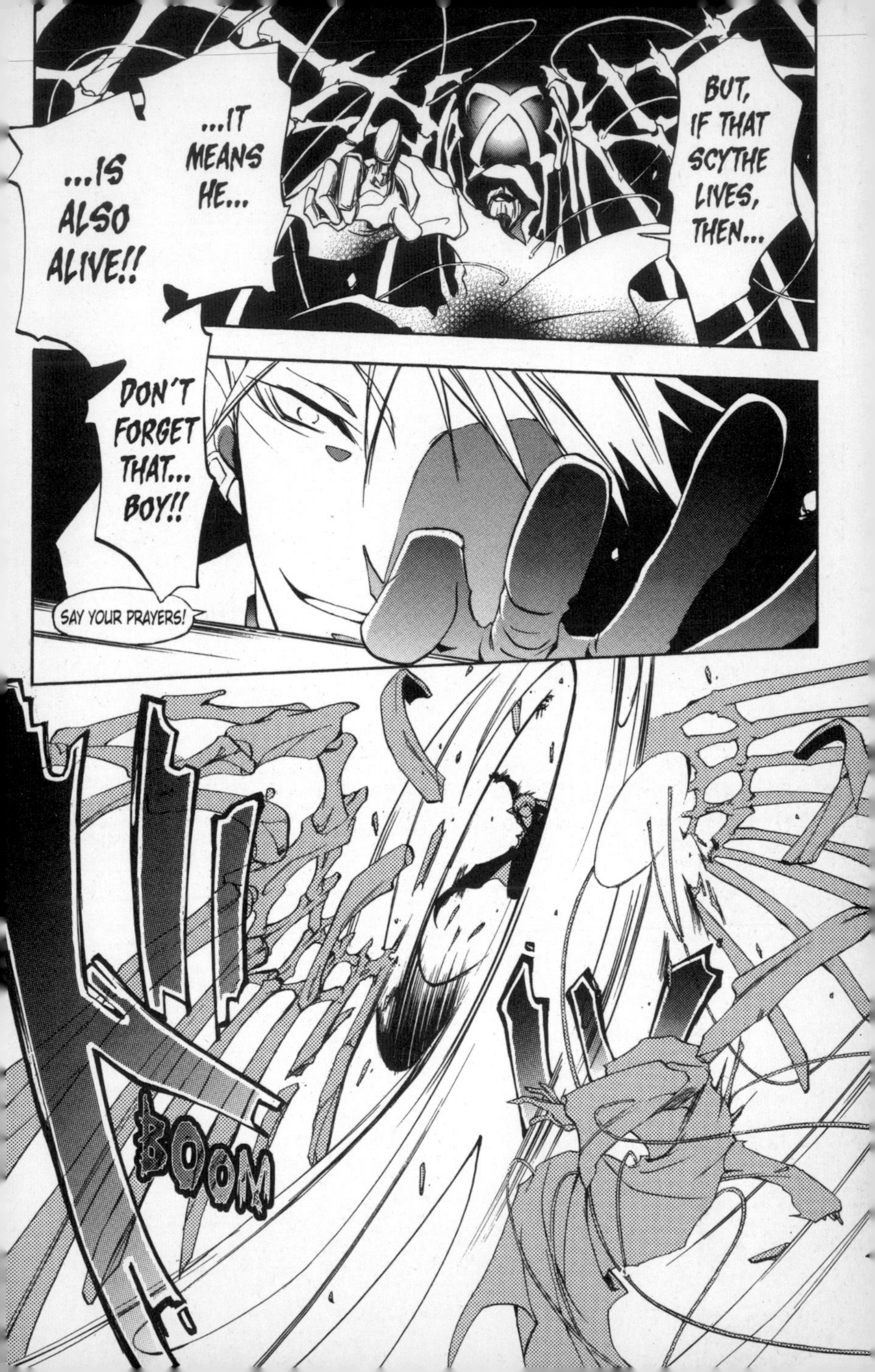
BUT, IF THAT SCYTHE LIVES, THEN...
...IT MEANS HE...
...IS ALSO ALIVE!!
DON'T FORGET THAT... BOY!!
SAY YOUR PRAYERS!
BOOM

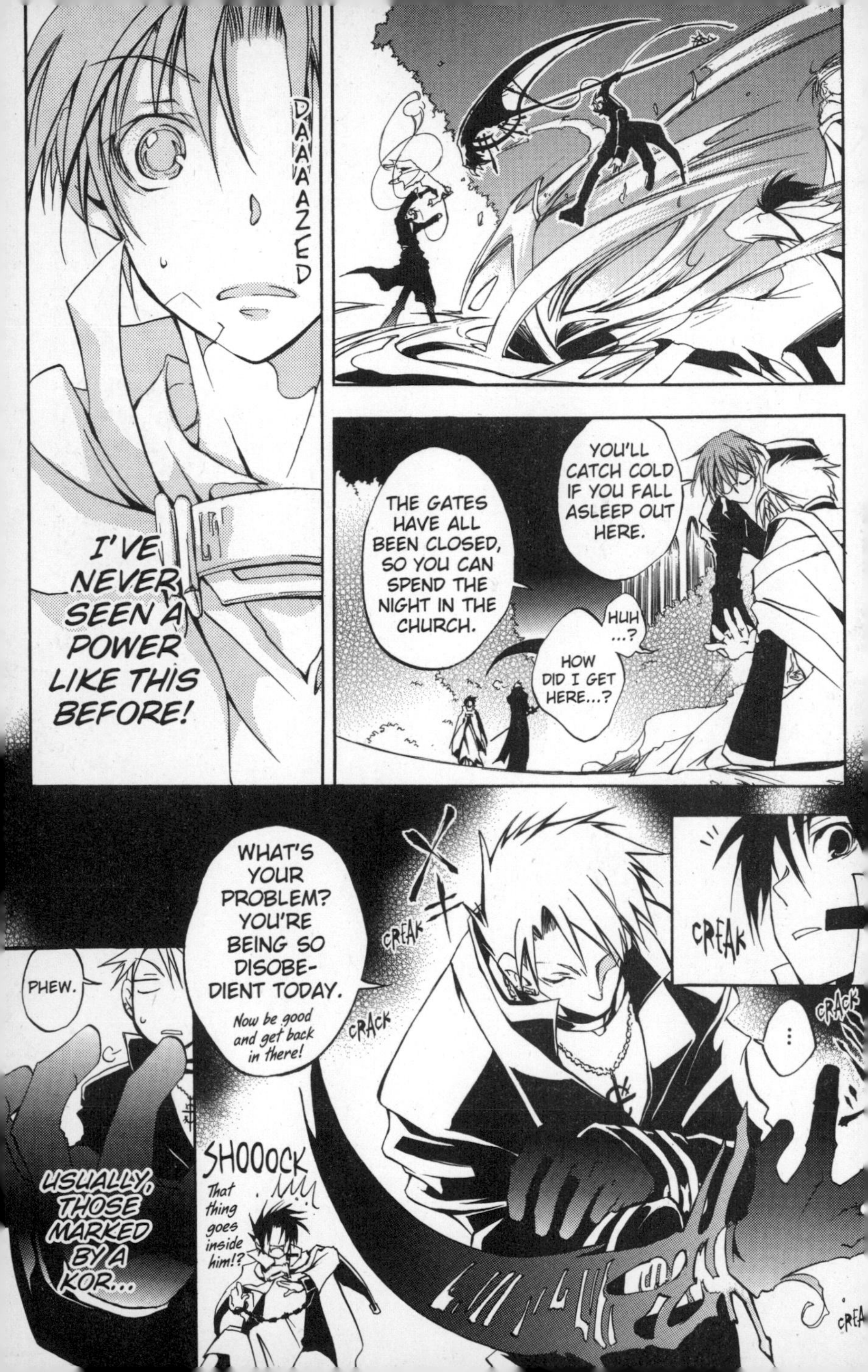
YOU'LL CATCH COLD IF YOU FALL ASLEEP OUT HERE.
THE GATES HAVE ALL BEEN CLOSED, SO YOU CAN SPEND THE NIGHT IN THE CHURCH.
HUH ...?
HOW DID I GET HERE...?
DAAAAAZED
I'VE NEVER SEEN A POWER LIKE THIS BEFORE!
CREAK
CRACK
...
CREAK
WHAT'S YOUR PROBLEM? YOU'RE BEING SO DISOBEDIENT TODAY.
Now be good and get back in there!
CRACK
CREA
PHEW.
SHOOOCK
That thing goes inside him!?
USUALLY, THOSE MARKED BY A KOR...

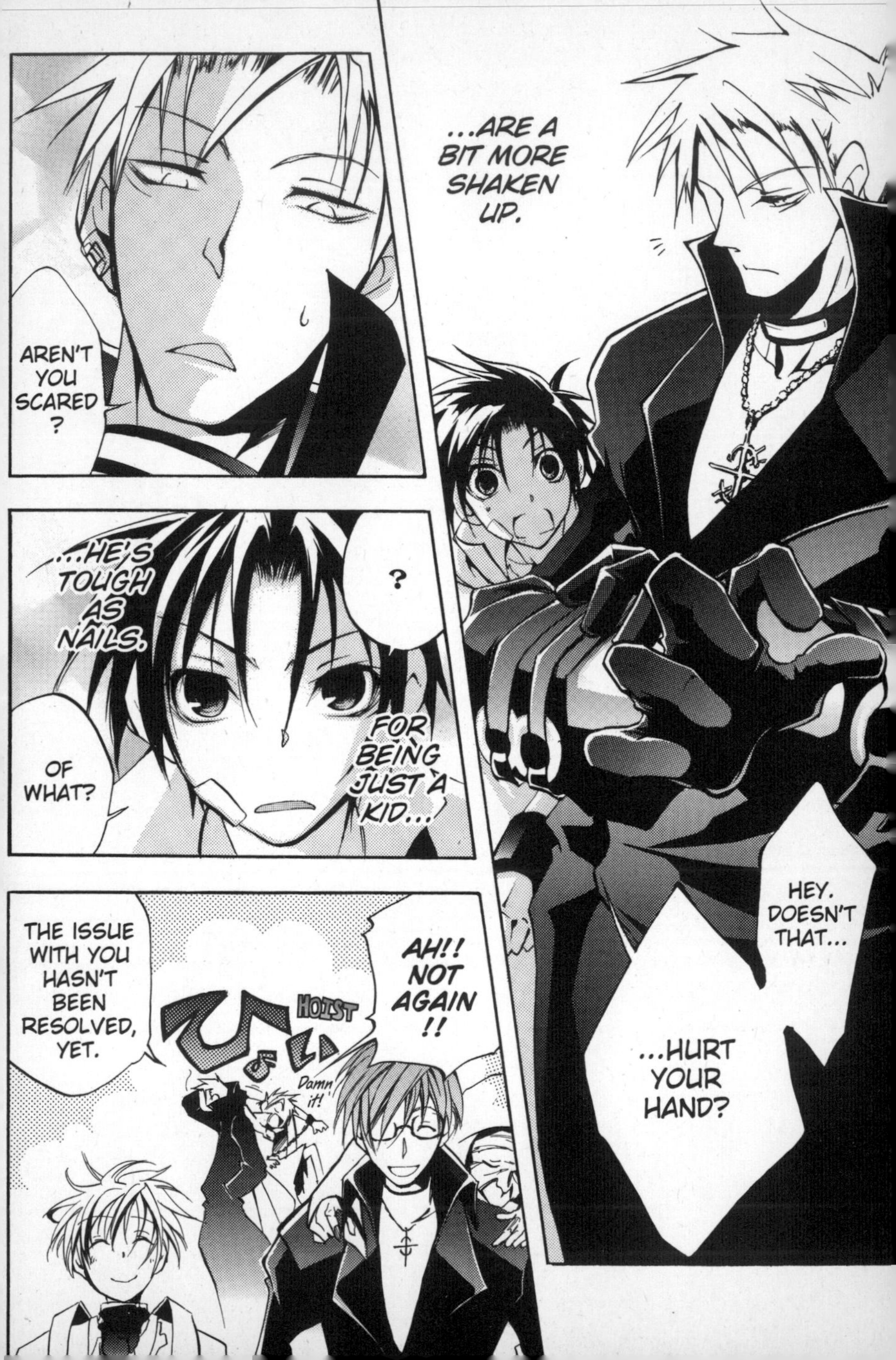
...ARE A BIT MORE SHAKEN UP.
HEY. DOESN'T THAT...
...HURT YOUR HAND?
AREN'T YOU SCARED?
?
...HE'S TOUGH AS NAILS.
FOR BEING JUST A KID...
OF WHAT?
AH!! NOT AGAIN!!
HOIST
THE ISSUE WITH YOU HASN'T BEEN RESOLVED, YET.
Damn it!

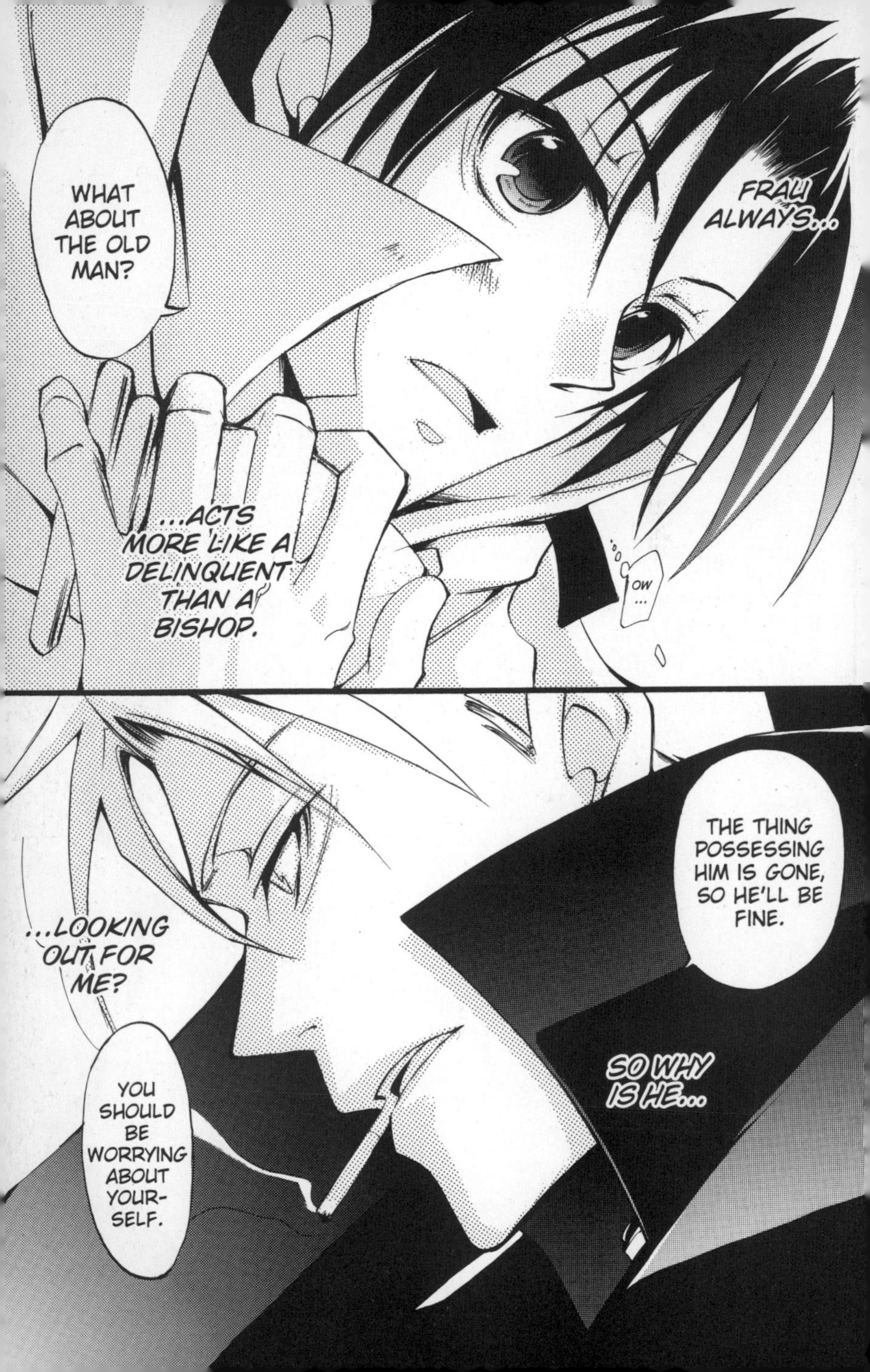
FRAU ALWAYS...
WHAT ABOUT THE OLD MAN?
...ACTS MORE LIKE A DELINQUENT THAN A BISHOP.
OW...
THE THING POSSESSING HIM IS GONE, SO HE'LL BE FINE.
SO WHY IS HE...
...LOOKING OUT FOR ME?
YOU SHOULD BE WORRYING ABOUT YOUR-SELF.

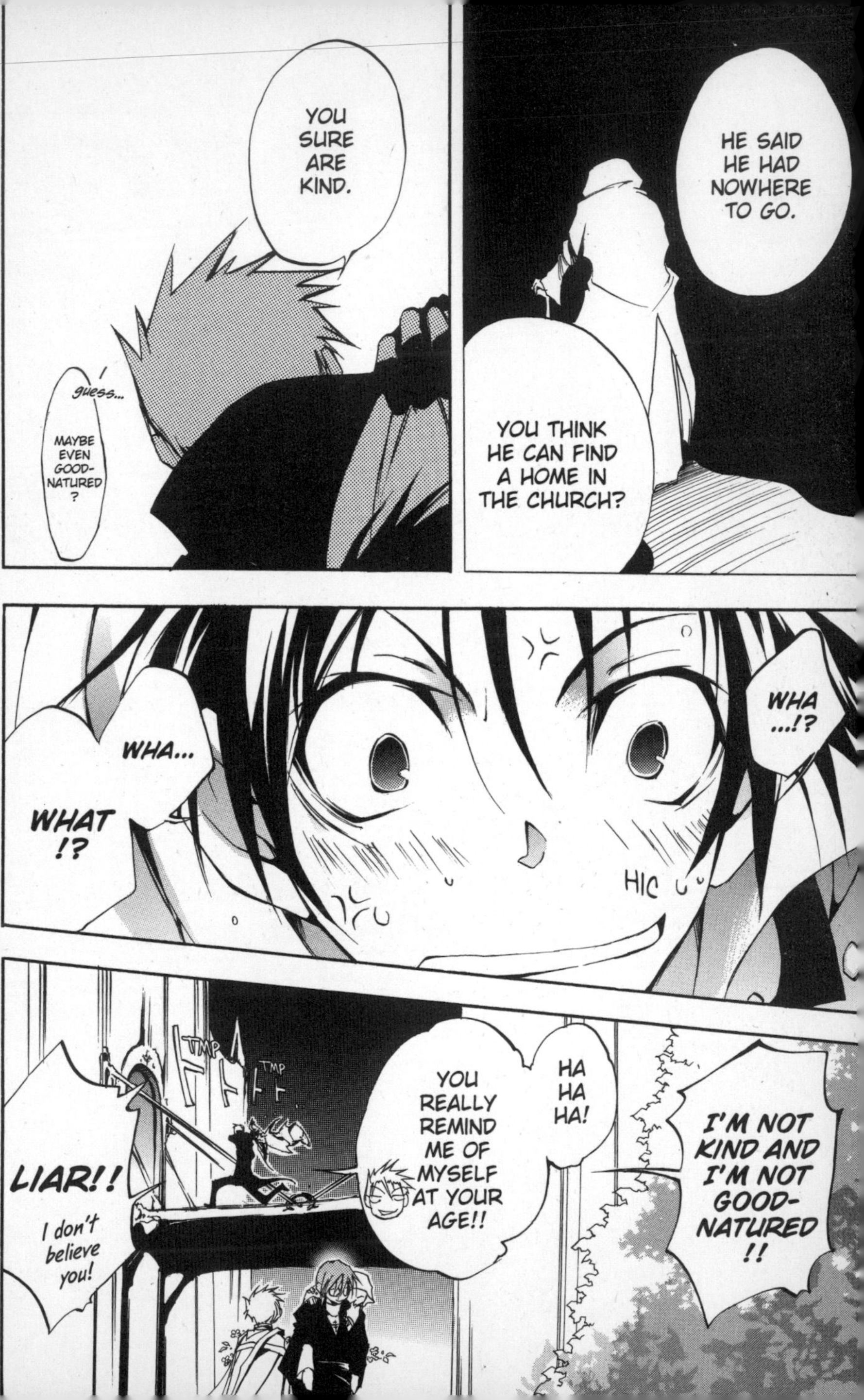
HE SAID HE HAD NOWHERE TO GO.
YOU THINK HE CAN FIND A HOME IN THE CHURCH?
YOU SURE ARE KIND.
I guess...
MAYBE EVEN GOOD-NATURED?
WHA ...!?
HIC
WHA...
WHAT!?
I'M NOT KIND AND I'M NOT GOOD-NATURED!!
HA HA HA!
YOU REALLY REMIND ME OF MYSELF AT YOUR AGE!!
TMP
TMP
LIAR!!
I don't believe you!

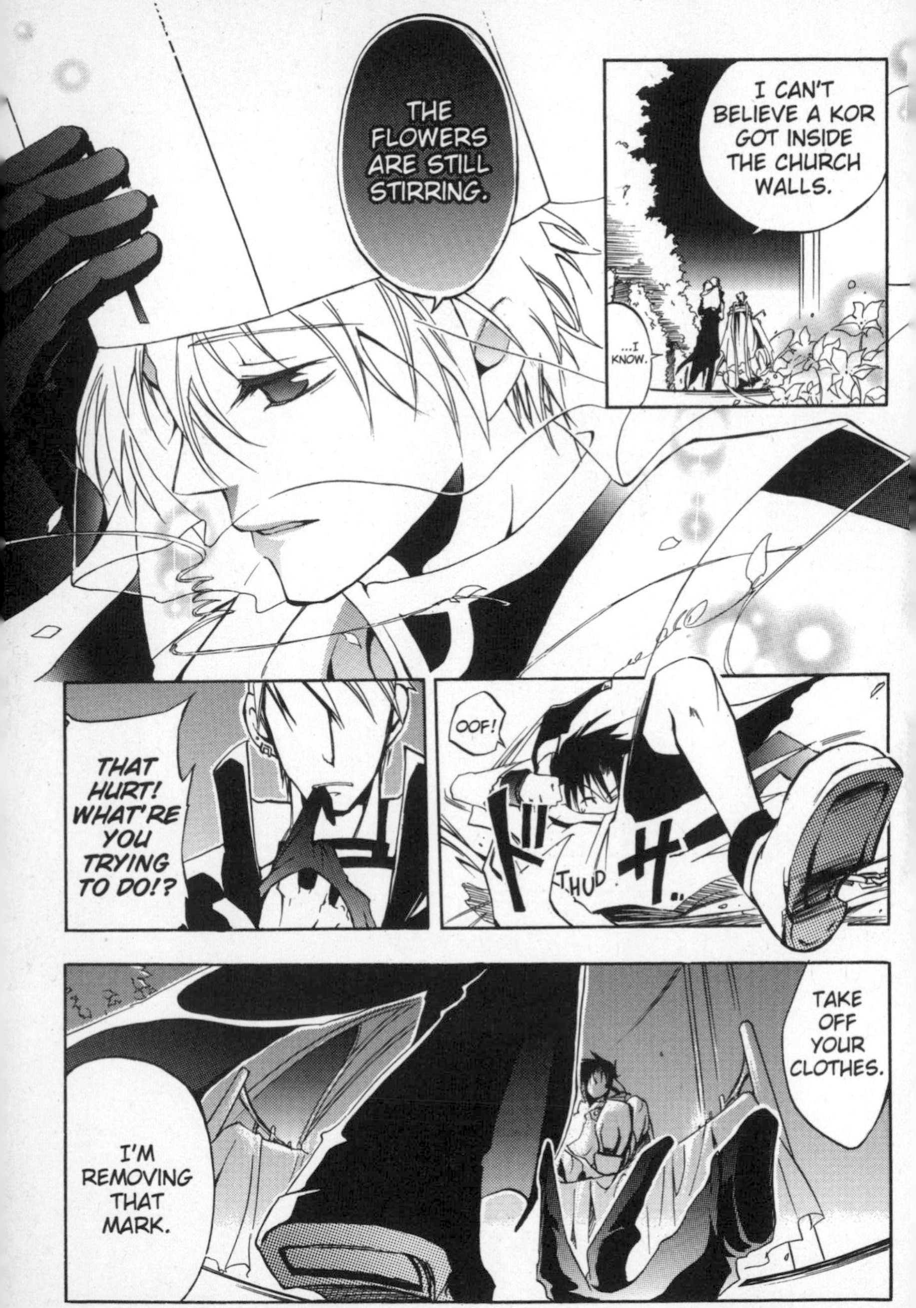
I CAN'T BELIEVE A KOR GOT INSIDE THE CHURCH WALLS.
...I KNOW.
THE FLOWERS ARE STILL STIRRING.
OOF!
THUD
THAT HURT! WHAT'RE YOU TRYING TO DO!?
TAKE OFF YOUR CLOTHES.
I'M REMOVING THAT MARK.

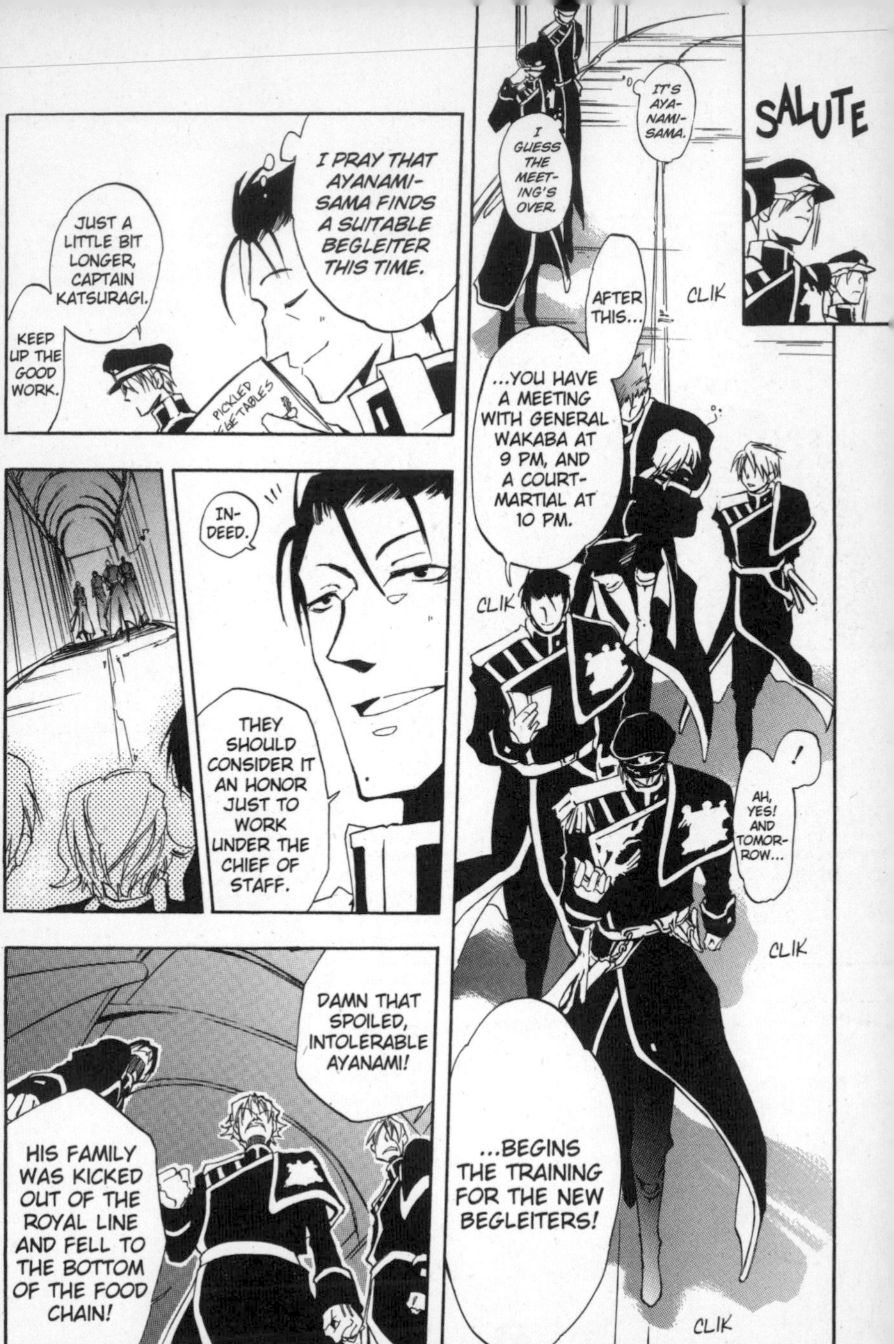
SALUTE
IT'S AYANAMI-SAMA.
I GUESS THE MEETING'S OVER.
CLIK
AFTER THIS...
...YOU HAVE A MEETING WITH GENERAL WAKABA AT 9 PM, AND A COURT-MARTIAL AT 10 PM.
CLIK
!
AH, YES! AND TOMORROW...
CLIK
...BEGINS THE TRAINING FOR THE NEW BEGLEITERS!
CLIK
I PRAY THAT AYANAMI-SAMA FINDS A SUITABLE BEGLEITER THIS TIME.
JUST A LITTLE BIT LONGER, CAPTAIN KATSURAGI.
KEEP UP THE GOOD WORK.
PICKLED VEGETABLES
IN-DEED.
THEY SHOULD CONSIDER IT AN HONOR JUST TO WORK UNDER THE CHIEF OF STAFF.
DAMN THAT SPOILED, INTOLERABLE AYANAMI!
HIS FAMILY WAS KICKED OUT OF THE ROYAL LINE AND FELL TO THE BOTTOM OF THE FOOD CHAIN!

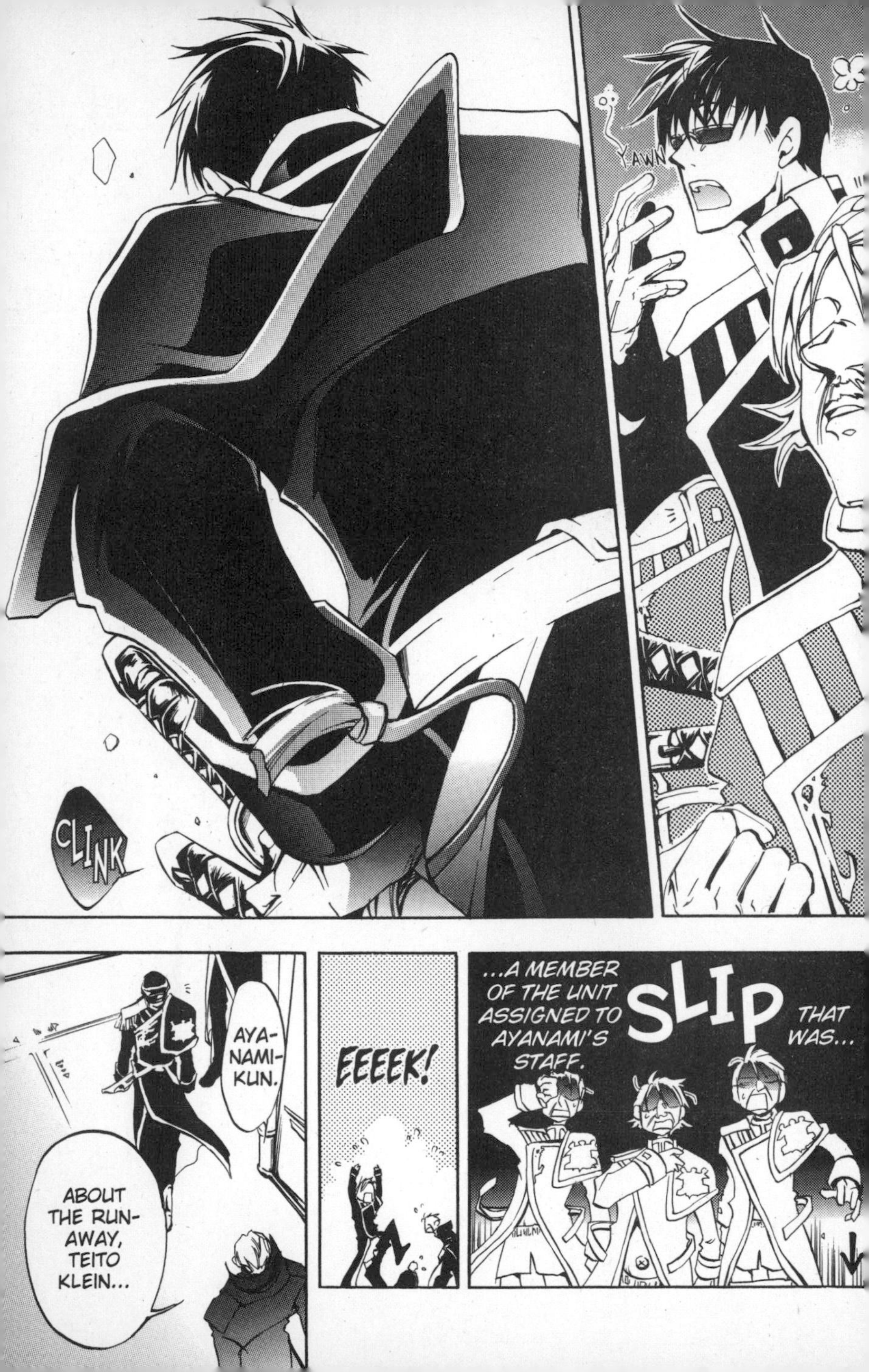
YAWN
CLINK
THAT WAS...
SLIP
...A MEMBER OF THE UNIT ASSIGNED TO AYANAMI'S STAFF.
EEEEK!
AYANAMI-KUN.
ABOUT THE RUNAWAY, TEITO KLEIN...

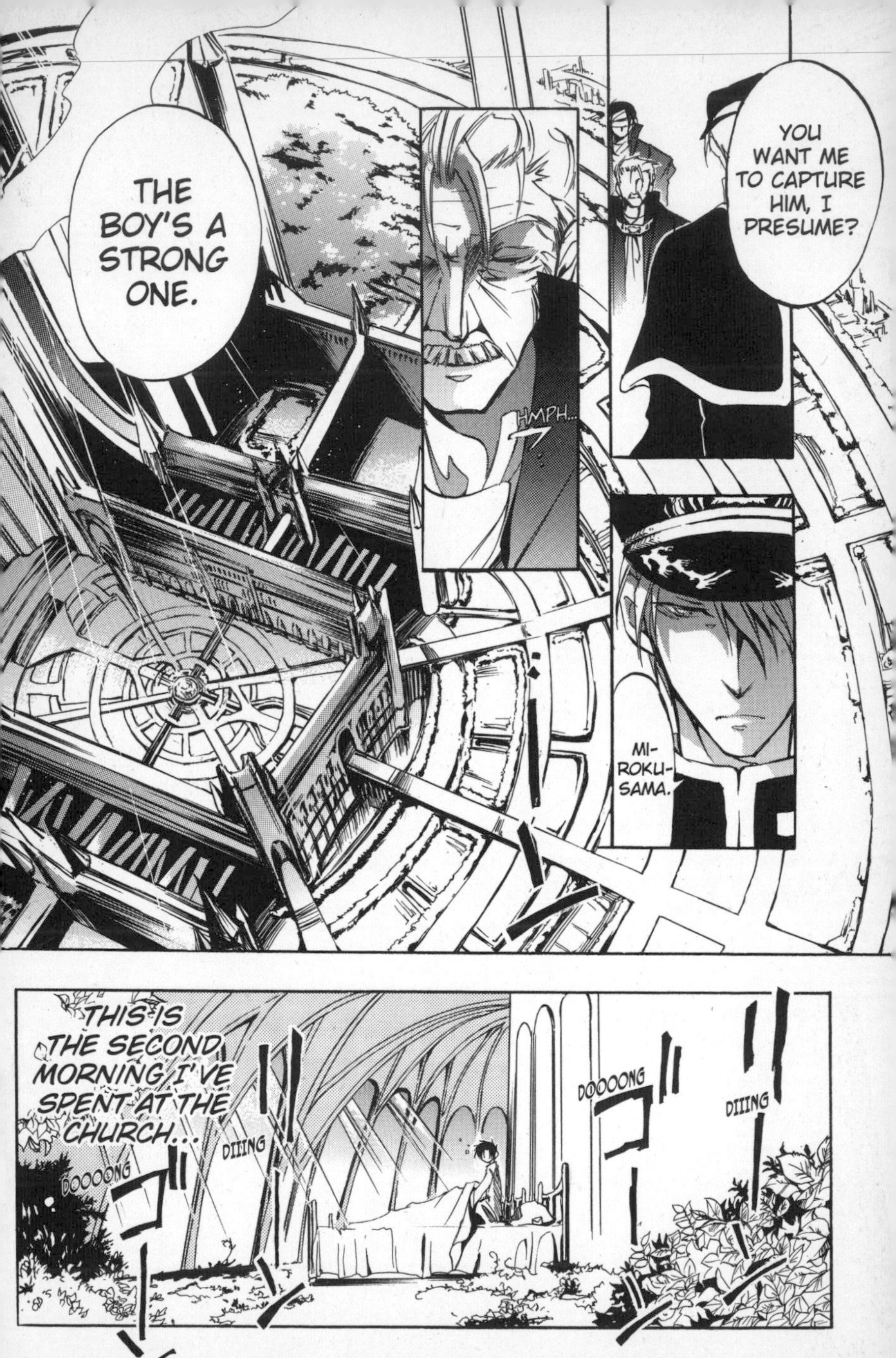
YOU WANT ME TO CAPTURE HIM, I PRESUME?
MI-ROKU-SAMA.
HMPH...
THE BOY'S A STRONG ONE.
DIIING
DOOOONG
DIIING
DOOOONG
THIS IS THE SECOND MORNING I'VE SPENT AT THE CHURCH...

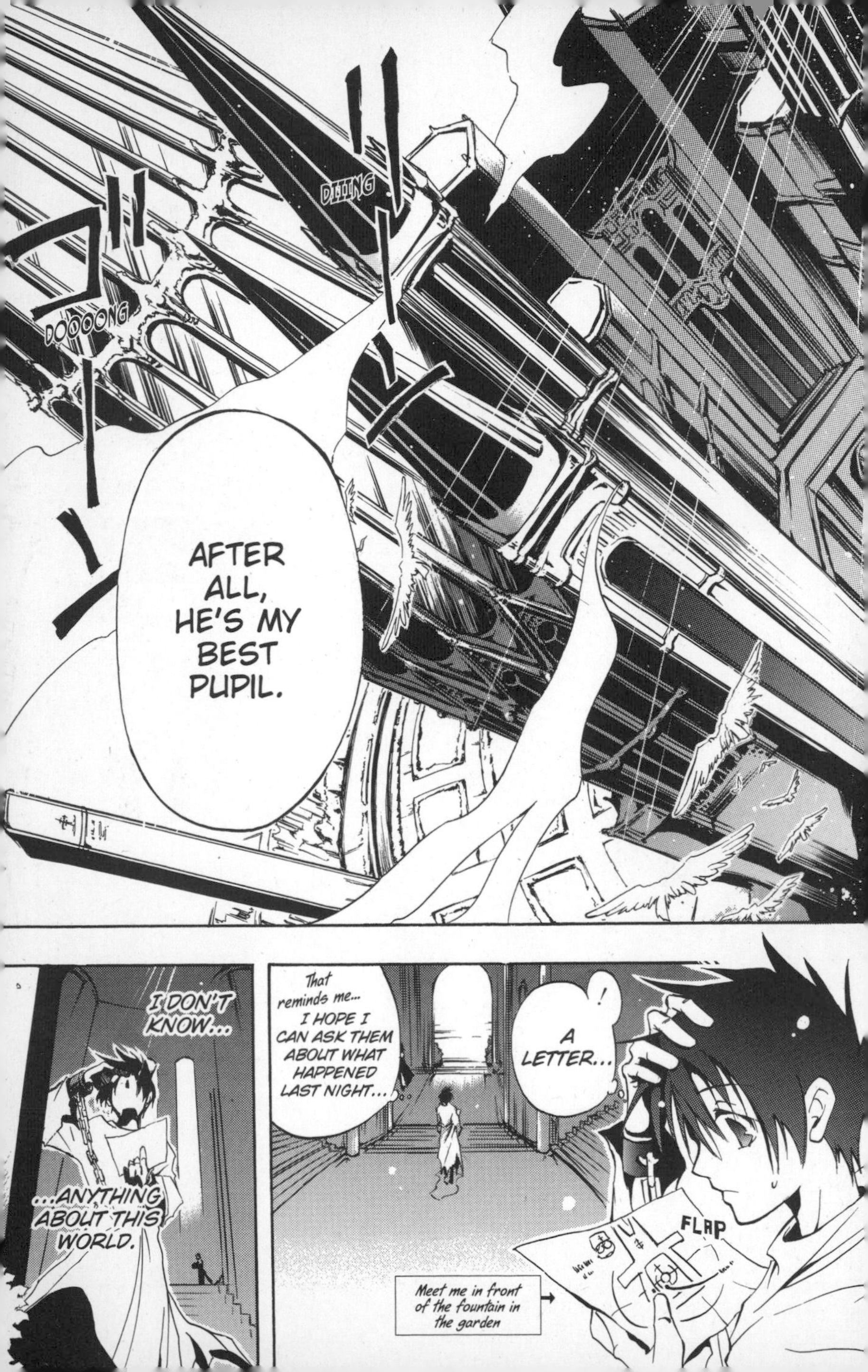
DIIING
DOOOONG
AFTER ALL, HE'S MY BEST PUPIL.
A LETTER...
FLAP
Meet me in front of the fountain in the garden
That reminds me... I HOPE I CAN ASK THEM ABOUT WHAT HAPPENED LAST NIGHT...
I DON'T KNOW...
...ANYTHING ABOUT THIS WORLD.

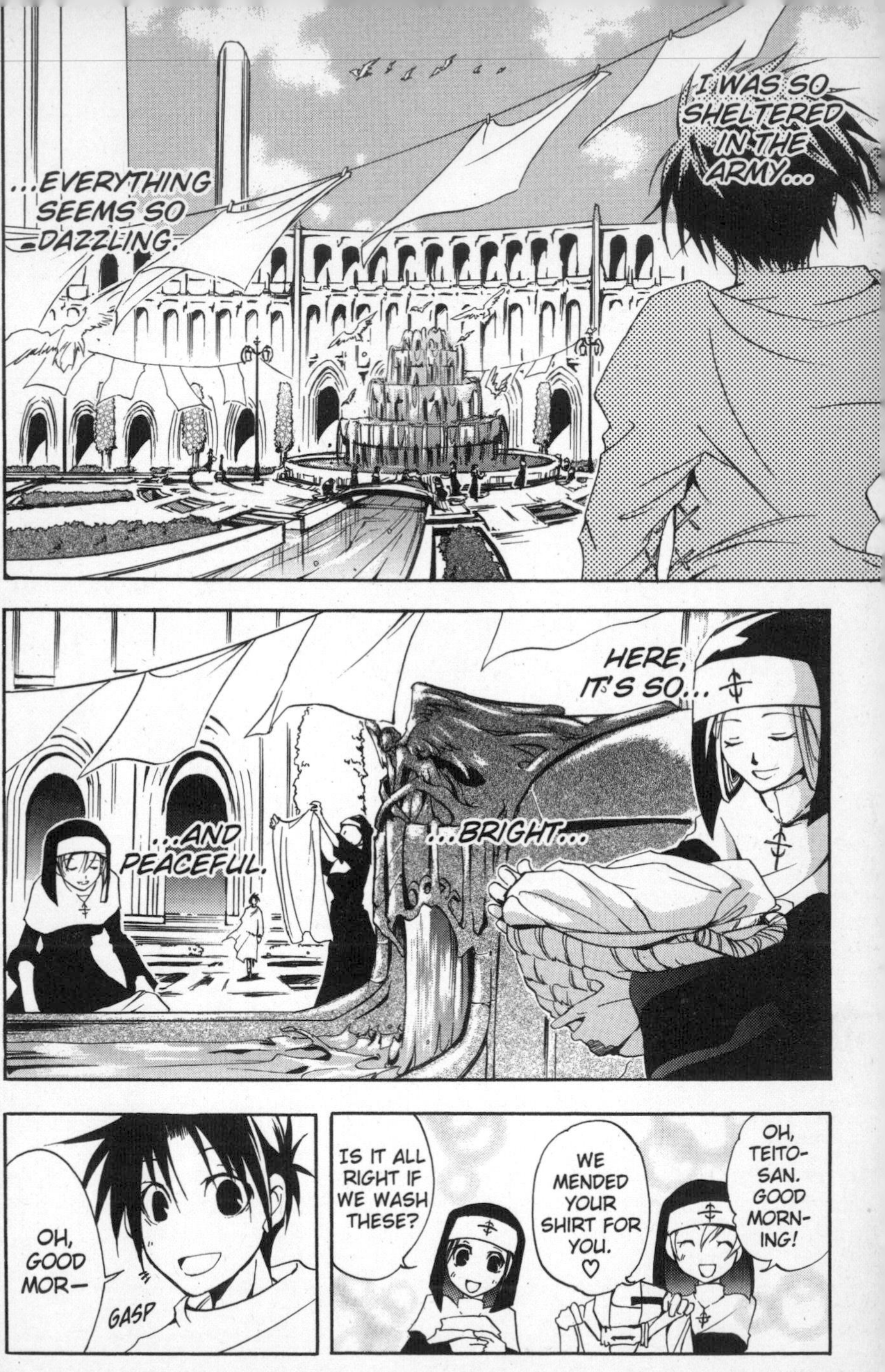
I WAS SO SHELTERED IN THE ARMY...
...EVERYTHING SEEMS SO DAZZLING.
HERE, IT'S SO...
...BRIGHT...
...AND PEACEFUL.
OH, TEITO-SAN. GOOD MORNING!
WE MENDED YOUR SHIRT FOR YOU. ♡
IS IT ALL RIGHT IF WE WASH THESE?
OH, GOOD MOR—
GASP

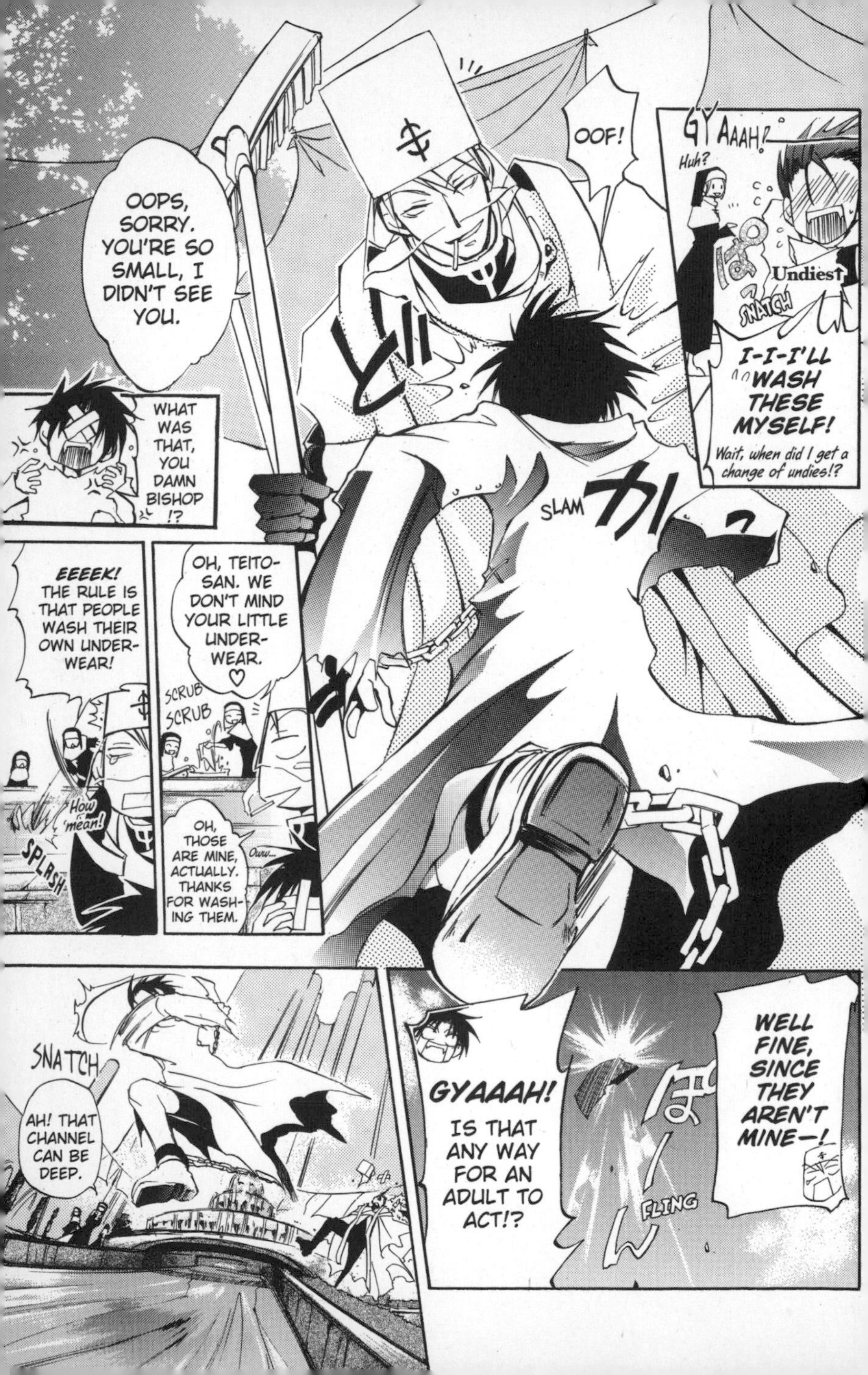
GYAAAH!
Huh?
Undies↑
SNATCH
I-I-I'LL WASH THESE MYSELF!
Wait, when did I get a change of undies!?
OOF!
OOPS, SORRY. YOU'RE SO SMALL, I DIDN'T SEE YOU.
SLAM
WHAT WAS THAT, YOU DAMN BISHOP!?
OH, TEITO-SAN. WE DON'T MIND YOUR LITTLE UNDERWEAR. ♡
SCRUB SCRUB
OH, THOSE ARE MINE, ACTUALLY. THANKS FOR WASHING THEM.
Oww...
EEEEK! THE RULE IS THAT PEOPLE WASH THEIR OWN UNDERWEAR!
How mean!
SPLASH
WELL FINE, SINCE THEY AREN'T MINE—!
GYAAAH!
IS THAT ANY WAY FOR AN ADULT TO ACT!?
FLING
SNATCH
AH! THAT CHANNEL CAN BE DEEP.

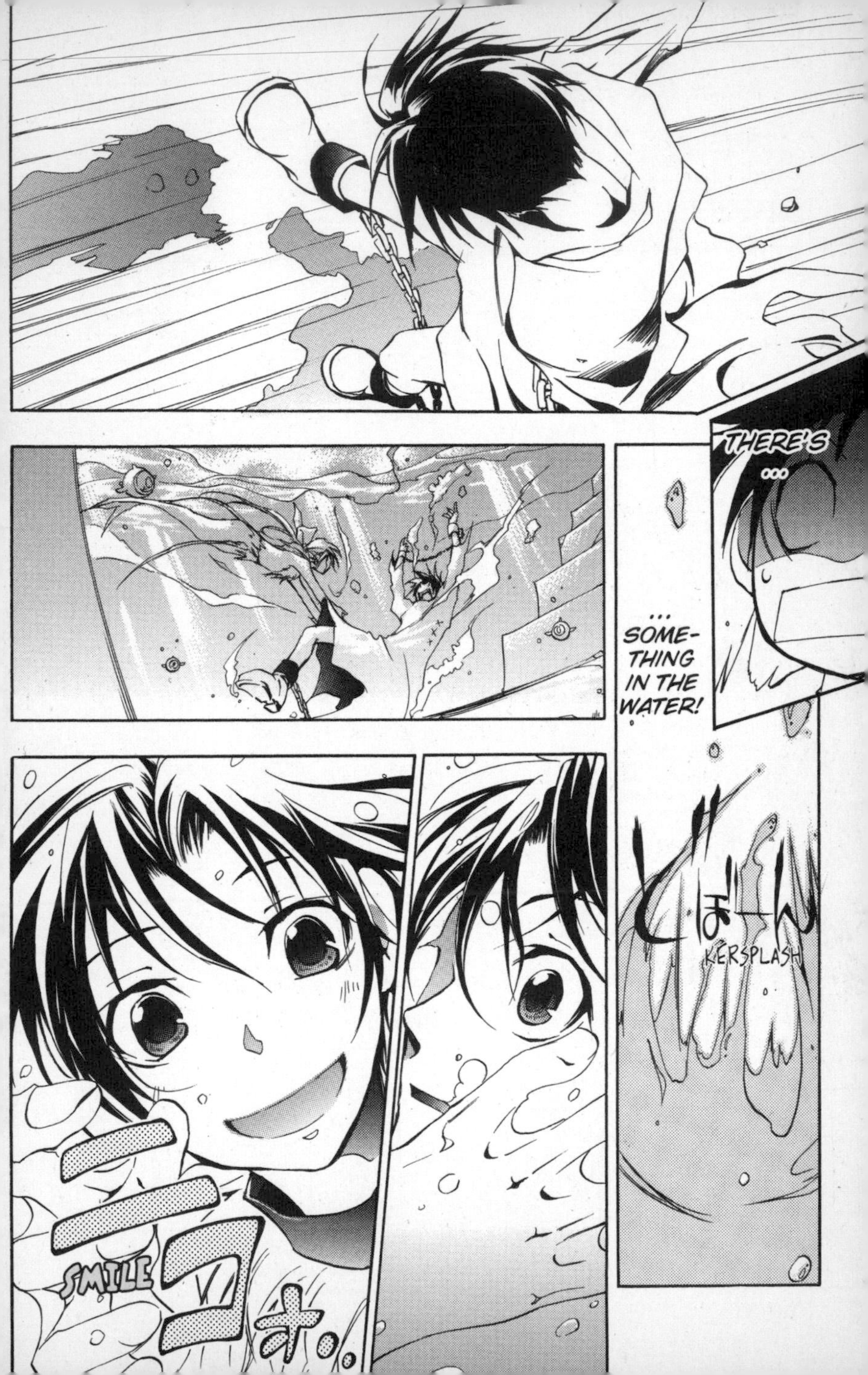
THERE'S ...
... SOME-THING IN THE WATER!
どぼーん
KERSPLASH
ニコォ。。
SMILE

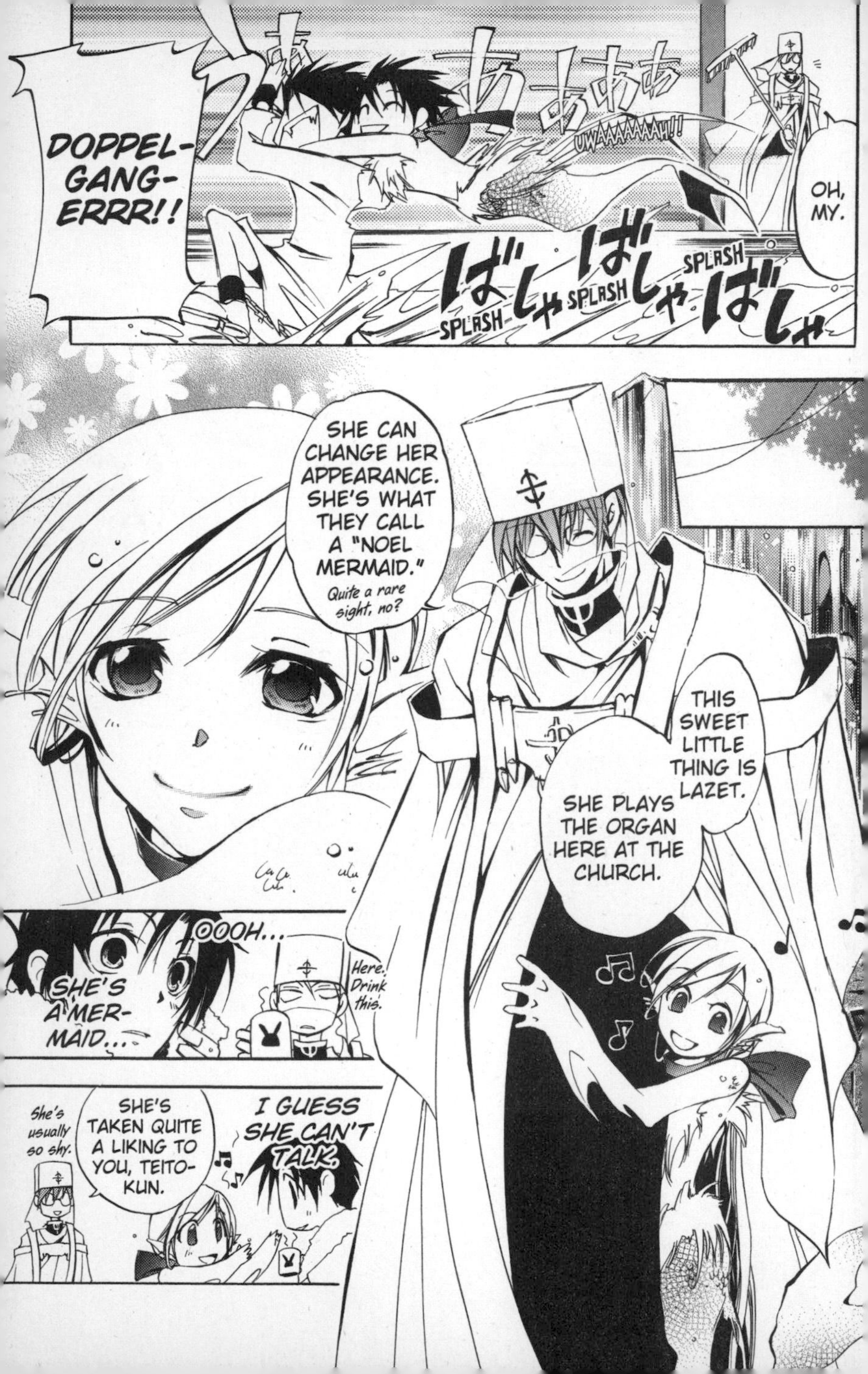
OH, MY.
UWAAAAAAAH!!
DOPPEL-GANG-ERRR!!
SPLASH
SPLASH
SPLASH
THIS SWEET LITTLE THING IS LAZET.
SHE PLAYS THE ORGAN HERE AT THE CHURCH.
SHE CAN CHANGE HER APPEARANCE. SHE'S WHAT THEY CALL A "NOEL MERMAID."
Quite a rare sight, no?
Here. Drink this.
OOOH...
SHE'S A MER-MAID...
I GUESS SHE CAN'T TALK.
SHE'S TAKEN QUITE A LIKING TO YOU, TEITO-KUN.
She's usually so shy.

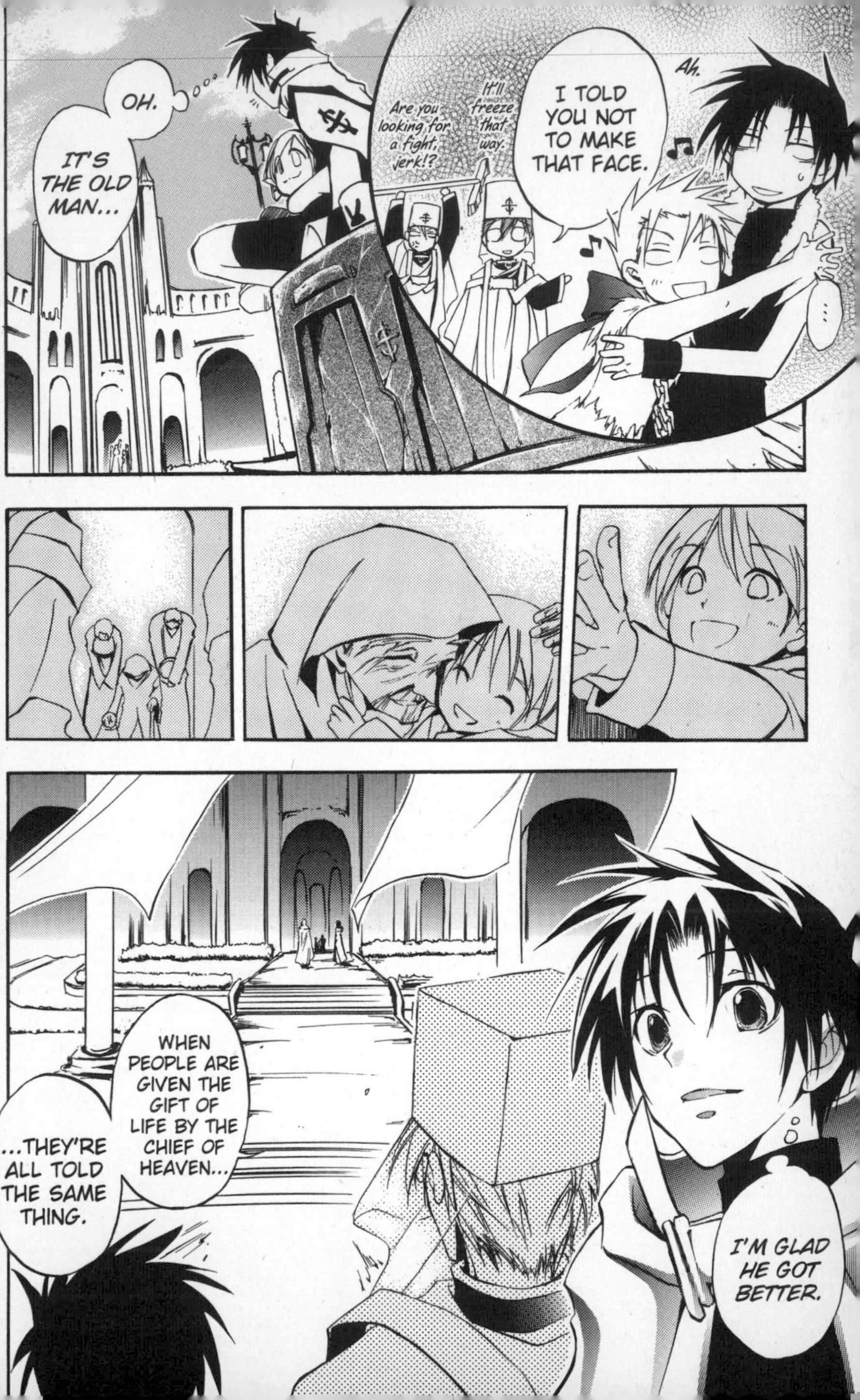
Ah.
I TOLD YOU NOT TO MAKE THAT FACE.
It'll freeze that way.
Are you looking for a fight, jerk!?
OH.
IT'S THE OLD MAN...
I'M GLAD HE GOT BETTER.
WHEN PEOPLE ARE GIVEN THE GIFT OF LIFE BY THE CHIEF OF HEAVEN...
...THEY'RE ALL TOLD THE SAME THING.

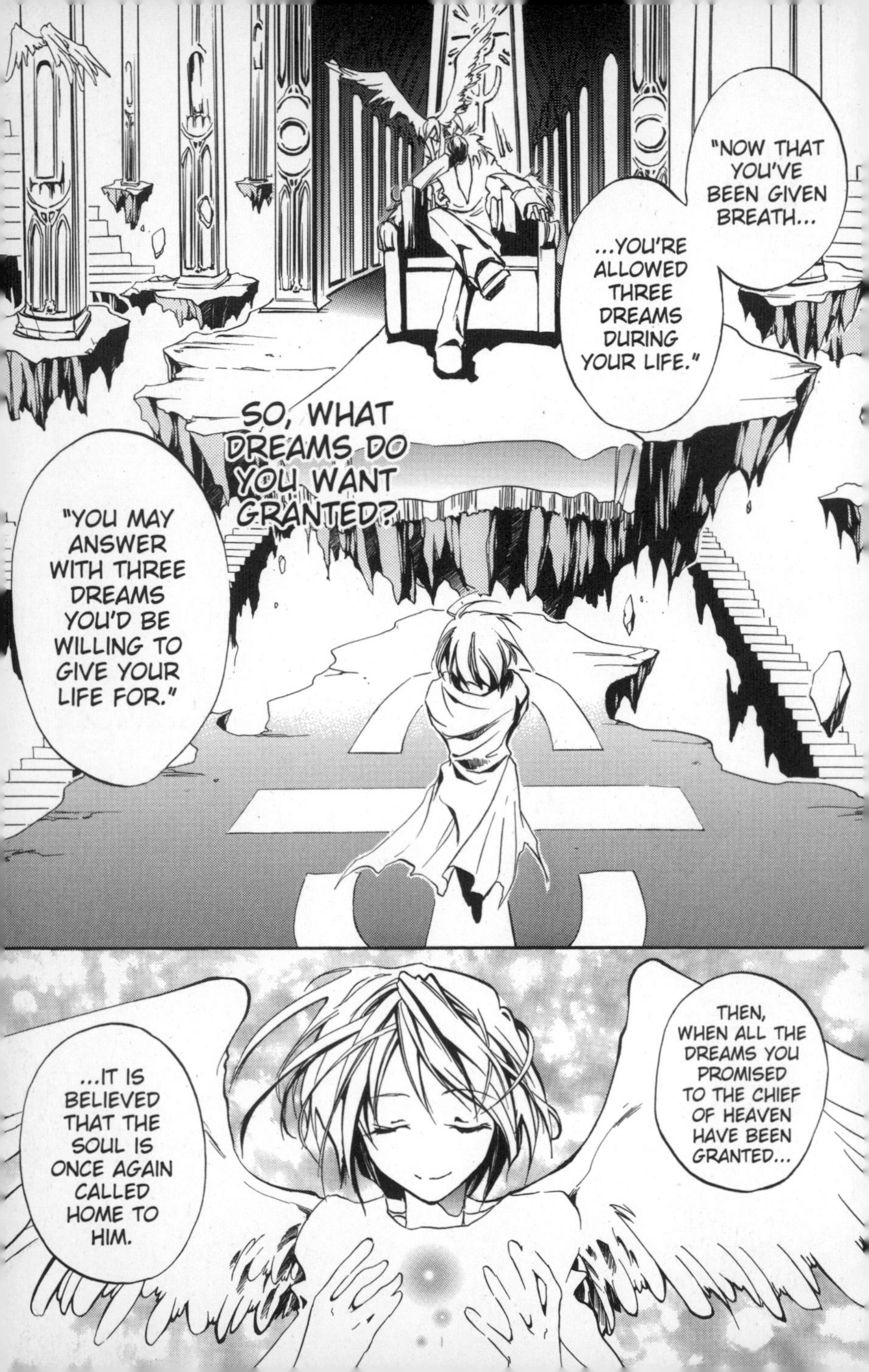
"NOW THAT YOU'VE BEEN GIVEN BREATH...
...YOU'RE ALLOWED THREE DREAMS DURING YOUR LIFE."
SO, WHAT DREAMS DO YOU WANT GRANTED?
"YOU MAY ANSWER WITH THREE DREAMS YOU'D BE WILLING TO GIVE YOUR LIFE FOR."
THEN, WHEN ALL THE DREAMS YOU PROMISED TO THE CHIEF OF HEAVEN HAVE BEEN GRANTED...
...IT IS BELIEVED THAT THE SOUL IS ONCE AGAIN CALLED HOME TO HIM.

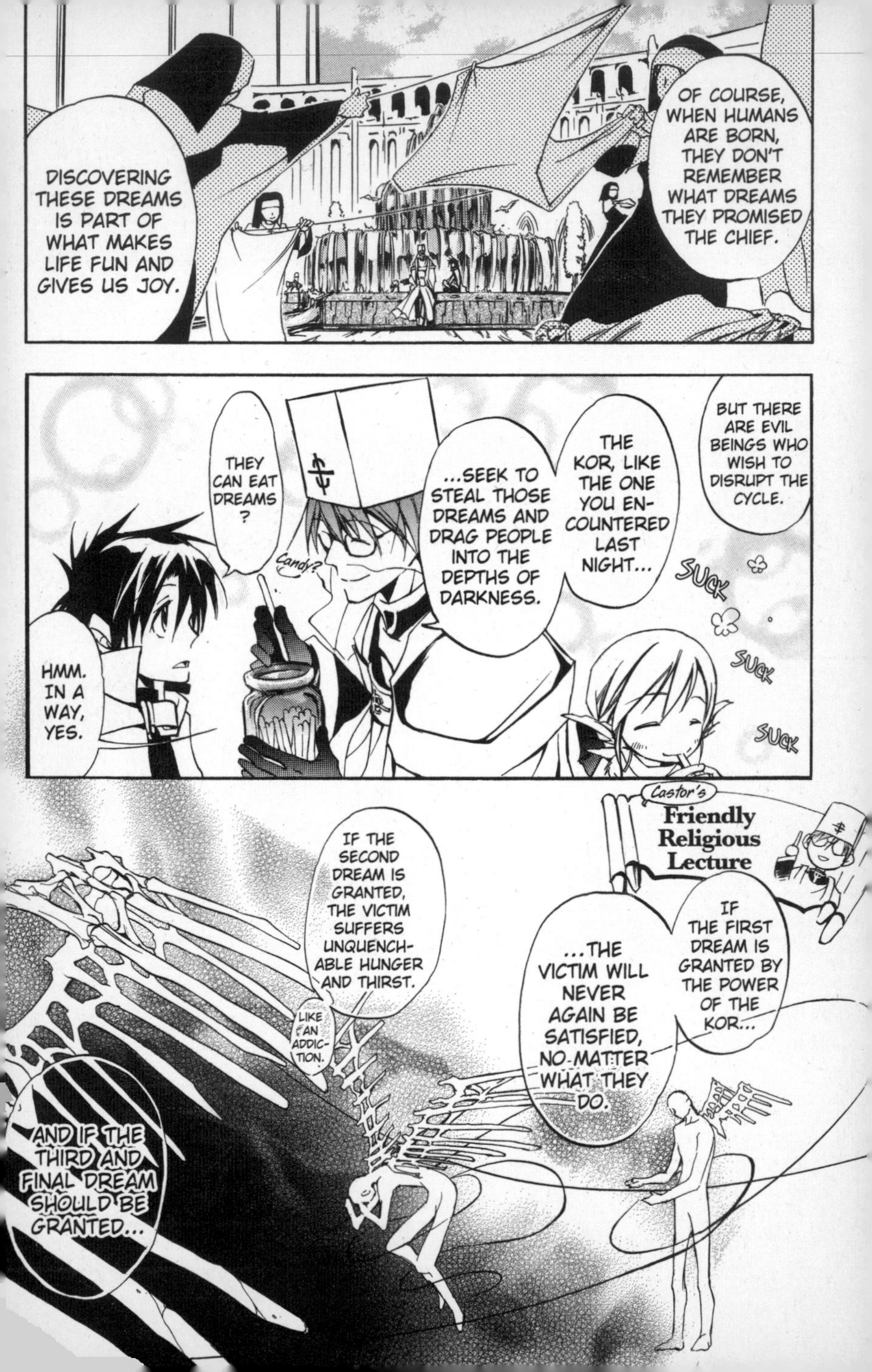

OF COURSE, WHEN HUMANS ARE BORN, THEY DON'T REMEMBER WHAT DREAMS THEY PROMISED THE CHIEF.
DISCOVERING THESE DREAMS IS PART OF WHAT MAKES LIFE FUN AND GIVES US JOY.
BUT THERE ARE EVIL BEINGS WHO WISH TO DISRUPT THE CYCLE.
THE KOR, LIKE THE ONE YOU EN-COUNTERED LAST NIGHT...
...SEEK TO STEAL THOSE DREAMS AND DRAG PEOPLE INTO THE DEPTHS OF DARKNESS.
SUCK
SUCK
SUCK
THEY CAN EAT DREAMS ?
Candy?
HMM. IN A WAY, YES.
Castor's Friendly Religious Lecture
IF THE FIRST DREAM IS GRANTED BY THE POWER OF THE KOR...
...THE VICTIM WILL NEVER AGAIN BE SATISFIED, NO MATTER WHAT THEY DO.
IF THE SECOND DREAM IS GRANTED, THE VICTIM SUFFERS UNQUENCH-ABLE HUNGER AND THIRST.
LIKE AN ADDIC-TION.
AND IF THE THIRD AND FINAL DREAM SHOULD BE GRANTED...

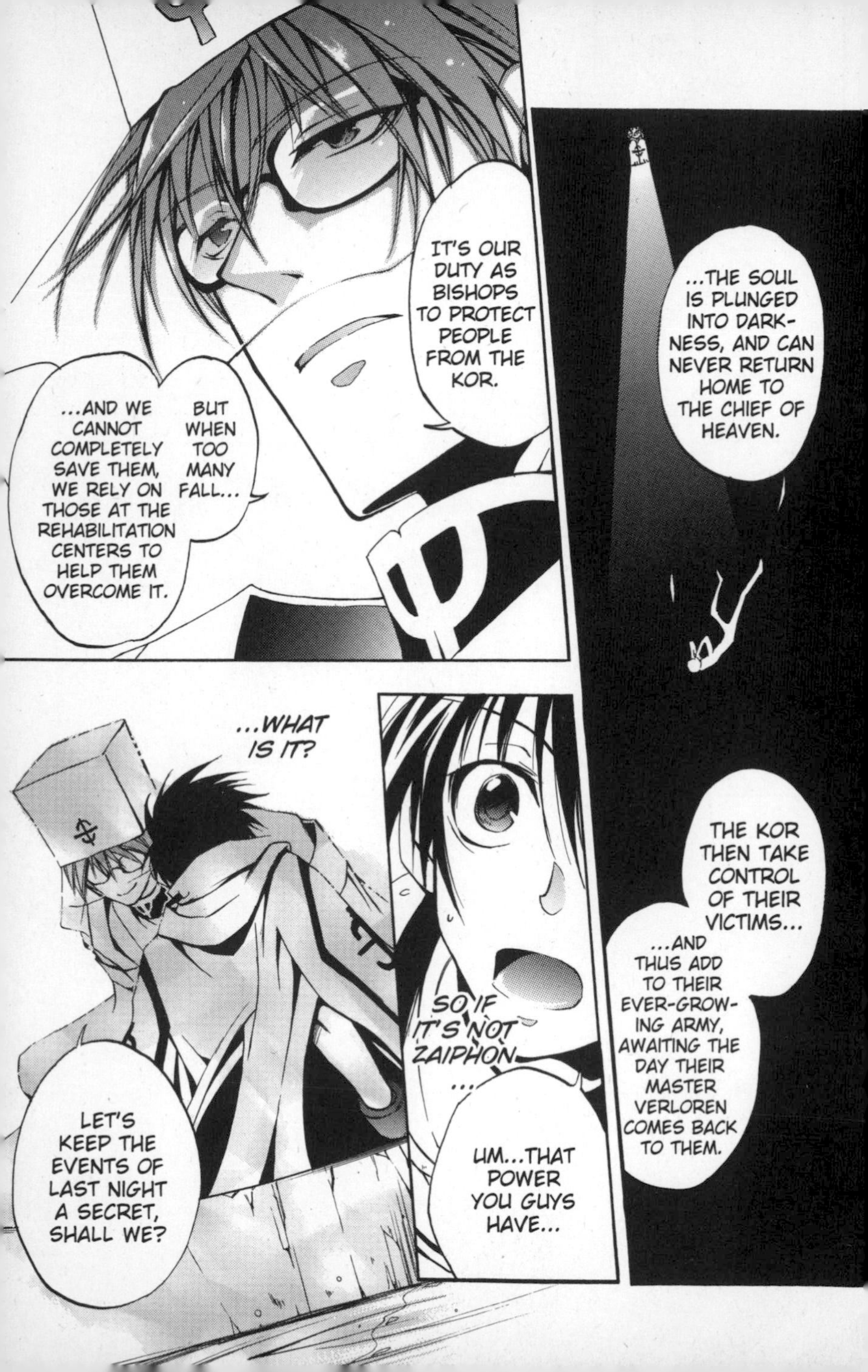
...THE SOUL IS PLUNGED INTO DARKNESS, AND CAN NEVER RETURN HOME TO THE CHIEF OF HEAVEN.
THE KOR THEN TAKE CONTROL OF THEIR VICTIMS...
...AND THUS ADD TO THEIR EVER-GROWING ARMY, AWAITING THE DAY THEIR MASTER VERLOREN COMES BACK TO THEM.
IT'S OUR DUTY AS BISHOPS TO PROTECT PEOPLE FROM THE KOR.
BUT WHEN TOO MANY FALL...
...AND WE CANNOT COMPLETELY SAVE THEM, WE RELY ON THOSE AT THE REHABILITATION CENTERS TO HELP THEM OVERCOME IT.
SO IF IT'S NOT ZAIPHON...
UM...THAT POWER YOU GUYS HAVE...
...WHAT IS IT?
LET'S KEEP THE EVENTS OF LAST NIGHT A SECRET, SHALL WE?

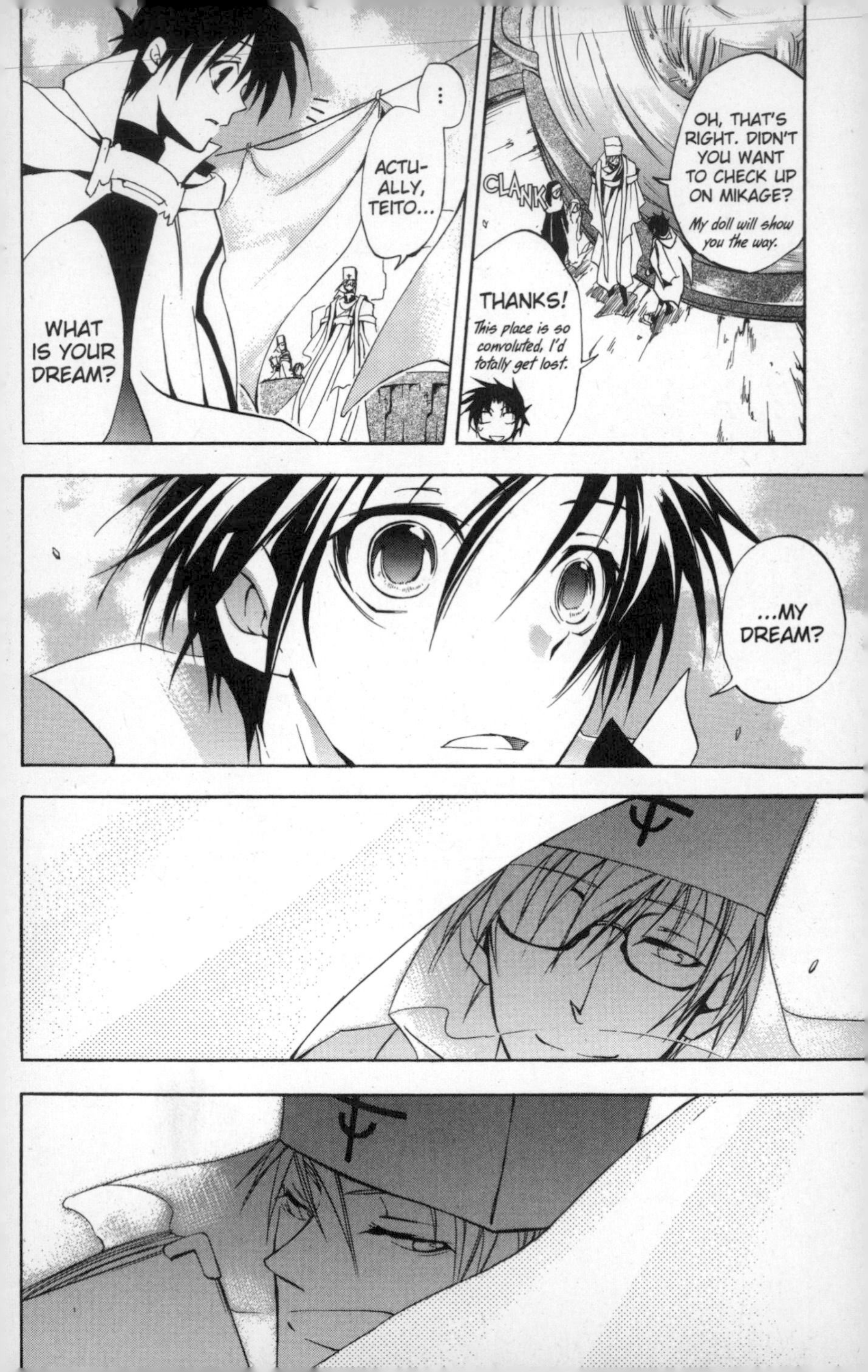
OH, THAT'S RIGHT. DIDN'T YOU WANT TO CHECK UP ON MIKAGE?
My doll will show you the way.
CLANK
THANKS!
This place is so convoluted, I'd totally get lost.
...
ACTU-ALLY, TEITO...
WHAT IS YOUR DREAM?
...MY DREAM?

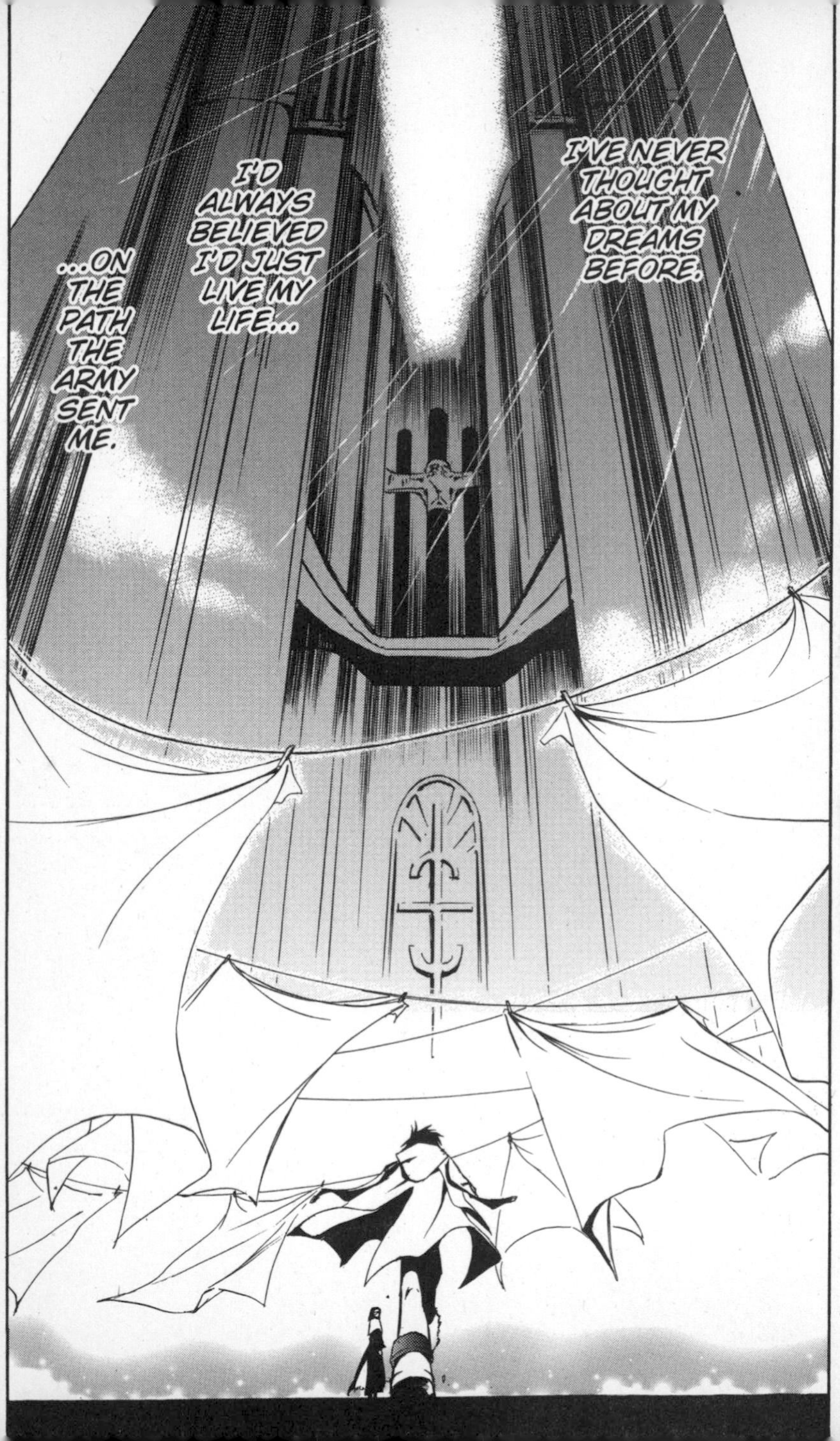
I'VE NEVER THOUGHT ABOUT MY DREAMS BEFORE.
I'D ALWAYS BELIEVED I'D JUST LIVE MY LIFE...
...ON THE PATH THE ARMY SENT ME.

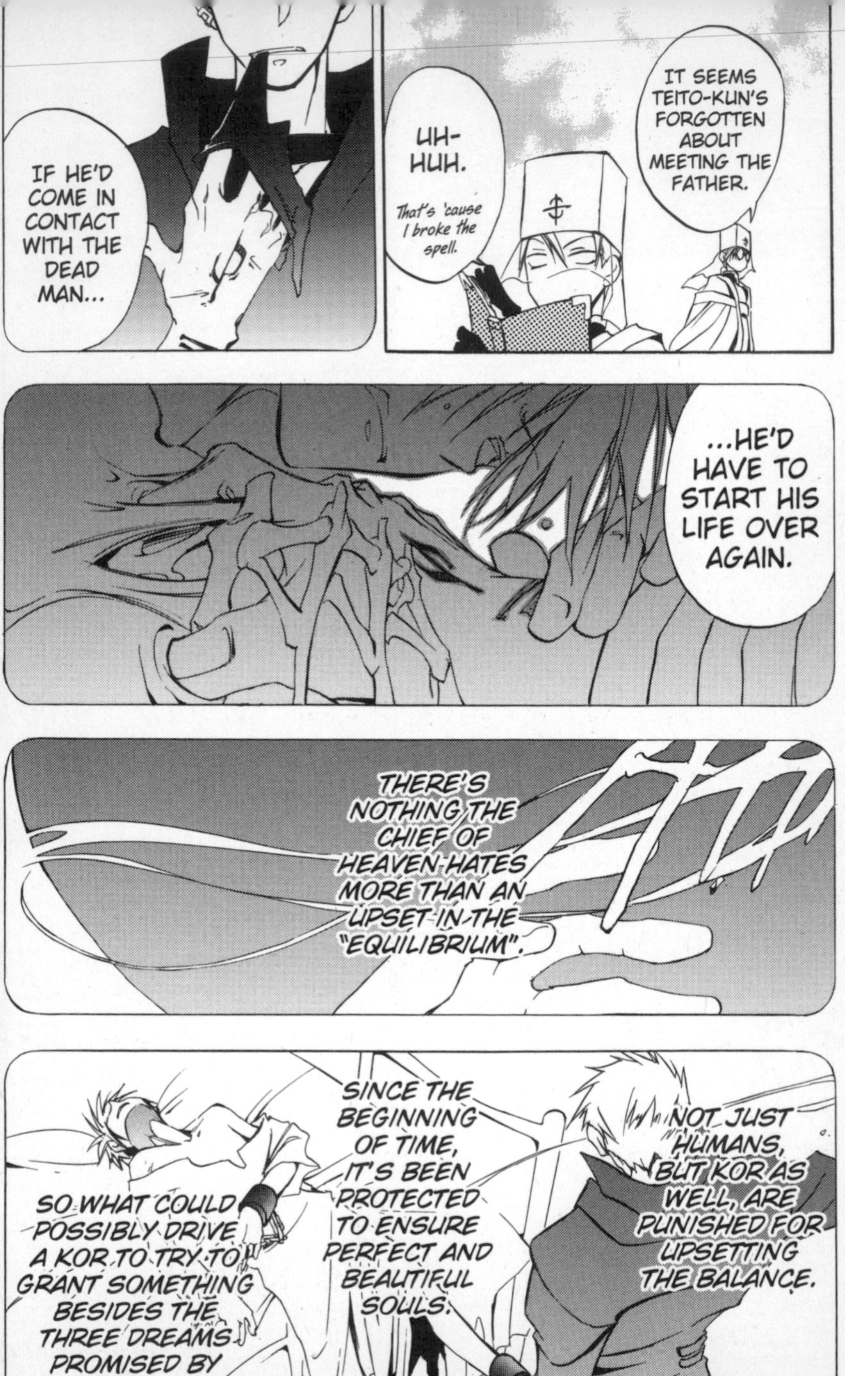
IT SEEMS TEITO-KUN'S FORGOTTEN ABOUT MEETING THE FATHER.
UH-HUH.
That's 'cause I broke the spell.
IF HE'D COME IN CONTACT WITH THE DEAD MAN...
...HE'D HAVE TO START HIS LIFE OVER AGAIN.
THERE'S NOTHING THE CHIEF OF HEAVEN HATES MORE THAN AN UPSET IN THE "EQUILIBRIUM".
NOT JUST HUMANS, BUT KOR AS WELL, ARE PUNISHED FOR UPSETTING THE BALANCE.
SINCE THE BEGINNING OF TIME, IT'S BEEN PROTECTED TO ENSURE PERFECT AND BEAUTIFUL SOULS.
SO WHAT COULD POSSIBLY DRIVE A KOR TO TRY TO GRANT SOMETHING BESIDES THE THREE DREAMS PROMISED BY GOD...?

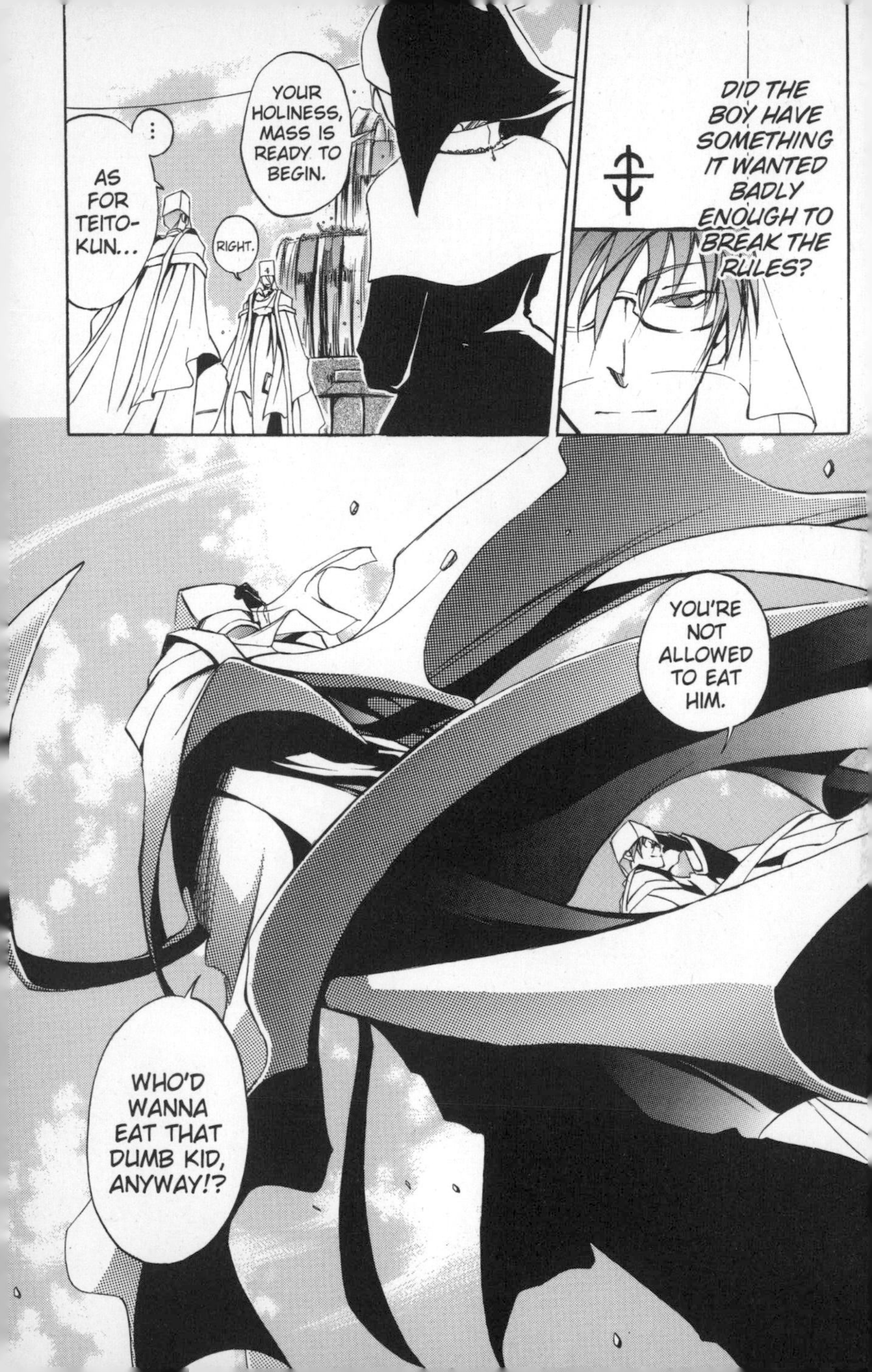
DID THE BOY HAVE SOMETHING IT WANTED BADLY ENOUGH TO BREAK THE RULES?
YOUR HOLINESS, MASS IS READY TO BEGIN.
...
AS FOR TEITO-KUN...
RIGHT.
YOU'RE NOT ALLOWED TO EAT HIM.
WHO'D WANNA EAT THAT DUMB KID, ANYWAY!?

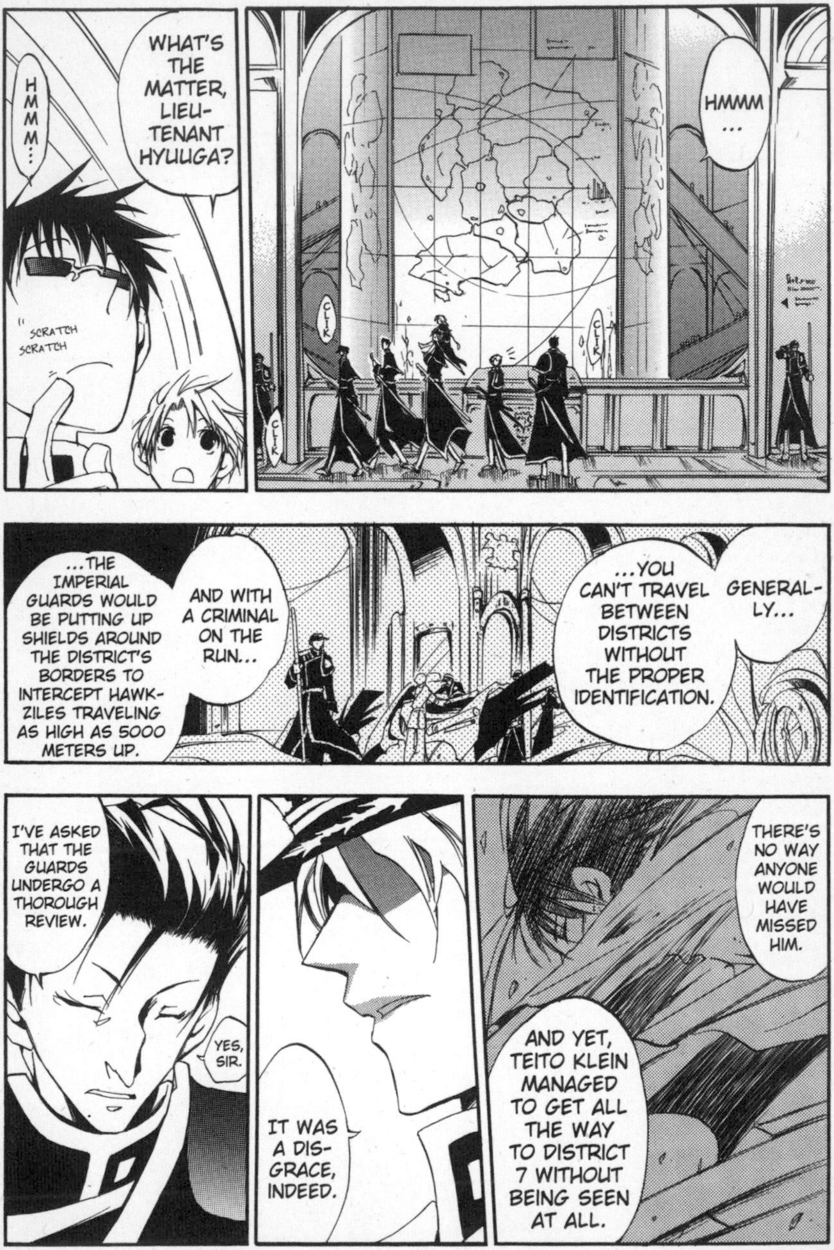
HMMM...
CLIK
CLIK
CLIK
WHAT'S THE MATTER, LIEUTENANT HYUUGA?
HMMM...
SCRATCH SCRATCH
GENERALLY...
...YOU CAN'T TRAVEL BETWEEN DISTRICTS WITHOUT THE PROPER IDENTIFICATION.
AND WITH A CRIMINAL ON THE RUN...
...THE IMPERIAL GUARDS WOULD BE PUTTING UP SHIELDS AROUND THE DISTRICT'S BORDERS TO INTERCEPT HAWKZILES TRAVELING AS HIGH AS 5000 METERS UP.
THERE'S NO WAY ANYONE WOULD HAVE MISSED HIM.
AND YET, TEITO KLEIN MANAGED TO GET ALL THE WAY TO DISTRICT 7 WITHOUT BEING SEEN AT ALL.
IT WAS A DISGRACE, INDEED.
I'VE ASKED THAT THE GUARDS UNDERGO A THOROUGH REVIEW.
YES, SIR.

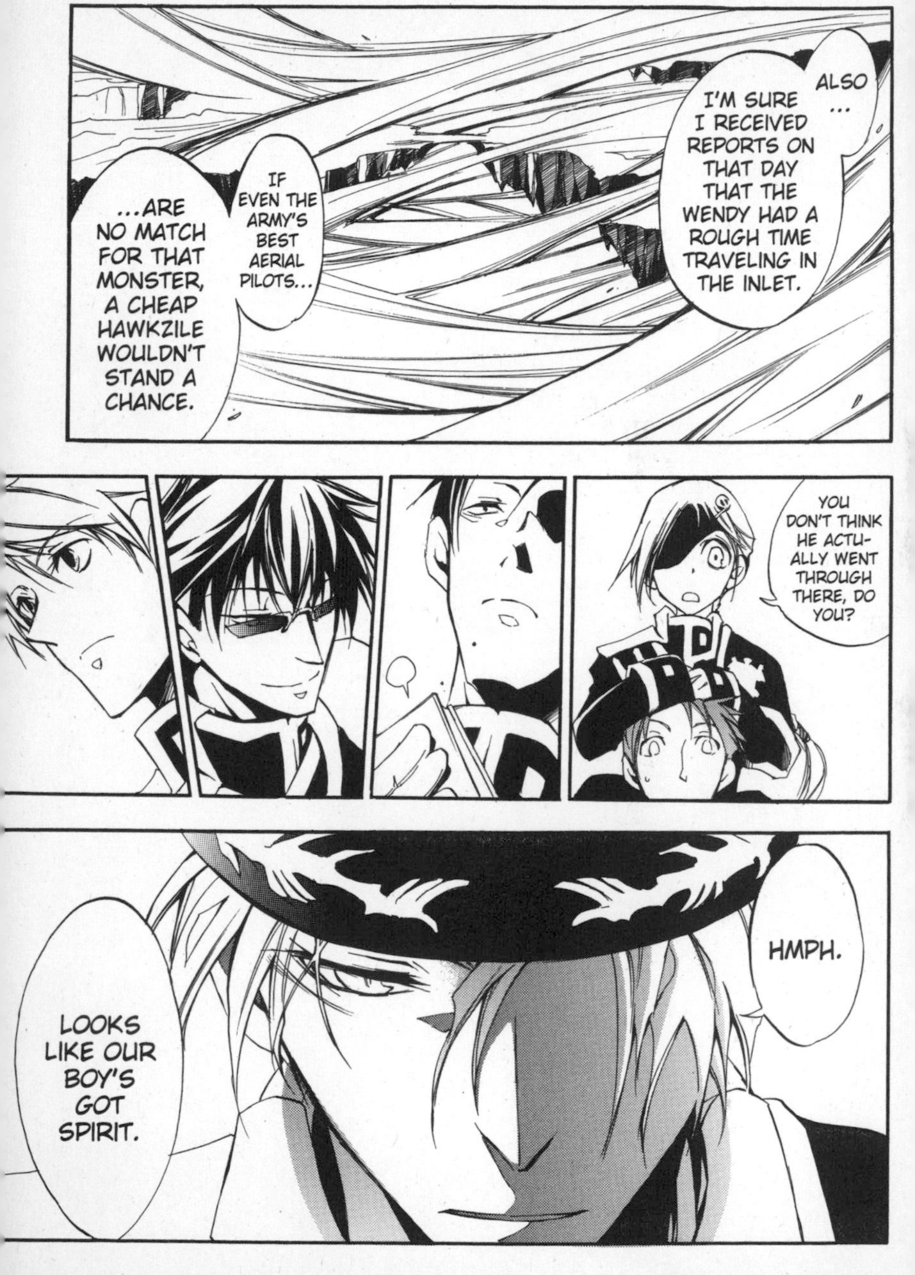
ALSO ... I'M SURE I RECEIVED REPORTS ON THAT DAY THAT THE WENDY HAD A ROUGH TIME TRAVELING IN THE INLET.
IF EVEN THE ARMY'S BEST AERIAL PILOTS...
...ARE NO MATCH FOR THAT MONSTER, A CHEAP HAWKZILE WOULDN'T STAND A CHANCE.
YOU DON'T THINK HE ACTUALLY WENT THROUGH THERE, DO YOU?
HMPH.
LOOKS LIKE OUR BOY'S GOT SPIRIT.

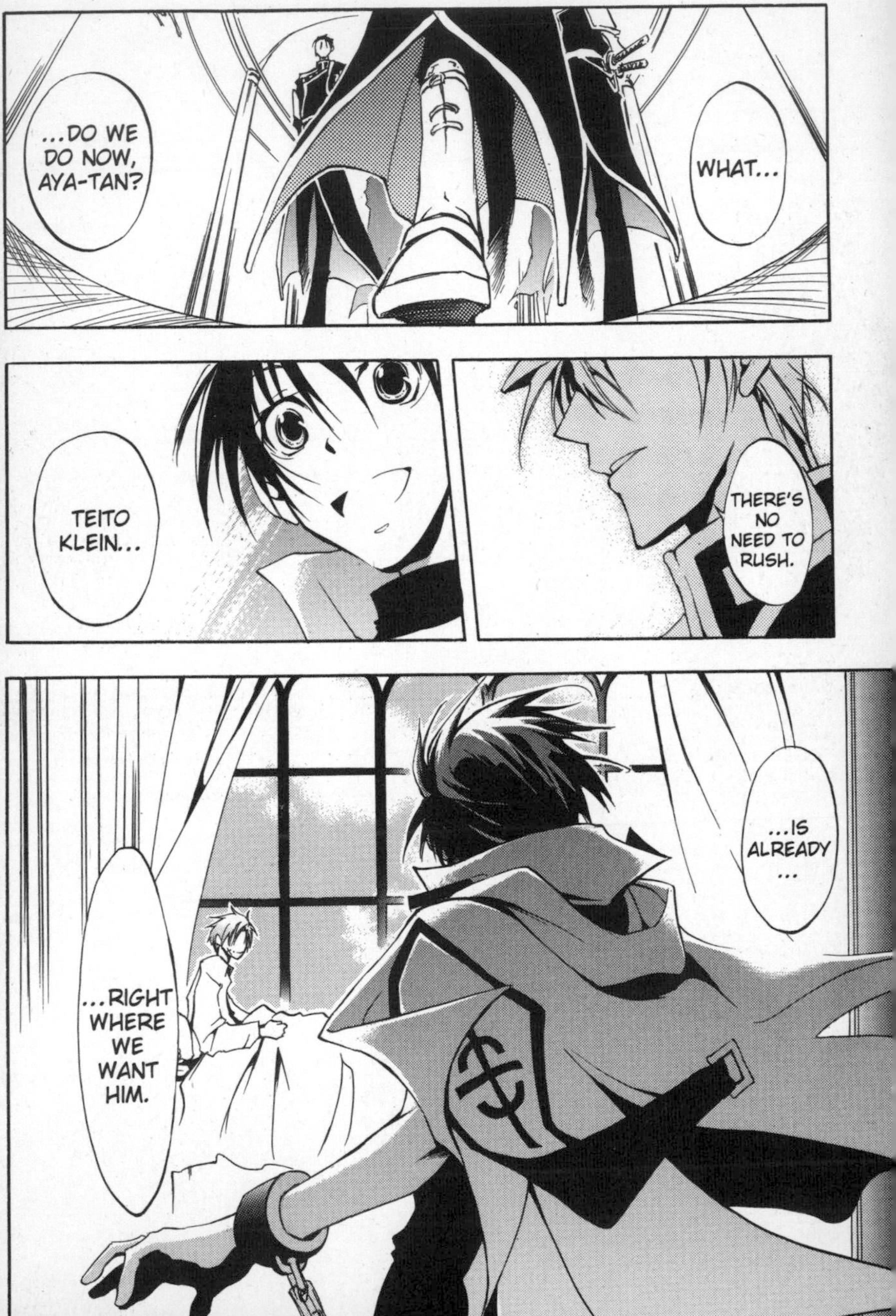
WHAT...
...DO WE DO NOW, AYA-TAN?
THERE'S NO NEED TO RUSH.
TEITO KLEIN...
...IS ALREADY ...
...RIGHT WHERE WE WANT HIM.

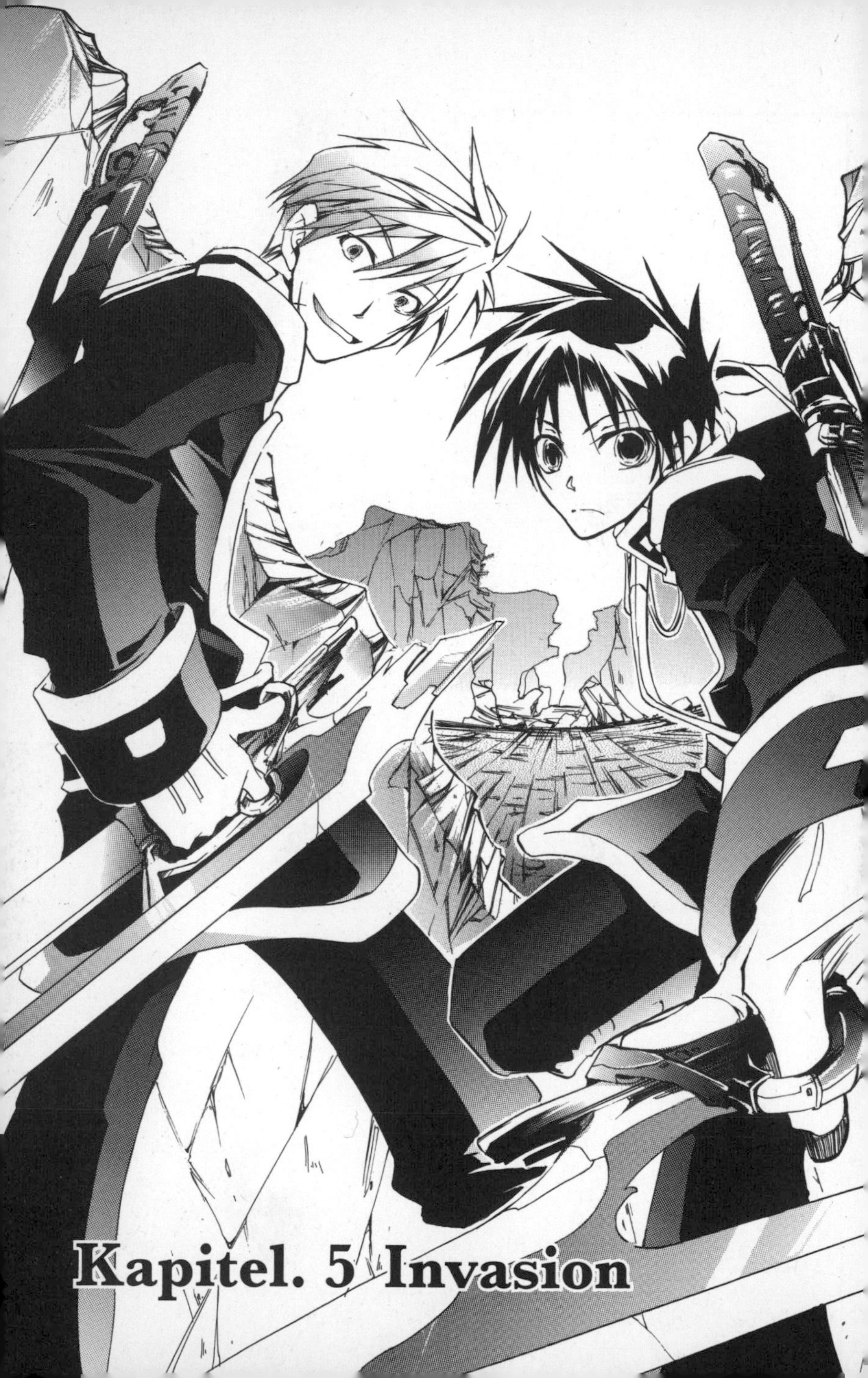
Kapitel. 5 Invasion

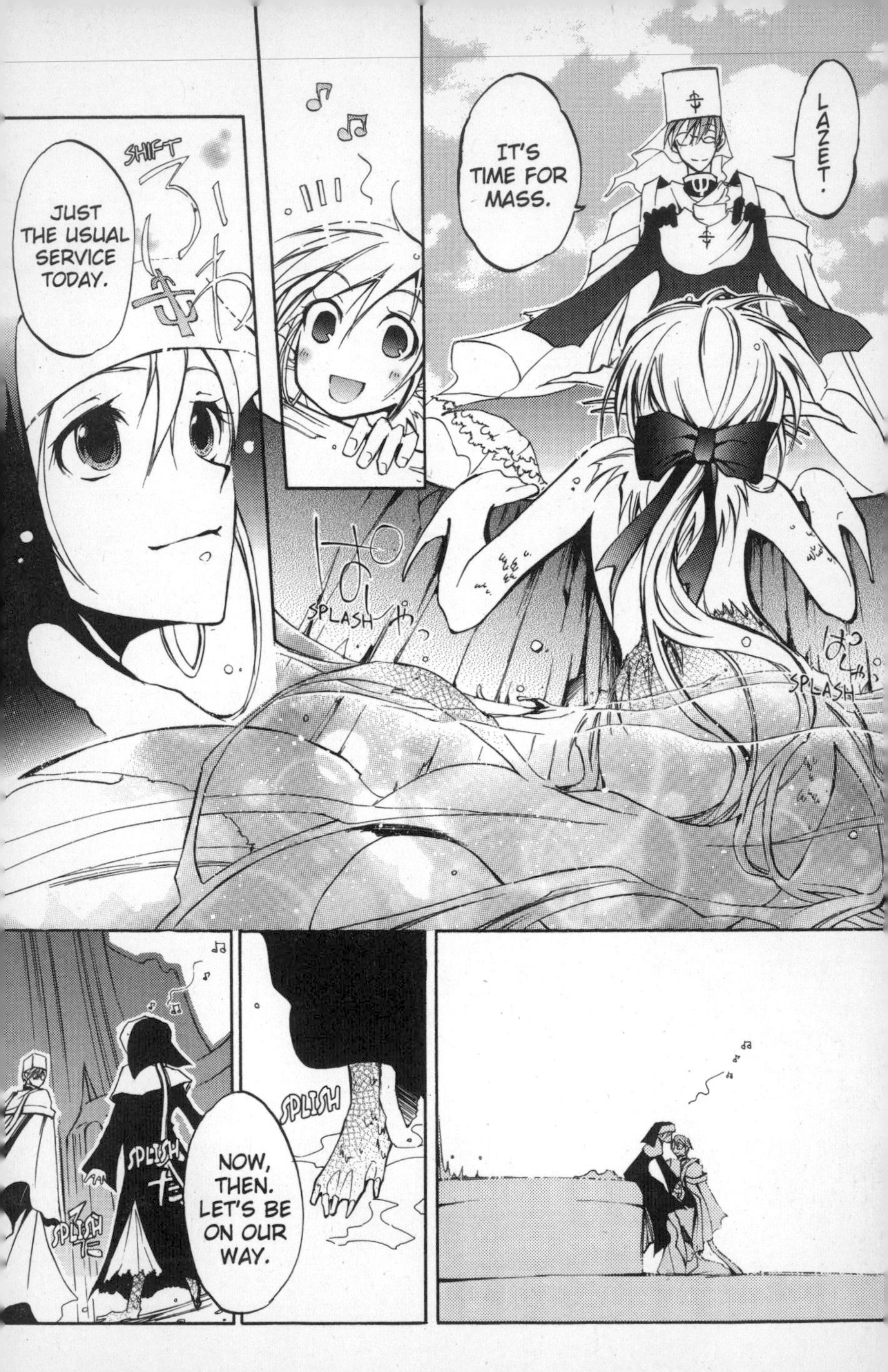
LAZET.
IT'S TIME FOR MASS.
SPLASH
SPLASH
SHIFT
JUST THE USUAL SERVICE TODAY.
SPLISH
NOW, THEN. LET'S BE ON OUR WAY.
SPLISH
SPLISH

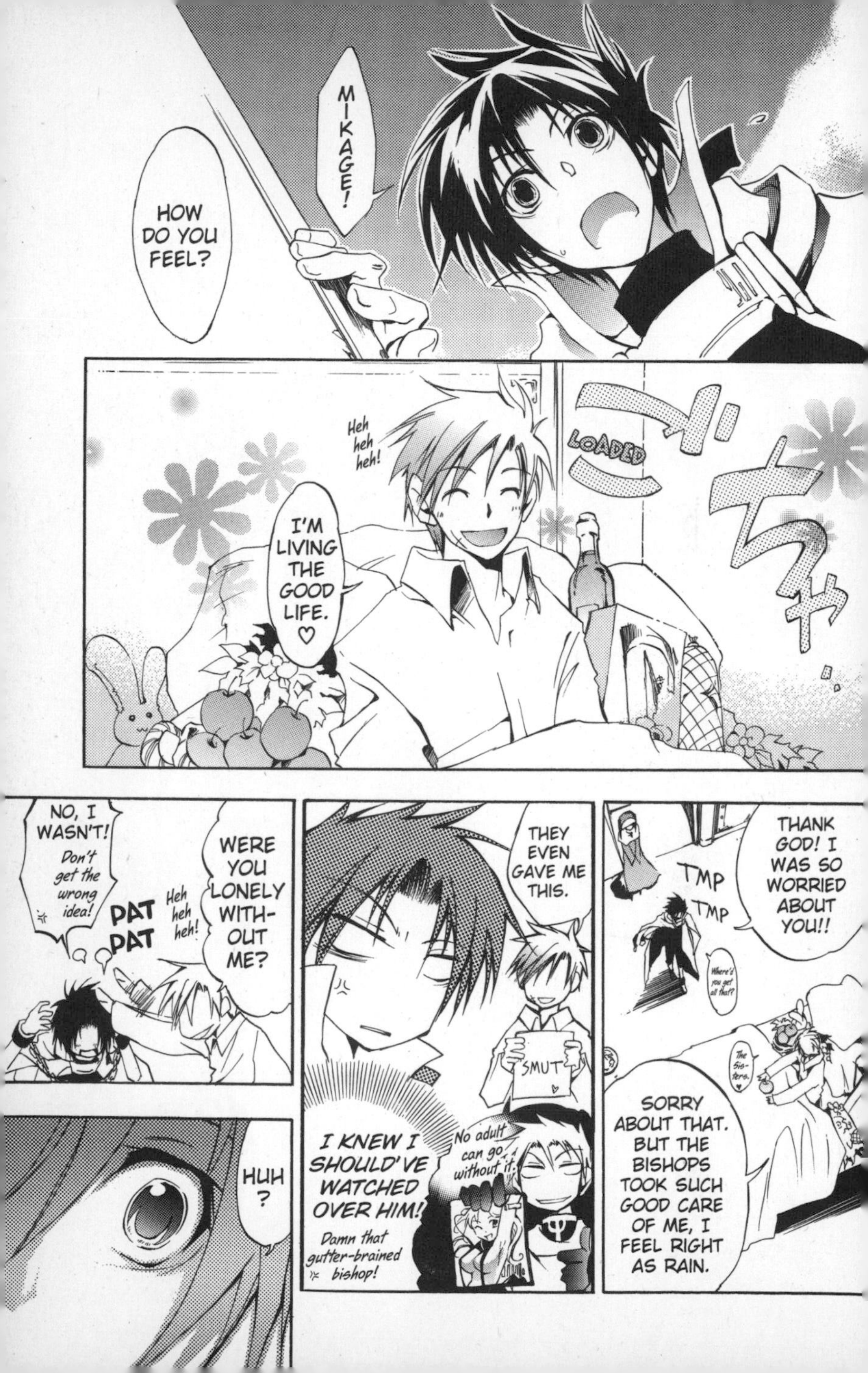

MIKAGE!
HOW DO YOU FEEL?
LOADED
Heh heh heh!
I'M LIVING THE GOOD LIFE. ♡
THANK GOD! I WAS SO WORRIED ABOUT YOU!!
TMP TMP
Where'd you get all that?
The Sisters. ♥
SORRY ABOUT THAT. BUT THE BISHOPS TOOK SUCH GOOD CARE OF ME, I FEEL RIGHT AS RAIN.
THEY EVEN GAVE ME THIS.
SMUT
No adult can go without it.
I KNEW I SHOULD'VE WATCHED OVER HIM!
Damn that gutter-brained bishop!
WERE YOU LONELY WITH-OUT ME?
Heh heh heh!
PAT PAT
NO, I WASN'T! Don't get the wrong idea!
HUH?

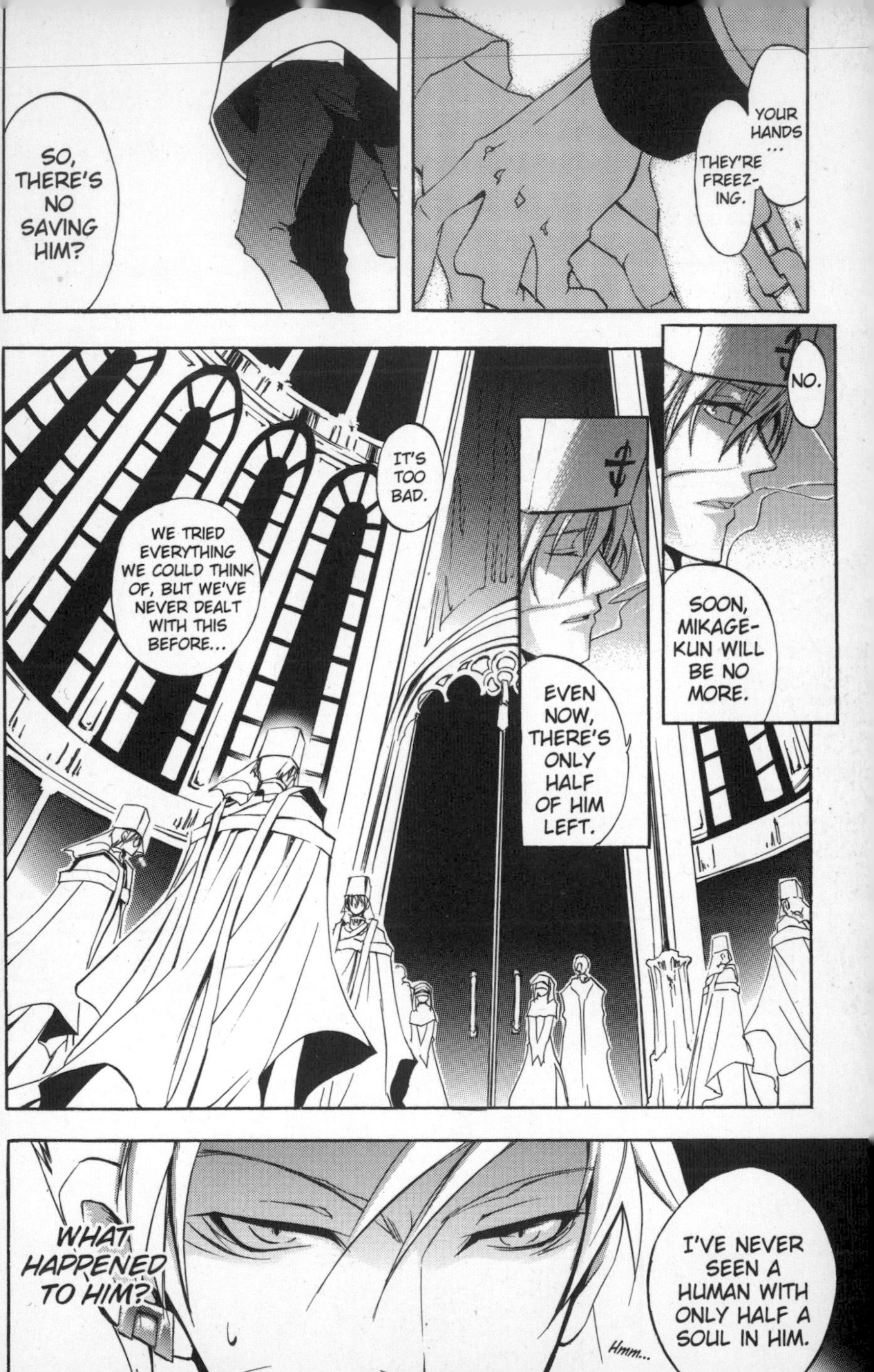

YOUR HANDS... THEY'RE FREEZ-ING.
SO, THERE'S NO SAVING HIM?
NO.
SOON, MIKAGE-KUN WILL BE NO MORE.
EVEN NOW, THERE'S ONLY HALF OF HIM LEFT.
IT'S TOO BAD.
WE TRIED EVERYTHING WE COULD THINK OF, BUT WE'VE NEVER DEALT WITH THIS BEFORE...
I'VE NEVER SEEN A HUMAN WITH ONLY HALF A SOUL IN HIM.
Hmm...
WHAT HAPPENED TO HIM?

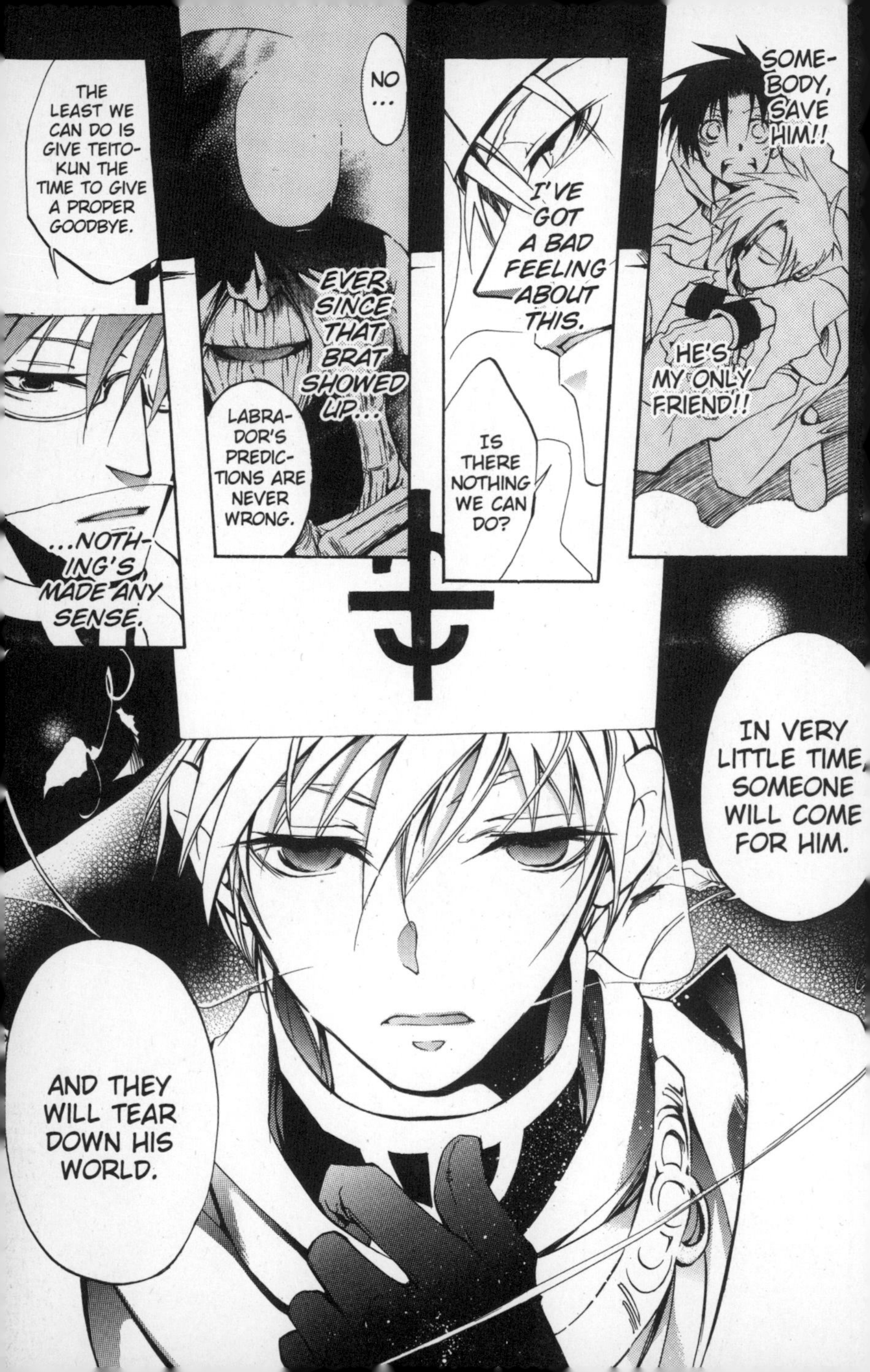

SOME-BODY, SAVE HIM!!
HE'S MY ONLY FRIEND!!
I'VE GOT A BAD FEELING ABOUT THIS.
IS THERE NOTHING WE CAN DO?
NO...
EVER SINCE THAT BRAT SHOWED UP...
LABRA-DOR'S PREDIC-TIONS ARE NEVER WRONG.
THE LEAST WE CAN DO IS GIVE TEITO-KUN THE TIME TO GIVE A PROPER GOODBYE.
...NOTH-ING'S MADE ANY SENSE.
IN VERY LITTLE TIME SOMEONE WILL COME FOR HIM.
AND THEY WILL TEAR DOWN HIS WORLD.

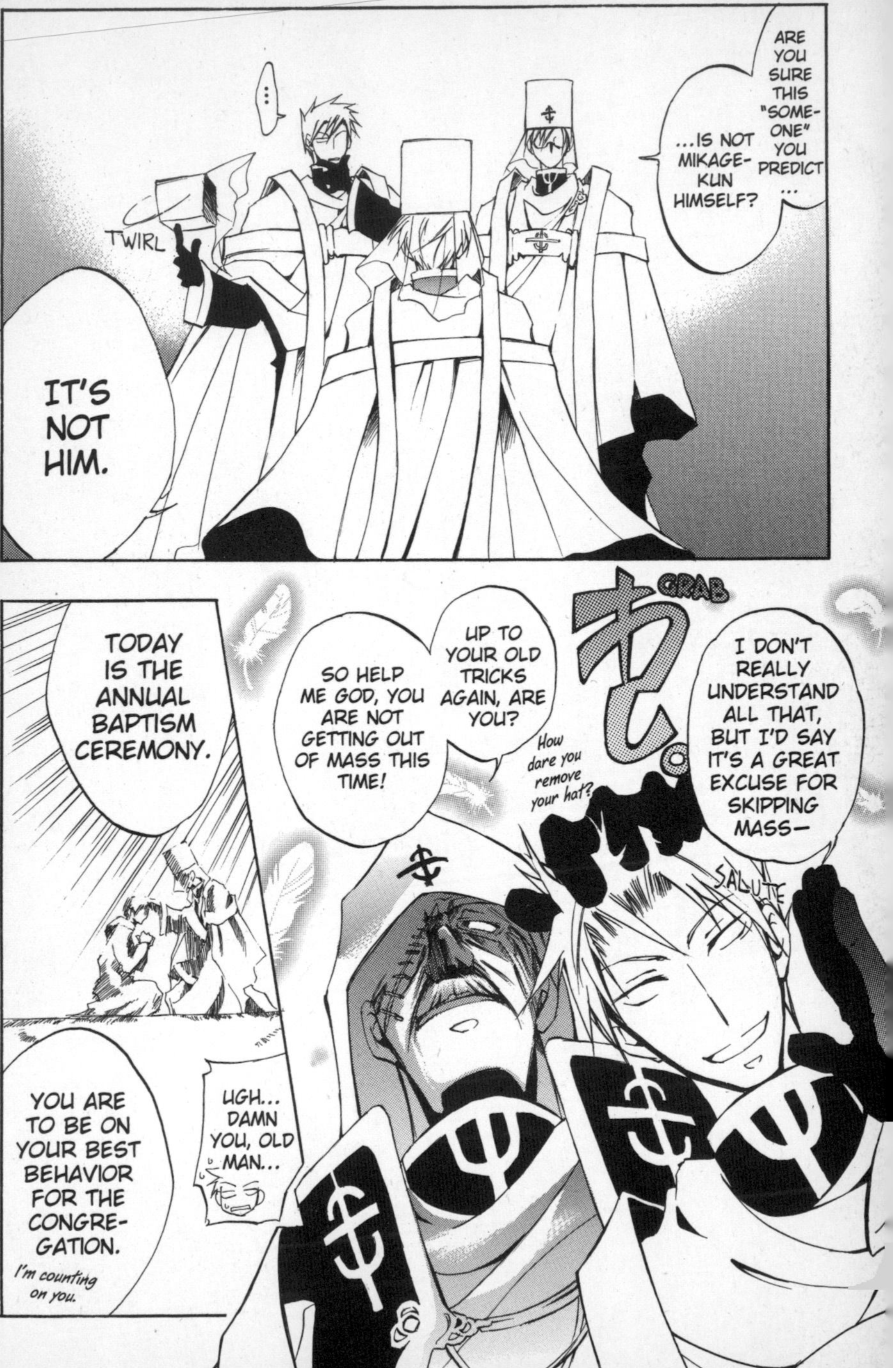
ARE YOU SURE THIS "SOME-ONE" YOU PREDICT ...
...IS NOT MIKAGE-KUN HIMSELF?
...
TWIRL
IT'S NOT HIM.
GRAB
I DON'T REALLY UNDERSTAND ALL THAT, BUT I'D SAY IT'S A GREAT EXCUSE FOR SKIPPING MASS—
How dare you remove your hat?
UP TO YOUR OLD TRICKS AGAIN, ARE YOU?
SO HELP ME GOD, YOU ARE NOT GETTING OUT OF MASS THIS TIME!
SALUTE
TODAY IS THE ANNUAL BAPTISM CEREMONY.
UGH... DAMN YOU, OLD MAN...
YOU ARE TO BE ON YOUR BEST BEHAVIOR FOR THE CONGREGATION.
I'm counting on you.

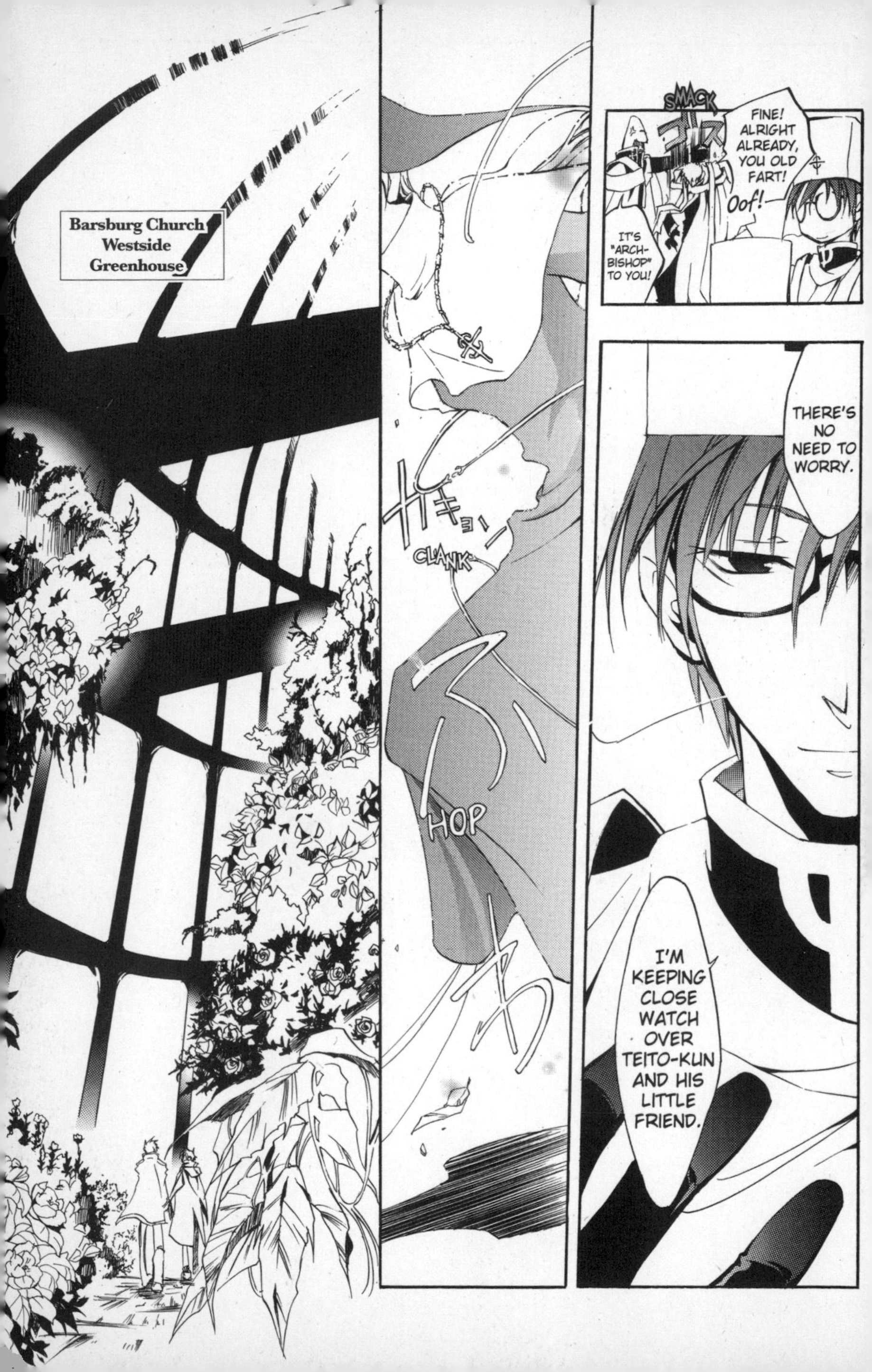
SMACK
FINE! ALRIGHT ALREADY, YOU OLD FART!
Oof!
IT'S "ARCH-BISHOP" TO YOU!
THERE'S NO NEED TO WORRY.
I'M KEEPING CLOSE WATCH OVER TEITO-KUN AND HIS LITTLE FRIEND.
CLANK
HOP
Barsburg Church Westside Greenhouse

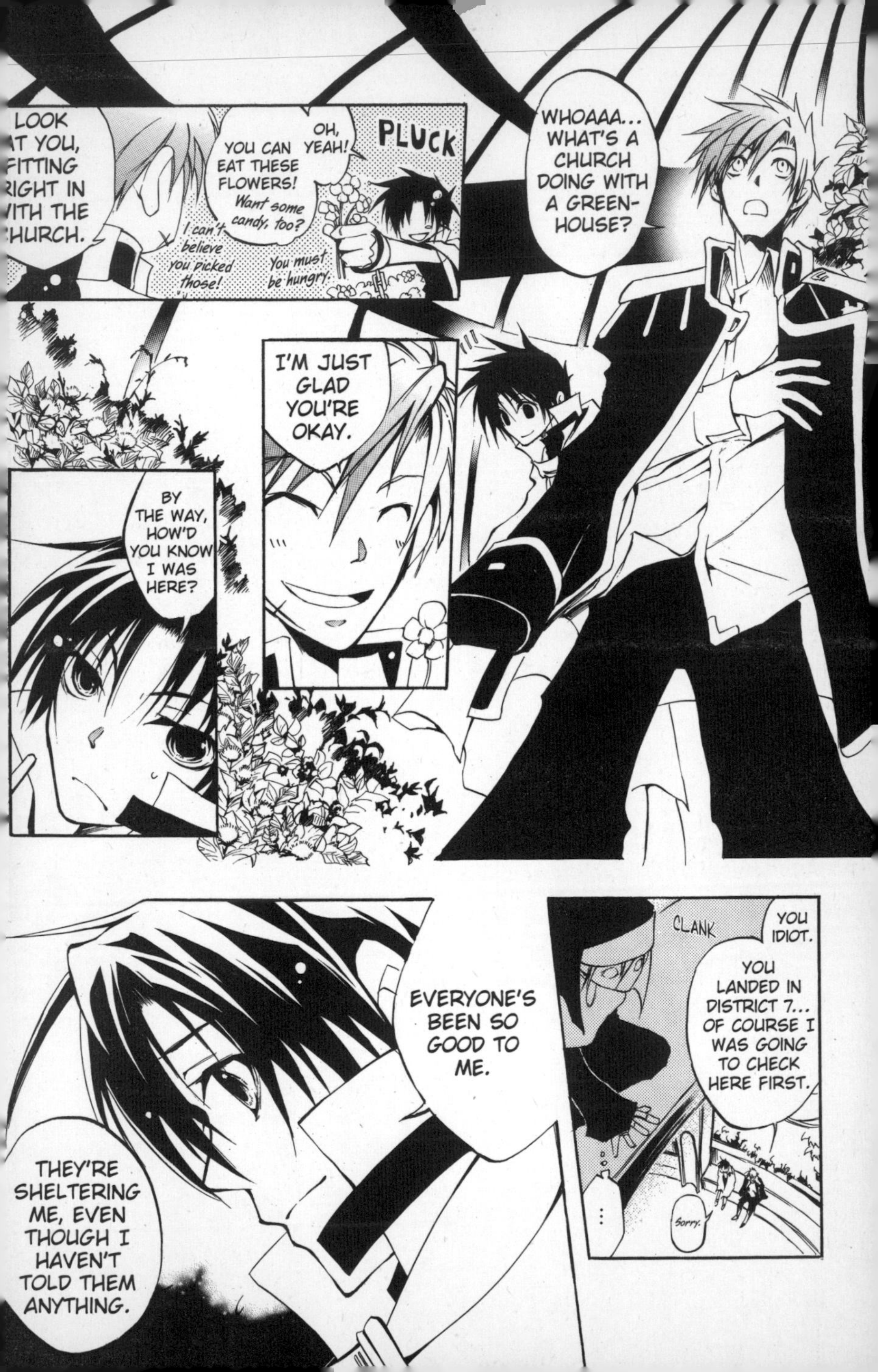
WHOAAA... WHAT'S A CHURCH DOING WITH A GREEN-HOUSE?
PLUCK
OH, YEAH!
YOU CAN EAT THESE FLOWERS!
Want some candy, too?
You must be hungry.
I can't believe you picked those!
LOOK AT YOU, FITTING RIGHT IN WITH THE CHURCH.
I'M JUST GLAD YOU'RE OKAY.
BY THE WAY, HOW'D YOU KNOW I WAS HERE?
CLANK
YOU IDIOT.
YOU LANDED IN DISTRICT 7... OF COURSE I WAS GOING TO CHECK HERE FIRST.
...
Sorry.
EVERYONE'S BEEN SO GOOD TO ME.
THEY'RE SHELTERING ME, EVEN THOUGH I HAVEN'T TOLD THEM ANYTHING.

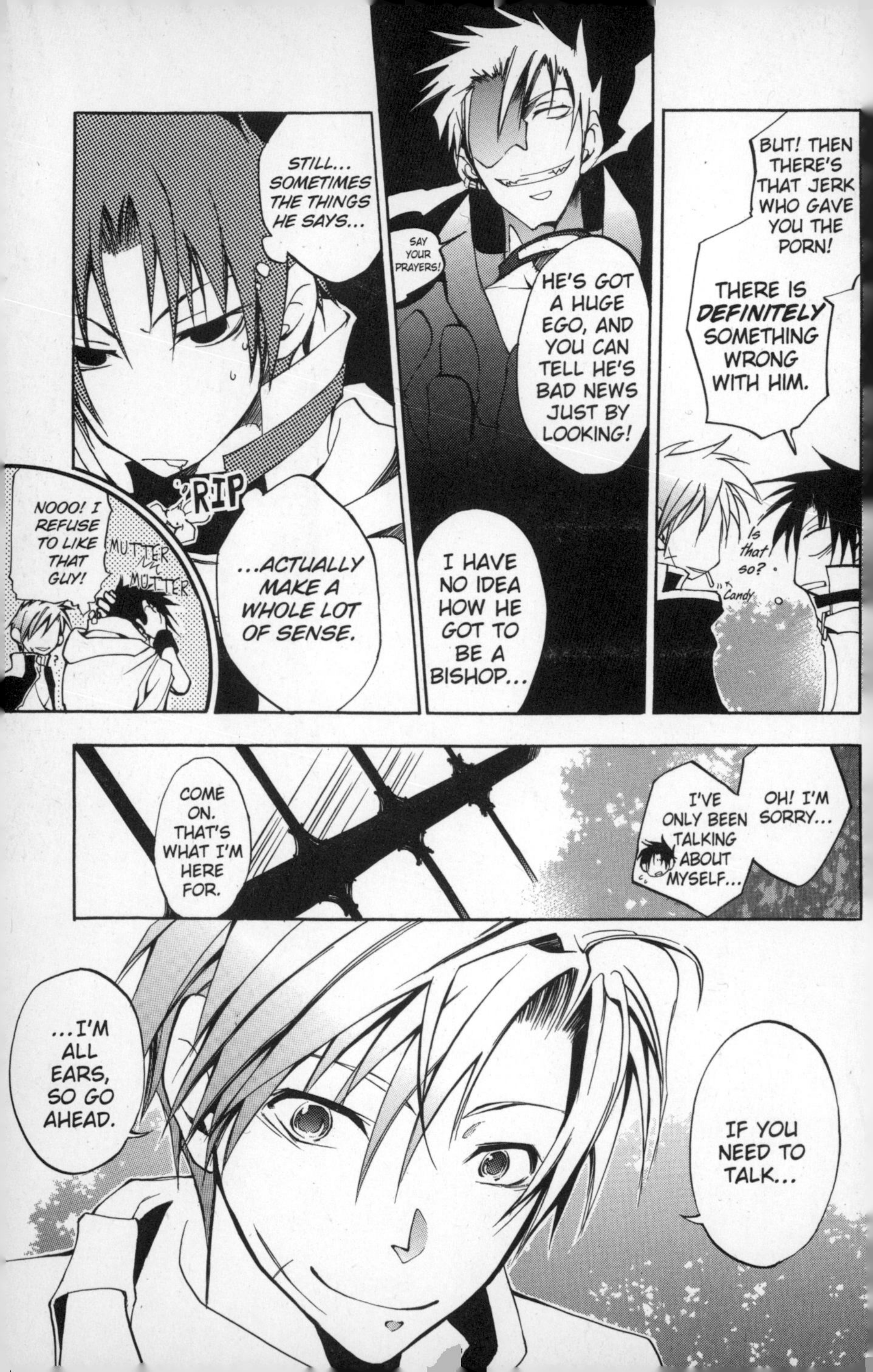
BUT! THEN THERE'S THAT JERK WHO GAVE YOU THE PORN!
THERE IS ***DEFINITELY*** SOMETHING WRONG WITH HIM.
Is that so?
Candy
SAY YOUR PRAYERS!
HE'S GOT A HUGE EGO, AND YOU CAN TELL HE'S BAD NEWS JUST BY LOOKING!
I HAVE NO IDEA HOW HE GOT TO BE A BISHOP...
STILL... SOMETIMES THE THINGS HE SAYS...
RIP
...ACTUALLY MAKE A WHOLE LOT OF SENSE.
NOOO! I REFUSE TO LIKE THAT GUY!
MUTTER MUTTER
OH! I'M SORRY...
I'VE ONLY BEEN TALKING ABOUT MYSELF...
COME ON. THAT'S WHAT I'M HERE FOR.
IF YOU NEED TO TALK...
...I'M ALL EARS, SO GO AHEAD.

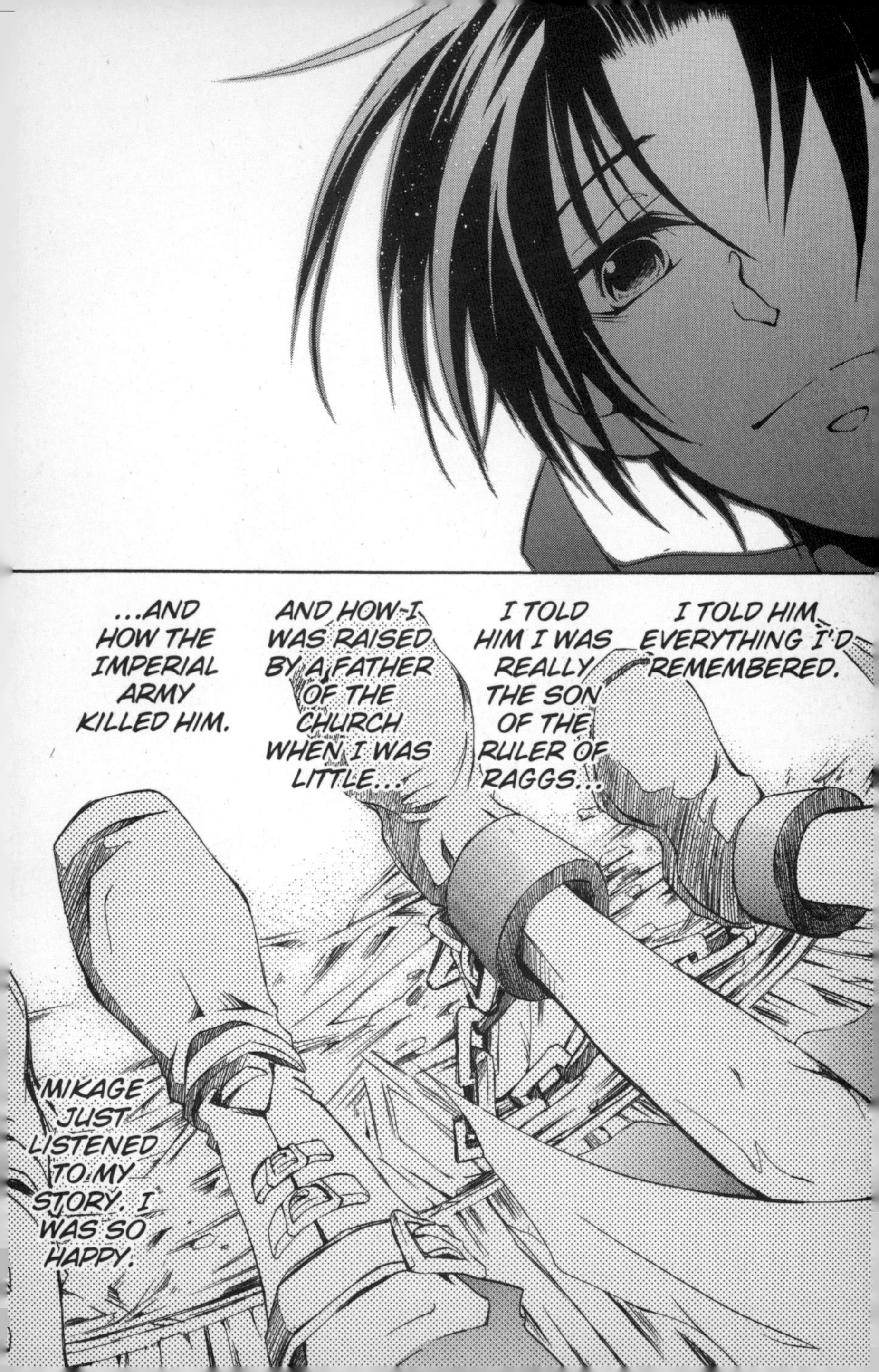
I TOLD HIM EVERYTHING I'D REMEMBERED.
I TOLD HIM I WAS REALLY THE SON OF THE RULER OF RAGGS...
AND HOW I WAS RAISED BY A FATHER OF THE CHURCH WHEN I WAS LITTLE...
...AND HOW THE IMPERIAL ARMY KILLED HIM.
MIKAGE JUST LISTENED TO MY STORY. I WAS SO HAPPY.

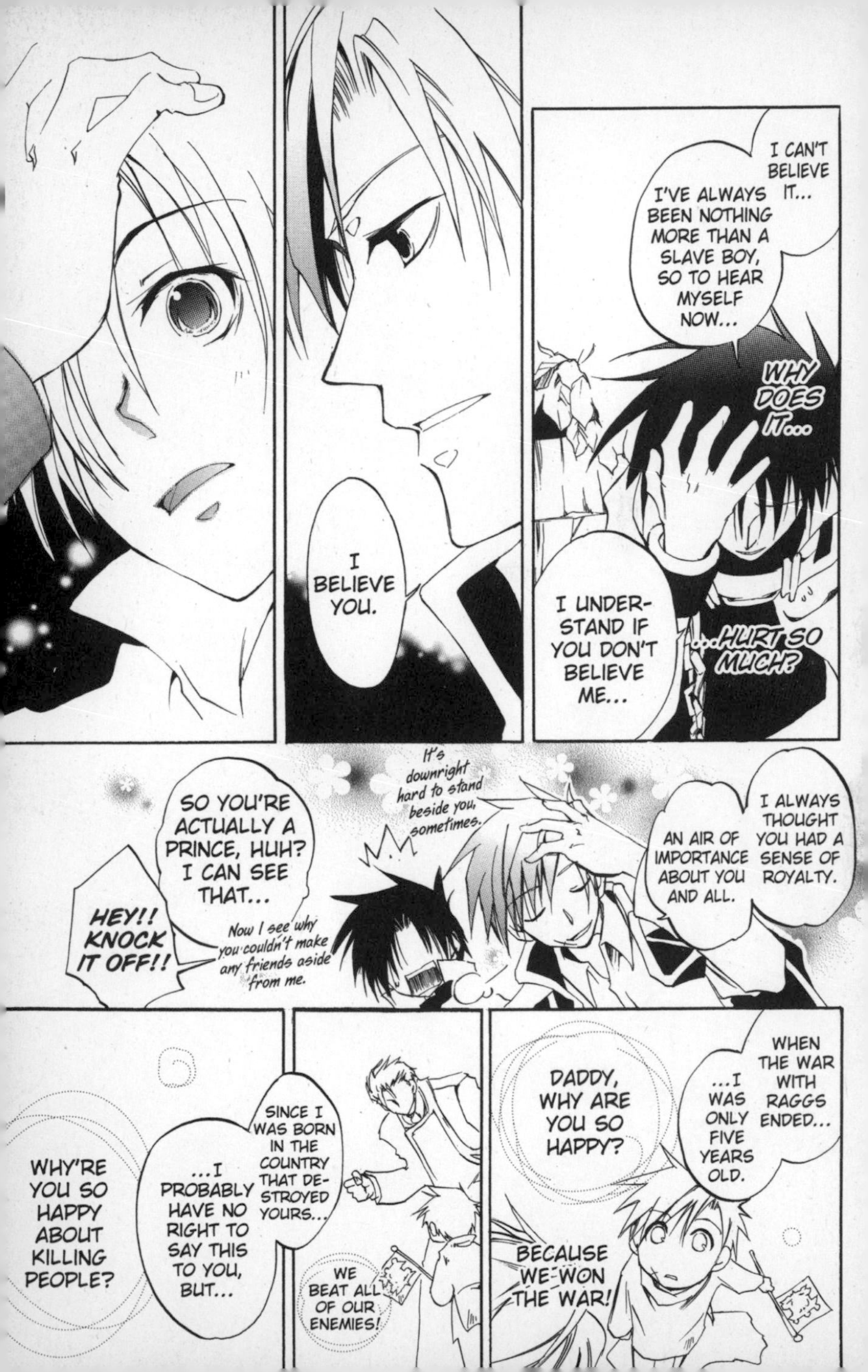
I CAN'T BELIEVE IT...
I'VE ALWAYS BEEN NOTHING MORE THAN A SLAVE BOY, SO TO HEAR MYSELF NOW...
WHY DOES IT...
...HURT SO MUCH?
I UNDERSTAND IF YOU DON'T BELIEVE ME...
I BELIEVE YOU.
I ALWAYS THOUGHT YOU HAD A SENSE OF ROYALTY.
AN AIR OF IMPORTANCE ABOUT YOU AND ALL.
It's downright hard to stand beside you, sometimes.
SO YOU'RE ACTUALLY A PRINCE, HUH? I CAN SEE THAT...
Now I see why you couldn't make any friends aside from me.
HEY!! KNOCK IT OFF!!
WHEN THE WAR WITH RAGGS ENDED...
...I WAS ONLY FIVE YEARS OLD.
DADDY, WHY ARE YOU SO HAPPY?
BECAUSE WE WON THE WAR!
SINCE I WAS BORN IN THE COUNTRY THAT DESTROYED YOURS...
WE BEAT ALL OF OUR ENEMIES!
...I PROBABLY HAVE NO RIGHT TO SAY THIS TO YOU, BUT...
WHY'RE YOU SO HAPPY ABOUT KILLING PEOPLE?

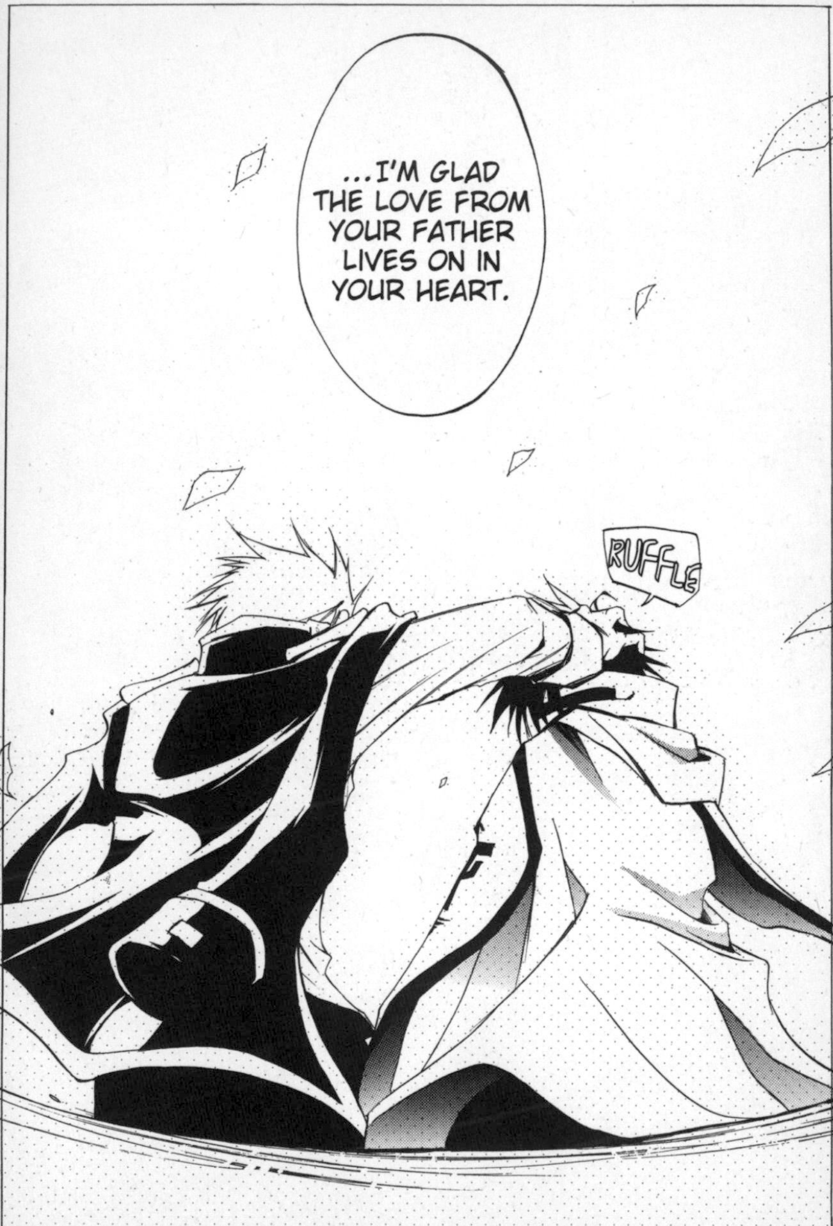
...I'M GLAD THE LOVE FROM YOUR FATHER LIVES ON IN YOUR HEART.
RUFFLE

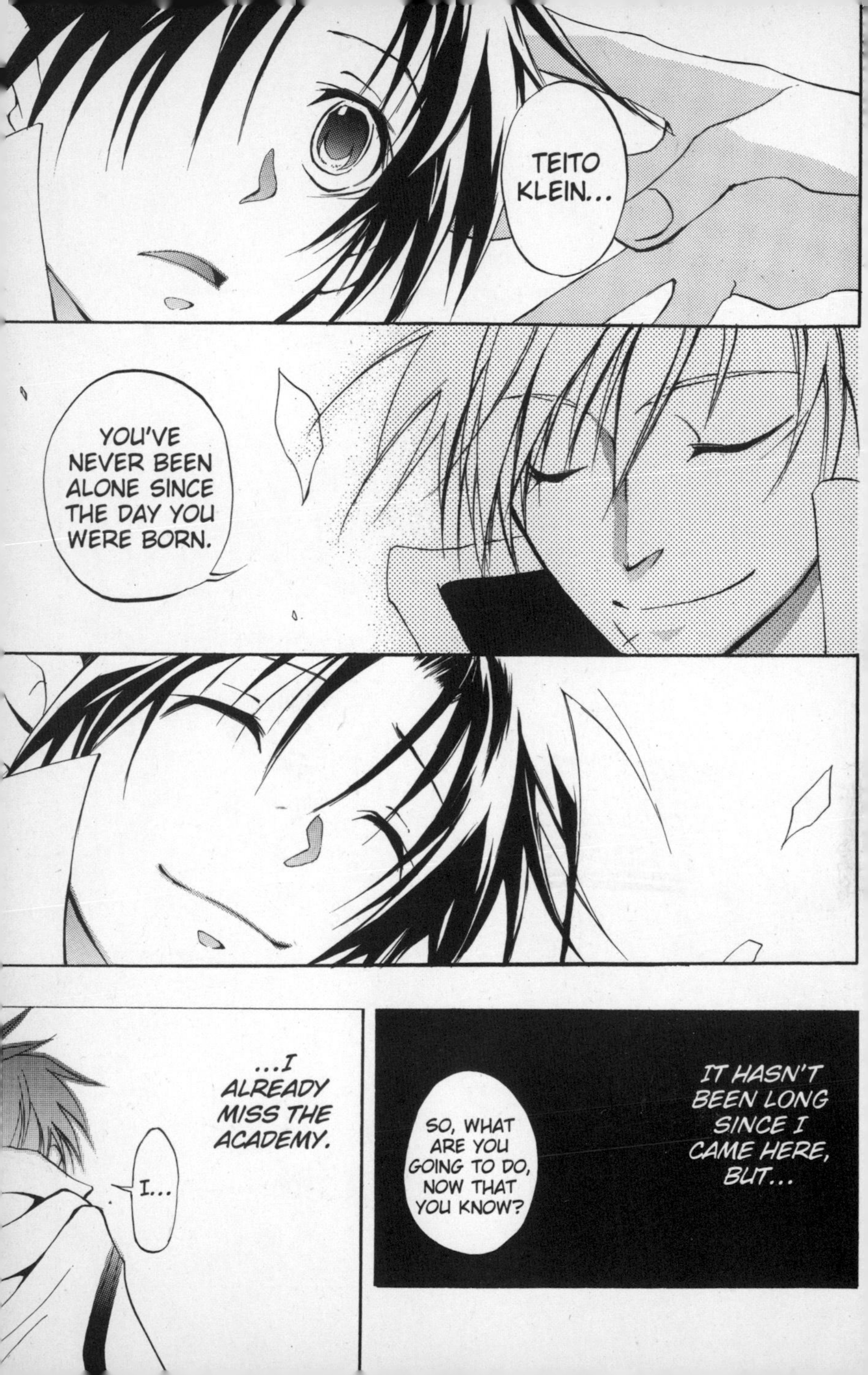
TEITO KLEIN...
YOU'VE NEVER BEEN ALONE SINCE THE DAY YOU WERE BORN.
IT HASN'T BEEN LONG SINCE I CAME HERE, BUT...
SO, WHAT ARE YOU GOING TO DO, NOW THAT YOU KNOW?
...I ALREADY MISS THE ACADEMY.
I...

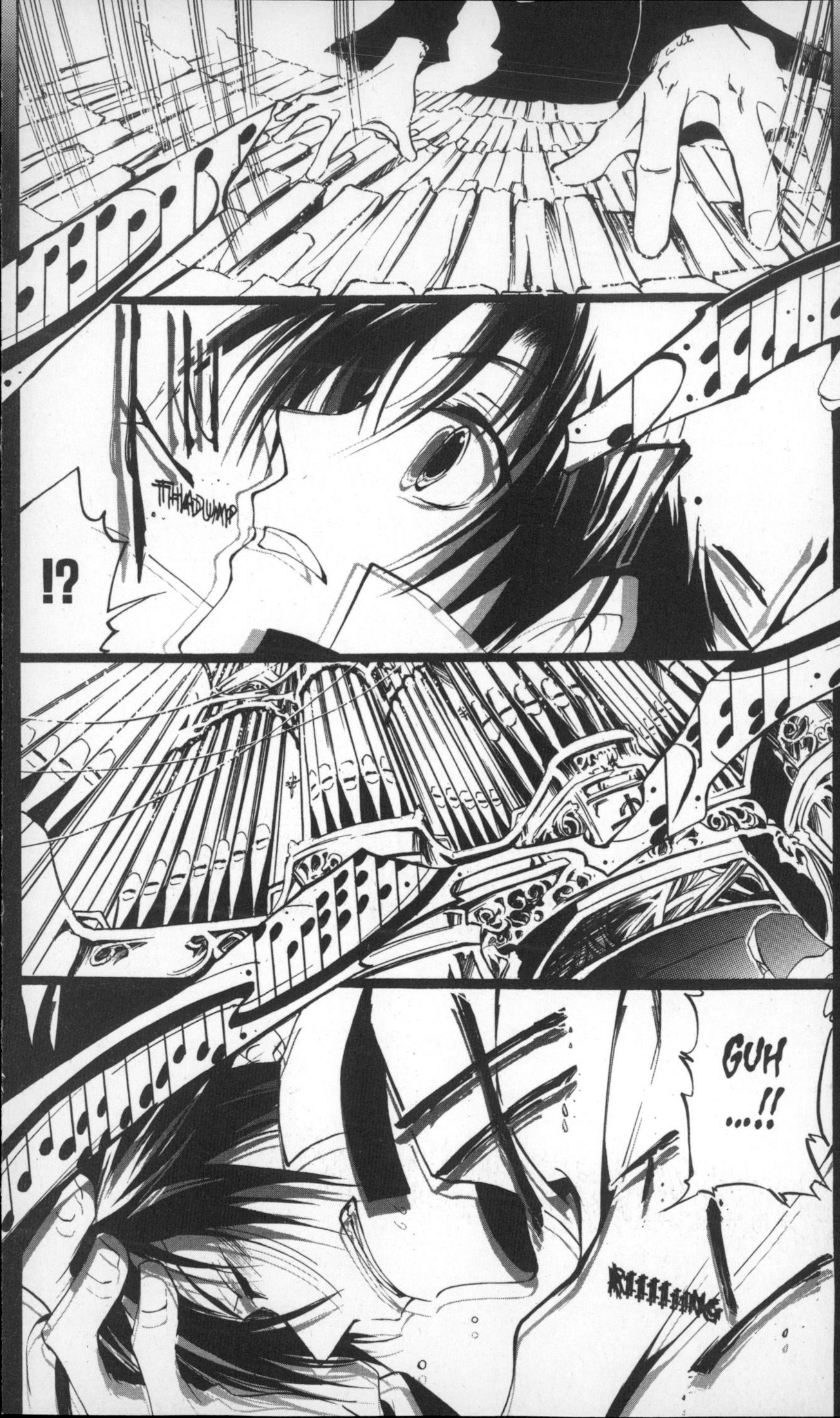
THADUMP
!?
GUH ...!!
RIIIIIIING

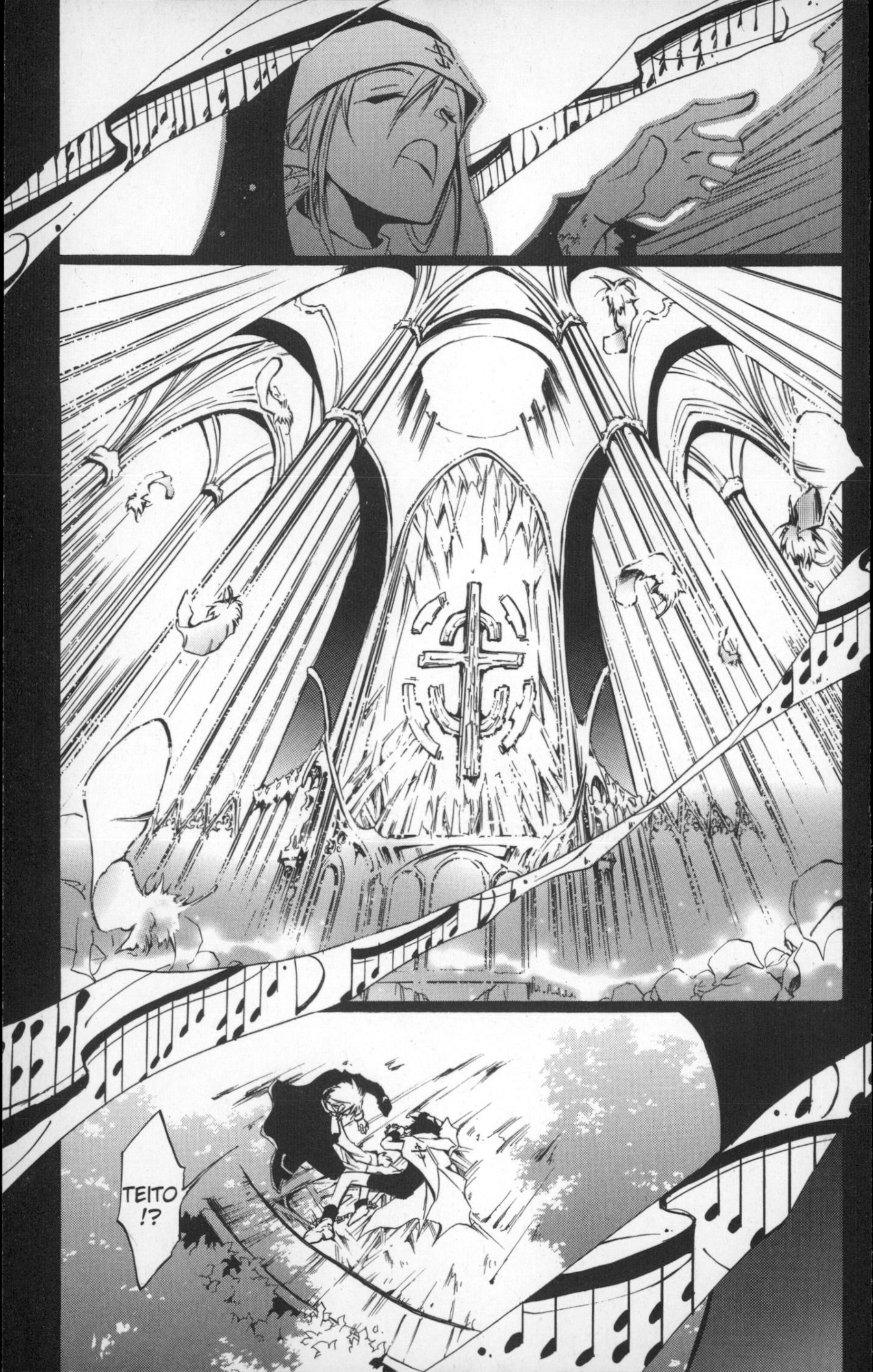
TEITO !?

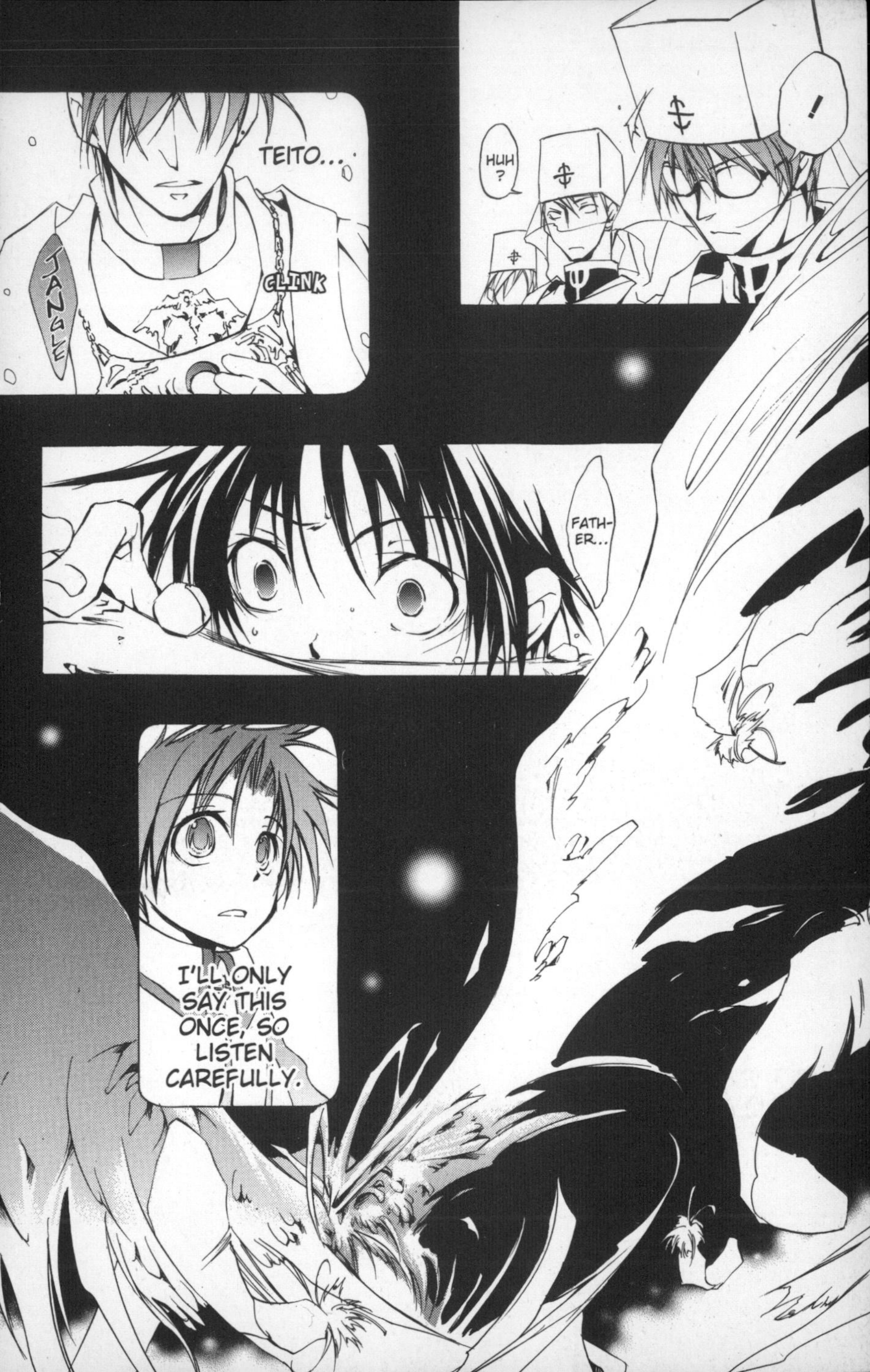
!
HUH ?
TEITO...
JANGLE
CLINK
FATHER- ER...
I'LL ONLY SAY THIS ONCE, SO LISTEN CAREFULLY.

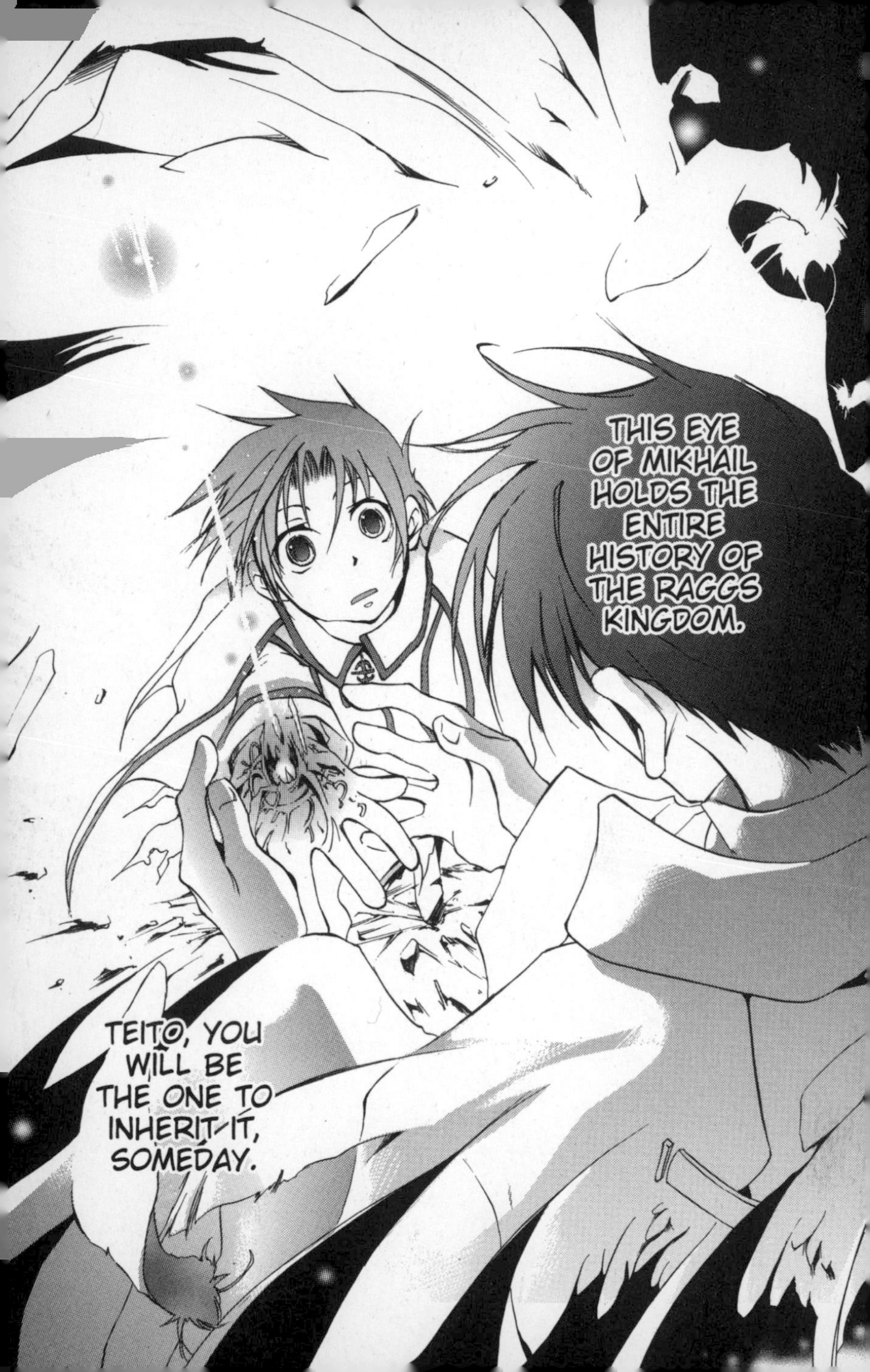
THIS EYE OF MIKHAIL HOLDS THE ENTIRE HISTORY OF THE RAGGS KINGDOM.
TEITO, YOU WILL BE THE ONE TO INHERIT IT, SOMEDAY.

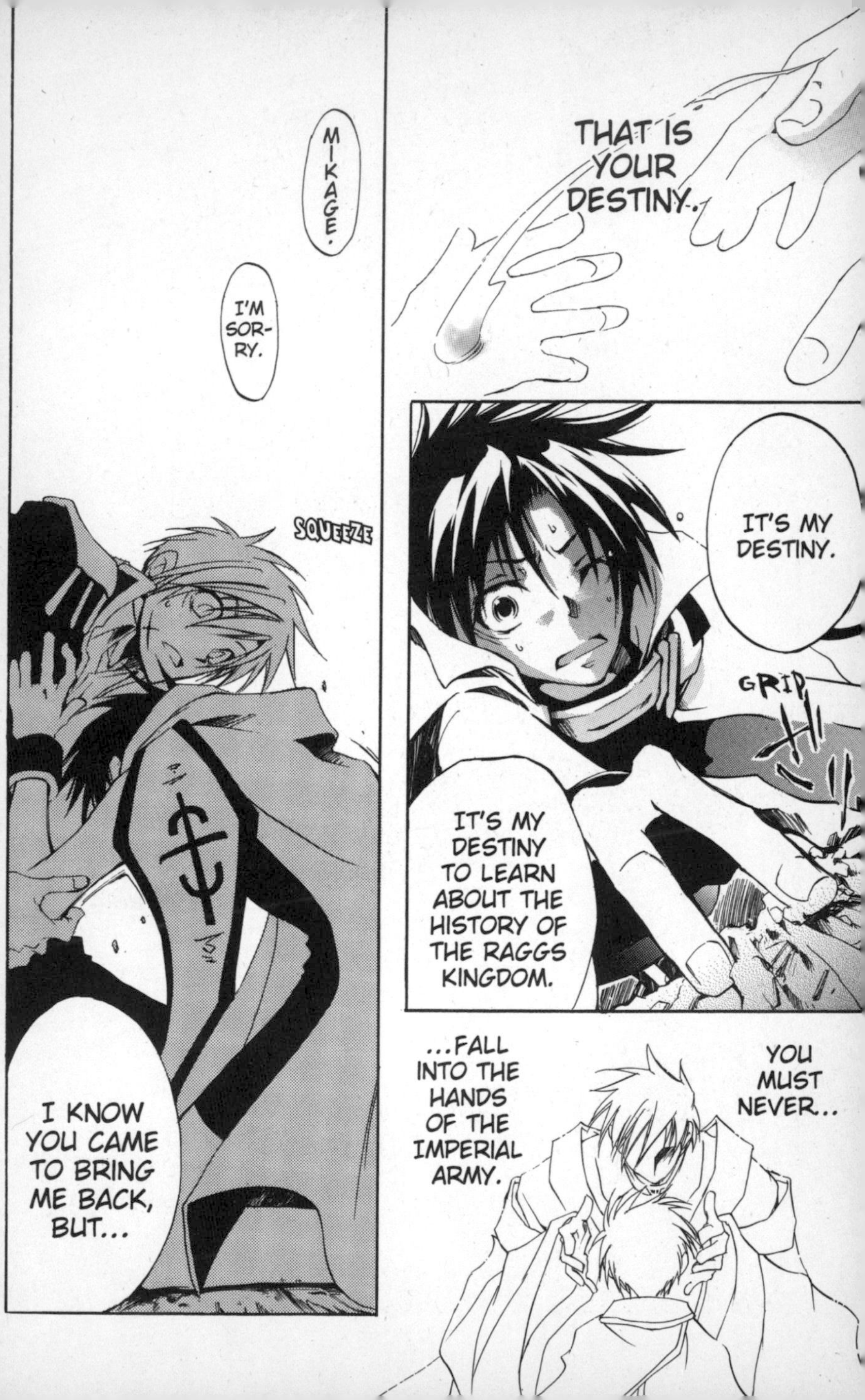
THAT IS YOUR DESTINY..
IT'S MY DESTINY.
GRIP
IT'S MY DESTINY TO LEARN ABOUT THE HISTORY OF THE RAGGS KINGDOM.
YOU MUST NEVER...
...FALL INTO THE HANDS OF THE IMPERIAL ARMY.
MIKAGE.
I'M SOR-RY.
SQUEEZE
I KNOW YOU CAME TO BRING ME BACK, BUT...

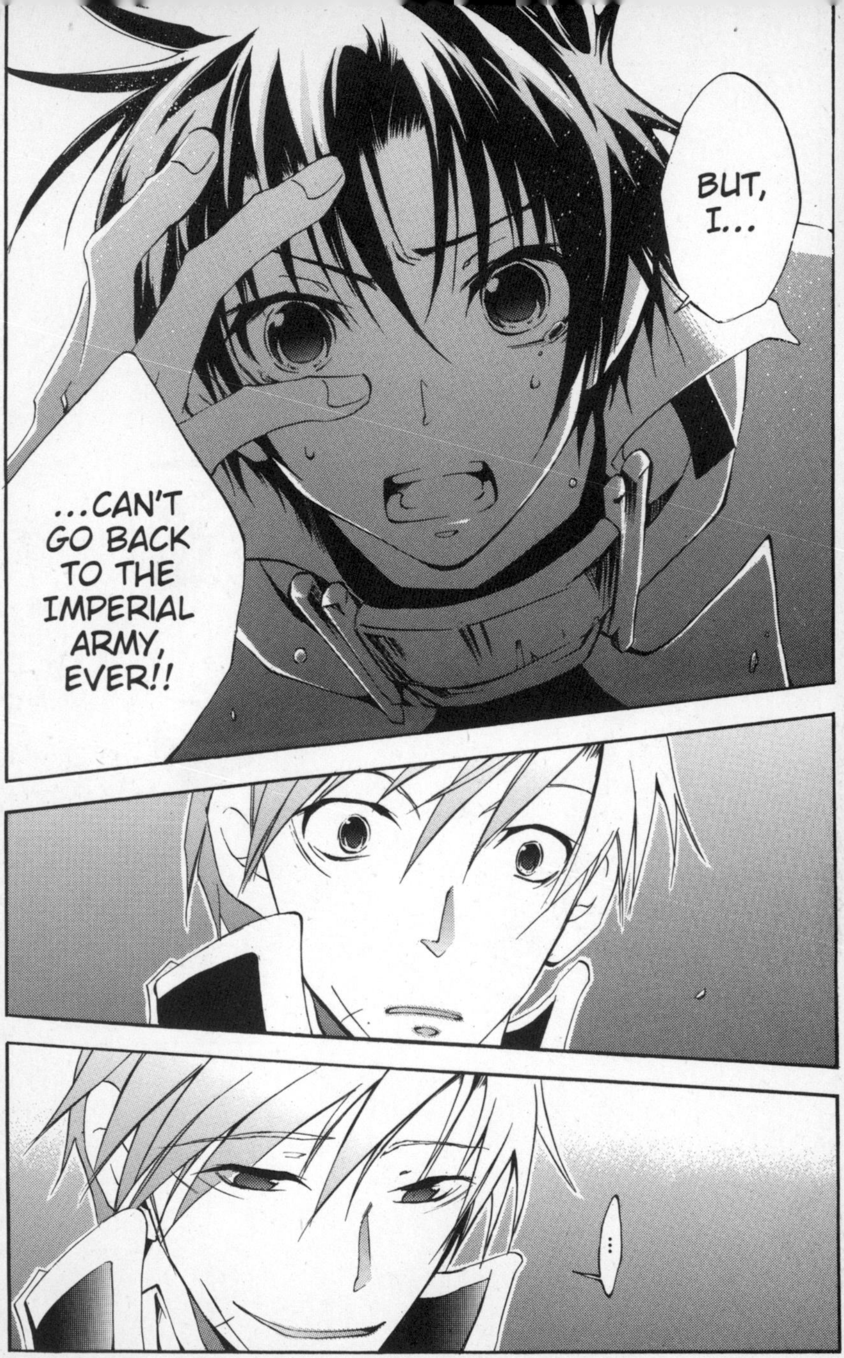
BUT, I...
...CAN'T GO BACK TO THE IMPERIAL ARMY, EVER!!
...

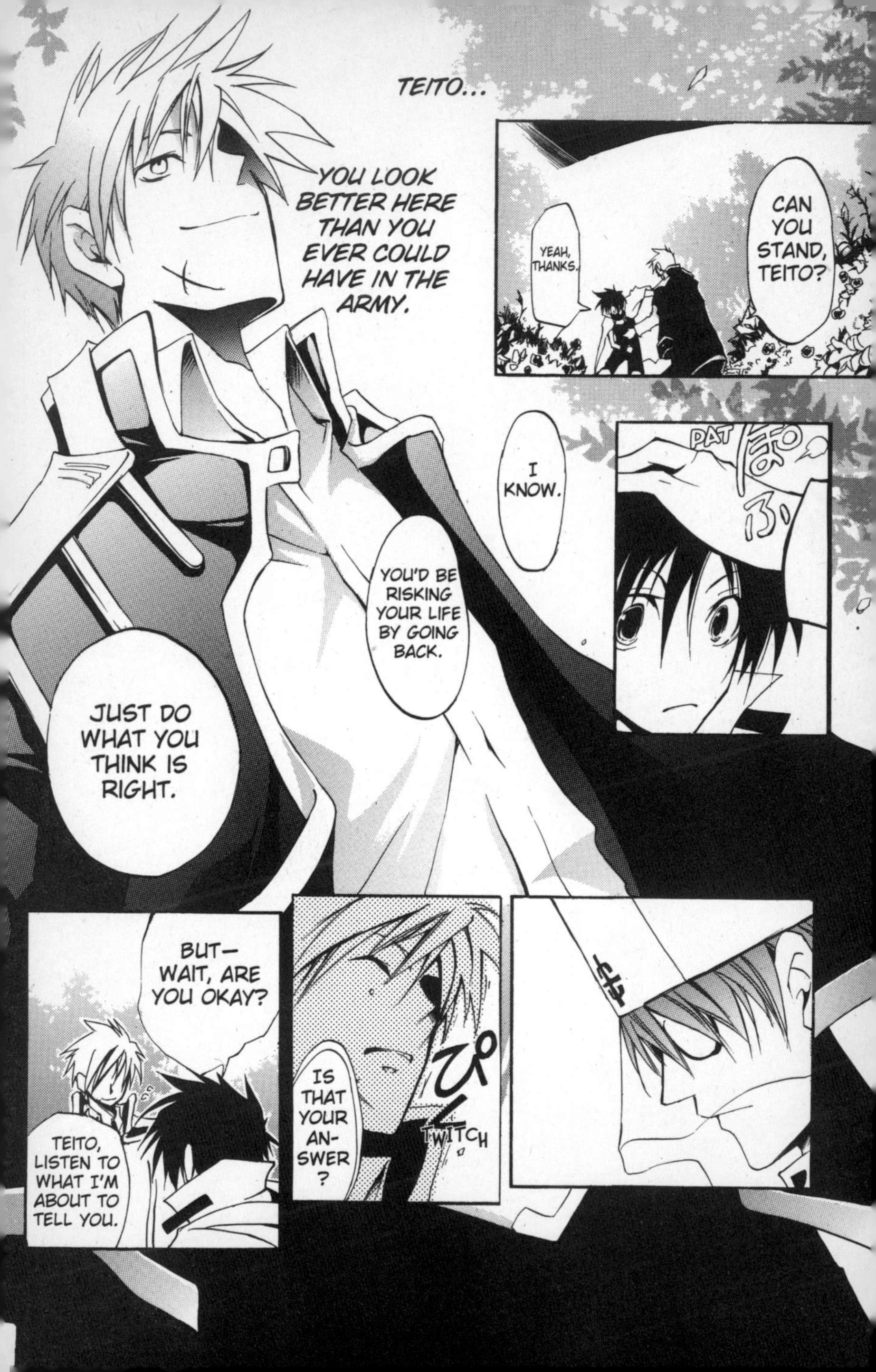
CAN YOU STAND, TEITO?
YEAH, THANKS.
PAT
I KNOW.
YOU'D BE RISKING YOUR LIFE BY GOING BACK.
TEITO...
YOU LOOK BETTER HERE THAN YOU EVER COULD HAVE IN THE ARMY.
JUST DO WHAT YOU THINK IS RIGHT.
IS THAT YOUR AN-SWER?
TWITCH
BUT— WAIT, ARE YOU OKAY?
TEITO, LISTEN TO WHAT I'M ABOUT TO TELL YOU.

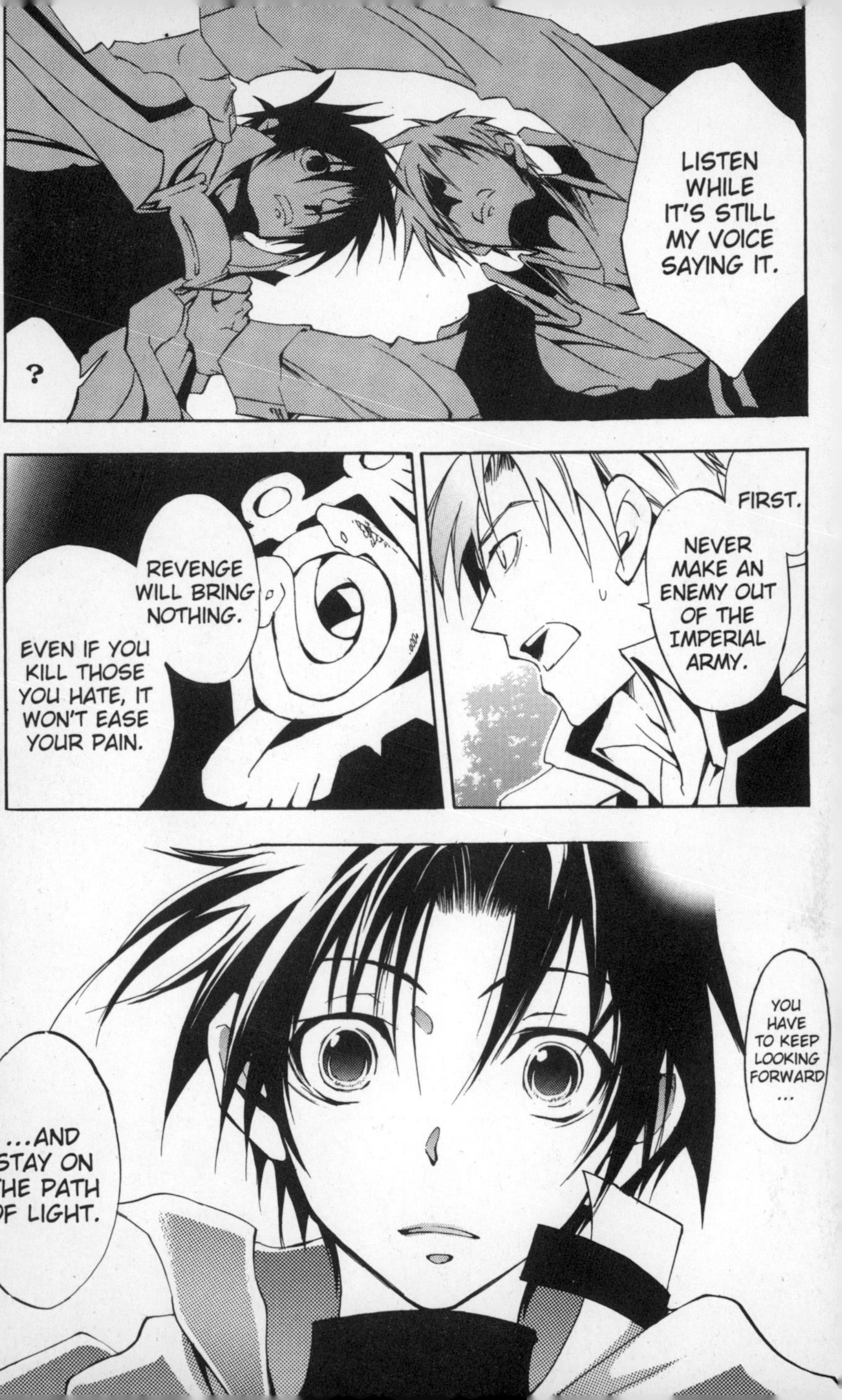
LISTEN WHILE IT'S STILL MY VOICE SAYING IT.
?
FIRST.
NEVER MAKE AN ENEMY OUT OF THE IMPERIAL ARMY.
REVENGE WILL BRING NOTHING.
EVEN IF YOU KILL THOSE YOU HATE, IT WON'T EASE YOUR PAIN.
YOU HAVE TO KEEP LOOKING FORWARD...
...AND STAY ON THE PATH OF LIGHT.

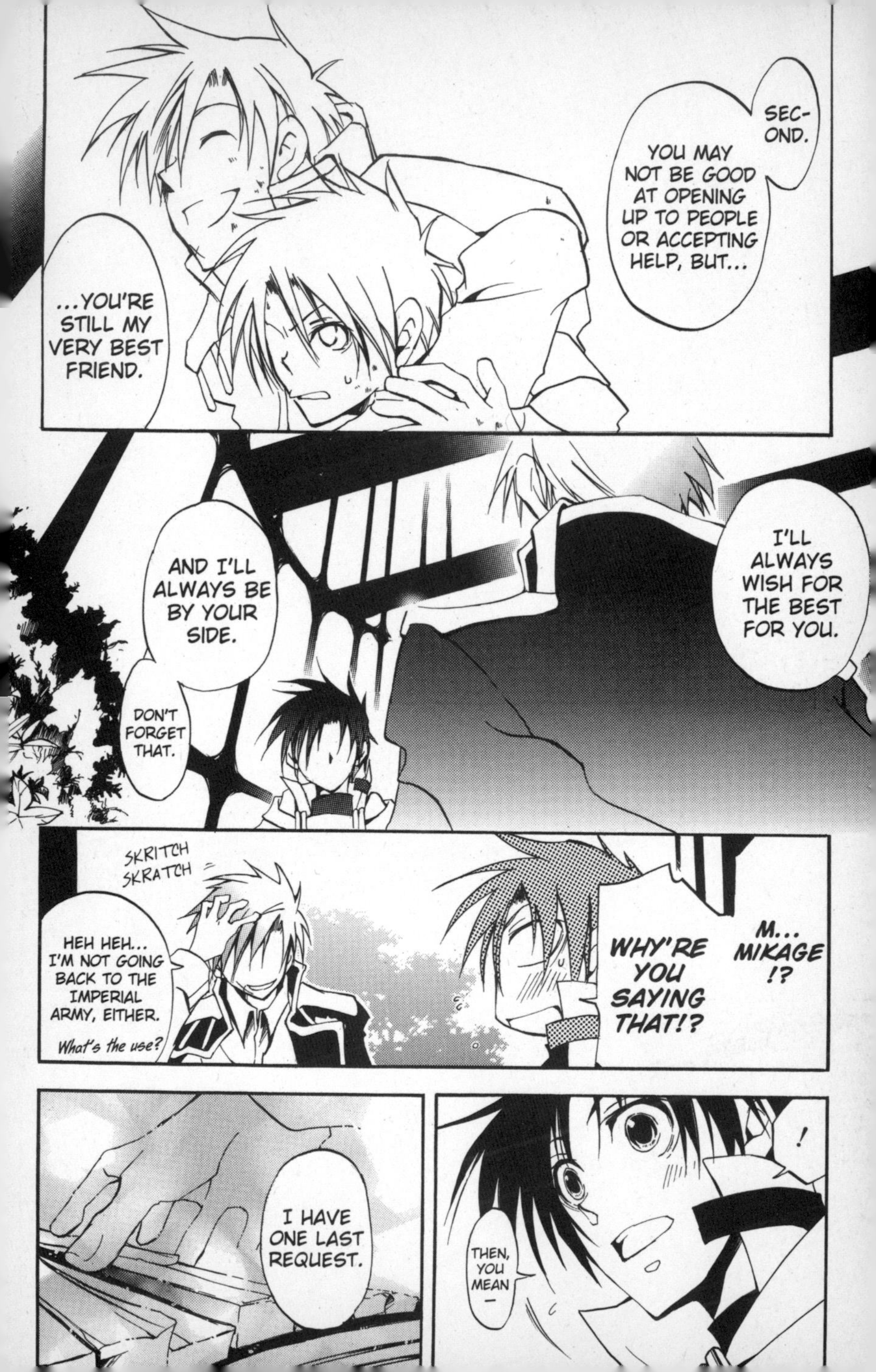
SEC-OND.
YOU MAY NOT BE GOOD AT OPENING UP TO PEOPLE OR ACCEPTING HELP, BUT...
...YOU'RE STILL MY VERY BEST FRIEND.
I'LL ALWAYS WISH FOR THE BEST FOR YOU.
AND I'LL ALWAYS BE BY YOUR SIDE.
DON'T FORGET THAT.
M... MIKAGE !?
WHY'RE YOU SAYING THAT!?
SKRITCH SKRATCH
HEH HEH... I'M NOT GOING BACK TO THE IMPERIAL ARMY, EITHER.
What's the use?
!
THEN, YOU MEAN —
I HAVE ONE LAST REQUEST.

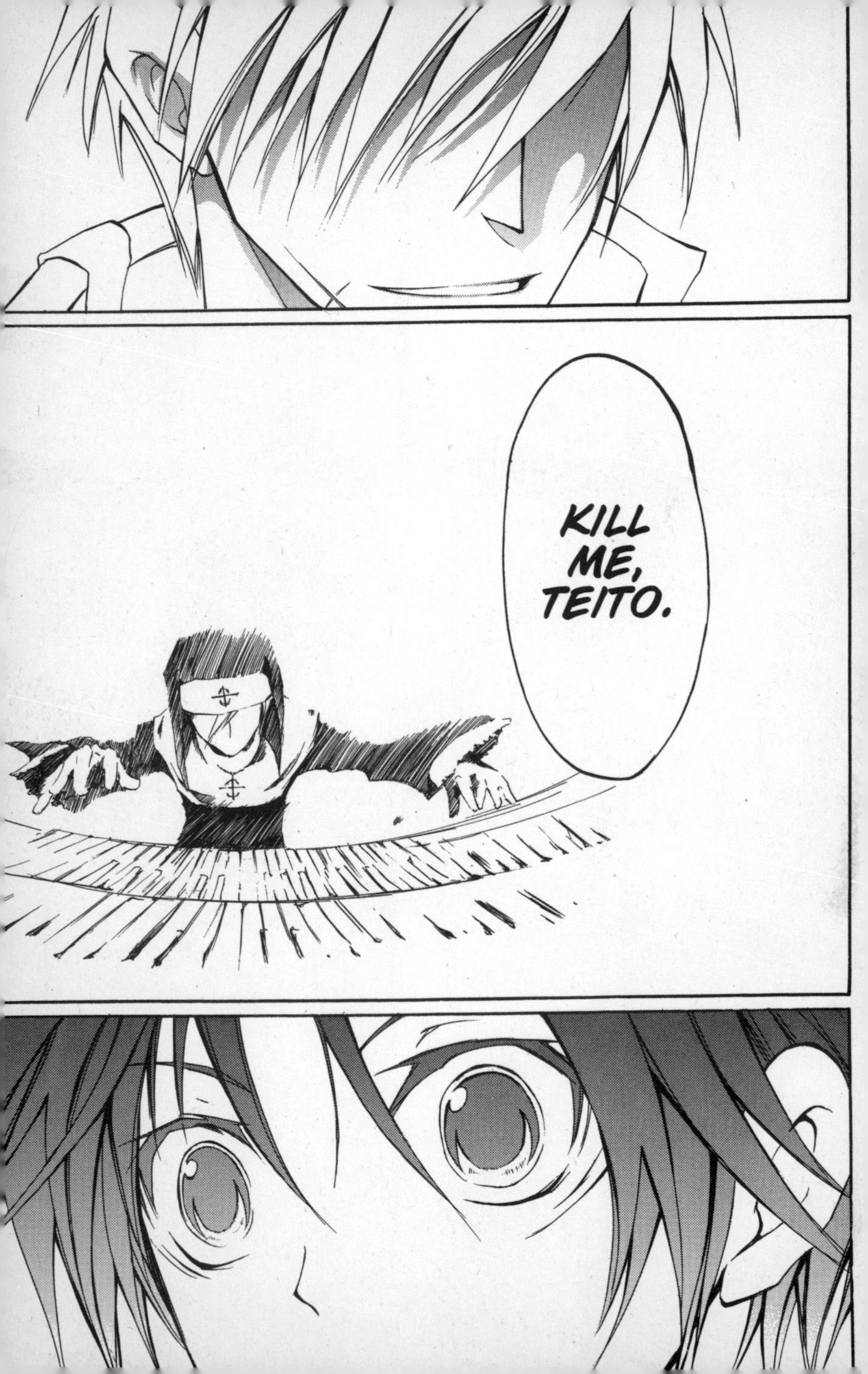
KILL ME, TEITO.

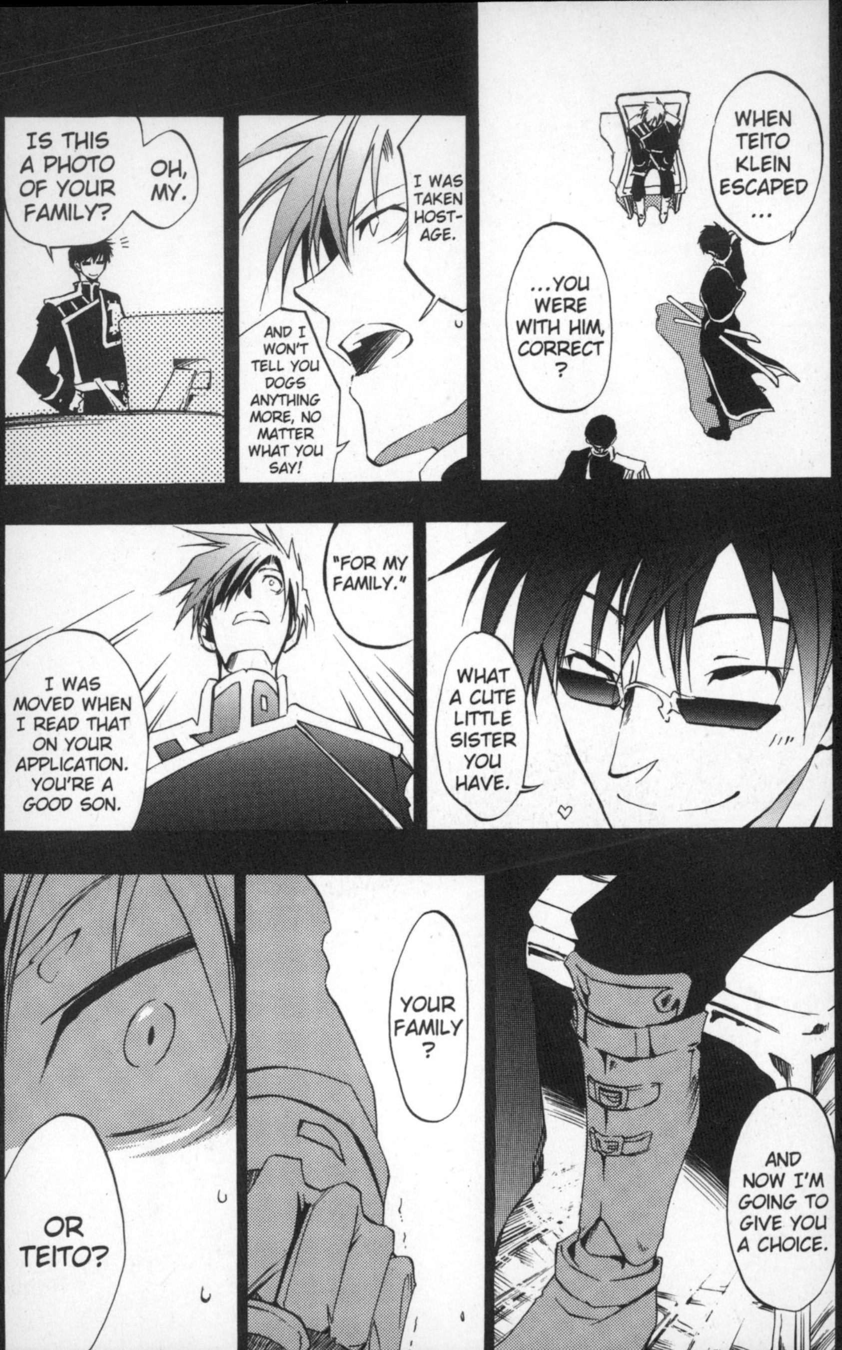
WHEN TEITO KLEIN ESCAPED ...
...YOU WERE WITH HIM, CORRECT ?
I WAS TAKEN HOST-AGE.
AND I WON'T TELL YOU DOGS ANYTHING MORE, NO MATTER WHAT YOU SAY!
OH, MY.
IS THIS A PHOTO OF YOUR FAMILY?
WHAT A CUTE LITTLE SISTER YOU HAVE.
"FOR MY FAMILY."
I WAS MOVED WHEN I READ THAT ON YOUR APPLICATION. YOU'RE A GOOD SON.
AND NOW I'M GOING TO GIVE YOU A CHOICE.
YOUR FAMILY ?
OR TEITO?

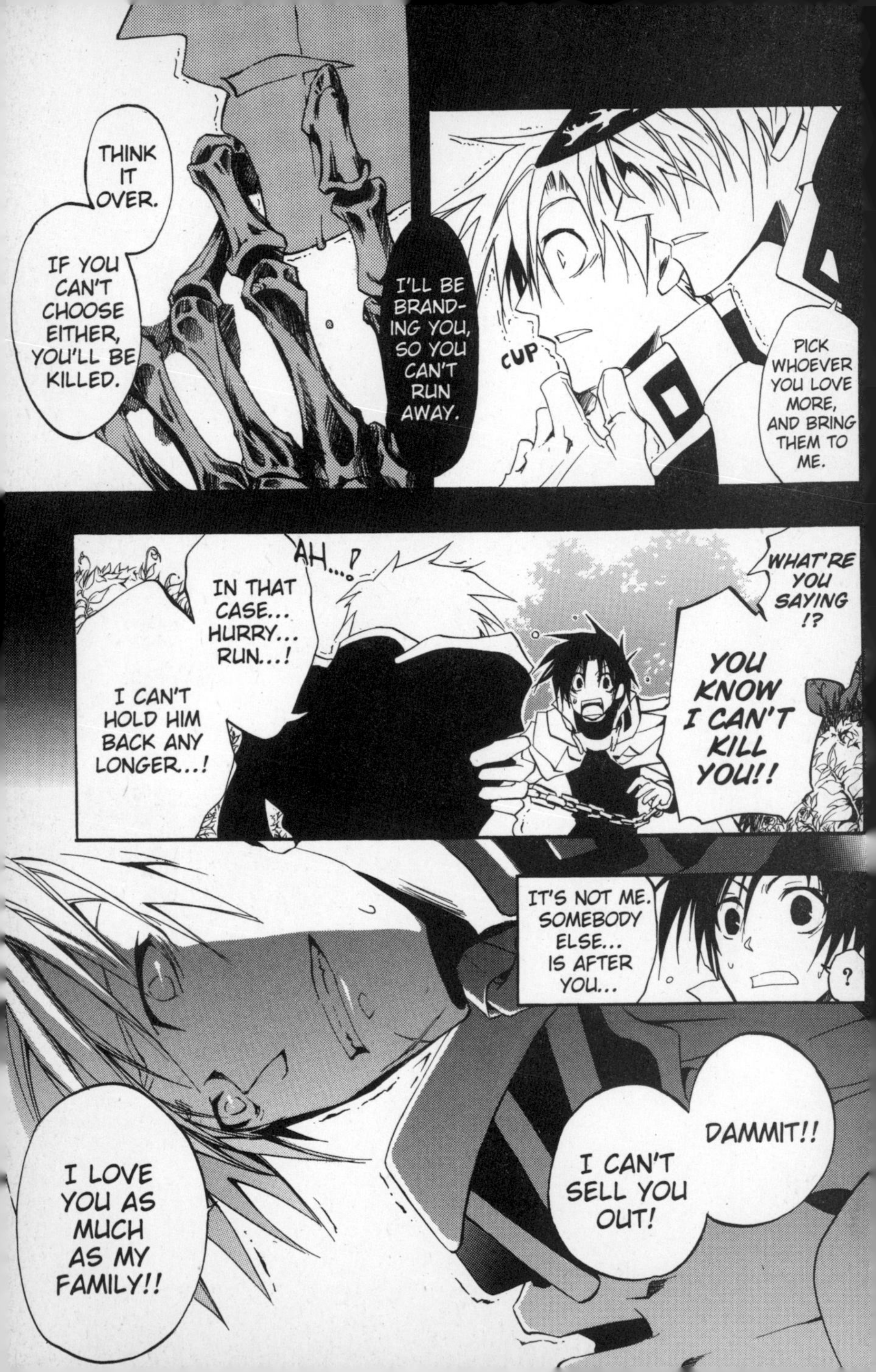
PICK WHOEVER YOU LOVE MORE, AND BRING THEM TO ME.
CUP
I'LL BE BRANDING YOU, SO YOU CAN'T RUN AWAY.
THINK IT OVER.
IF YOU CAN'T CHOOSE EITHER, YOU'LL BE KILLED.
WHAT'RE YOU SAYING !?
YOU KNOW I CAN'T KILL YOU!!
AH...!
IN THAT CASE... HURRY... RUN...!
I CAN'T HOLD HIM BACK ANY LONGER...!
IT'S NOT ME. SOMEBODY ELSE... IS AFTER YOU...
?
DAMMIT!!
I CAN'T SELL YOU OUT!
I LOVE YOU AS MUCH AS MY FAMILY!!

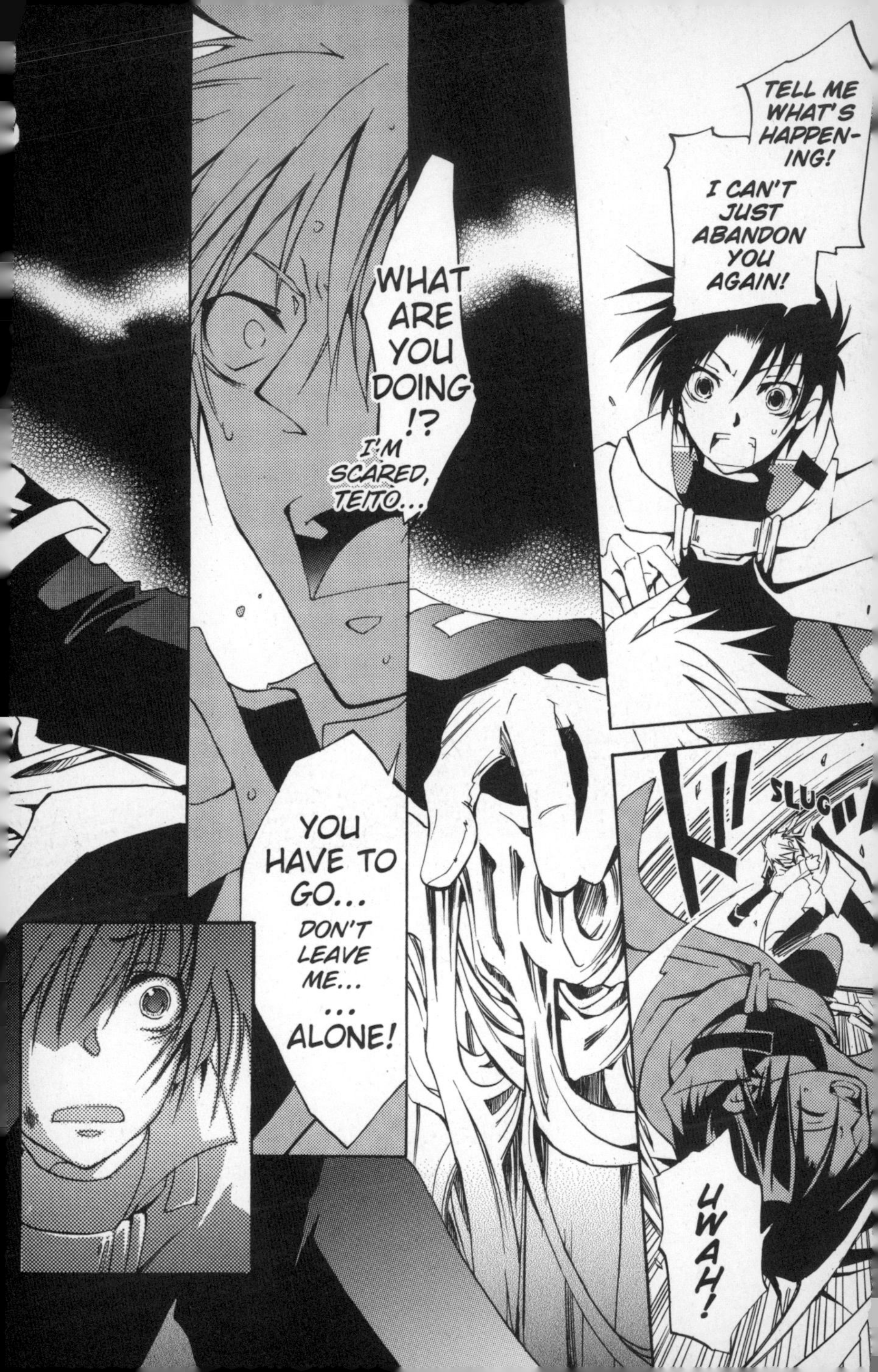
TELL ME WHAT'S HAPPENING!
I CAN'T JUST ABANDON YOU AGAIN!
WHAT ARE YOU DOING!?
I'M SCARED, TEITO...
SLUG!!
UWAH!
YOU HAVE TO GO...
DON'T LEAVE ME...
...ALONE!

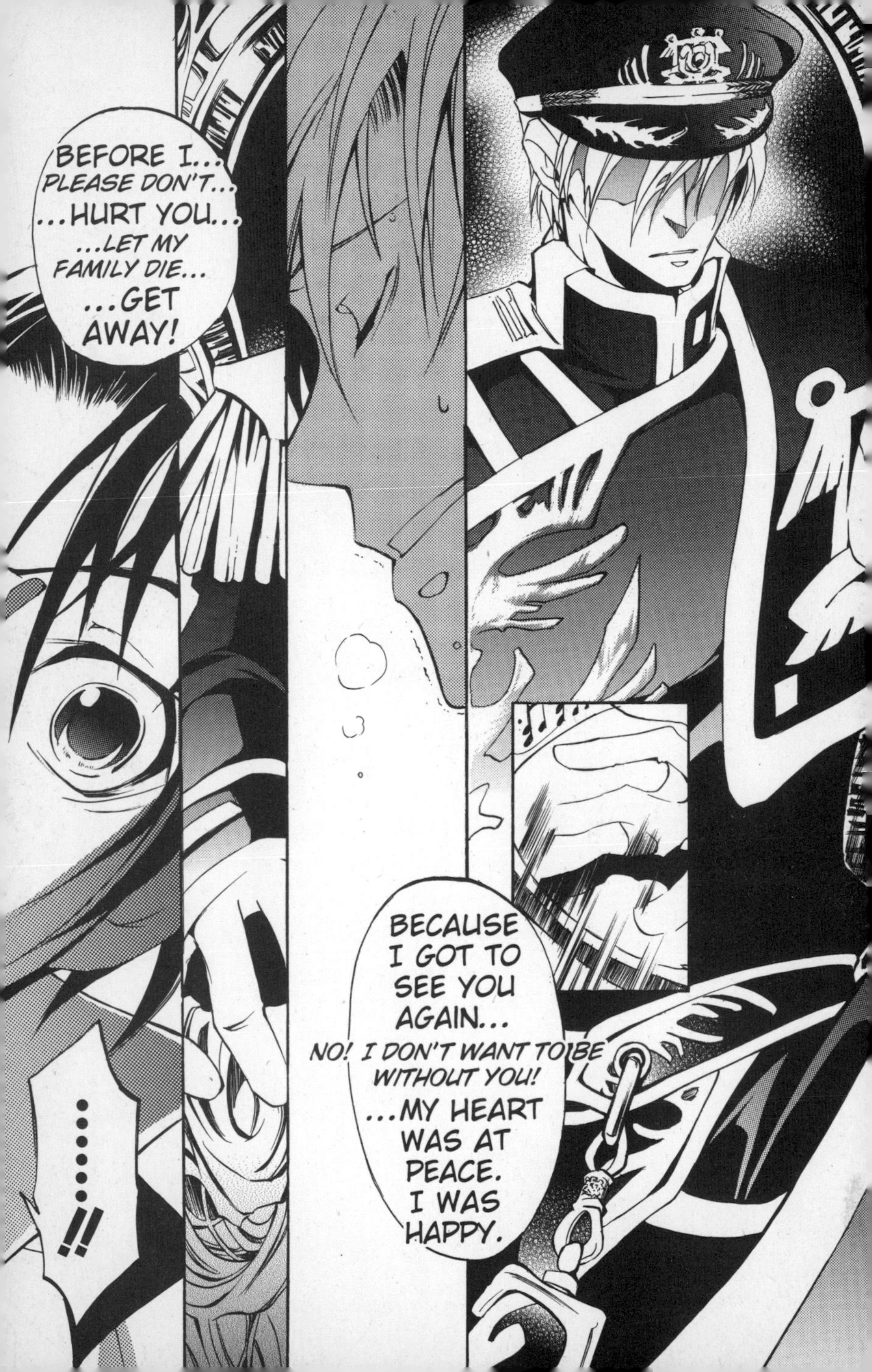
BECAUSE I GOT TO SEE YOU AGAIN... NO! I DON'T WANT TO BE WITHOUT YOU! ...MY HEART WAS AT PEACE. I WAS HAPPY.
BEFORE I... PLEASE DON'T... ...HURT YOU... ...LET MY FAMILY DIE... ...GET AWAY!
......!!

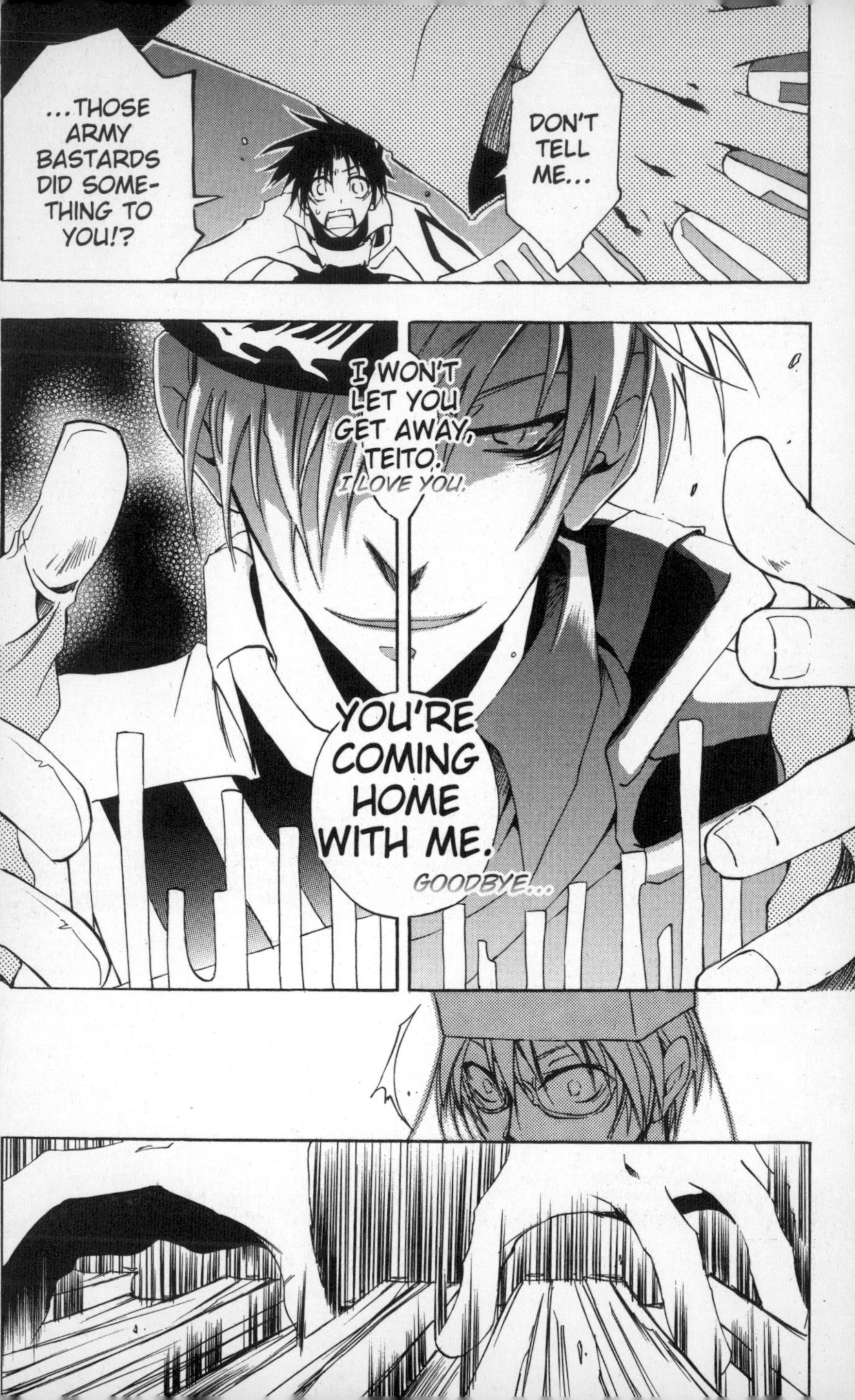
DON'T TELL ME...
...THOSE ARMY BASTARDS DID SOME-THING TO YOU!?
I WON'T LET YOU GET AWAY, TEITO.
I LOVE YOU.
YOU'RE COMING HOME WITH ME.
GOODBYE...

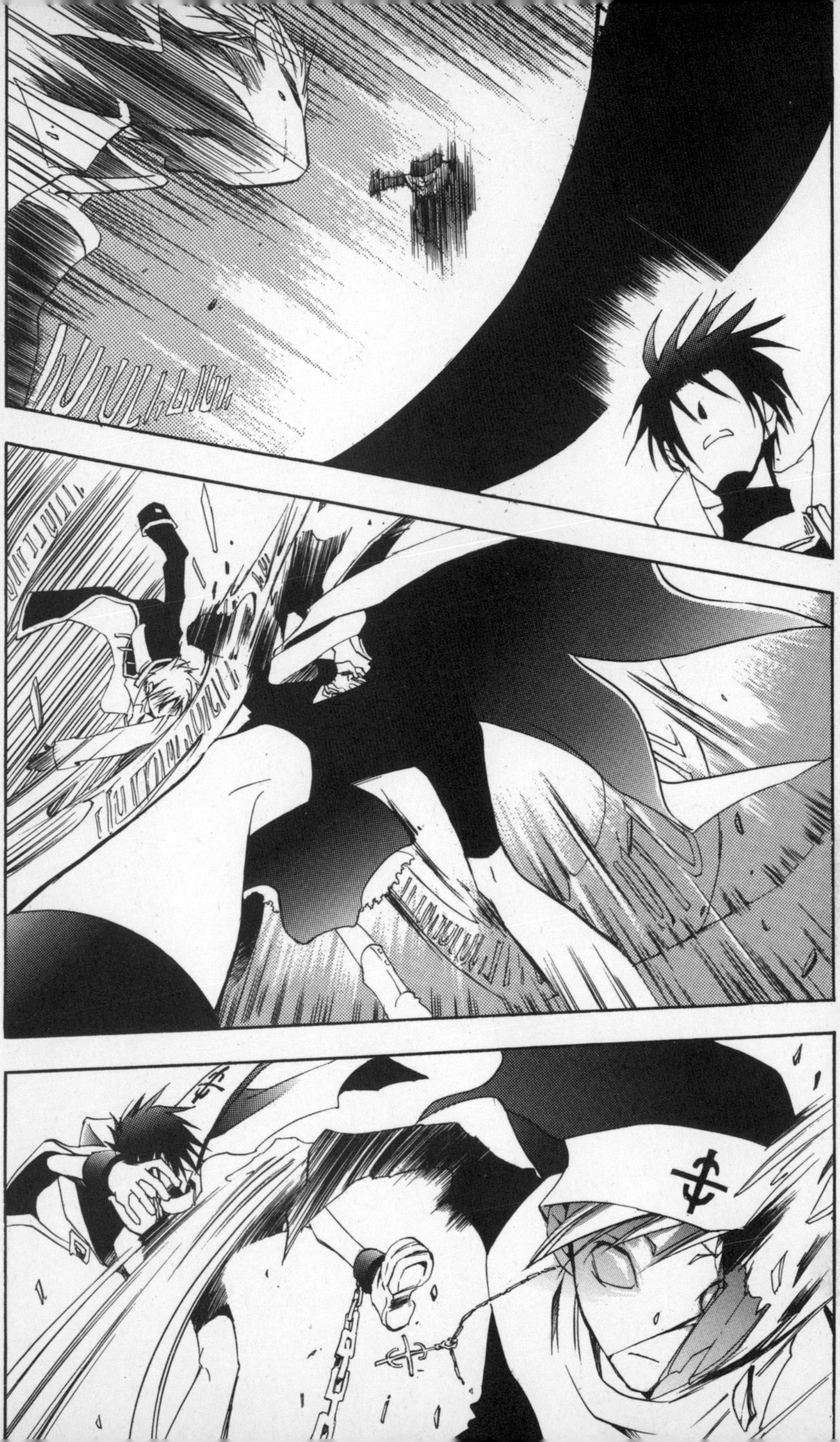

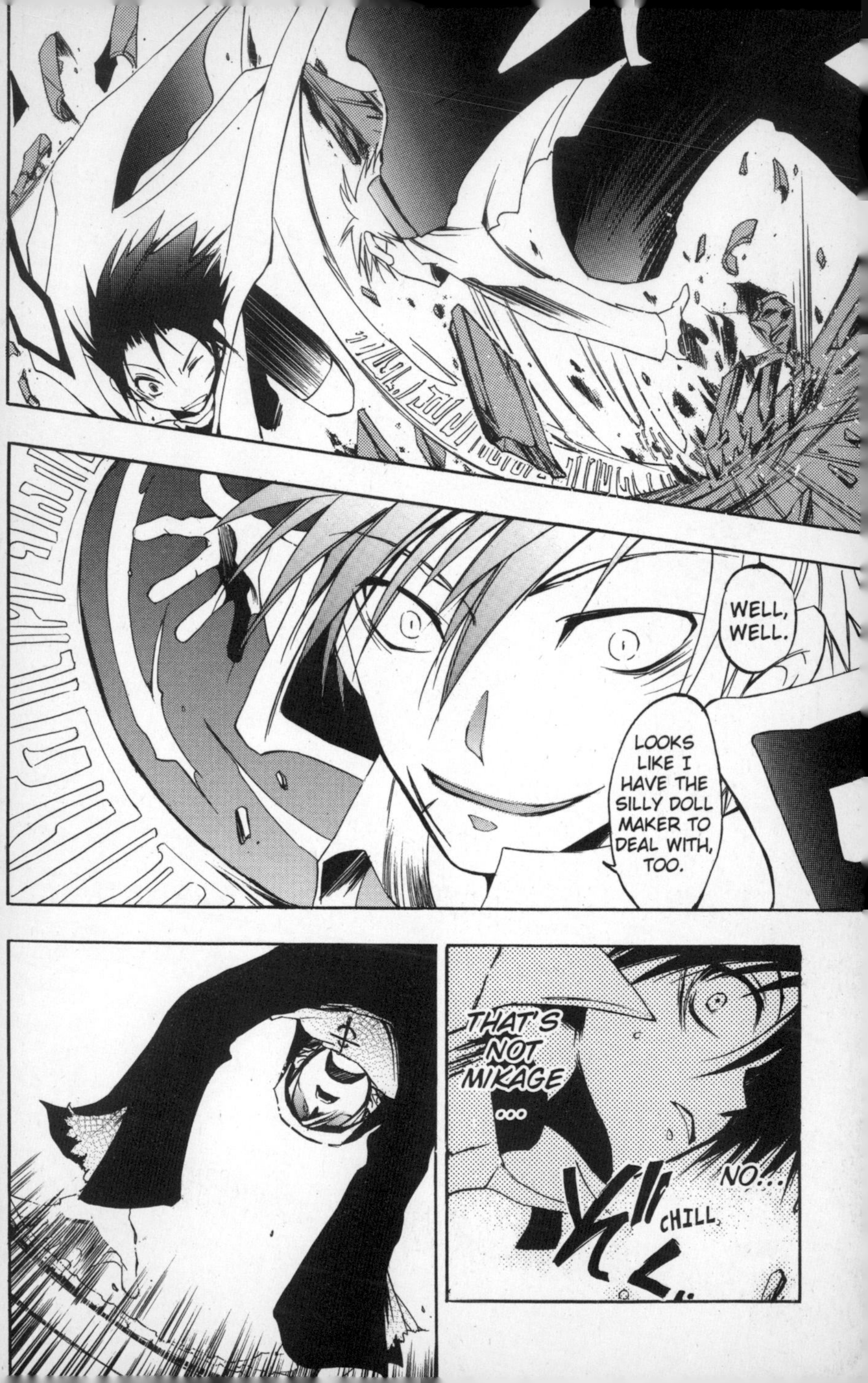
WELL, WELL.
LOOKS LIKE I HAVE THE SILLY DOLL MAKER TO DEAL WITH, TOO.
THAT'S NOT MIKAGE...
NO...
CHILL

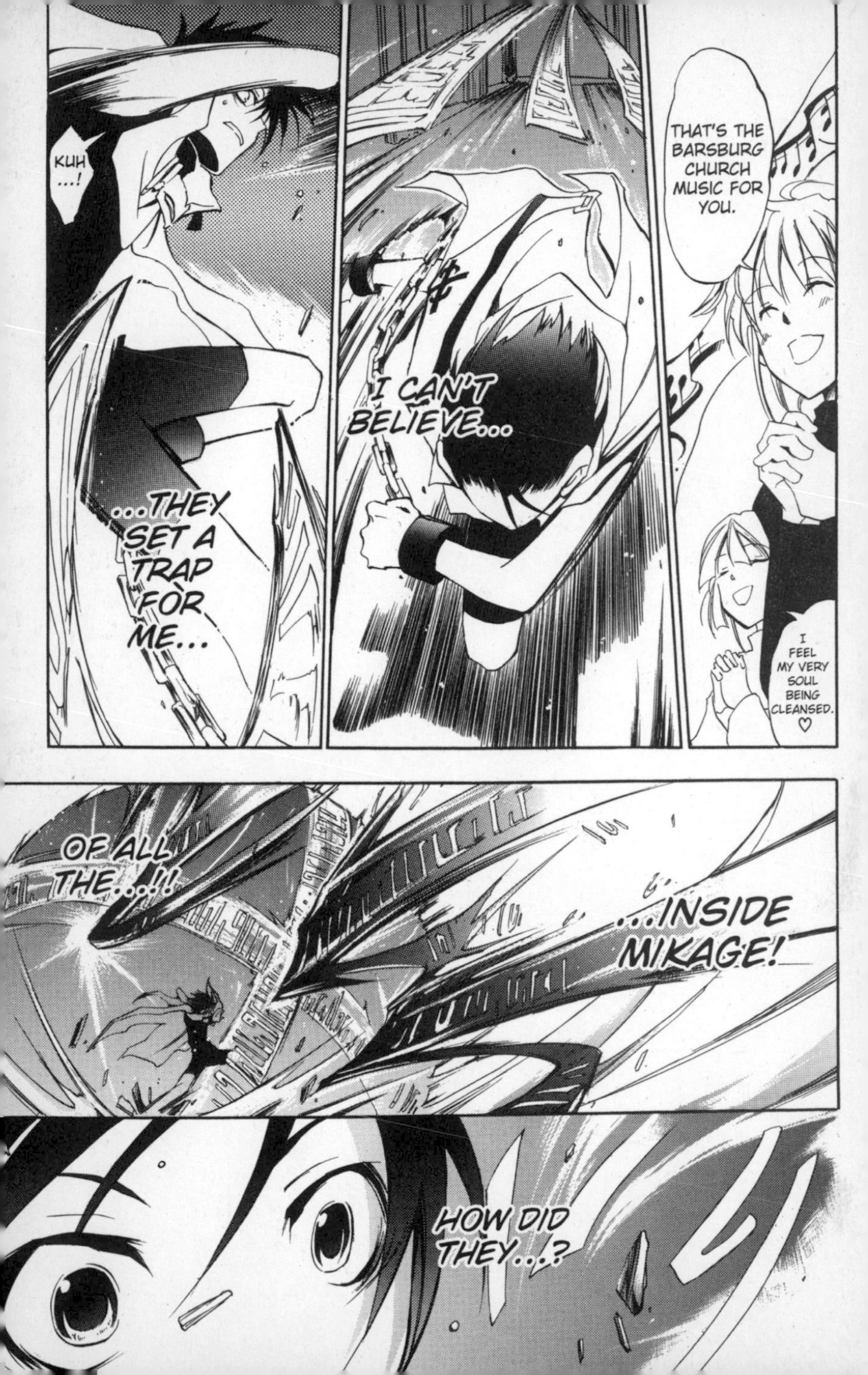
THAT'S THE BARSBURG CHURCH MUSIC FOR YOU.
I FEEL MY VERY SOUL BEING CLEANSED. ♡
I CAN'T BELIEVE...
KUH ...!
...THEY SET A TRAP FOR ME...
...INSIDE MIKAGE!
OF ALL THE...!!
HOW DID THEY...?

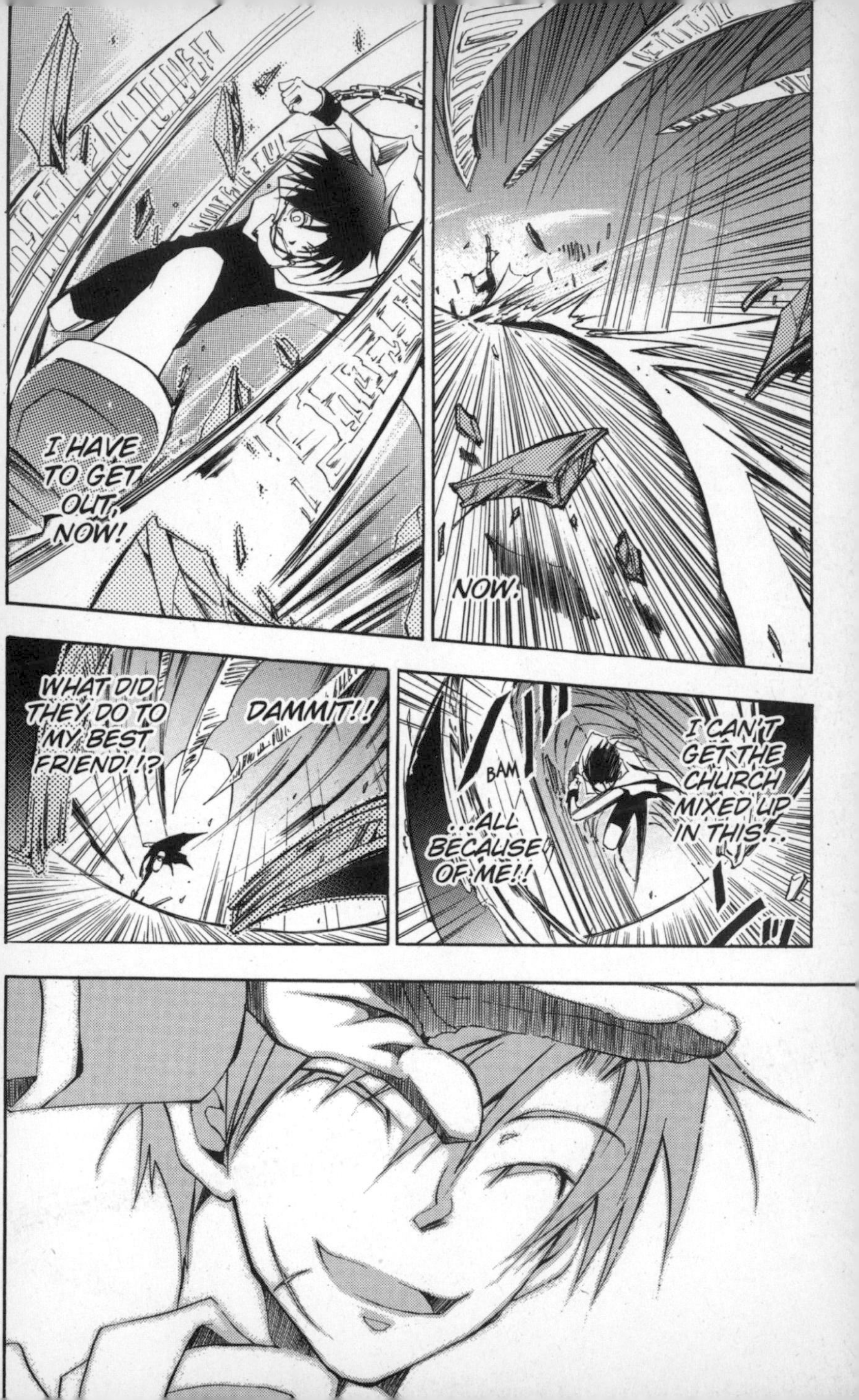
NOW.
I HAVE TO GET OUT, NOW!
I CAN'T GET THE CHURCH MIXED UP IN THIS...
BAM
...ALL BECAUSE OF ME!!
DAMMIT!!
WHAT DID THEY DO TO MY BEST FRIEND!!?

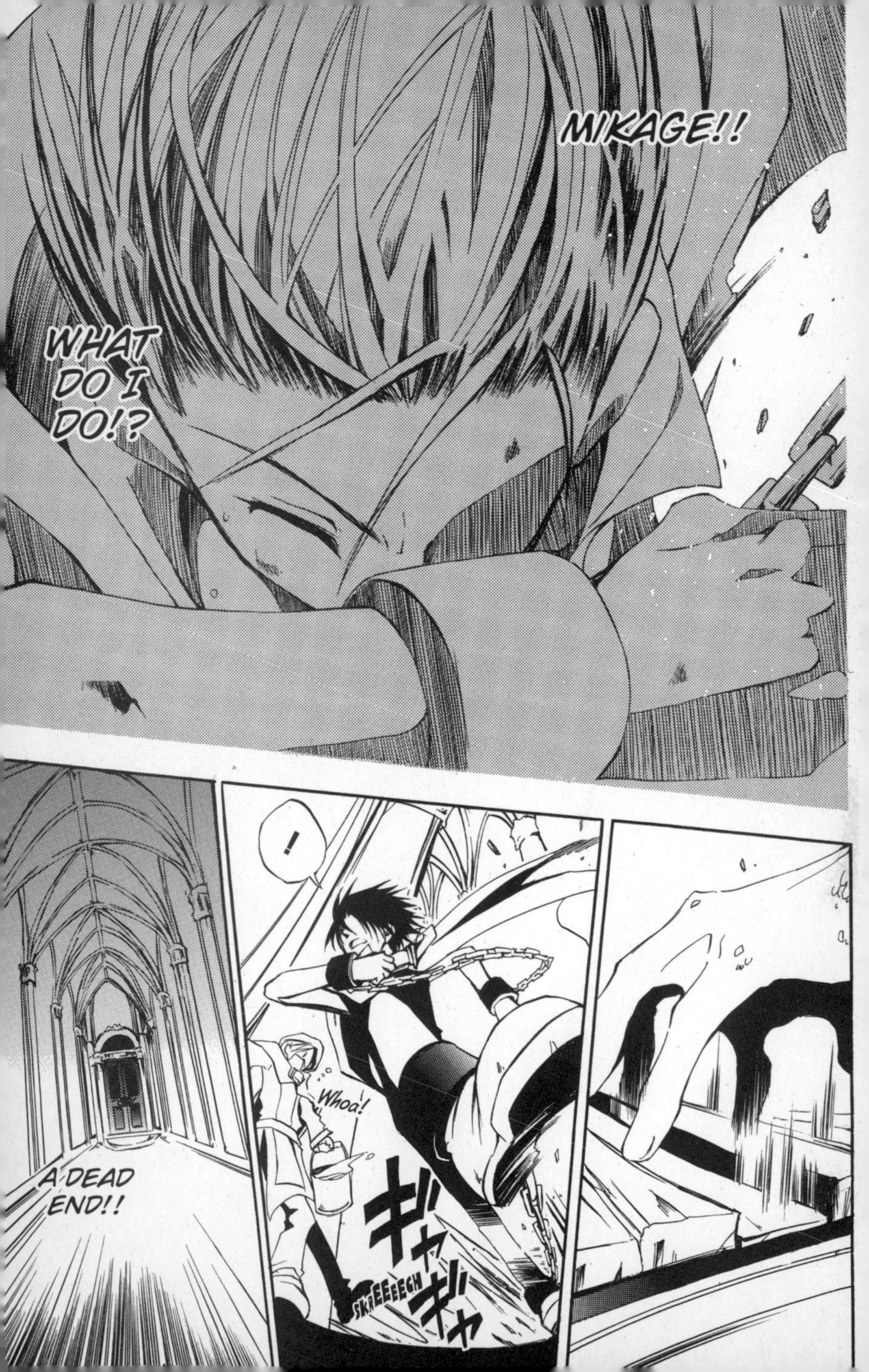
MIKAGE!!
WHAT DO I DO!?
!
Whoa!
ギャギャ
SKREEEEECH
A DEAD END!!

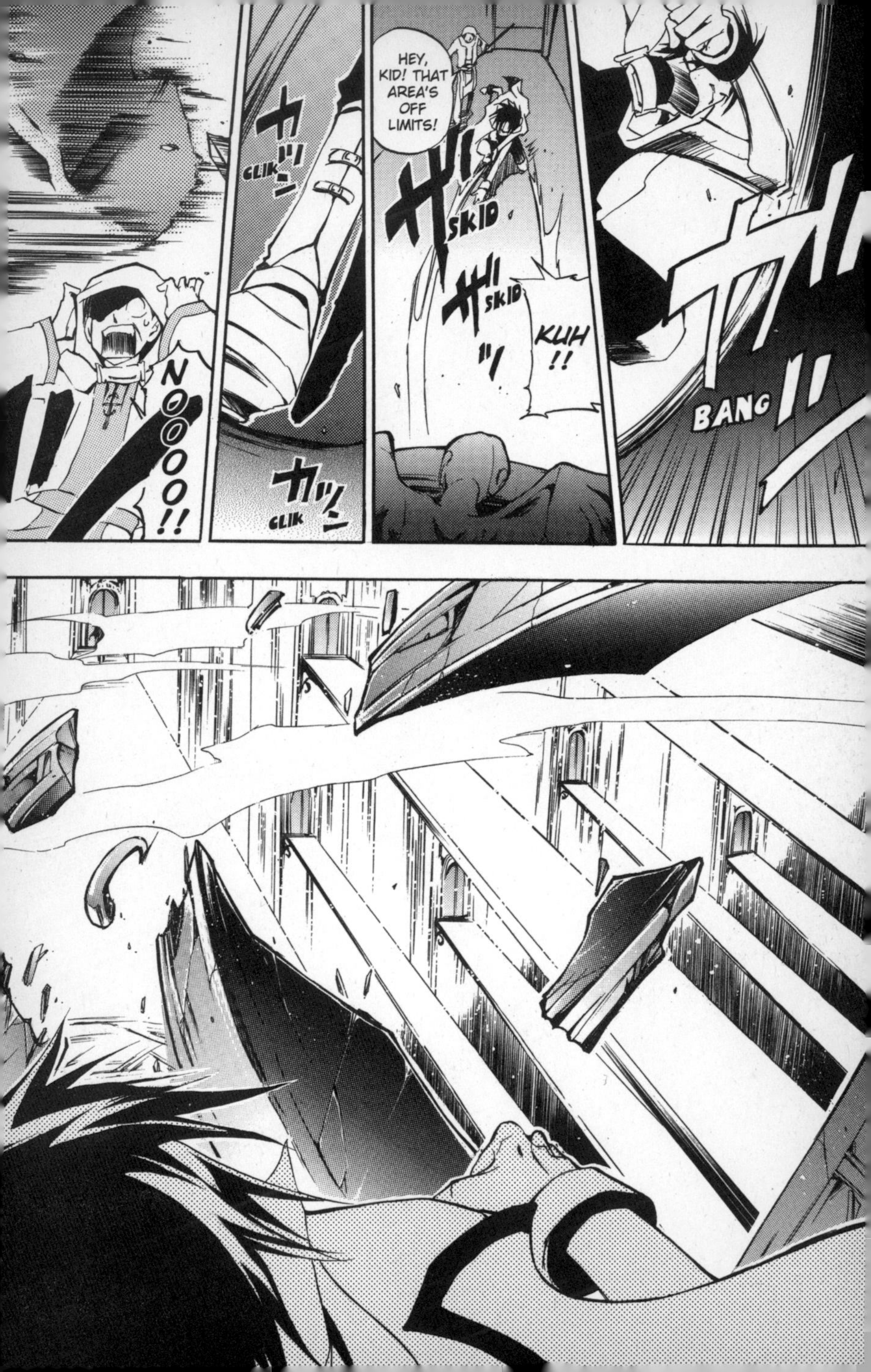
BANG
HEY, KID! THAT AREA'S OFF LIMITS!
SKID
SKID
KUH!!
CLIK
CLIK
NOOOOO!!

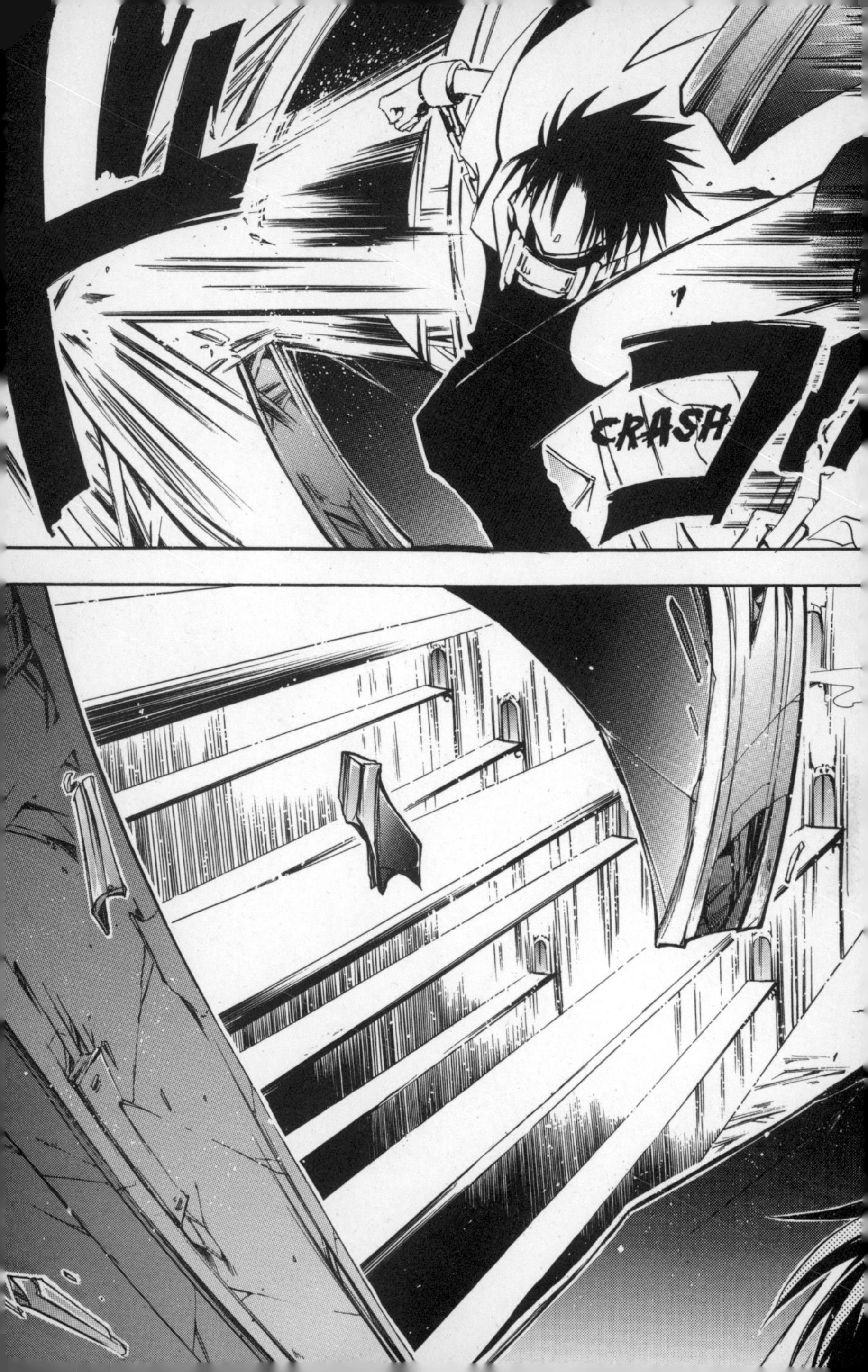
CRASH

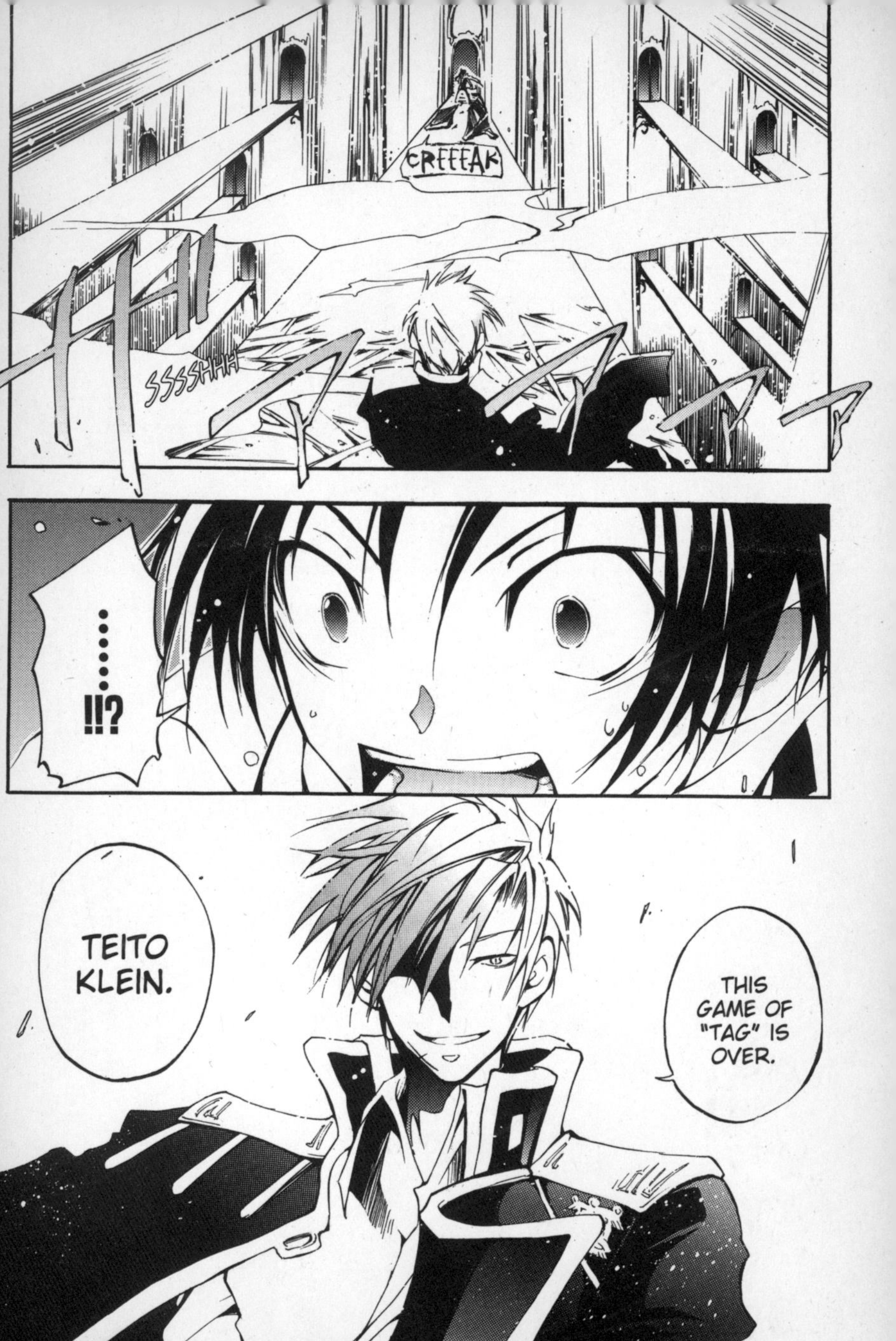
CREEEAK
SSSSSHHH
......!!?
TEITO KLEIN.
THIS GAME OF "TAG" IS OVER.

07-GHOST [1] END

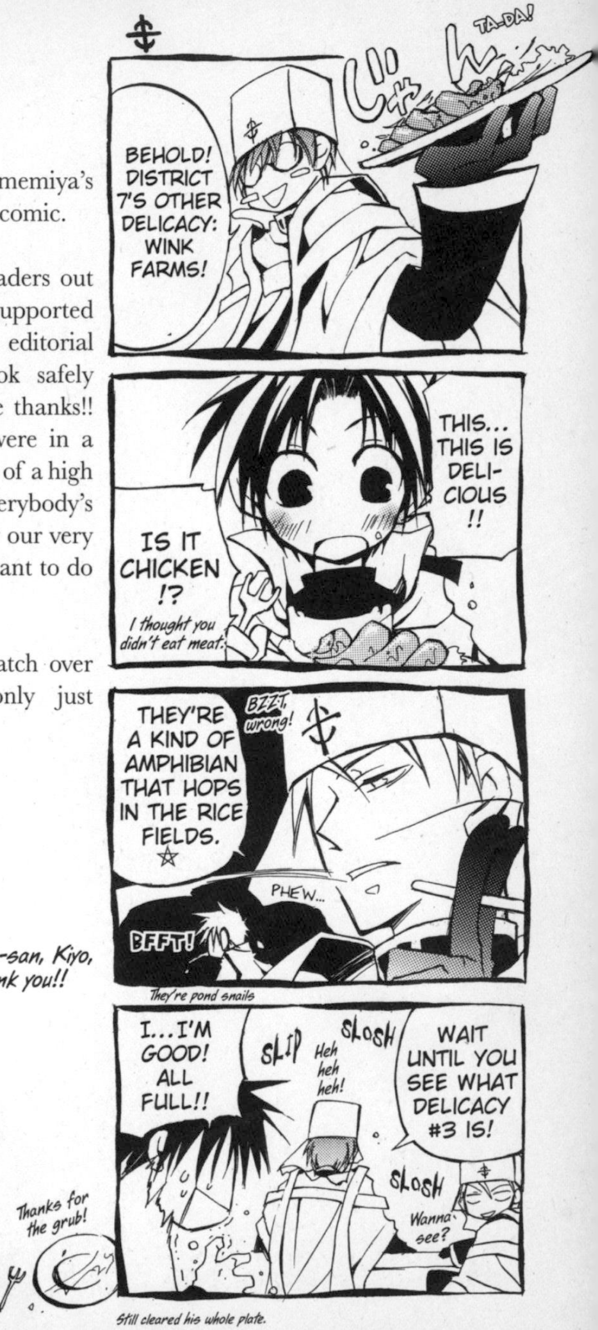
TA-DA!
じゃん
BEHOLD! DISTRICT 7'S OTHER DELICACY: WINK FARMS!
THIS... THIS IS DELICIOUS!!
IS IT CHICKEN!?
I thought you didn't eat meat.
BZZT, wrong!
THEY'RE A KIND OF AMPHIBIAN THAT HOPS IN THE RICE FIELDS. ☆
PHEW...
BFFT!
They're pond snails
WAIT UNTIL YOU SEE WHAT DELICACY #3 IS!
SLOSH
Heh heh heh!
SLIP
I...I'M GOOD! ALL FULL!!
SLOSH
Wanna see?
Thanks for the grub!
Still cleared his whole plate.

07-GHOST is Yuki Amemiya's and Yukino Ichihara's first comic.

It's all thanks to you readers out there, our friends who supported us, and everyone from the editorial department that this book safely made it. Our most sincere thanks!! At times, it felt like we were in a three-legged race at the top of a high cliff (sob), but thanks to everybody's help, we were able to draw our very own manga. It makes us want to do even better for next time.

We hope you'll keep watch over Teito's journey that's only just begun.

Special thanks

AD, Zenko, Abo, Ranmaru, Hiro-san, Kiyo, Ochi-kun, and our families. Thank you!!

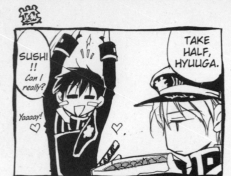

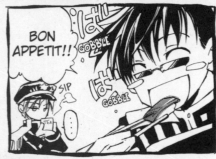

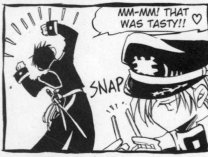

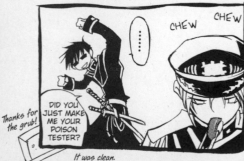

POSTSCRIPT

TAKE HALF, HYUUGA.
SUSHI!!
Can I really?
Yaaaay!
GOBBLE
BON APPETIT!!
GOBBLE
SIP
TEA
. . . .
MM-MM! THAT WAS TASTY!!
SNAP
CHEW
CHEW
......
DID YOU JUST MAKE ME YOUR POISON TESTER?
Thanks for the grub!
It was clean.

Thank you! *October 2005*

Amemiya & Ichihara

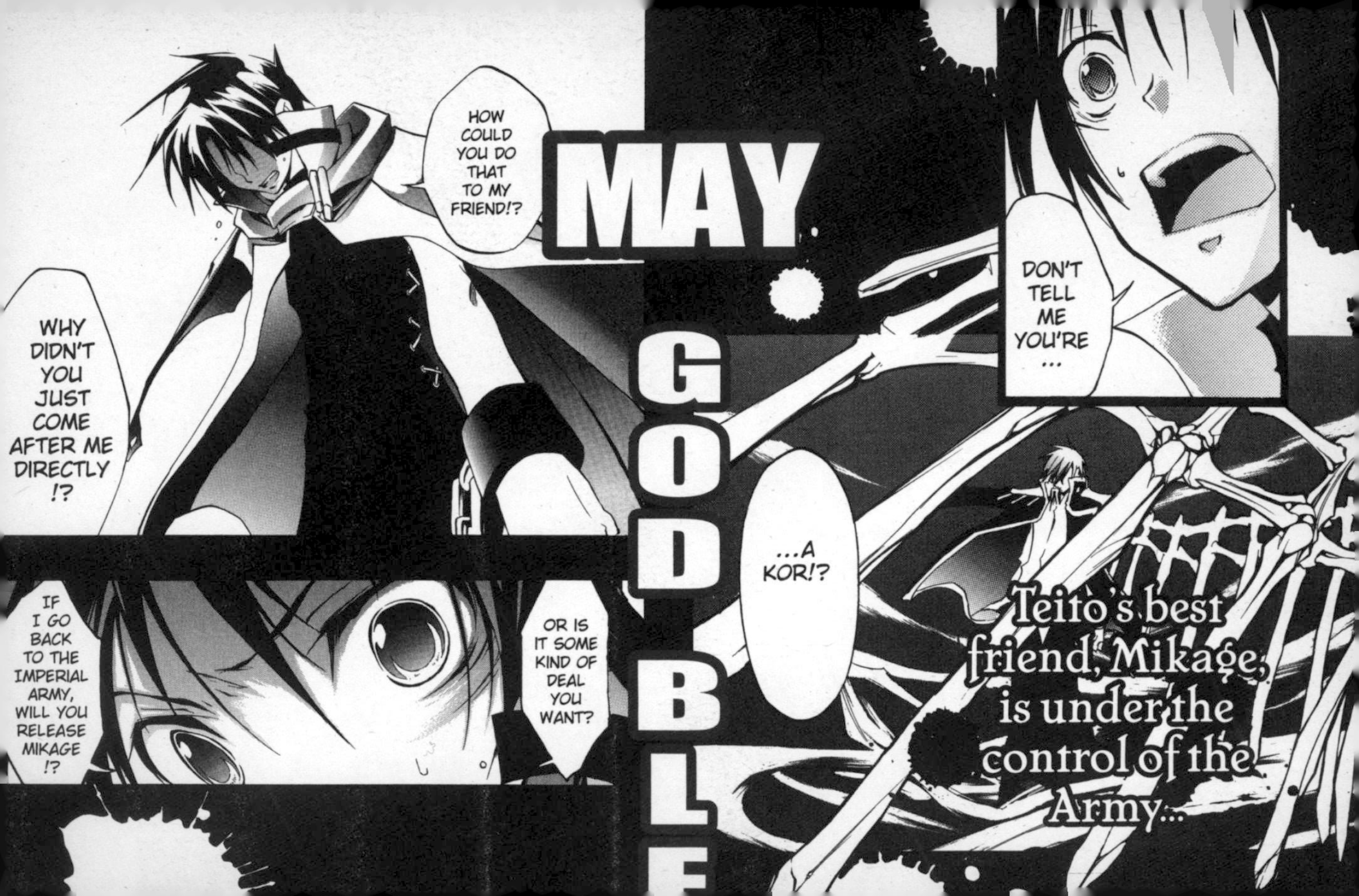
DON'T TELL ME YOU'RE ...
...A KOR!?
Teito's best friend, Mikage, is under the control of the Army...
MAY GOD BLE
HOW COULD YOU DO THAT TO MY FRIEND!?
WHY DIDN'T YOU JUST COME AFTER ME DIRECTLY !?
OR IS IT SOME KIND OF DEAL YOU WANT?
IF I GO BACK TO THE IMPERIAL ARMY, WILL YOU RELEASE MIKAGE !?

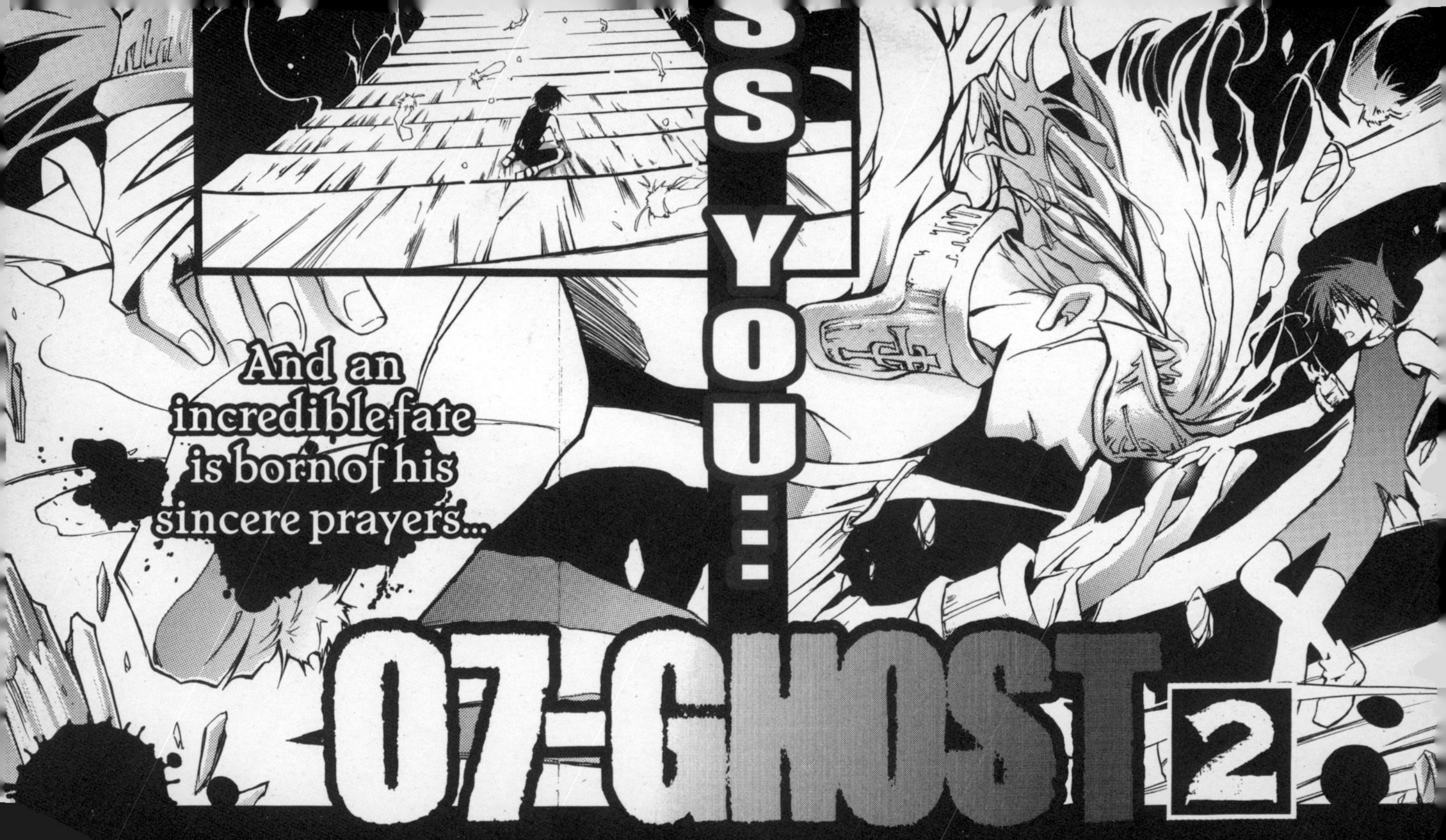
S YOU…
And an incredible fate is born of his sincere prayers...
07-GHOST 2

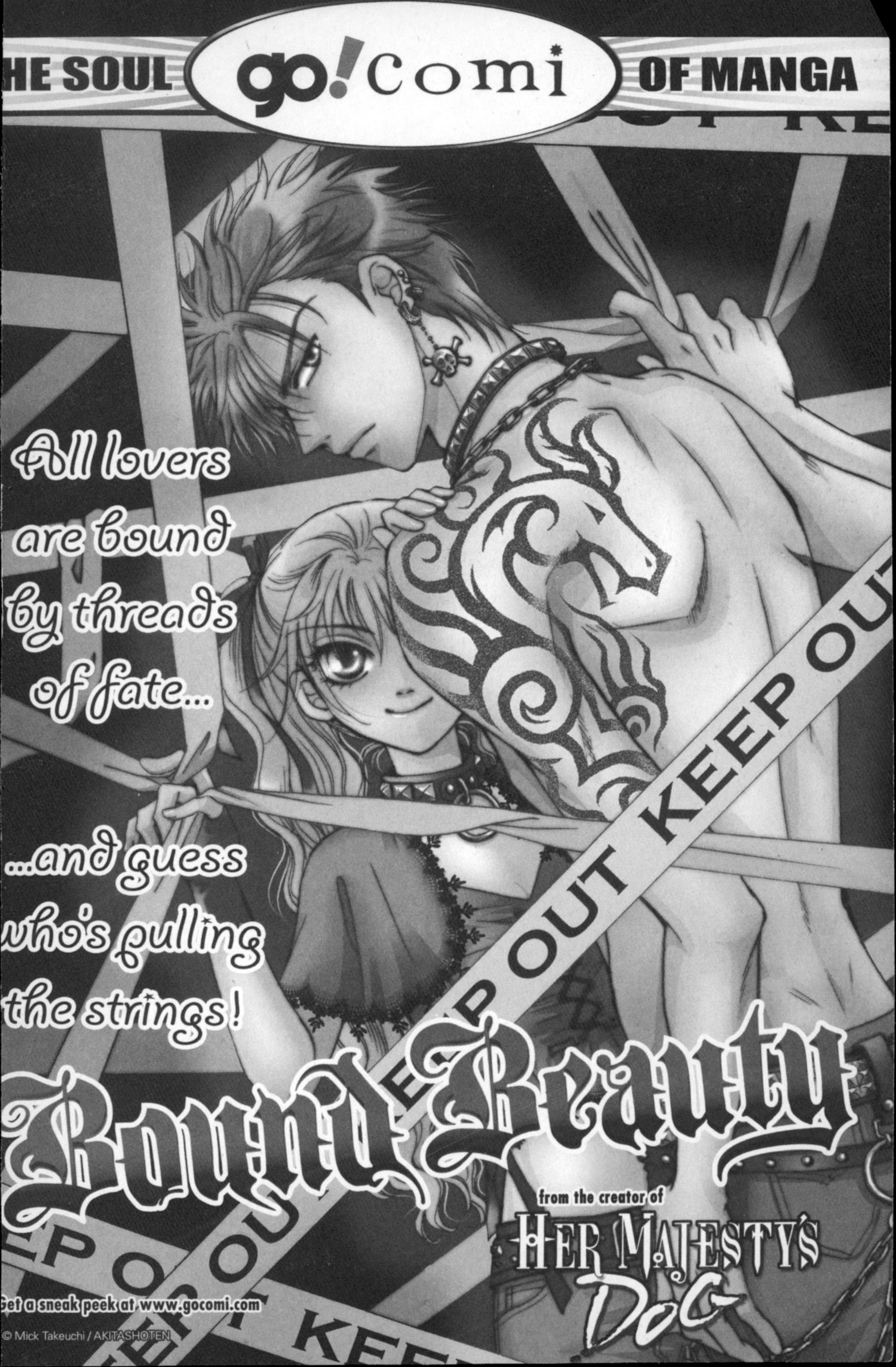
HE SOUL go!comi OF MANGA
All lovers are bound by threads of fate...
...and guess who's pulling the strings!
KEEP OUT KEEP OUT
Bound Beauty
from the creator of
HER MAJESTY'S DOG
Get a sneak peek at www.gocomi.com
© Mick Takeuchi / AKITASHOTEN

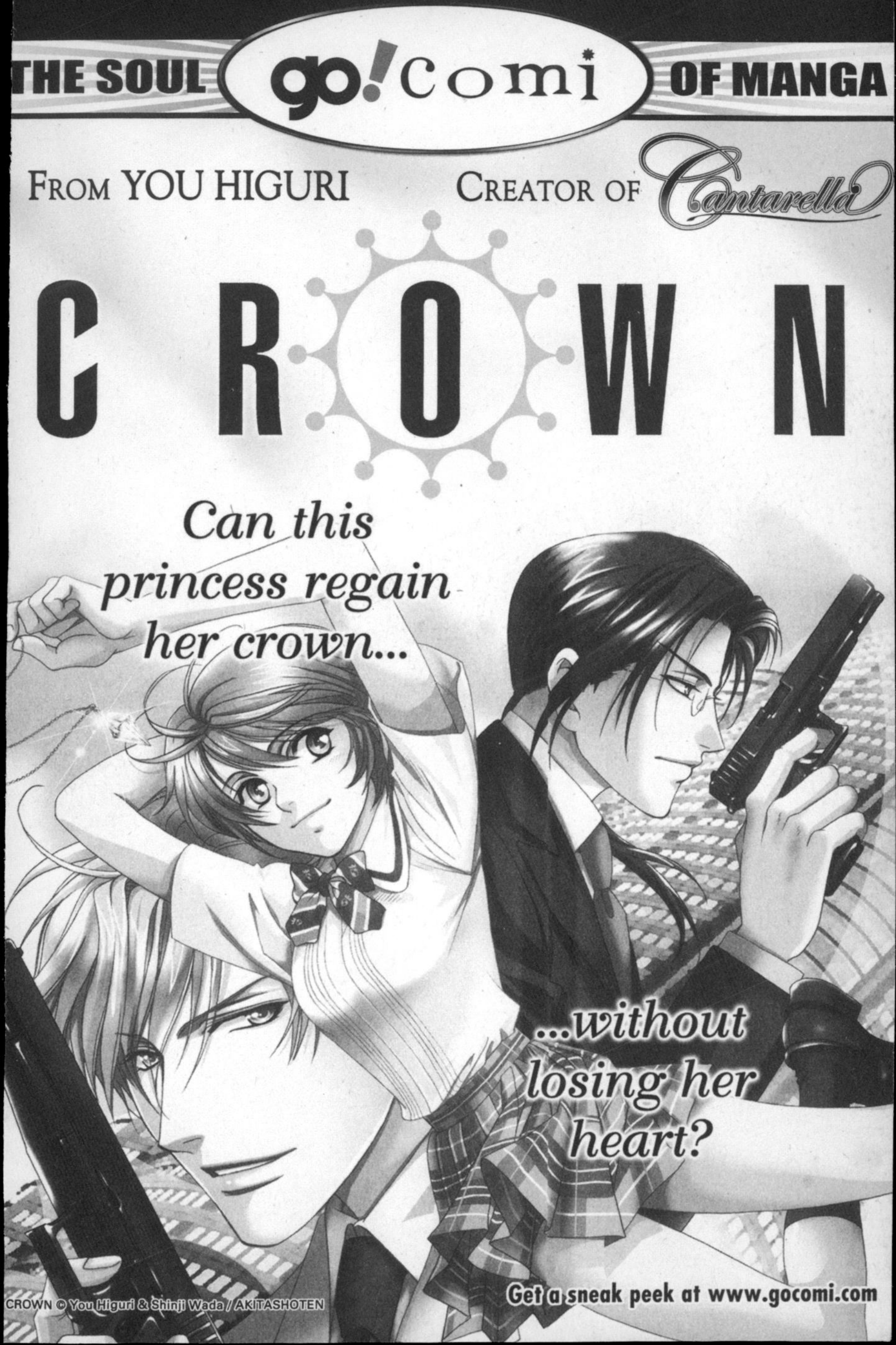
THE SOUL go!comi OF MANGA
FROM YOU HIGURI
CREATOR OF Cantarella
CROWN
Can this princess regain her crown...
...without losing her heart?
CROWN © You Higuri & Shinji Wada / AKITASHOTEN
Get a sneak peek at www.gocomi.com

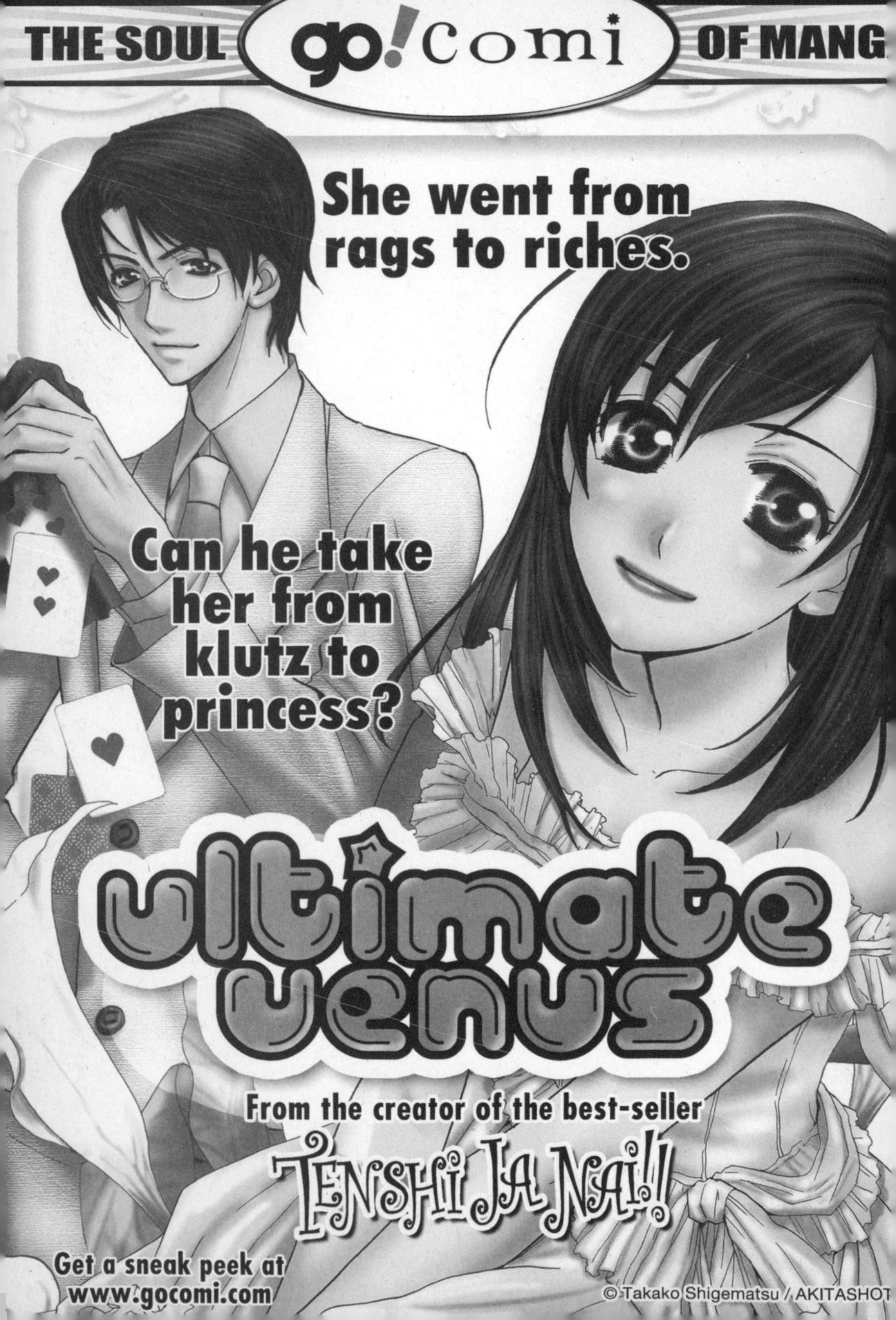
THE SOUL
go!comi
OF MANG
She went from rags to riches.
Can he take her from klutz to princess?
ultimate venus
From the creator of the best-seller
TENSHI JA NAI!!
Get a sneak peek at www.gocomi.com
© Takako Shigematsu / AKITASHOT

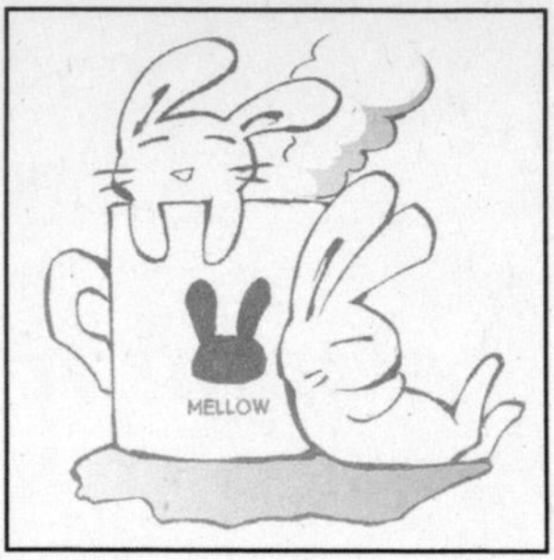
MELLOW

YUKI AMEMIYA
YUKINO ICHIHARA

Greetings. This is our first book, ever.
Which is such a momentous feat for us that
we feel nearly paralyzed with terror.
You have no idea how many people saved
our sorry butts during the whole process... ;_;
Thank you. Thank you.
We'd be so happy if you could enjoy this
work...even if just a smidge.